W9-CNX-089

Dragon Goes House-Hunting

4

Story by
KAWO TANUKI

Art by
CHOCO AYA

CHARACTERS

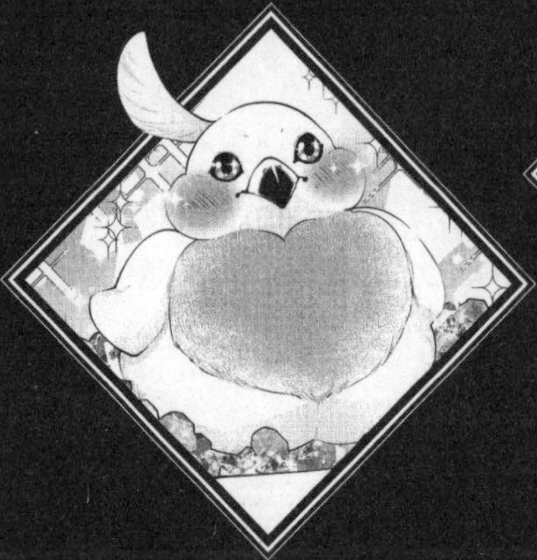

Pip

A chick adopted by Letty. His extraordinarily long full name won't fit into this space, but begins with Piyovelt Phelpia Pi.

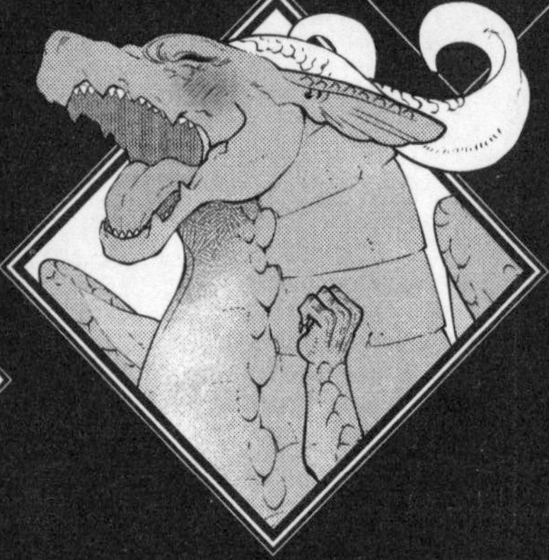

Letty

A dragon searching for his ideal home. He's picked up the nickname "Flame Dragon King" of late, which makes him even more nervous than usual.

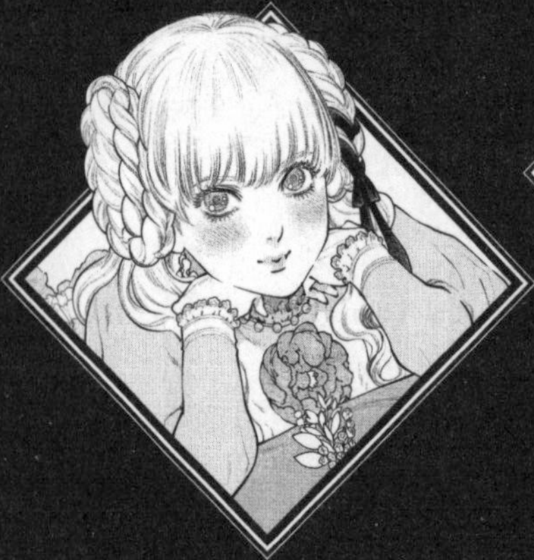

Nell

A naughty princess from a human kingdom. Loves baths. Traveled with the others for a while and may yet meet up with them again.

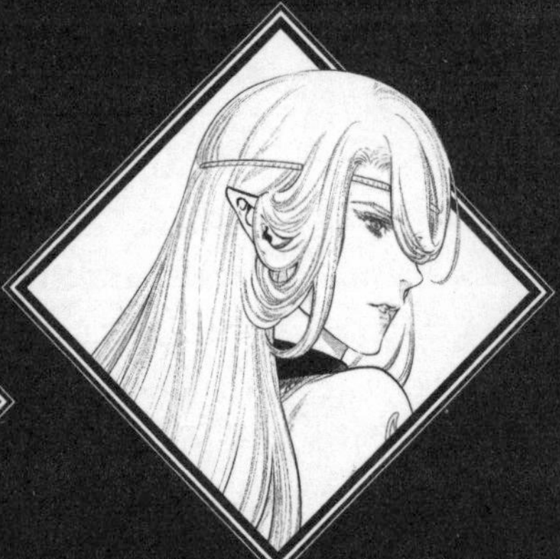

Dearia

A handsome male elf, Letty's friend, and an architect, builder, realtor, and (despite Letty's misunderstanding about this) some kind of Dark Lord.

STORY

Letty seeks a home where even a weak, cowardly dragon like himself can live his life in peace and quiet. With Dearia and Pip, he travels the world viewing all sorts of potential properties.

Along the way, Letty took in Nell, a princess who ran away from home only to wind up kidnapped. The group's travels then took them to an underground labyrinth located under Nell's old home. Somehow, they ended up barricaded inside the royal palace and Letty had to reconcile Nell and her father....

After bidding farewell to the princess, Letty and company continued on their house-hunting adventure, which was still far from being even halfway done!

Contents

House 16: Pip Goes Off to Play

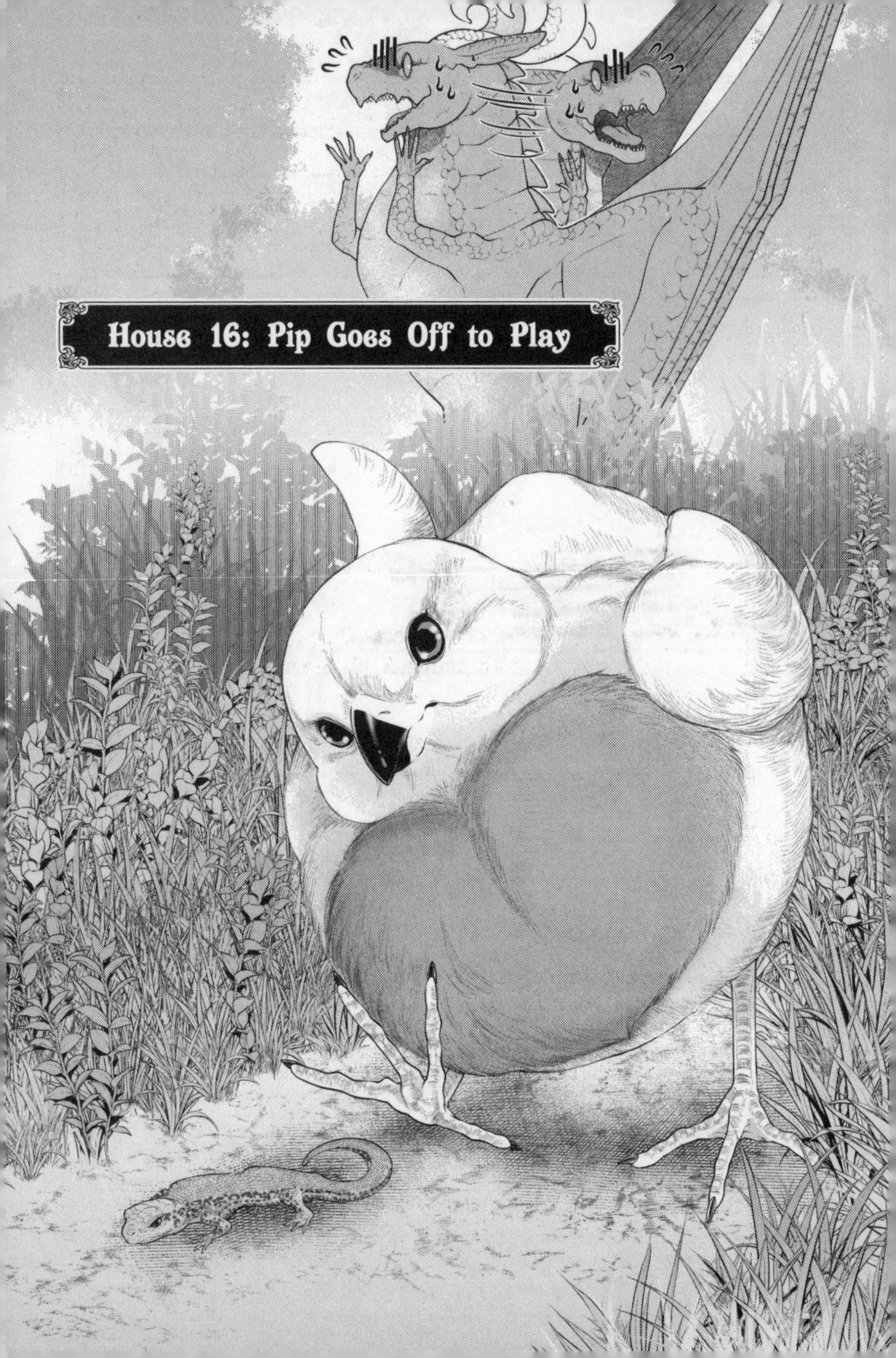

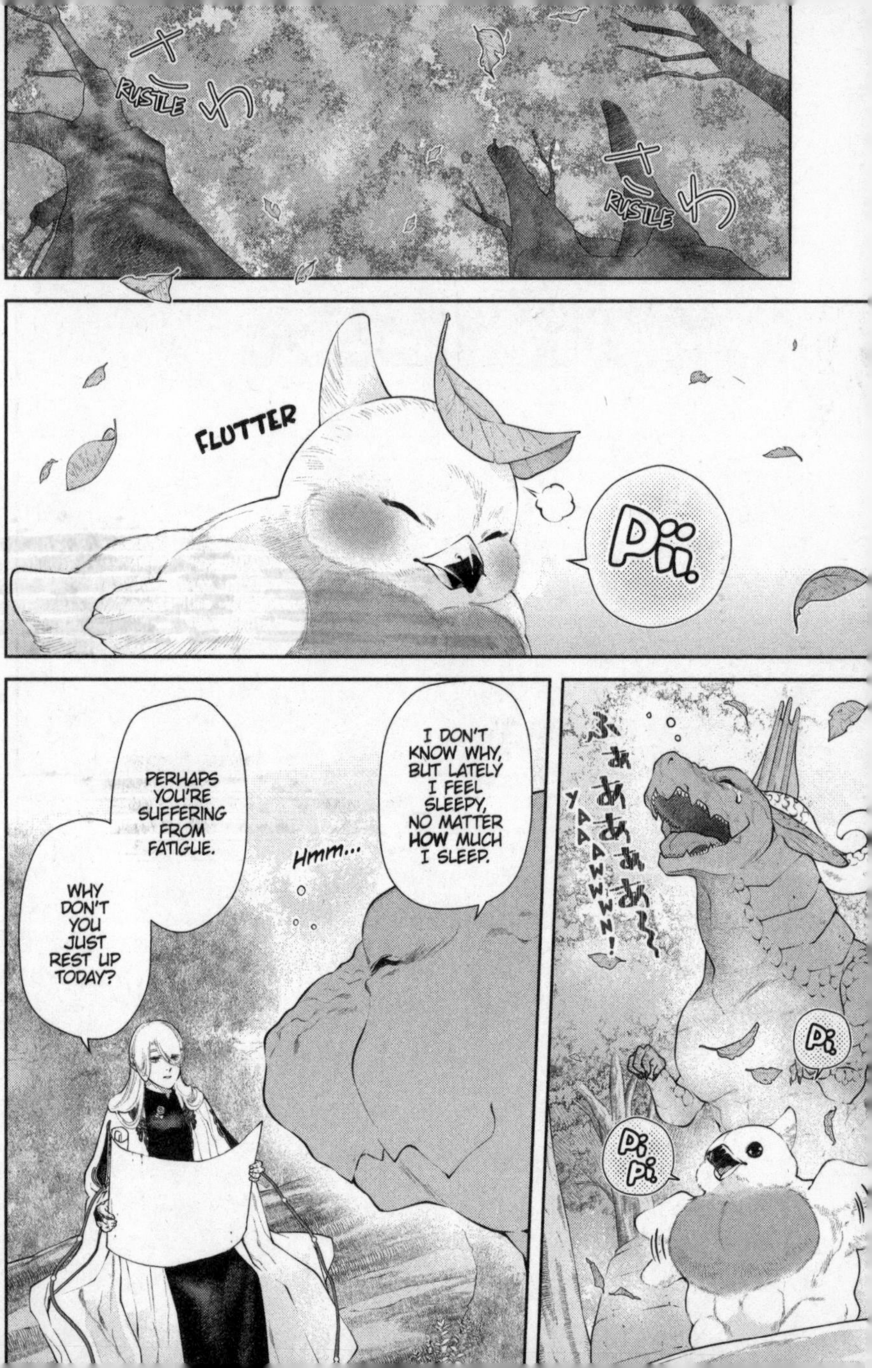
RUSTLE
RUSTLE
FLUTTER
Pii.
YAAAWWN!
Pi.
Pi pi.
I DON'T KNOW WHY, BUT LATELY I FEEL SLEEPY, NO MATTER HOW MUCH I SLEEP.
Hmm...
PERHAPS YOU'RE SUFFERING FROM FATIGUE.
WHY DON'T YOU JUST REST UP TODAY?

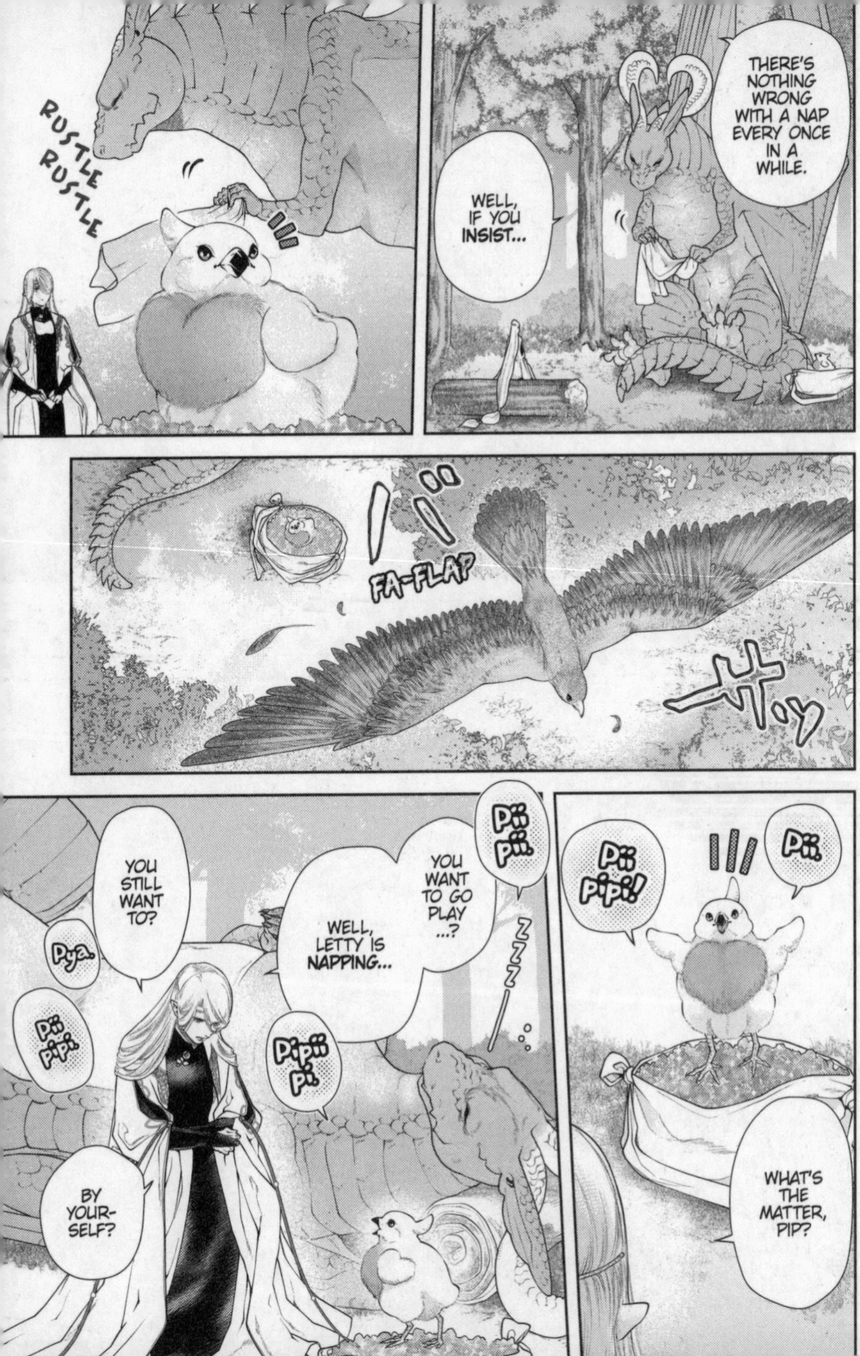
THERE'S NOTHING WRONG WITH A NAP EVERY ONCE IN A WHILE.
WELL, IF YOU INSIST...
RUSTLE RUSTLE
FA-FLAP
Pii.
Pii pipi!
WHAT'S THE MATTER, PIP?
Pii pii.
YOU WANT TO GO PLAY ...?
ZZZ
WELL, LETTY IS NAPPING...
Pipii pi.
YOU STILL WANT TO?
Pya.
Pii pipi.
BY YOUR-SELF?

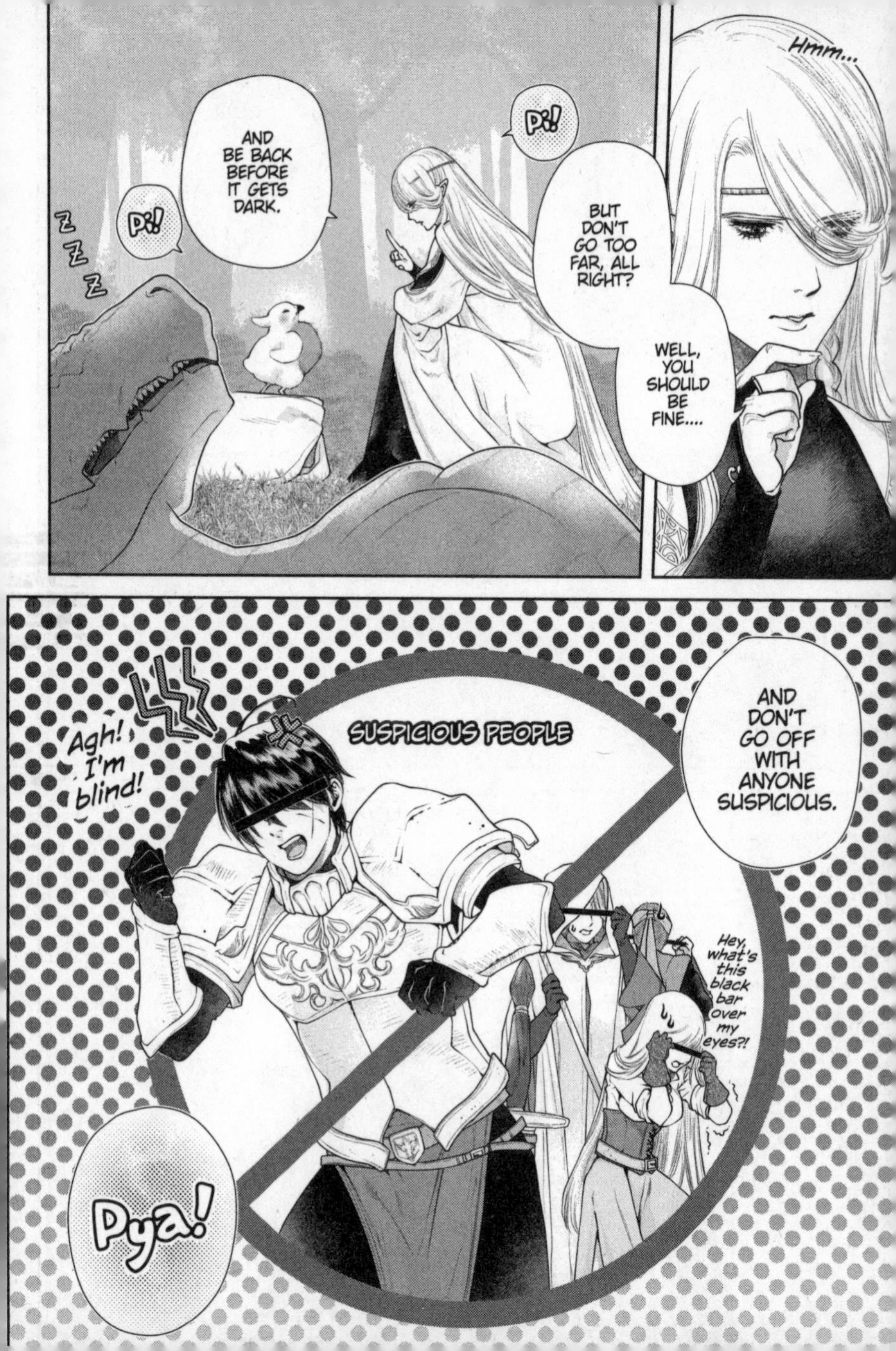
Hmmm...
WELL, YOU SHOULD BE FINE....
BUT DON'T GO TOO FAR, ALL RIGHT?
Pi!
AND BE BACK BEFORE IT GETS DARK.
Pi!
Z Z Z
AND DON'T GO OFF WITH ANYONE SUSPICIOUS.
SUSPICIOUS PEOPLE
Agh! I'm blind!
Hey, what's this black bar over my eyes?!
Pya!

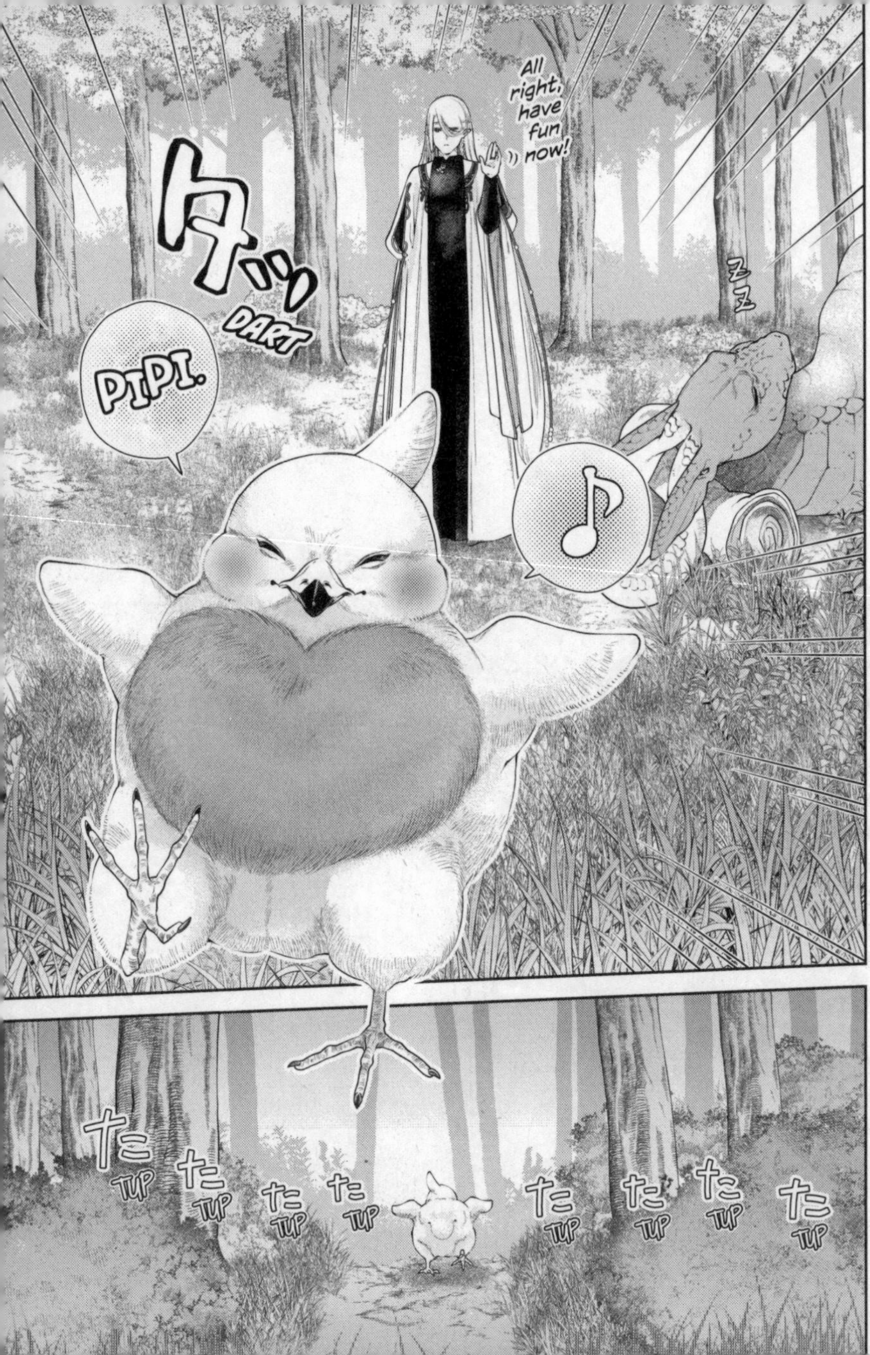
All right, have fun now!
タッ
DART
PIPI.
♪
Z Z
たた
TUP
たた
TUP
たた
TUP
たた
TUP
たた
TUP
たた
TUP
たた
TUP
たた
TUP

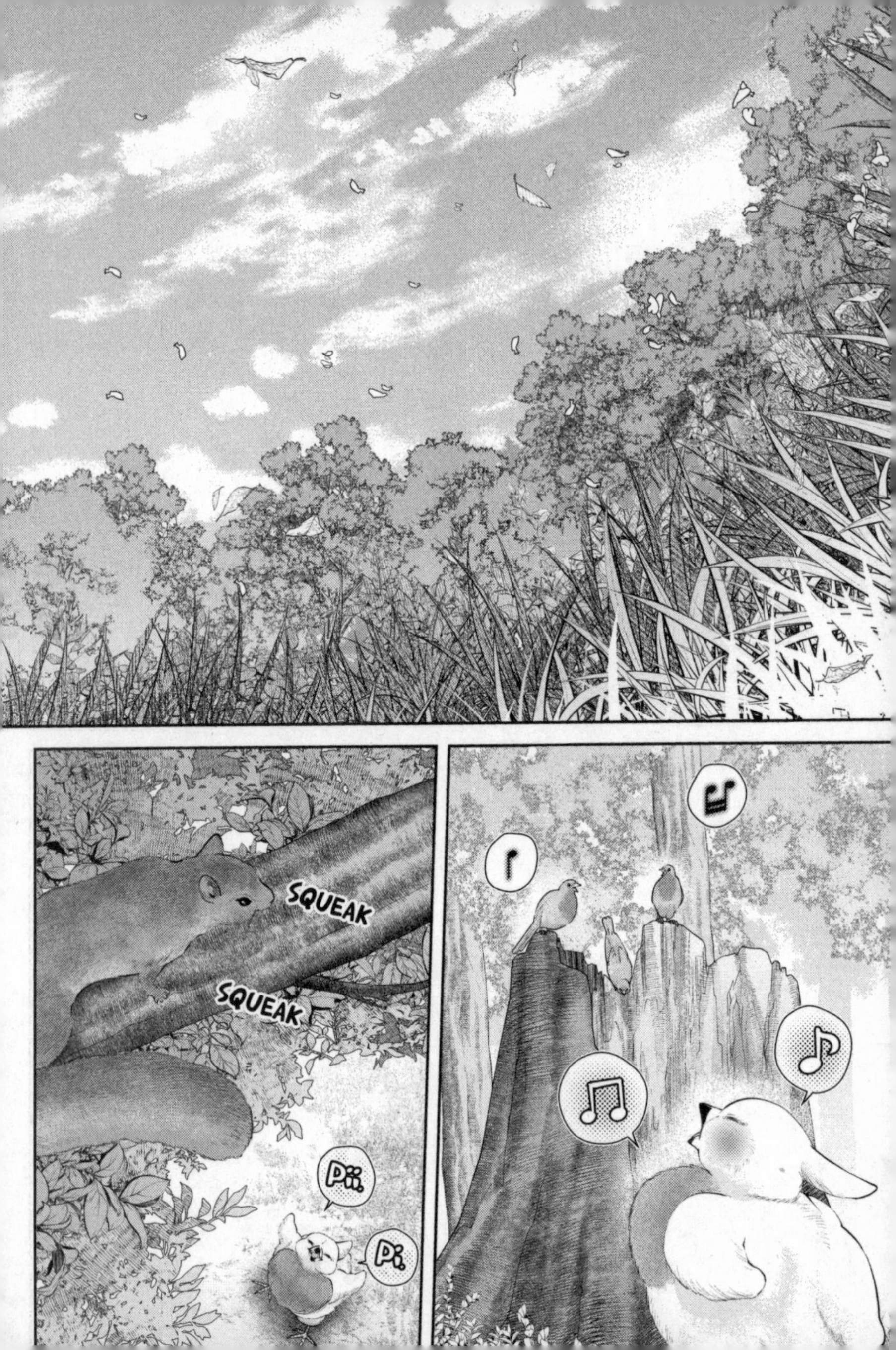
SQUEAK
SQUEAK
Pii.
Pi.

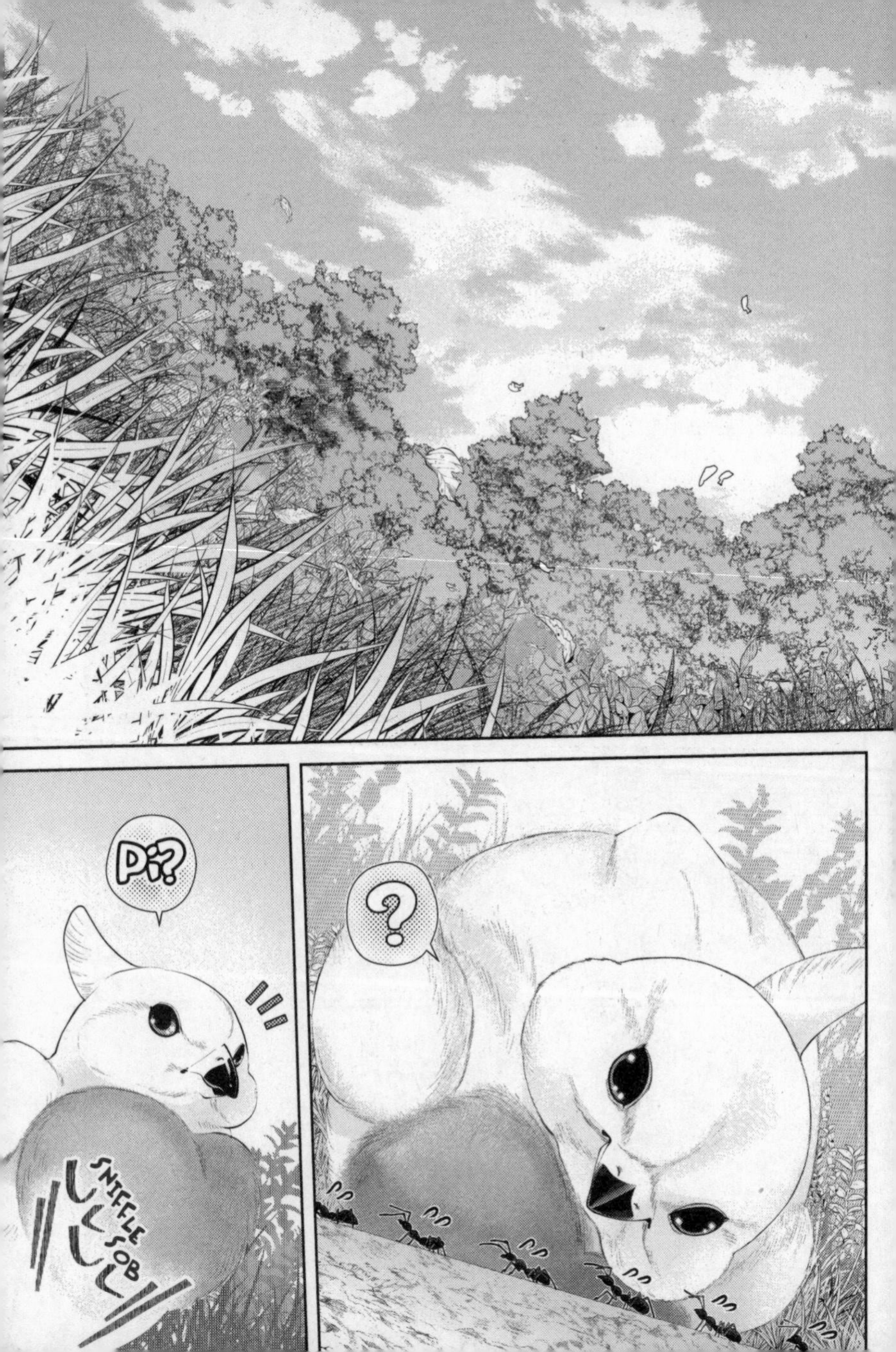
?
Pi?
SNIFFLE SOB
しくしく

Peek-A-Boo

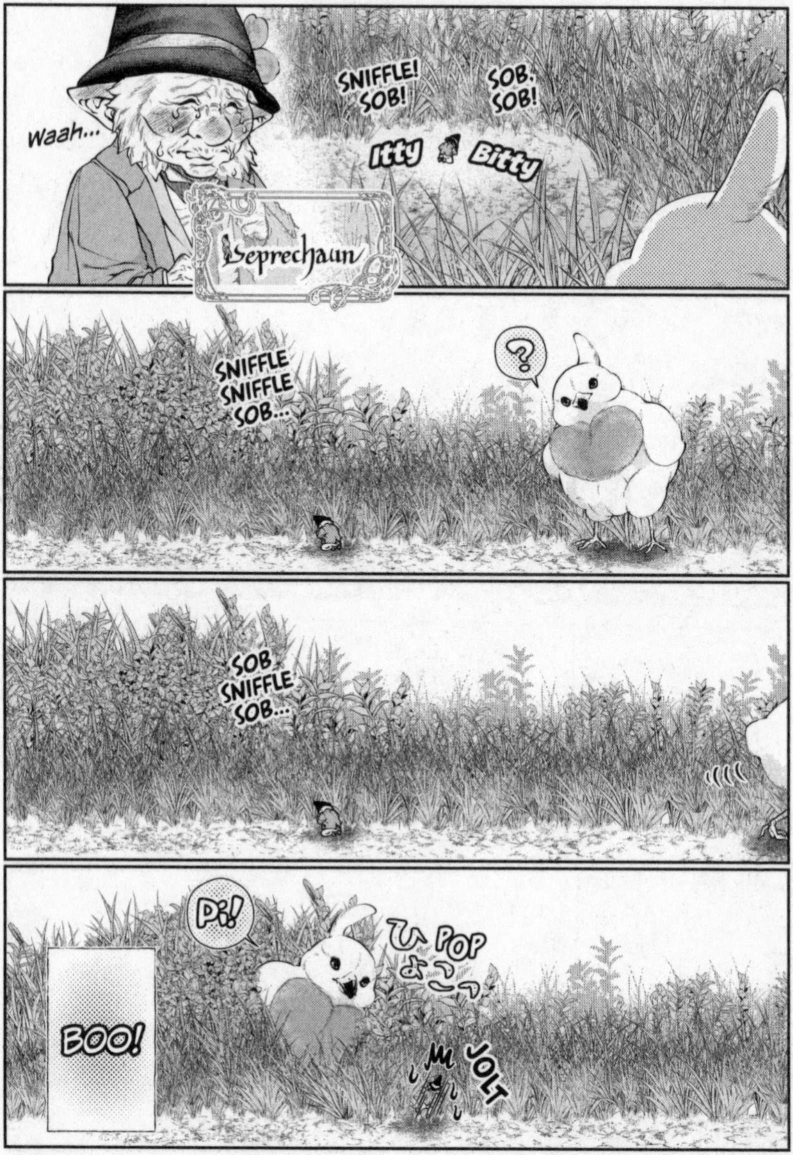

Waah...
SNIFFLE! SOB!
SOB. SOB!
Itty Bitty
Leprechaun
SNIFFLE SNIFFLE SOB...
?
SOB SNIFFLE SOB...
Pi!
ひょこっ POP
BOO!
JOLT

Always Everywhere Annoying

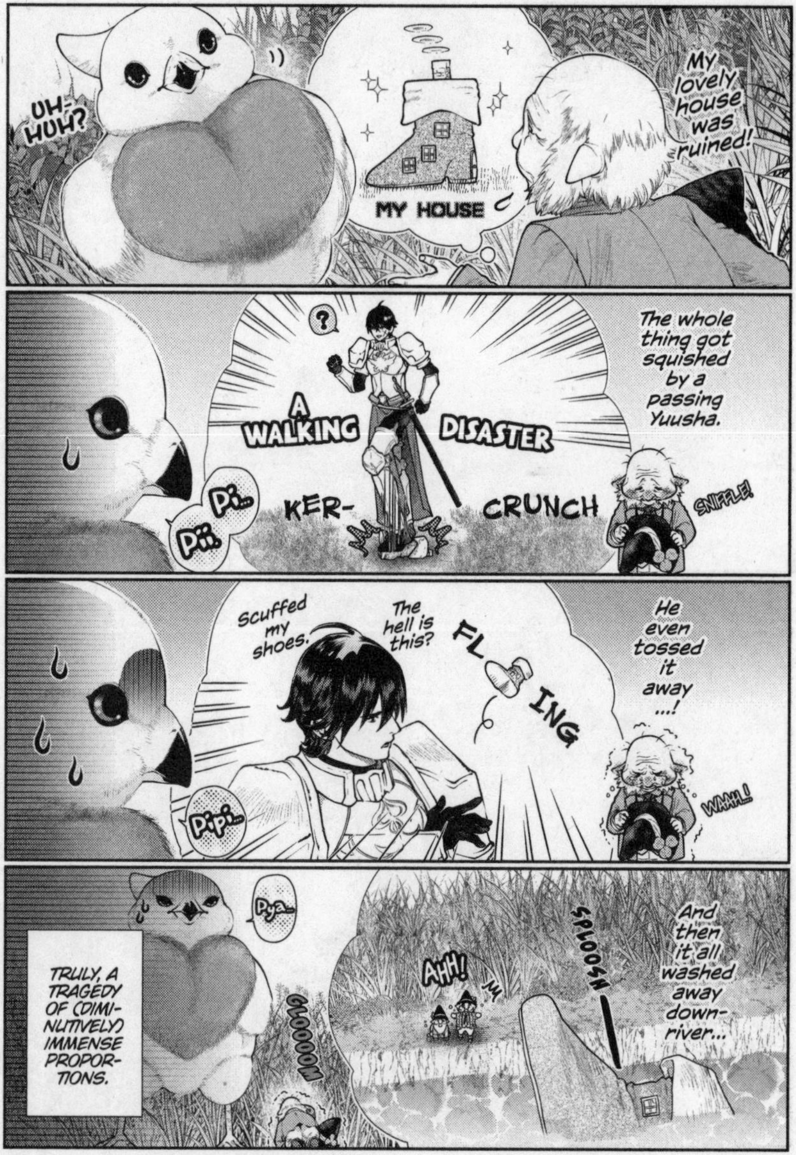

My lovely house was ruined!
MY HOUSE
UH-HUH?
The whole thing got squished by a passing Yuusha.
SNIFFLE!
A WALKING DISASTER
?
KER-CRUNCH
Pi...
Pii.
He even tossed it away...!
WAHH!
FLING
The hell is this?
Scuffed my shoes.
Pipi...
And then it all washed away down-river...
SPLOOSH
AHH!
Pya...
WOOOOOO
TRULY, A TRAGEDY OF (DIMINUTIVELY) IMMENSE PROPORTIONS.

A Misunderstanding

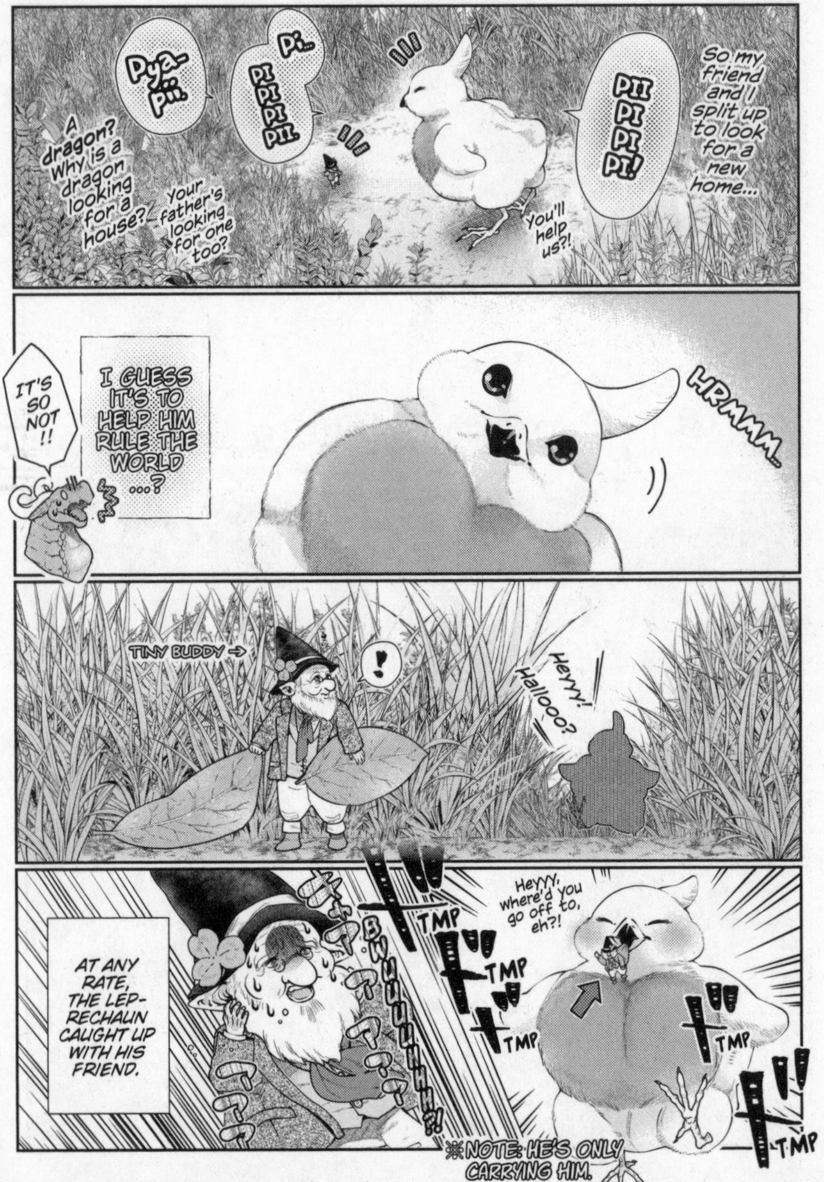

Pya-... pii.
Pi... PI PI PI PII.
!!!
A dragon? Why is a dragon looking for a house?
Your father's looking for one too?
PII PI PI PI!
So my friend and I split up to look for a new home...
You'll help us?!
I GUESS IT'S TO HELP HIM RULE THE WORLD ...?
IT'S SO NOT !!
HRMMM...
TINY BUDDY →
!
Heyyy! Hallooo?
AT ANY RATE, THE LEP-RECHAUN CAUGHT UP WITH HIS FRIEND.
Heyyy, where'd you go off to, eh?!
TMP
TMP
TMP
TMP
TMP
※NOTE: HE'S ONLY CARRYING HIM.

Your True Desire Is Close

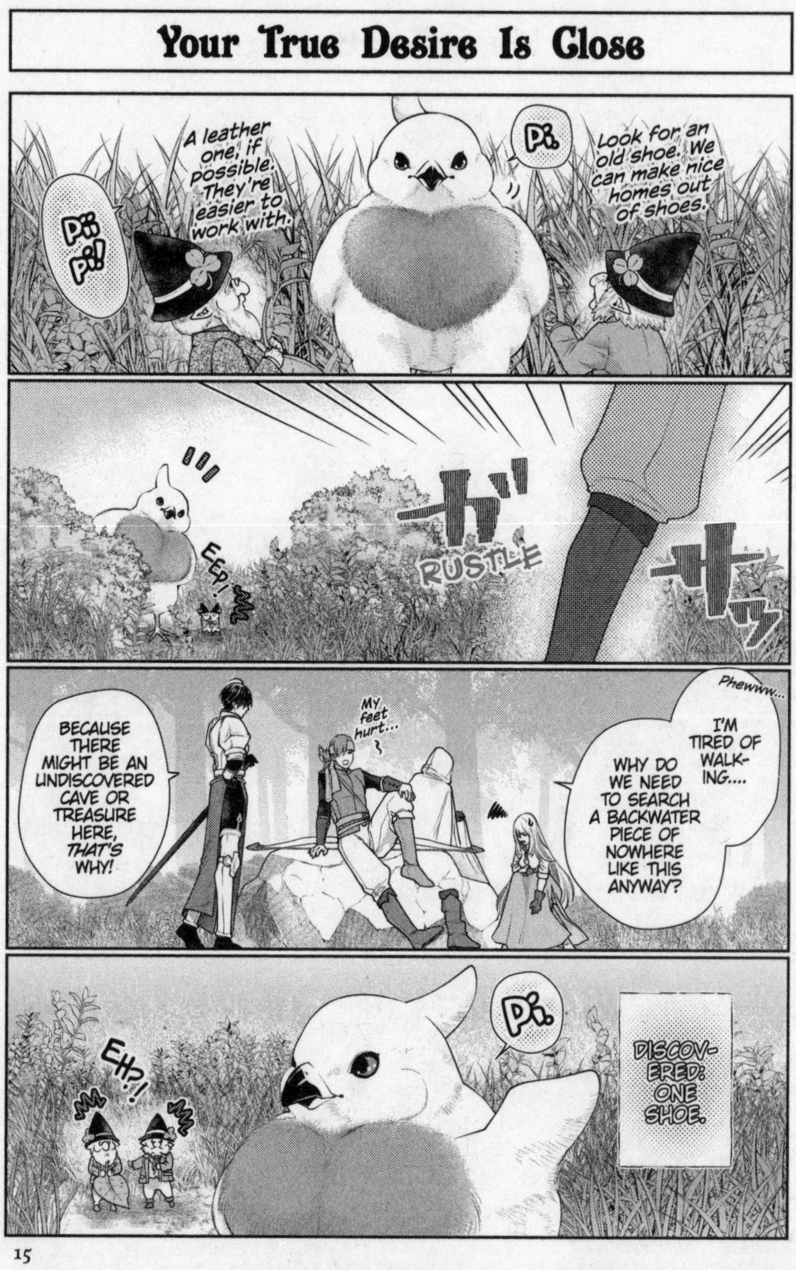
Look for an old shoe. We can make nice homes out of shoes.
Pi.
A leather one, if possible. They're easier to work with.
Pi pi!
ガサッ
RUSTLE
!!!
EEEP!
Phewww...
I'M TIRED OF WALK-ING....
WHY DO WE NEED TO SEARCH A BACKWATER PIECE OF NOWHERE LIKE THIS ANYWAY?
My feet hurt...
BECAUSE THERE MIGHT BE AN UNDISCOVERED CAVE OR TREASURE HERE, *THAT'S* WHY!
DISCOV-ERED: ONE SHOE.
Pi.
EH?!

I Know

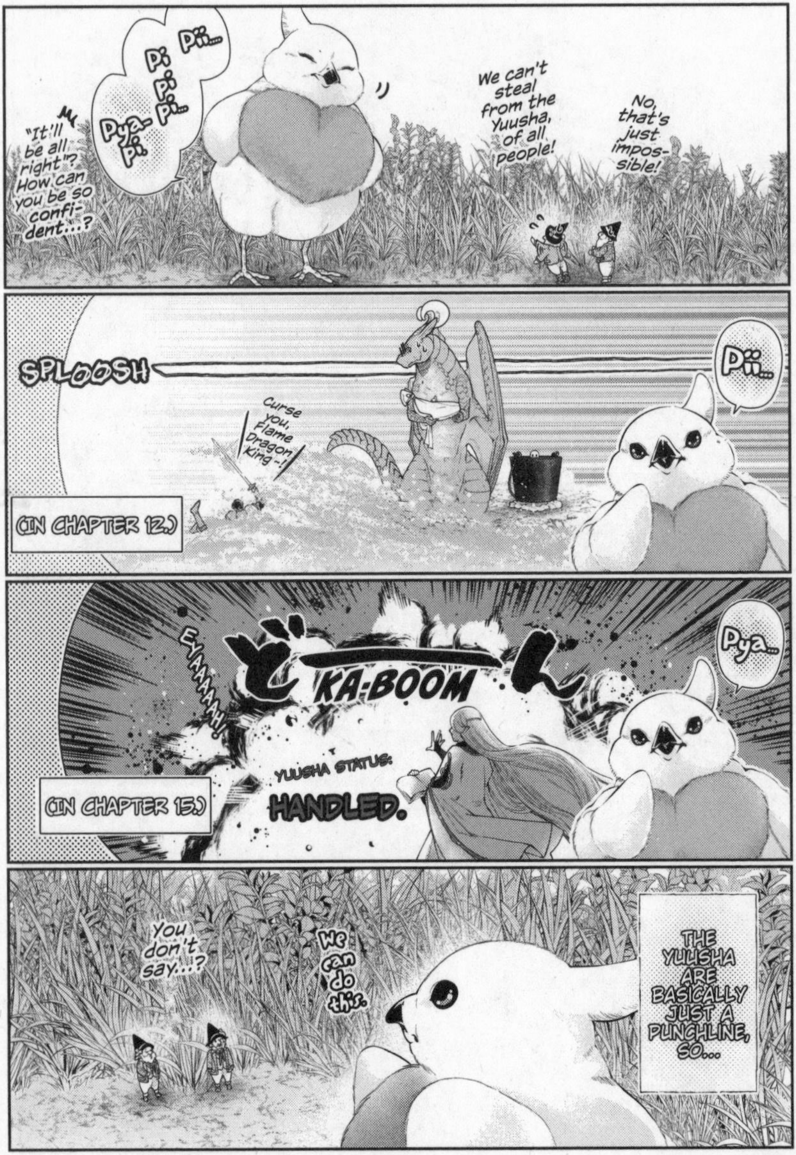

No, that's just impos-sible!
We can't steal from the Yuusha, of all people!
Pii... Pi pi pi... Pya-pi.
"It'll be all right"? How can you be so confi-dent...?
Pii...
SPLOOSH
Curse you, Flame Dragon King~!
(IN CHAPTER 12.)
Pya...
KA-BOOM
EYAAAAAH!
YUUSHA STATUS:
HANDLED.
(IN CHAPTER 15.)
THE YUUSHA ARE BASICALLY JUST A PUNCHLINE, SO...
We can do this.
You don't say...?

Child of the Flame Dragon King

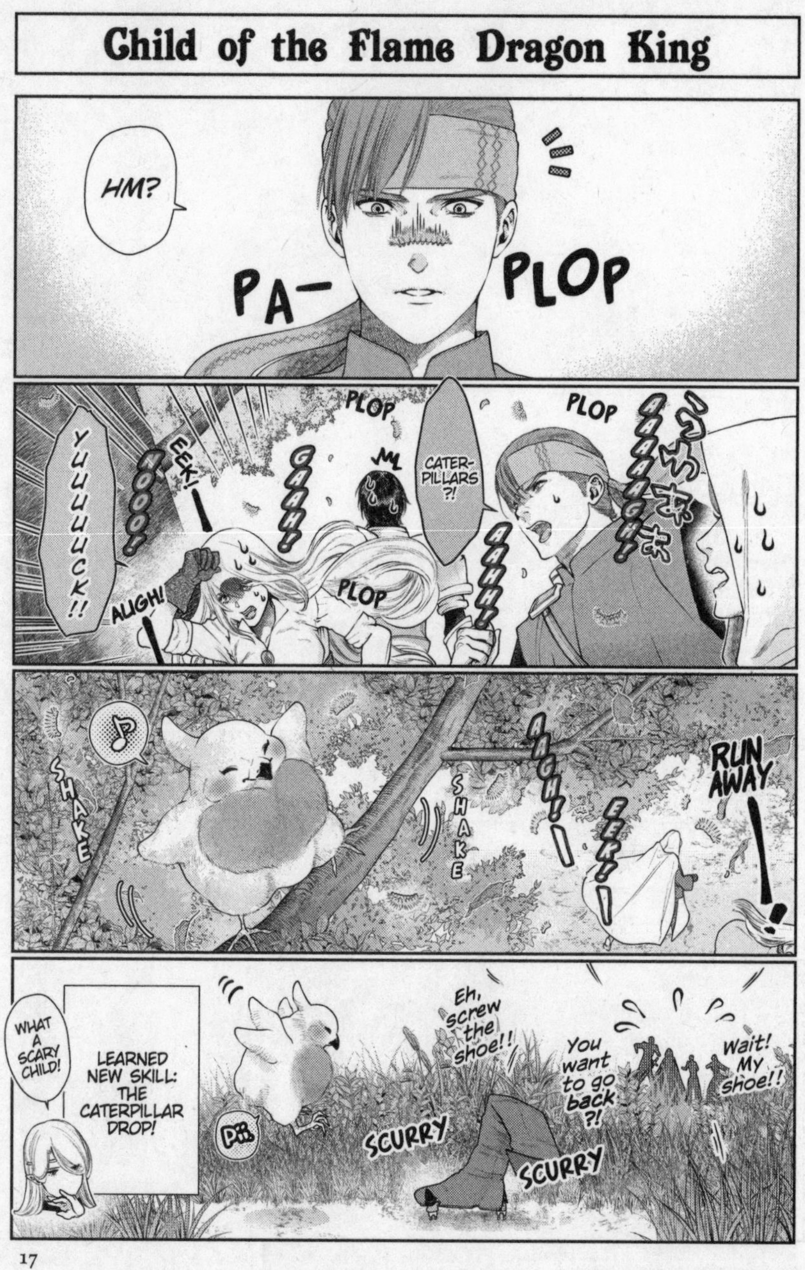
HM?
PA—
PLOP
YUUUUUUCK!!
NOOOO!
EEK!
AUGH!
GAAH!
PLOP
PLOP
CATER-PILLARS?!
AAHH!
PLOP
AAAAAAGH!
SHAKE
SHAKE
AAGH!
EEK!
RUN AWAY
WHAT A SCARY CHILD!
LEARNED NEW SKILL: THE CATERPILLAR DROP!
Pii
SCURRY
Eh, screw the shoe!!
SCURRY
You want to go back?!
Wait! My shoe!!

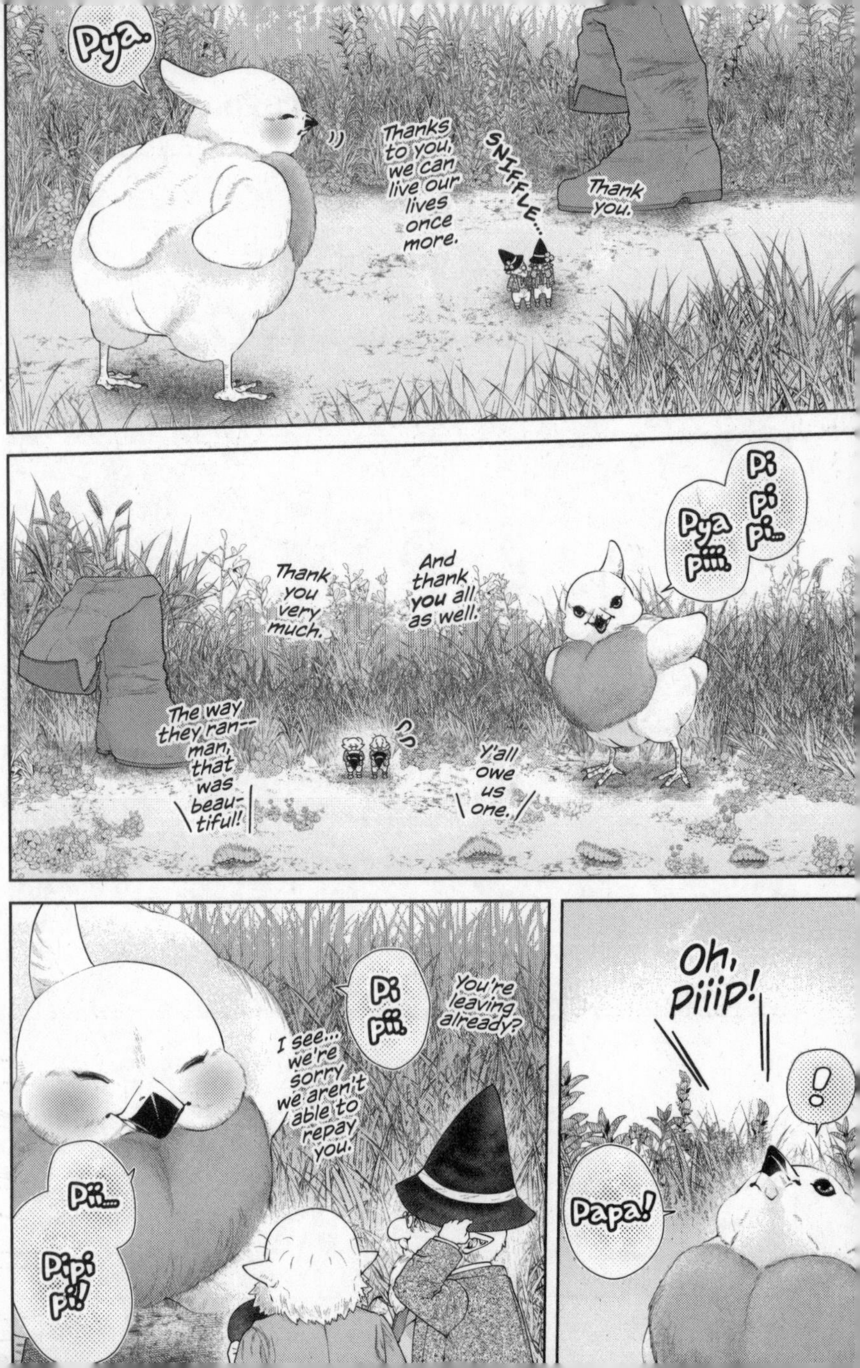
Thank you.
SNIFFLE...
Thanks to you, we can live our lives once more.
Pya.
Pi pi pi...
Pya piiii.
And thank you all as well.
Thank you very much.
Y'all owe us one.
The way they ran--man, that was beautiful!
Oh, Piiip!
!
Papa!
You're leaving already?
Pi pii.
I see... we're sorry we aren't able to repay you.
Pii...
Pipi pi!

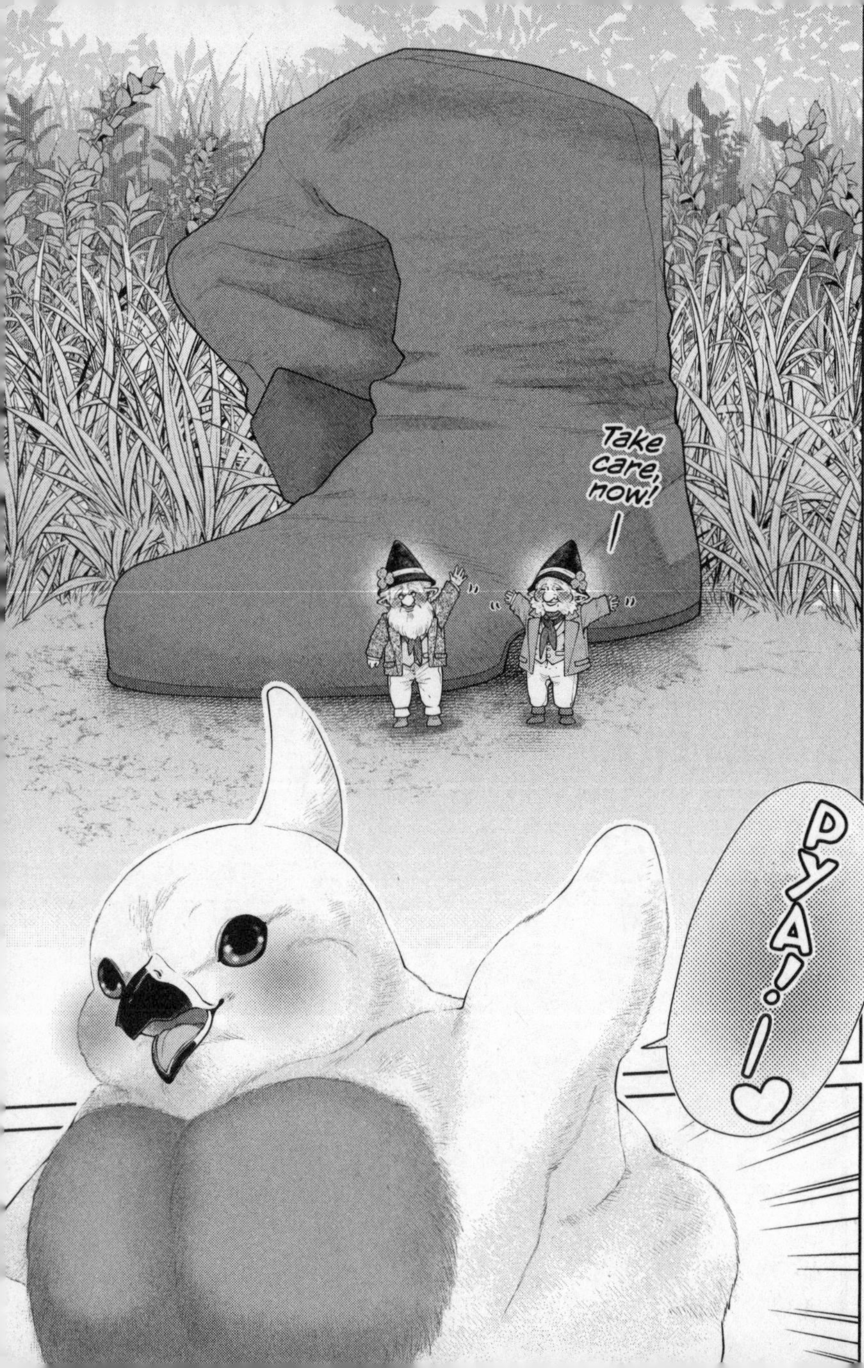
Take care, now!
PYA!—♥

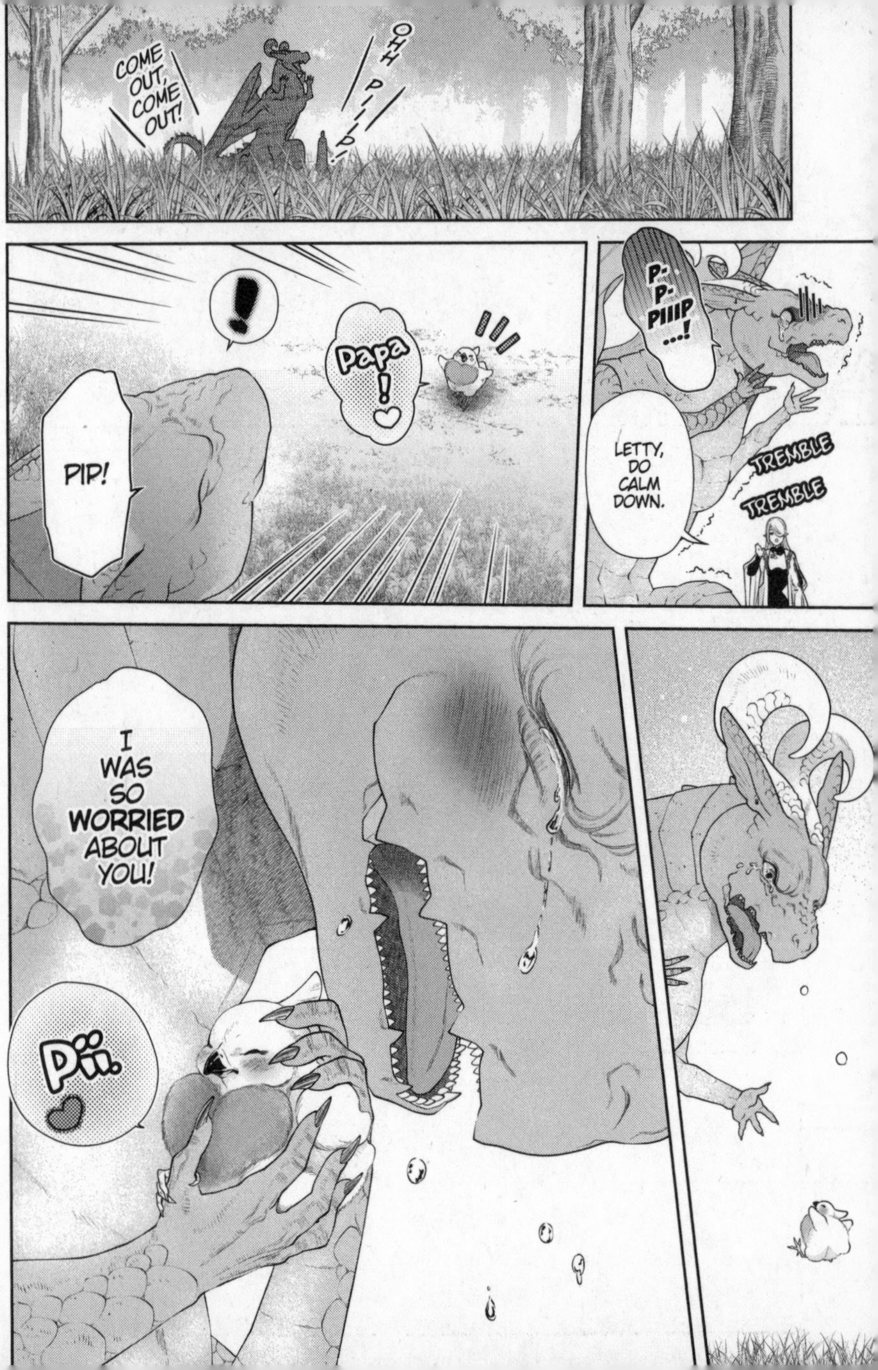
OHH P-I-I-P!
COME OUT, COME OUT!
!!!
Papa!
!
PIP!
P-P-PIIIP...!
LETTY, DO CALM DOWN.
TREMBLE
TREMBLE
I WAS SO WORRIED ABOUT YOU!
Pii.

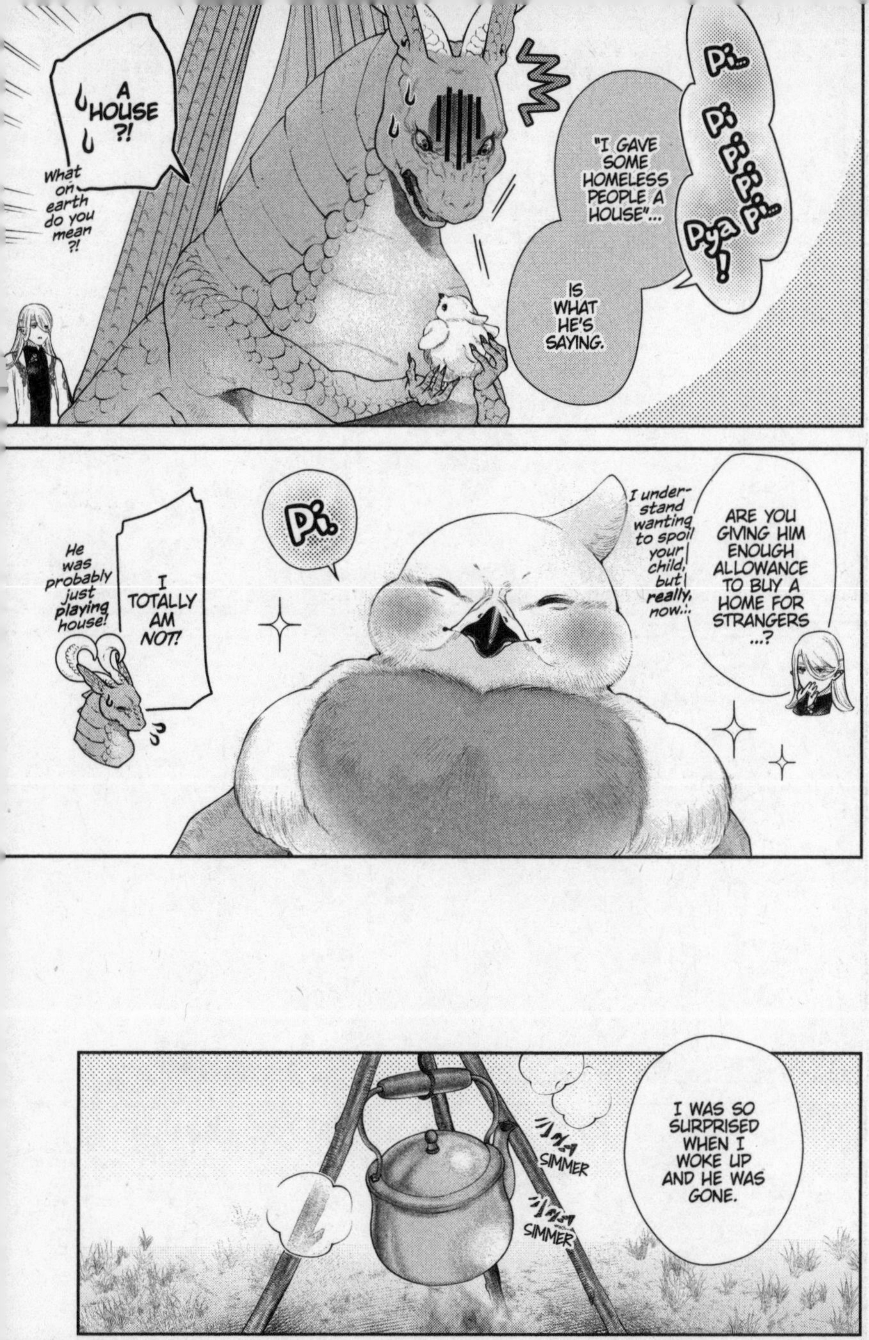
Pi... Pi pi pi pi... Pya!
"I GAVE SOME HOMELESS PEOPLE A HOUSE"...
IS WHAT HE'S SAYING.
A HOUSE?!
What on earth do you mean?!
ARE YOU GIVING HIM ENOUGH ALLOWANCE TO BUY A HOME FOR STRANGERS...?
I understand wanting to spoil your child, but really, now...
Pi.
I TOTALLY AM NOT!
He was probably just playing house!
I WAS SO SURPRISED WHEN I WOKE UP AND HE WAS GONE.
SIMMER
SIMMER

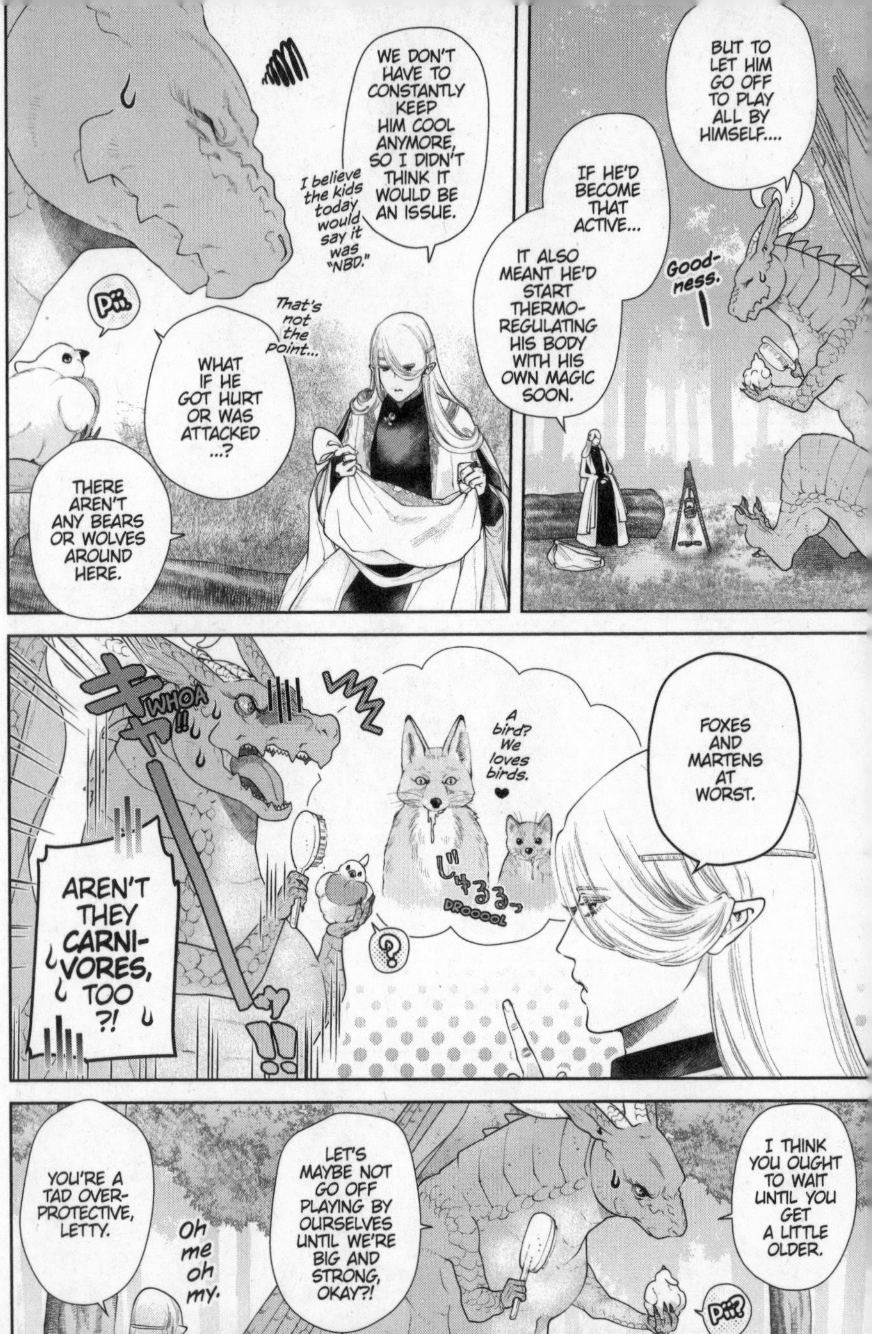

BUT TO LET HIM GO OFF TO PLAY ALL BY HIMSELF....
Goodness.
IF HE'D BECOME THAT ACTIVE...
IT ALSO MEANT HE'D START THERMO-REGULATING HIS BODY WITH HIS OWN MAGIC SOON.
WE DON'T HAVE TO CONSTANTLY KEEP HIM COOL ANYMORE, SO I DIDN'T THINK IT WOULD BE AN ISSUE.
I believe the kids today would say it was "NBD."
That's not the point...
WHAT IF HE GOT HURT OR WAS ATTACKED ...?
Pii.
THERE AREN'T ANY BEARS OR WOLVES AROUND HERE.
FOXES AND MARTENS AT WORST.
A bird? We loves birds.
じゅるる
DROOOOL
キャ
WHOA!!
ARE'NT THEY CARNI-VORES, TOO?!
?
I THINK YOU OUGHT TO WAIT UNTIL YOU GET A LITTLE OLDER.
Pii?
LET'S MAYBE NOT GO OFF PLAYING BY OURSELVES UNTIL WE'RE BIG AND STRONG, OKAY?!
Oh me oh my.
YOU'RE A TAD OVER-PROTECTIVE, LETTY.

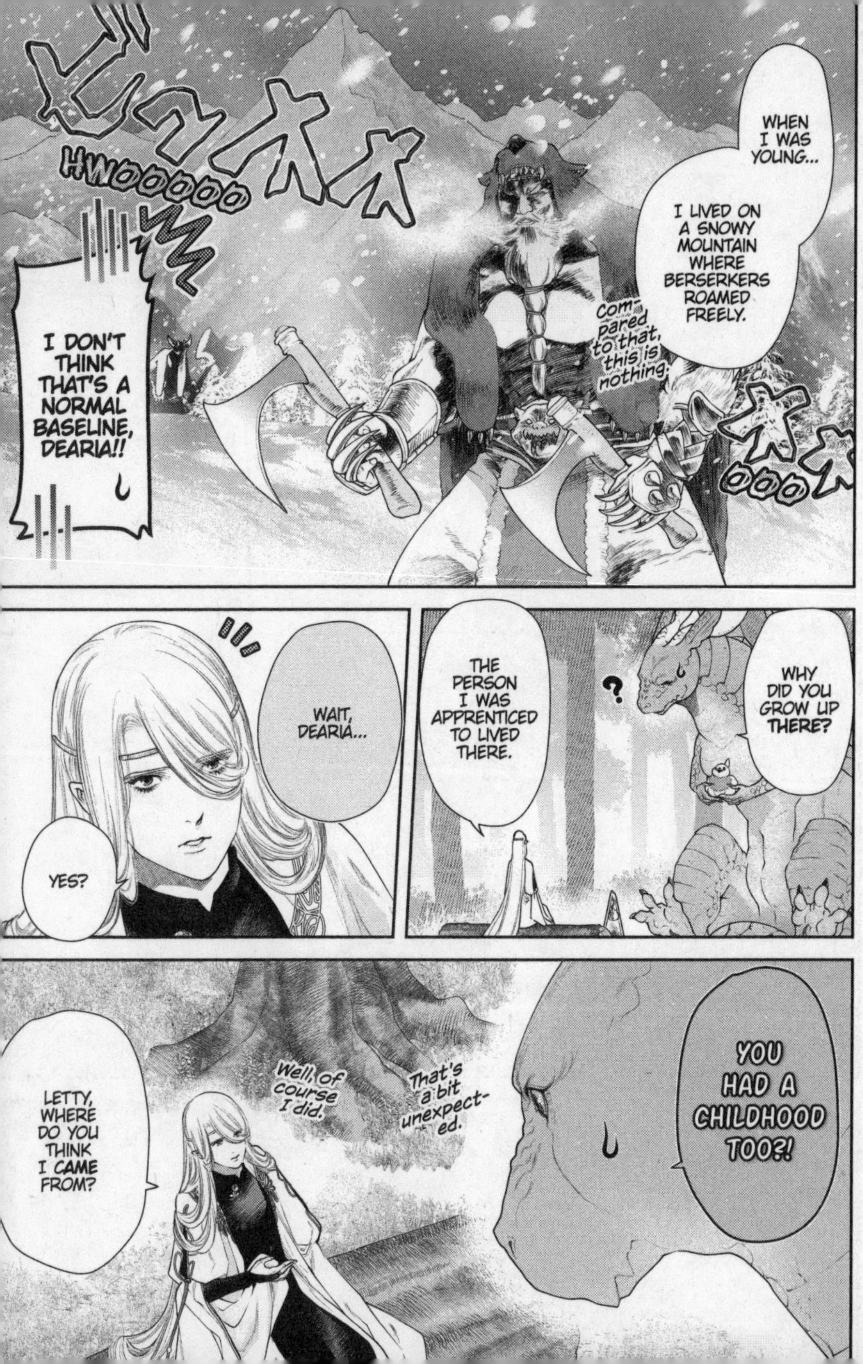
WHEN I WAS YOUNG...
I LIVED ON A SNOWY MOUNTAIN WHERE BERSERKERS ROAMED FREELY.
Compared to that, this is nothing.
HWOOOOOO
OOO
I DON'T THINK THAT'S A NORMAL BASELINE, DEARIA!!
WHY DID YOU GROW UP THERE?
THE PERSON I WAS APPRENTICED TO LIVED THERE.
WAIT, DEARIA...
YES?
YOU HAD A CHILDHOOD TOO?!
That's a bit unexpected.
Well, of course I did.
LETTY, WHERE DO YOU THINK I CAME FROM?

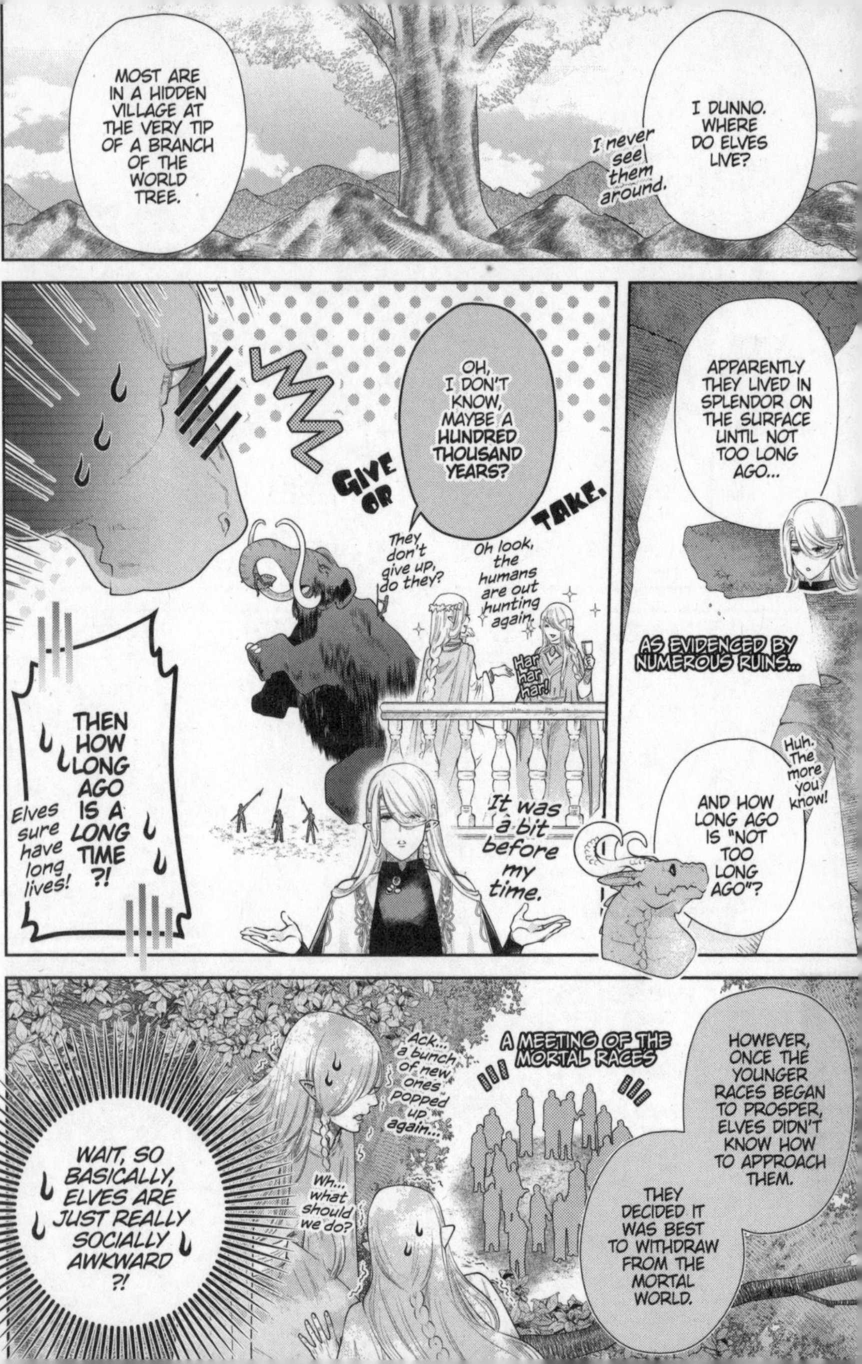
I DUNNO. WHERE DO ELVES LIVE?
I never see them around.
MOST ARE IN A HIDDEN VILLAGE AT THE VERY TIP OF A BRANCH OF THE WORLD TREE.
APPARENTLY THEY LIVED IN SPLENDOR ON THE SURFACE UNTIL NOT TOO LONG AGO...
AS EVIDENCED BY NUMEROUS RUINS...
AND HOW LONG AGO IS "NOT TOO LONG AGO"?
Huh. The more you know!
OH, I DON'T KNOW, MAYBE A HUNDRED THOUSAND YEARS?
GIVE OR TAKE.
It was a bit before my time.
Oh look, the humans are out hunting again.
They don't give up, do they?
Har har har!
THEN HOW LONG AGO IS A LONG TIME?!
Elves sure have long lives!
HOWEVER, ONCE THE YOUNGER RACES BEGAN TO PROSPER, ELVES DIDN'T KNOW HOW TO APPROACH THEM.
THEY DECIDED IT WAS BEST TO WITHDRAW FROM THE MORTAL WORLD.
A MEETING OF THE MORTAL RACES
Ack... a bunch of new ones popped up again...
Wh... what should we do?
WAIT, SO BASICALLY, ELVES ARE JUST REALLY SOCIALLY AWKWARD?!

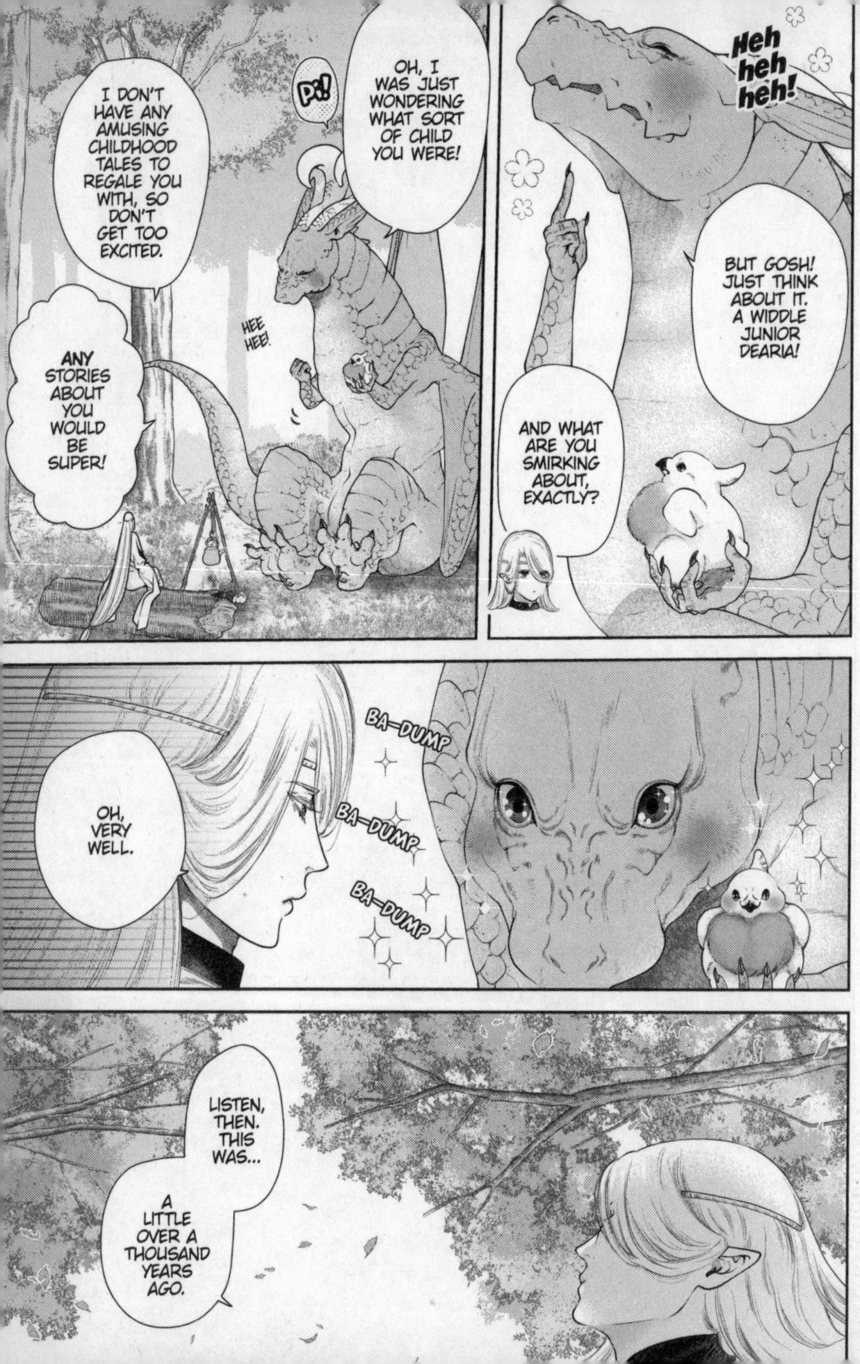

Heh heh heh!
BUT GOSH! JUST THINK ABOUT IT. A WIDDLE JUNIOR DEARIA!
AND WHAT ARE YOU SMIRKING ABOUT, EXACTLY?
Pi!
OH, I WAS JUST WONDERING WHAT SORT OF CHILD YOU WERE!
I DON'T HAVE ANY AMUSING CHILDHOOD TALES TO REGALE YOU WITH, SO DON'T GET TOO EXCITED.
HEE HEE!
ANY STORIES ABOUT YOU WOULD BE SUPER!
BA-DUMP
BA-DUMP
BA-DUMP
OH, VERY WELL.
LISTEN, THEN. THIS WAS...
A LITTLE OVER A THOUSAND YEARS AGO.

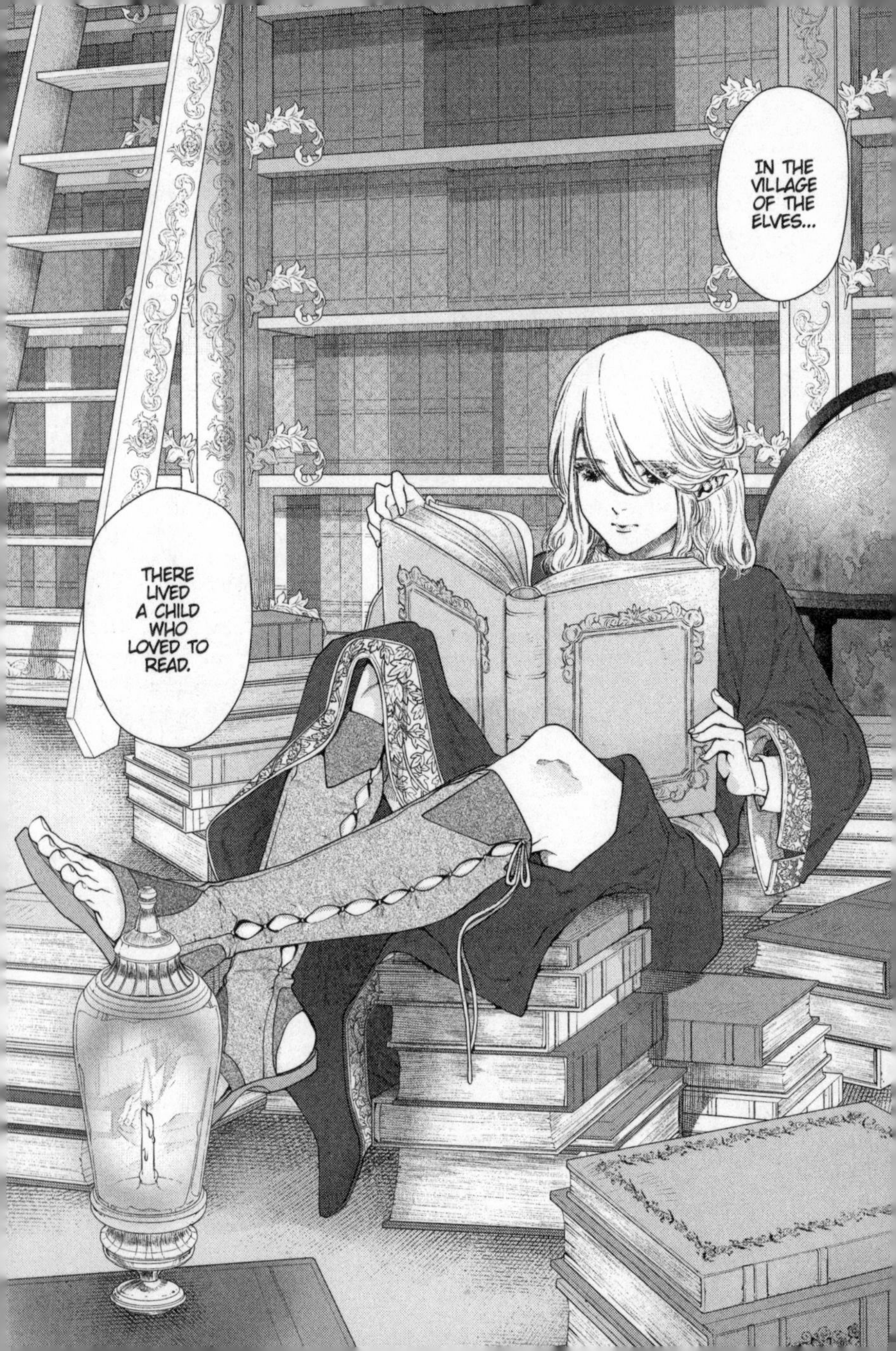
IN THE VILLAGE OF THE ELVES...
THERE LIVED A CHILD WHO LOVED TO READ.

Grown Up

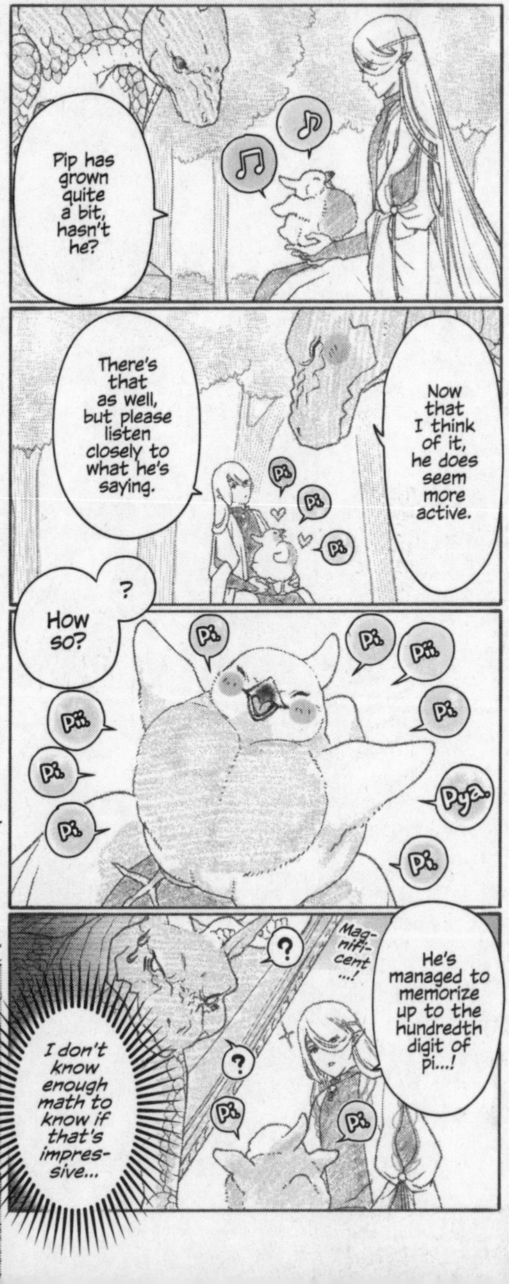
Pip has grown quite a bit, hasn't he?
Now that I think of it, he does seem more active.
There's that as well, but please listen closely to what he's saying.
Pi.
Pi.
Pi.
How so?
?
Pi.
Pi.
Pii.
Pi.
Pya.
Pi.
Pi.
Pi.
Pi.
He's managed to memorize up to the hundredth digit of pi...!
Magnificent...!
?
?
I don't know enough math to know if that's impressive...
Pi.
Pi.

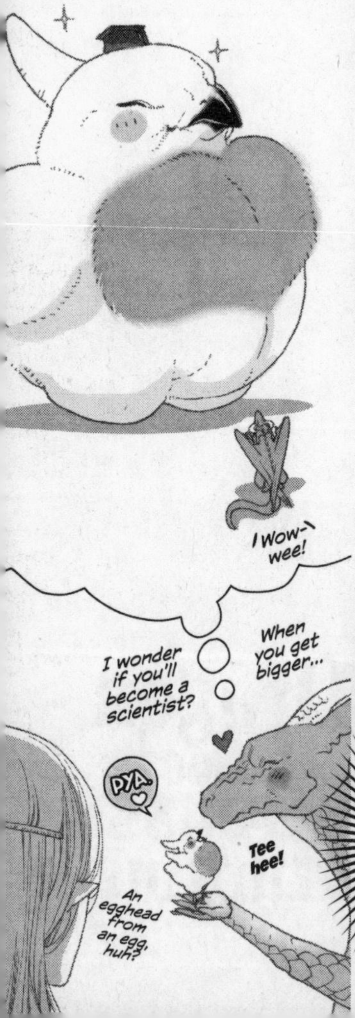
Wow-wee!
When you get bigger...
I wonder if you'll become a scientist?
PYA.
Tee hee!
An egghead from an egg, huh?

Dragon
Goes
House-
Hunting

House 17: An Unbreakable Home

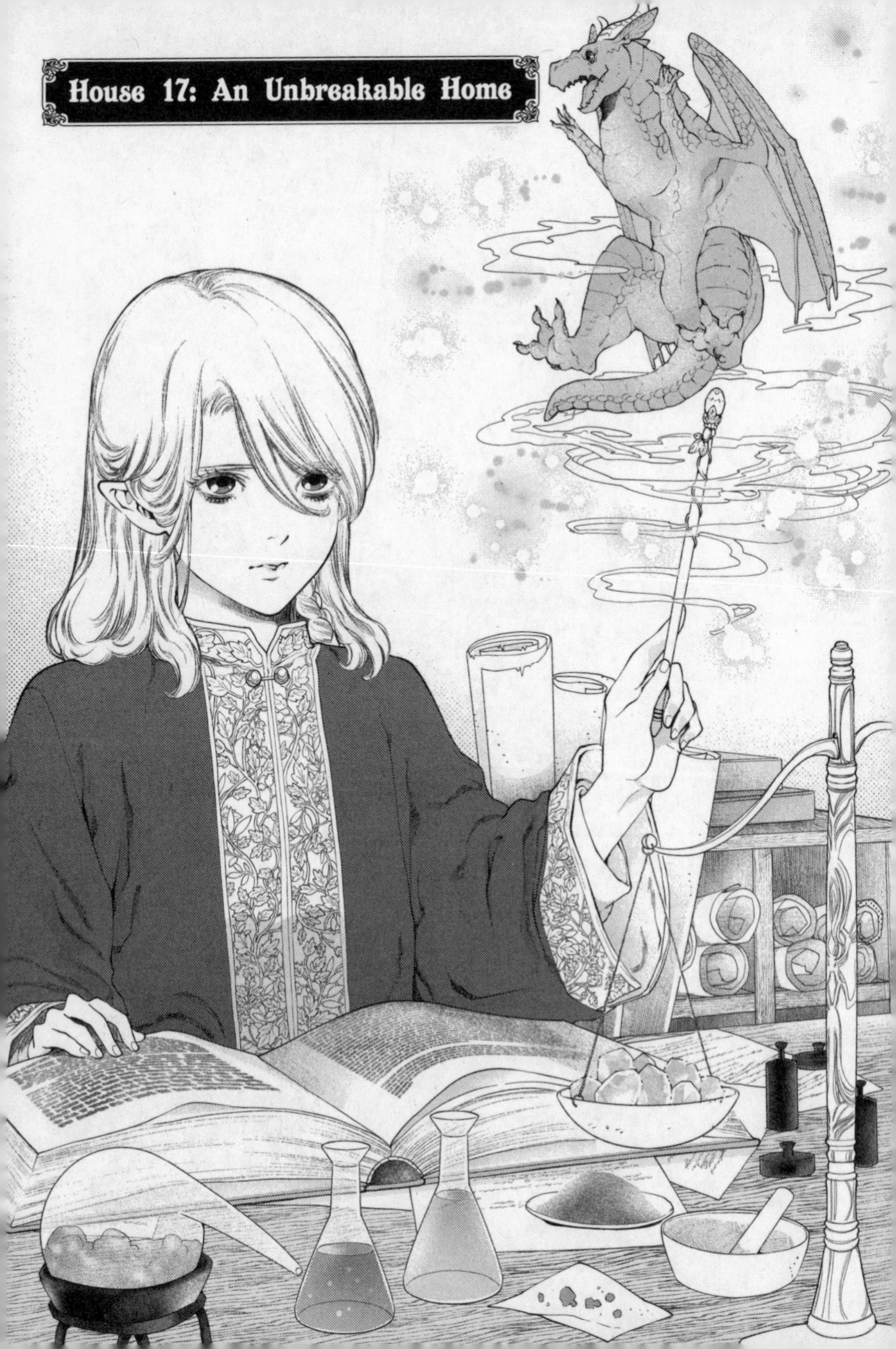

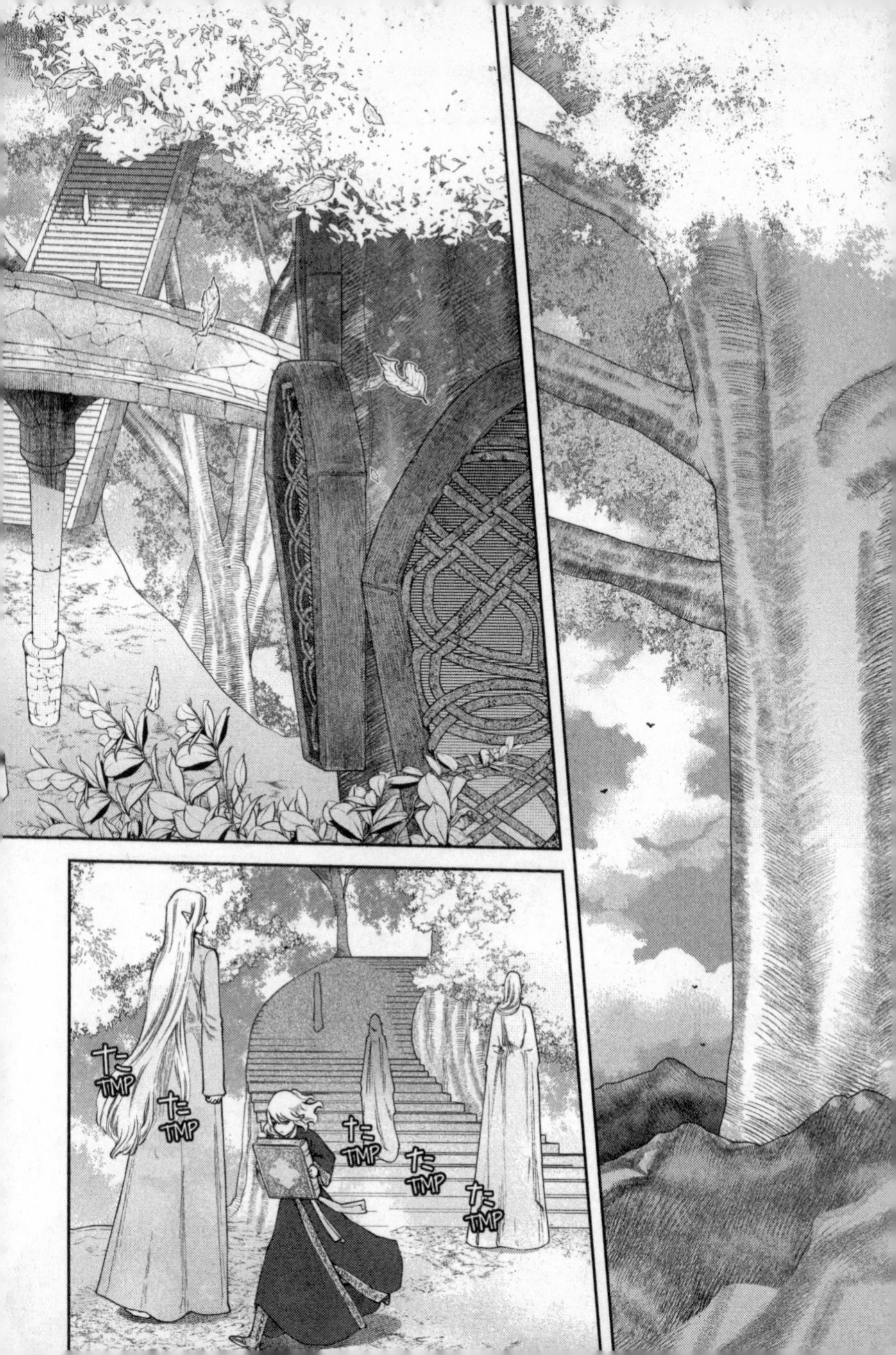
たっ
TMP
たっ
TMP
たっ
TMP
たっ
TMP
たっ
TMP

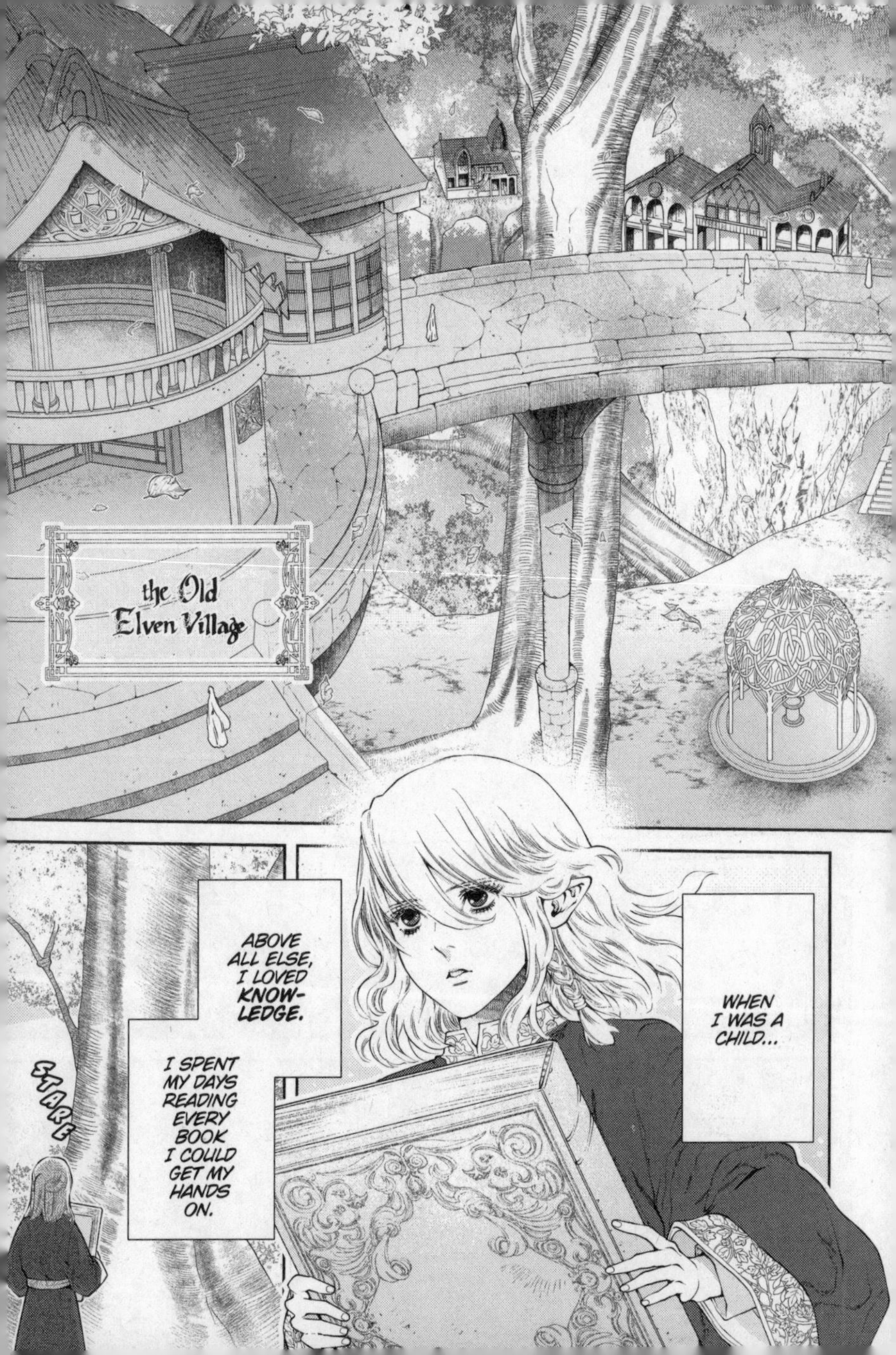
the Old Elven Village
WHEN I WAS A CHILD...
ABOVE ALL ELSE, I LOVED KNOWLEDGE.
I SPENT MY DAYS READING EVERY BOOK I COULD GET MY HANDS ON.
STARE

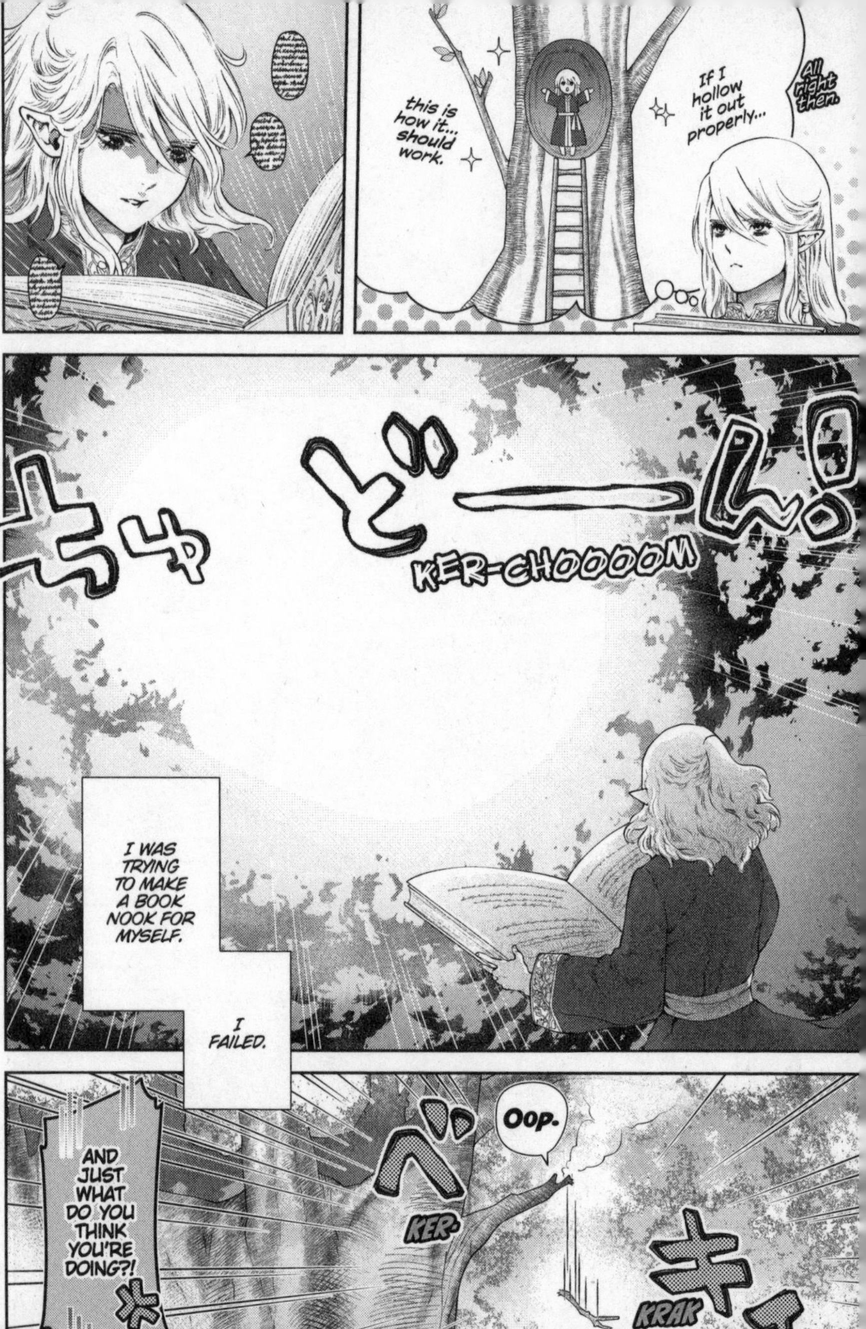
All right then.
If I hollow it out properly...
this is how it... should work.
ちゅどーーん!
KER-CHOOOOOM
I WAS TRYING TO MAKE A BOOK NOOK FOR MYSELF.
I FAILED.
Oop.
べ
KER-
キ
KRAK
AND JUST WHAT DO YOU THINK YOU'RE DOING?!

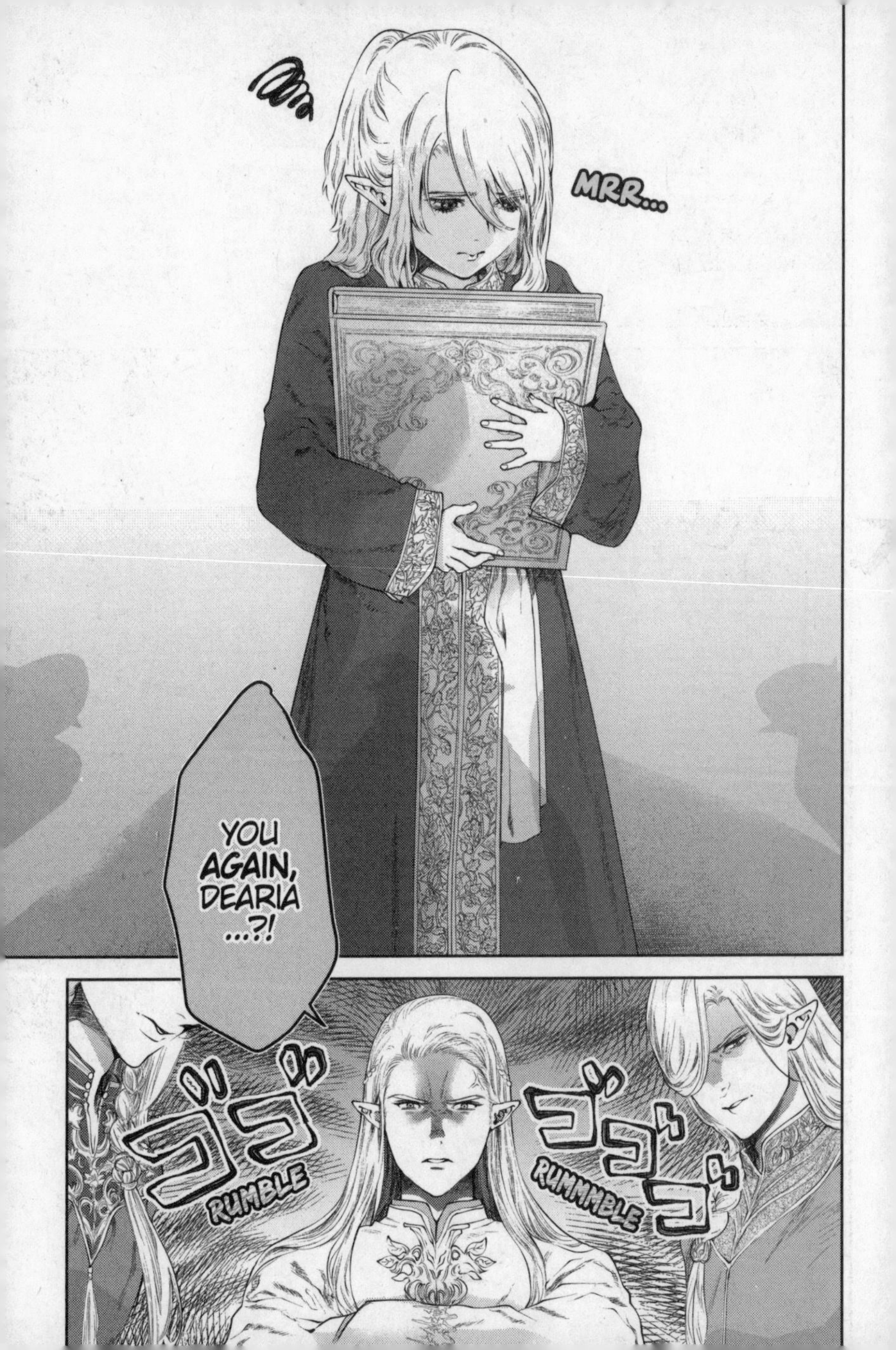
MRR...
YOU AGAIN, DEARIA ...?!
ゴゴ
RUMBLE
ゴゴゴ
RUMMMBLE

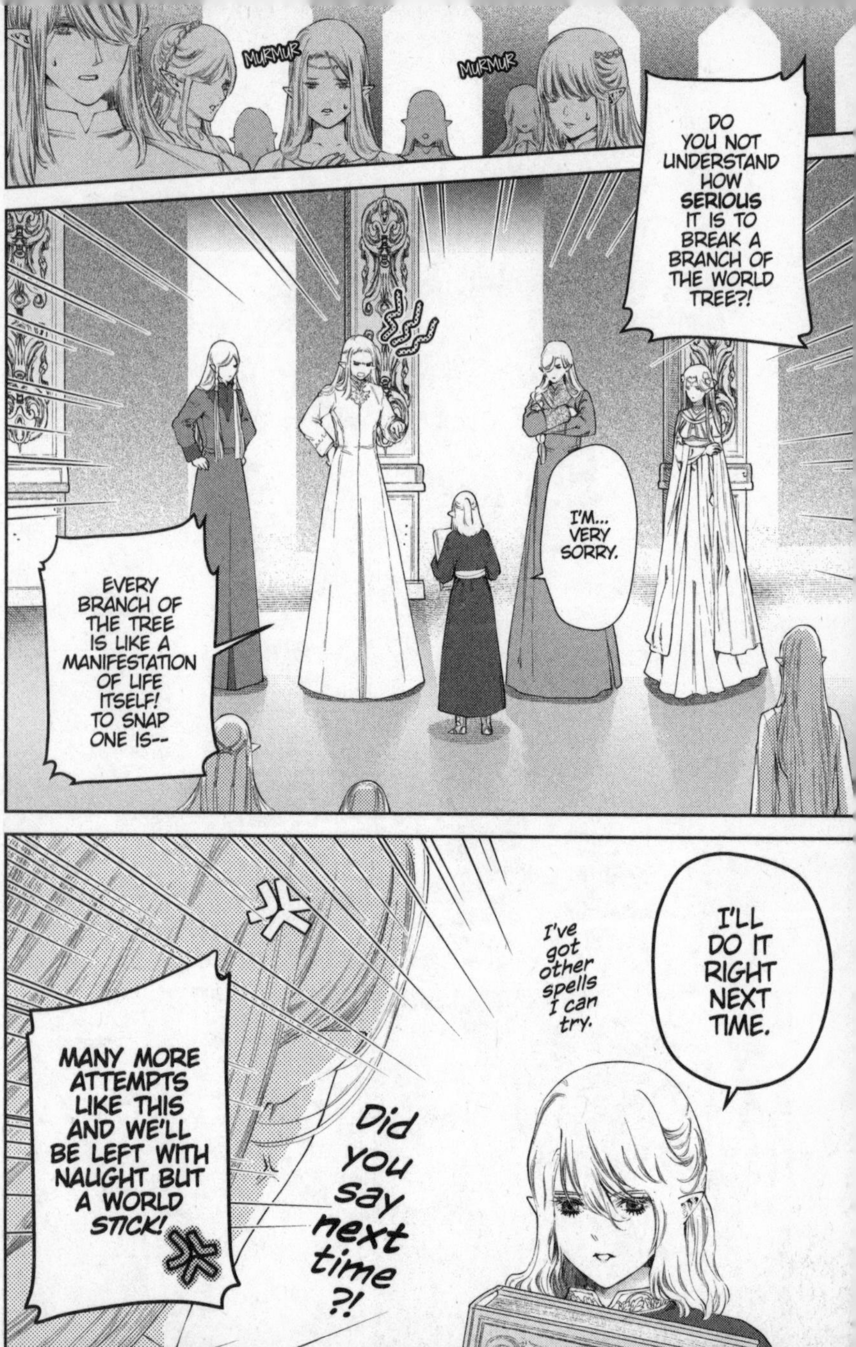
MURMUR
MURMUR
DO YOU NOT UNDERSTAND HOW SERIOUS IT IS TO BREAK A BRANCH OF THE WORLD TREE?!
I'M... VERY SORRY.
EVERY BRANCH OF THE TREE IS LIKE A MANIFESTATION OF LIFE ITSELF! TO SNAP ONE IS--
I'LL DO IT RIGHT NEXT TIME.
I've got other spells I can try.
Did you say next time?!
MANY MORE ATTEMPTS LIKE THIS AND WE'LL BE LEFT WITH NAUGHT BUT A WORLD STICK!

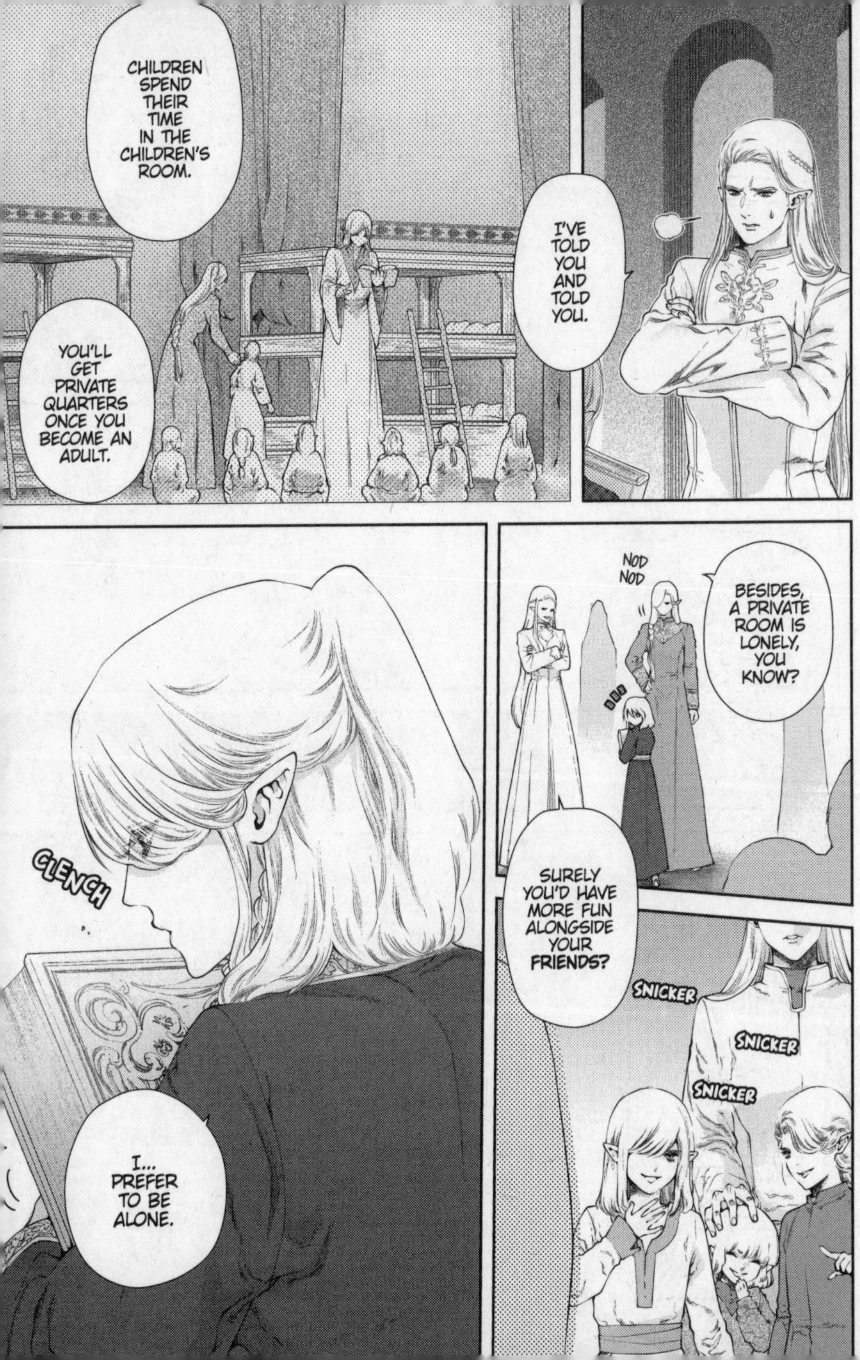
I'VE TOLD YOU AND TOLD YOU.
CHILDREN SPEND THEIR TIME IN THE CHILDREN'S ROOM.
YOU'LL GET PRIVATE QUARTERS ONCE YOU BECOME AN ADULT.
NOD NOD
BESIDES, A PRIVATE ROOM IS LONELY, YOU KNOW?
SURELY YOU'D HAVE MORE FUN ALONGSIDE YOUR FRIENDS?
SNICKER
SNICKER
SNICKER
CLENCH
I... PREFER TO BE ALONE.

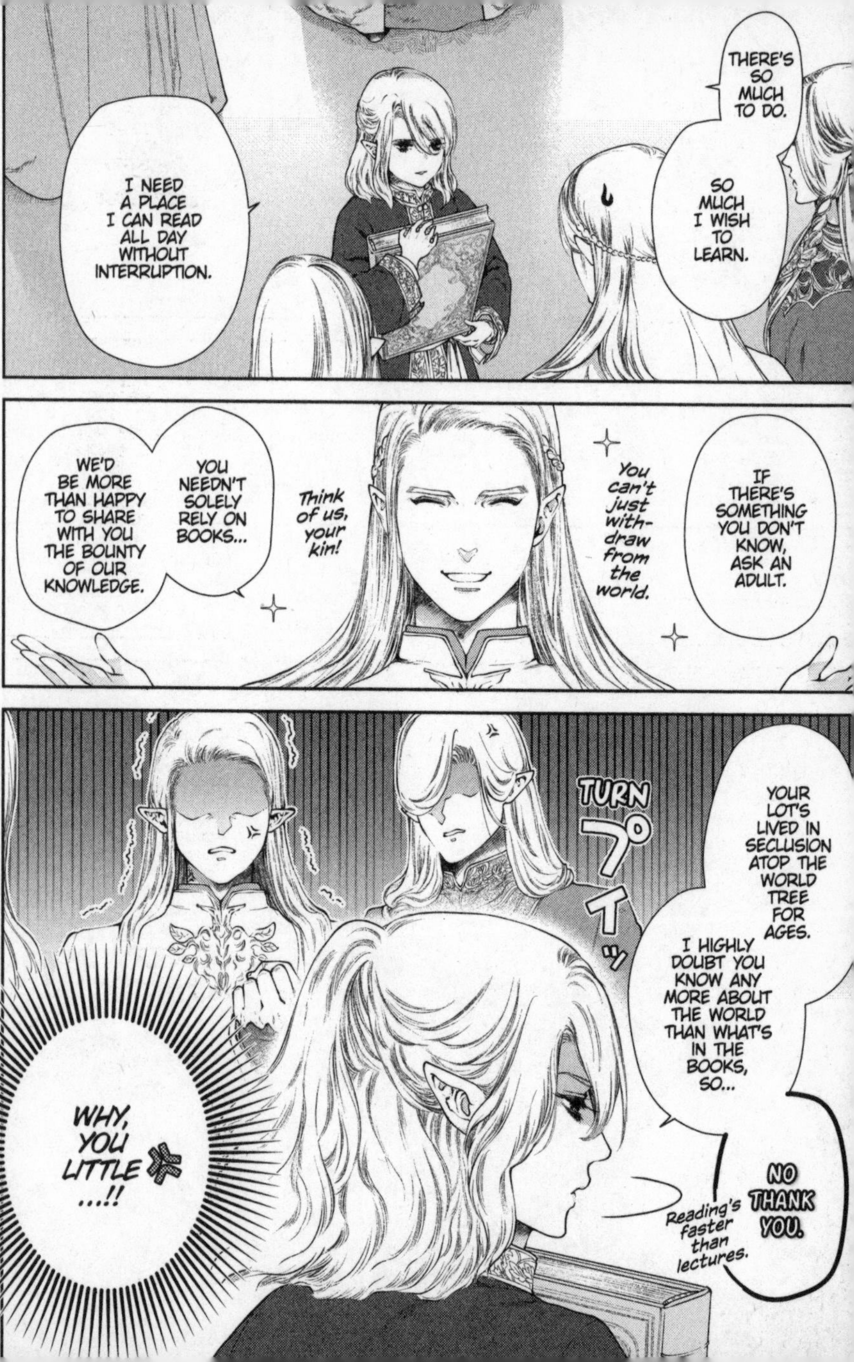
THERE'S SO MUCH TO DO.
SO MUCH I WISH TO LEARN.
I NEED A PLACE I CAN READ ALL DAY WITHOUT INTERRUPTION.
IF THERE'S SOMETHING YOU DON'T KNOW, ASK AN ADULT.
You can't just with-draw from the world.
Think of us, your kin!
YOU NEEDN'T SOLELY RELY ON BOOKS...
WE'D BE MORE THAN HAPPY TO SHARE WITH YOU THE BOUNTY OF OUR KNOWLEDGE.
TURN
プイッ
YOUR LOT'S LIVED IN SECLUSION ATOP THE WORLD TREE FOR AGES.
I HIGHLY DOUBT YOU KNOW ANY MORE ABOUT THE WORLD THAN WHAT'S IN THE BOOKS, SO...
NO THANK YOU.
Reading's faster than lectures.
WHY, YOU LITTLE ...!!

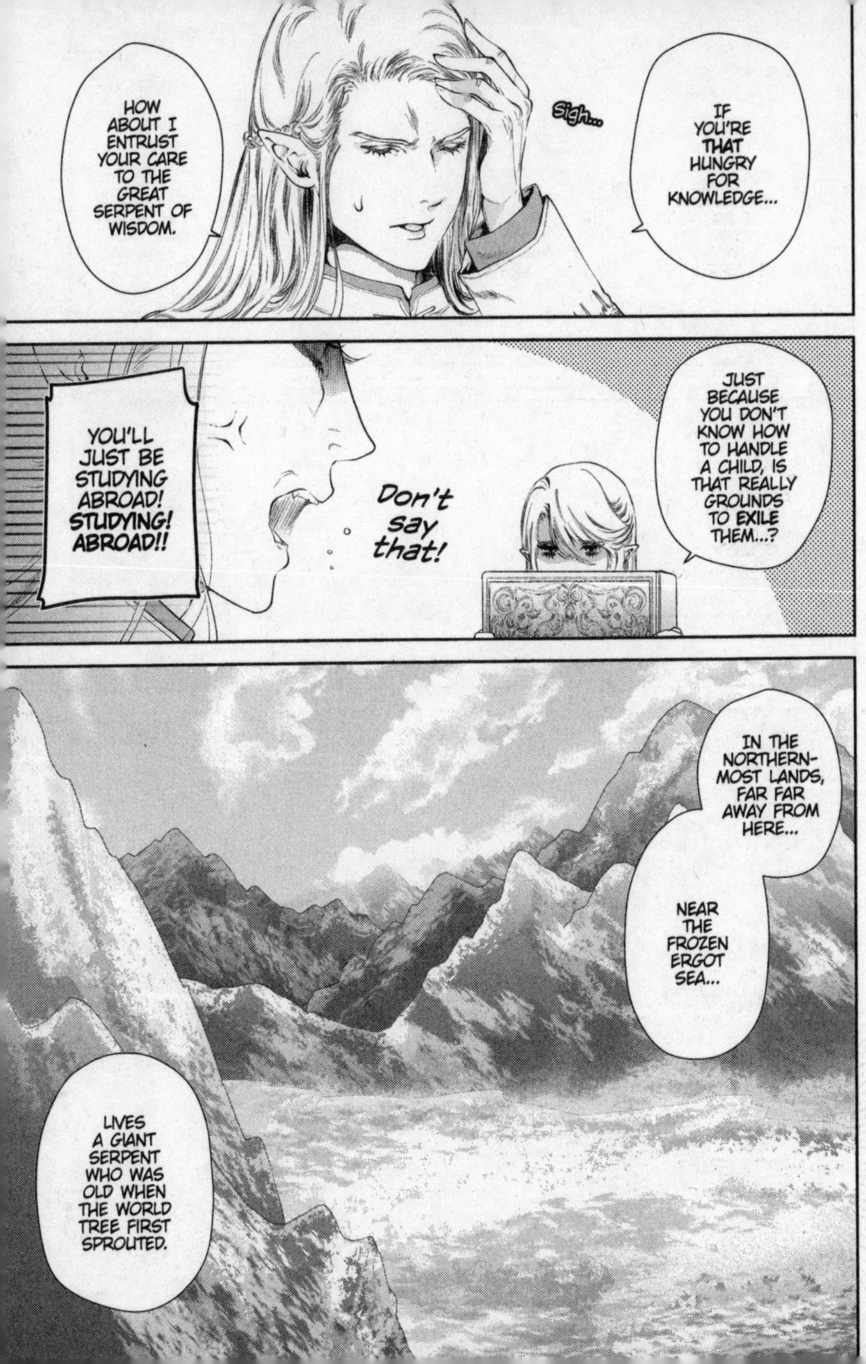
IF YOU'RE THAT HUNGRY FOR KNOWLEDGE...
Sigh...
HOW ABOUT I ENTRUST YOUR CARE TO THE GREAT SERPENT OF WISDOM.
JUST BECAUSE YOU DON'T KNOW HOW TO HANDLE A CHILD, IS THAT REALLY GROUNDS TO EXILE THEM...?
Don't say that!
YOU'LL JUST BE STUDYING ABROAD! STUDYING! ABROAD!!
IN THE NORTHERN-MOST LANDS, FAR FAR AWAY FROM HERE...
NEAR THE FROZEN ERGOT SEA...
LIVES A GIANT SERPENT WHO WAS OLD WHEN THE WORLD TREE FIRST SPROUTED.

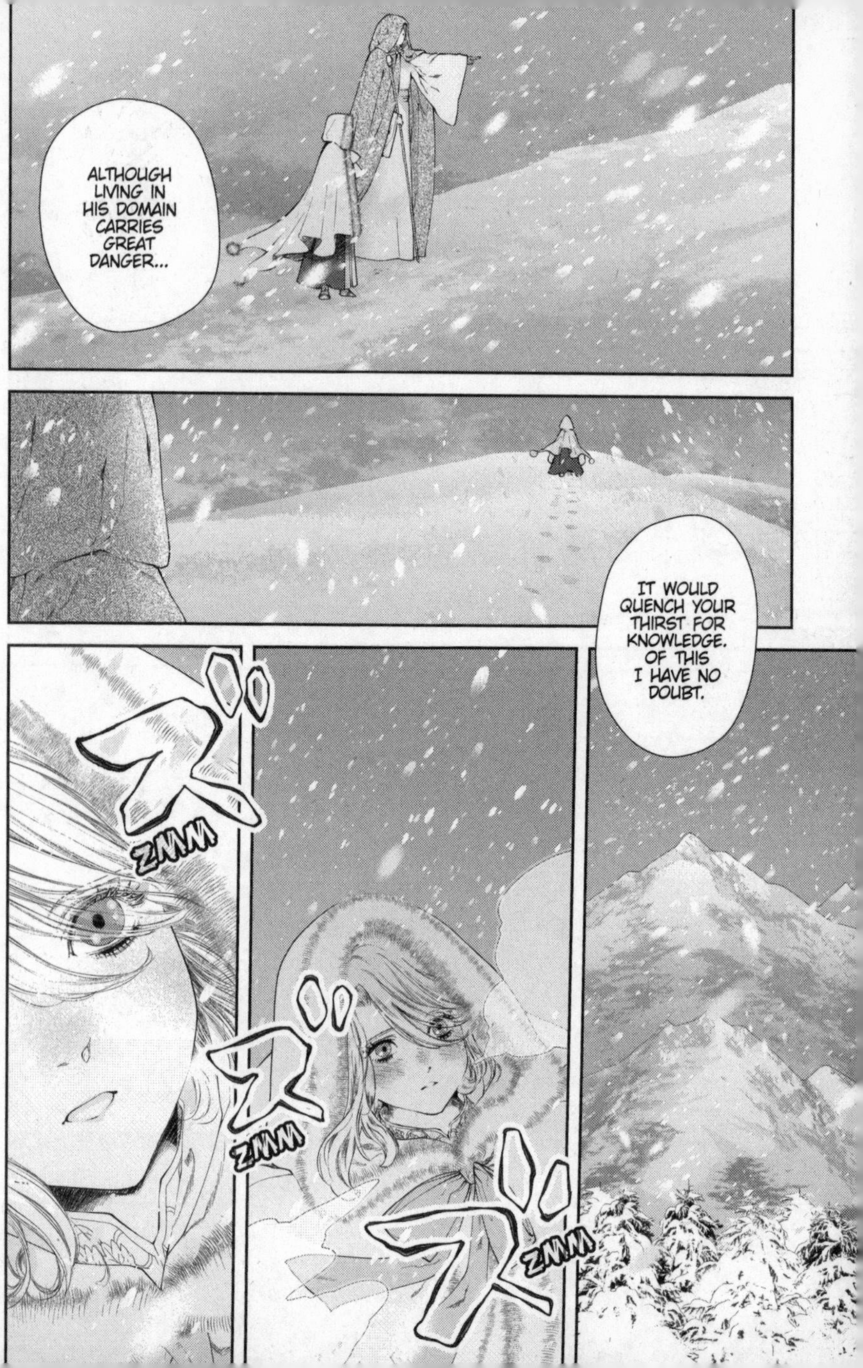

ALTHOUGH LIVING IN HIS DOMAIN CARRIES GREAT DANGER...
IT WOULD QUENCH YOUR THIRST FOR KNOWLEDGE. OF THIS I HAVE NO DOUBT.
ZMMM
ZMMM
ZMMM

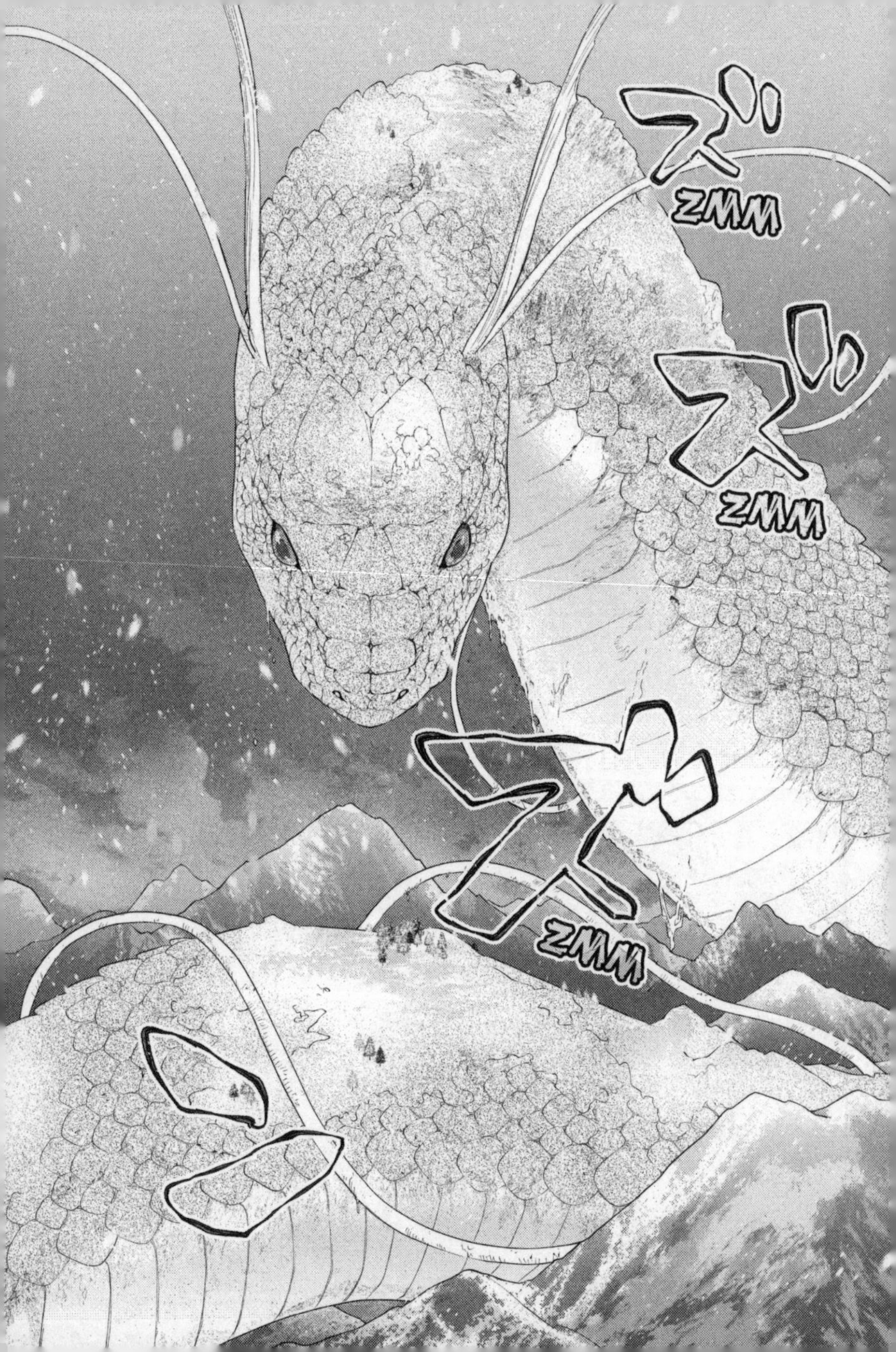
ズ
ZMMM
ズ
ZMMM
ズ
ZMMM
ン

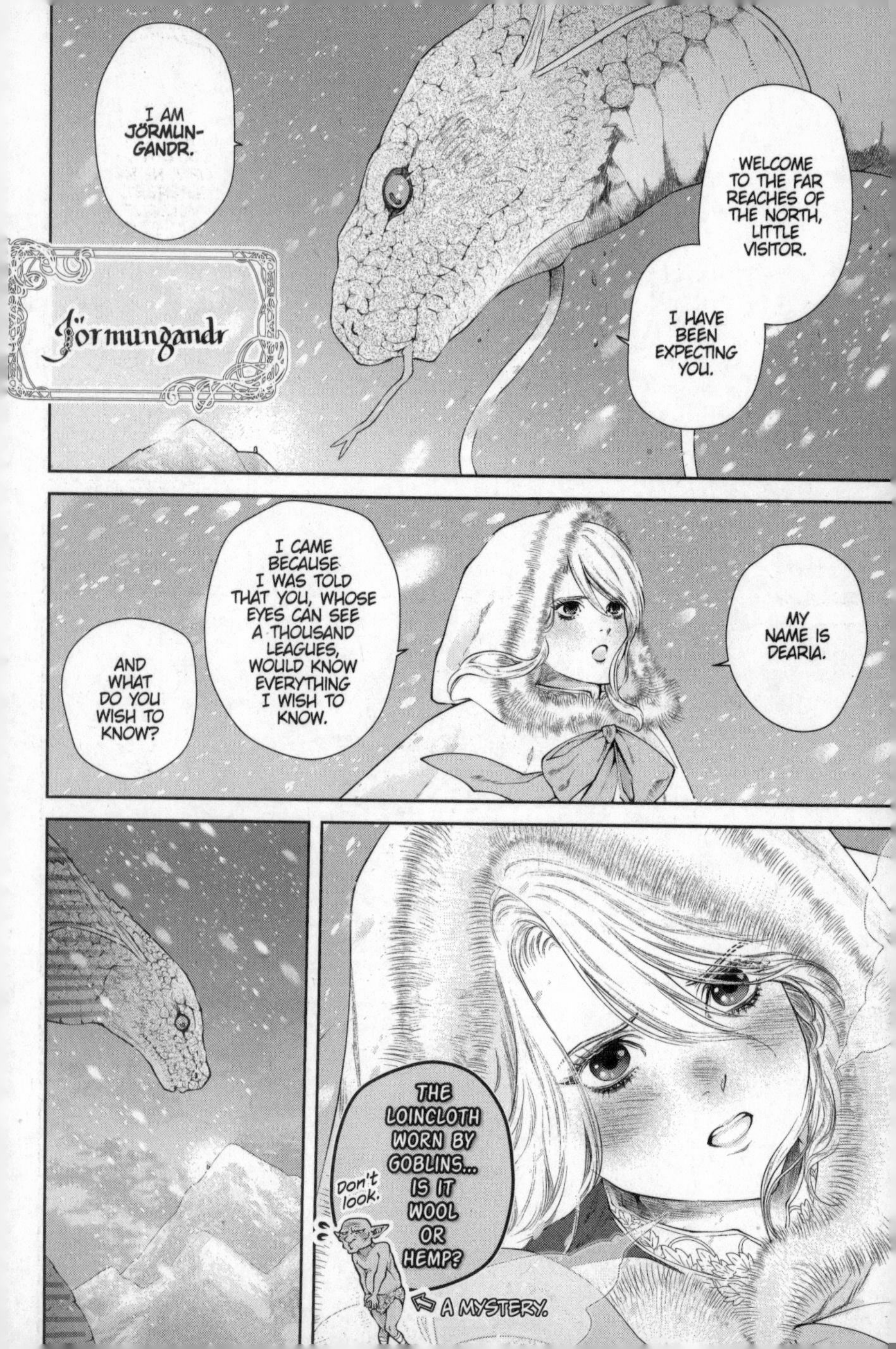
I AM JÖRMUN-GANDR.
Jörmungandr
WELCOME TO THE FAR REACHES OF THE NORTH, LITTLE VISITOR.
I HAVE BEEN EXPECTING YOU.
MY NAME IS DEARIA.
I CAME BECAUSE I WAS TOLD THAT YOU, WHOSE EYES CAN SEE A THOUSAND LEAGUES, WOULD KNOW EVERYTHING I WISH TO KNOW.
AND WHAT DO YOU WISH TO KNOW?
THE LOINCLOTH WORN BY GOBLINS... IS IT WOOL OR HEMP?
Don't look.
A MYSTERY.

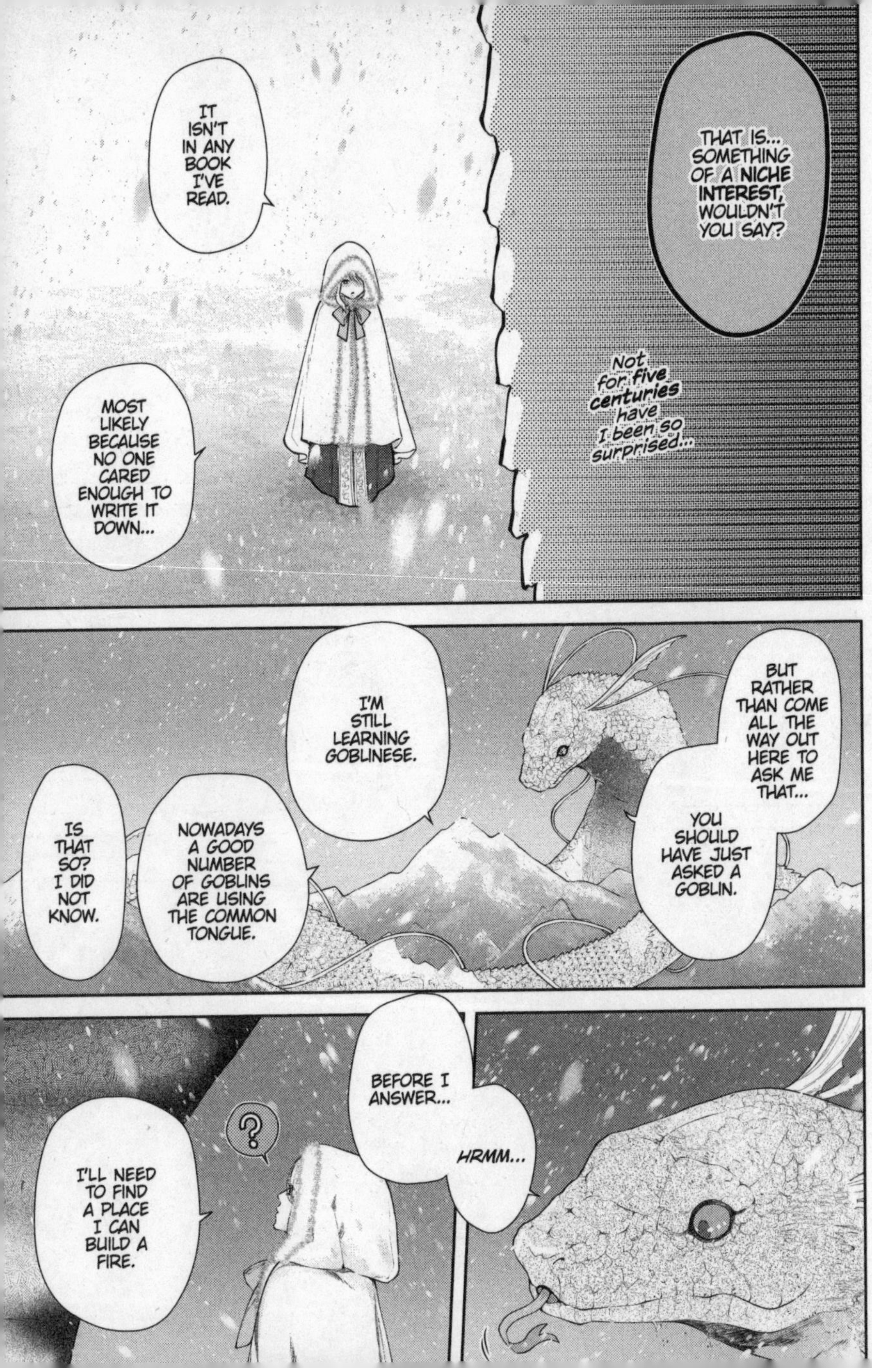
THAT IS... SOMETHING OF A NICHE INTEREST, WOULDN'T YOU SAY?
Not for five centuries have I been so surprised...
IT ISN'T IN ANY BOOK I'VE READ.
MOST LIKELY BECAUSE NO ONE CARED ENOUGH TO WRITE IT DOWN...
BUT RATHER THAN COME ALL THE WAY OUT HERE TO ASK ME THAT...
YOU SHOULD HAVE JUST ASKED A GOBLIN.
I'M STILL LEARNING GOBLINESE.
NOWADAYS A GOOD NUMBER OF GOBLINS ARE USING THE COMMON TONGUE.
IS THAT SO? I DID NOT KNOW.
BEFORE I ANSWER...
HRMM...
?
I'LL NEED TO FIND A PLACE I CAN BUILD A FIRE.

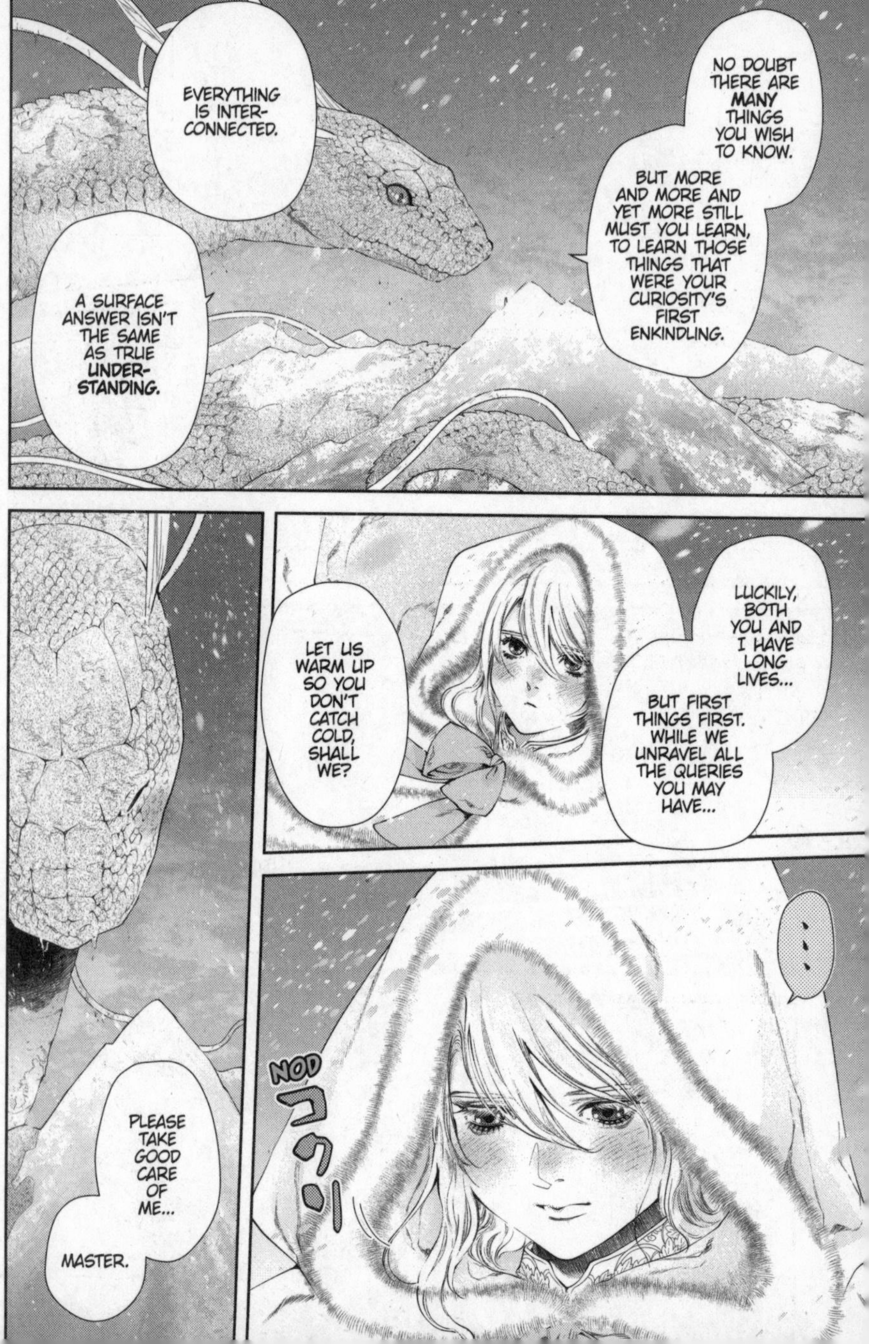
NO DOUBT THERE ARE MANY THINGS YOU WISH TO KNOW.
BUT MORE AND MORE AND YET MORE STILL MUST YOU LEARN, TO LEARN THOSE THINGS THAT WERE YOUR CURIOSITY'S FIRST ENKINDLING.
EVERYTHING IS INTER-CONNECTED.
A SURFACE ANSWER ISN'T THE SAME AS TRUE UNDER-STANDING.
LUCKILY, BOTH YOU AND I HAVE LONG LIVES...
BUT FIRST THINGS FIRST. WHILE WE UNRAVEL ALL THE QUERIES YOU MAY HAVE...
LET US WARM UP SO YOU DON'T CATCH COLD, SHALL WE?
...
NOD
PLEASE TAKE GOOD CARE OF ME...
MASTER.

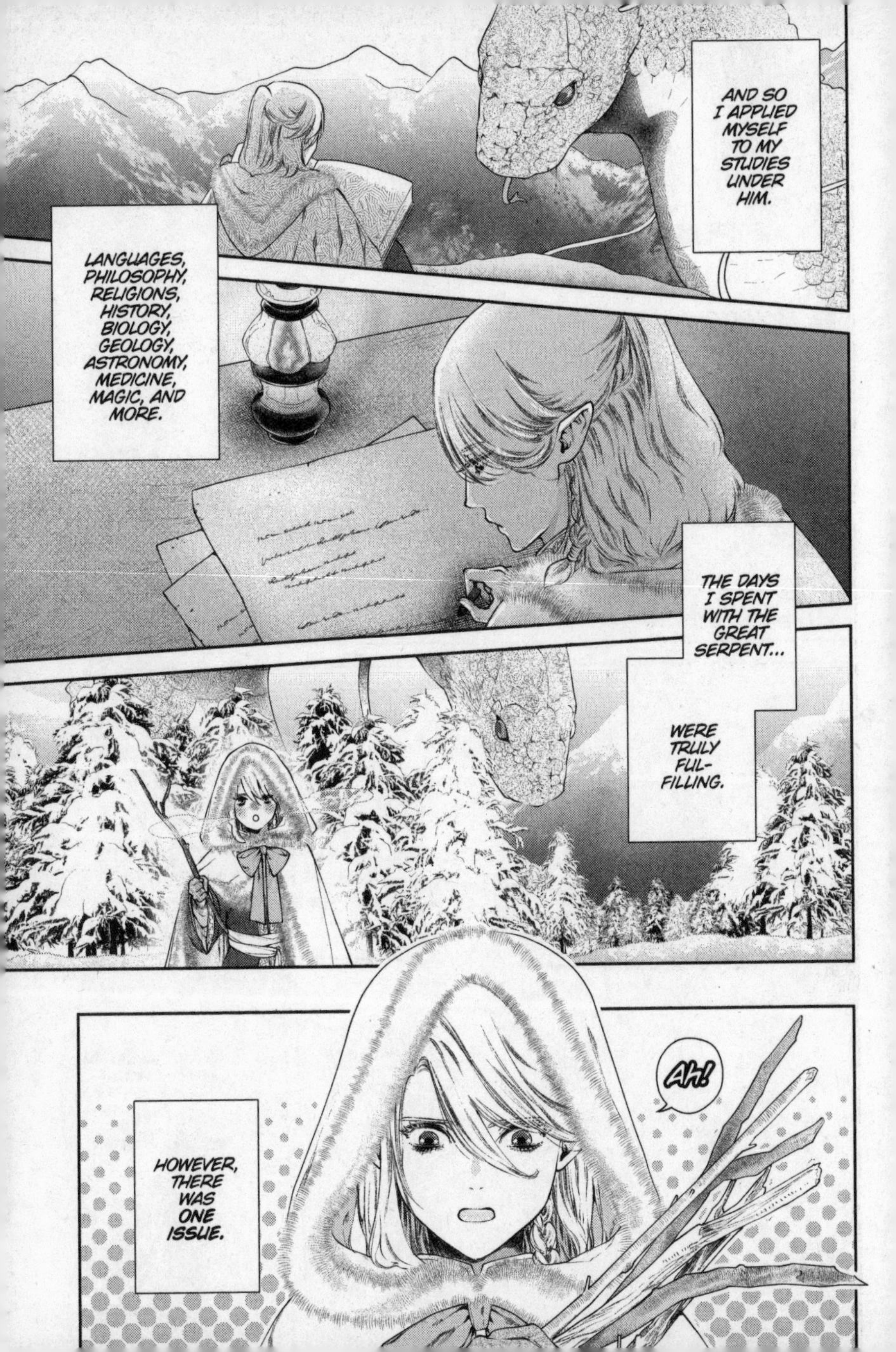
AND SO I APPLIED MYSELF TO MY STUDIES UNDER HIM.
LANGUAGES, PHILOSOPHY, RELIGIONS, HISTORY, BIOLOGY, GEOLOGY, ASTRONOMY, MEDICINE, MAGIC, AND MORE.
THE DAYS I SPENT WITH THE GREAT SERPENT...
WERE TRULY FUL-FILLING.
Ah!
HOWEVER, THERE WAS ONE ISSUE.

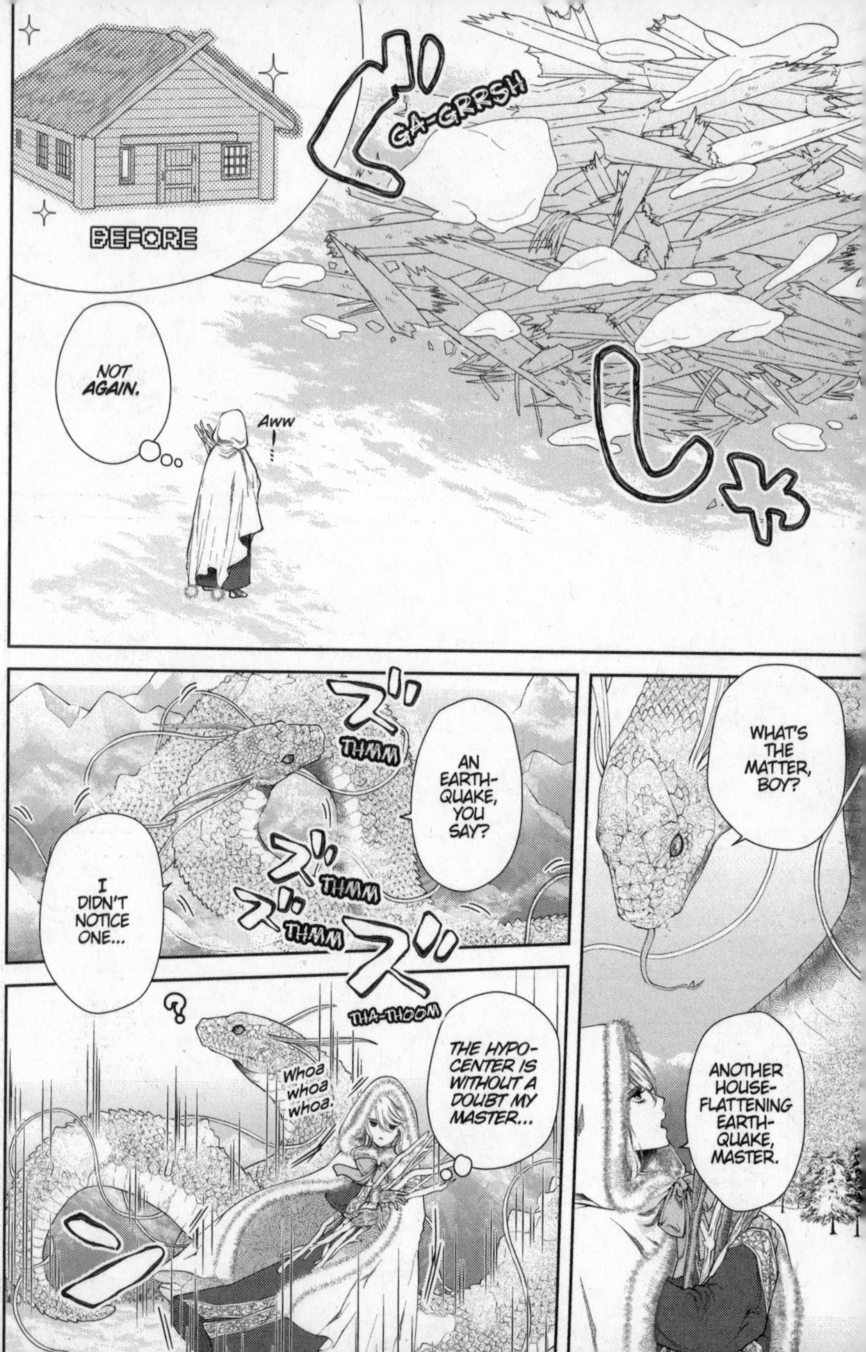
BEFORE
GA-GRRSH
NOT AGAIN.
Aww!
WHAT'S THE MATTER, BOY?
ANOTHER HOUSE-FLATTENING EARTH-QUAKE, MASTER.
AN EARTH-QUAKE, YOU SAY?
THMM
THMM
THMM
I DIDN'T NOTICE ONE...
THA-THOOM
THE HYPO-CENTER IS WITHOUT A DOUBT MY MASTER...
Whoa whoa whoa.

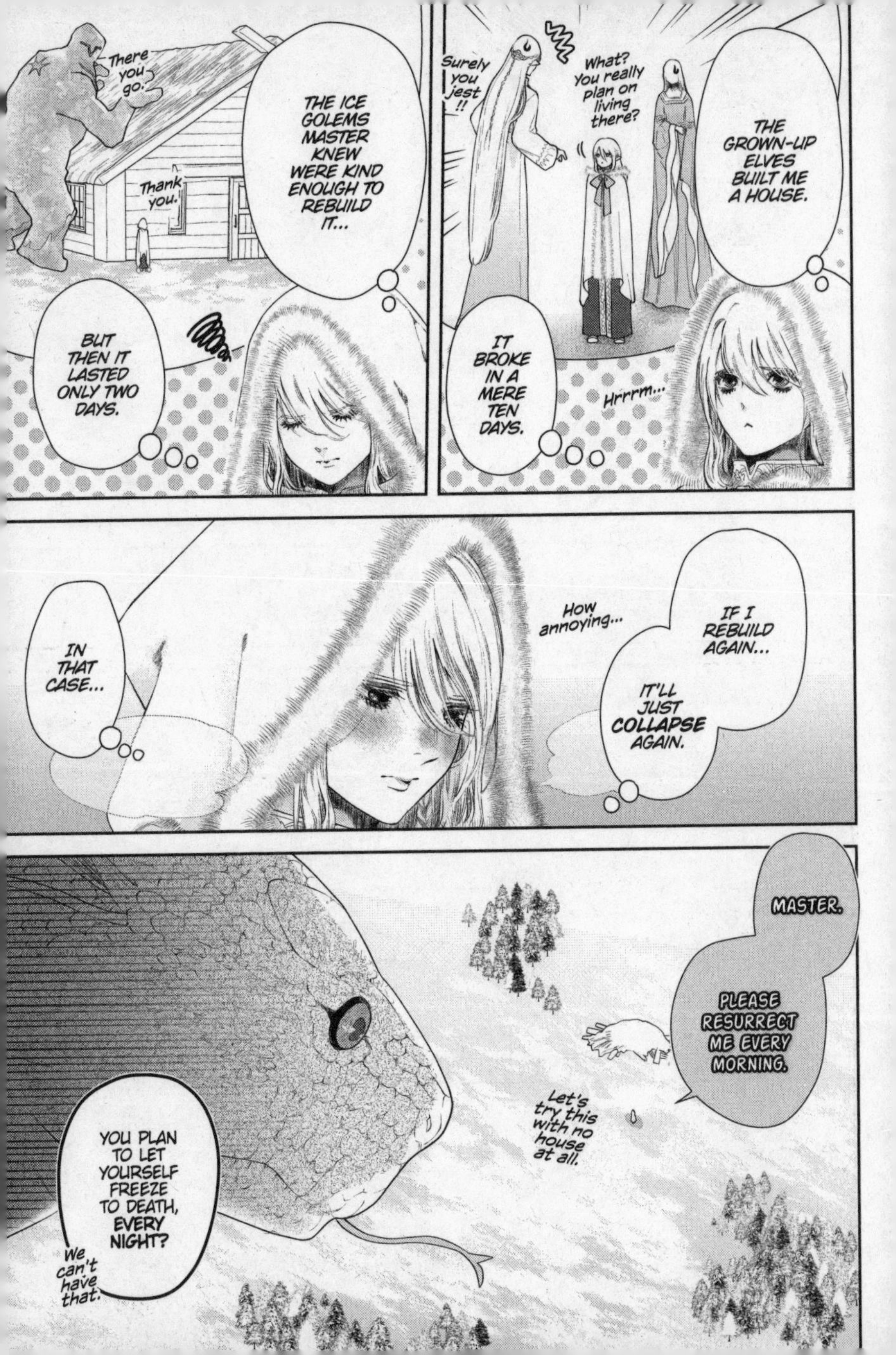
THE GROWN-UP ELVES BUILT ME A HOUSE.
What? You really plan on living there?
Surely you jest!!
Hrrrm...
IT BROKE IN A MERE TEN DAYS.
THE ICE GOLEMS MASTER KNEW WERE KIND ENOUGH TO REBUILD IT...
There you go.
Thank you.
BUT THEN IT LASTED ONLY TWO DAYS.
IF I REBUILD AGAIN...
IT'LL JUST COLLAPSE AGAIN.
How annoying...
IN THAT CASE...
MASTER.
PLEASE RESURRECT ME EVERY MORNING.
Let's try this with no house at all.
YOU PLAN TO LET YOURSELF FREEZE TO DEATH, EVERY NIGHT?
We can't have that.

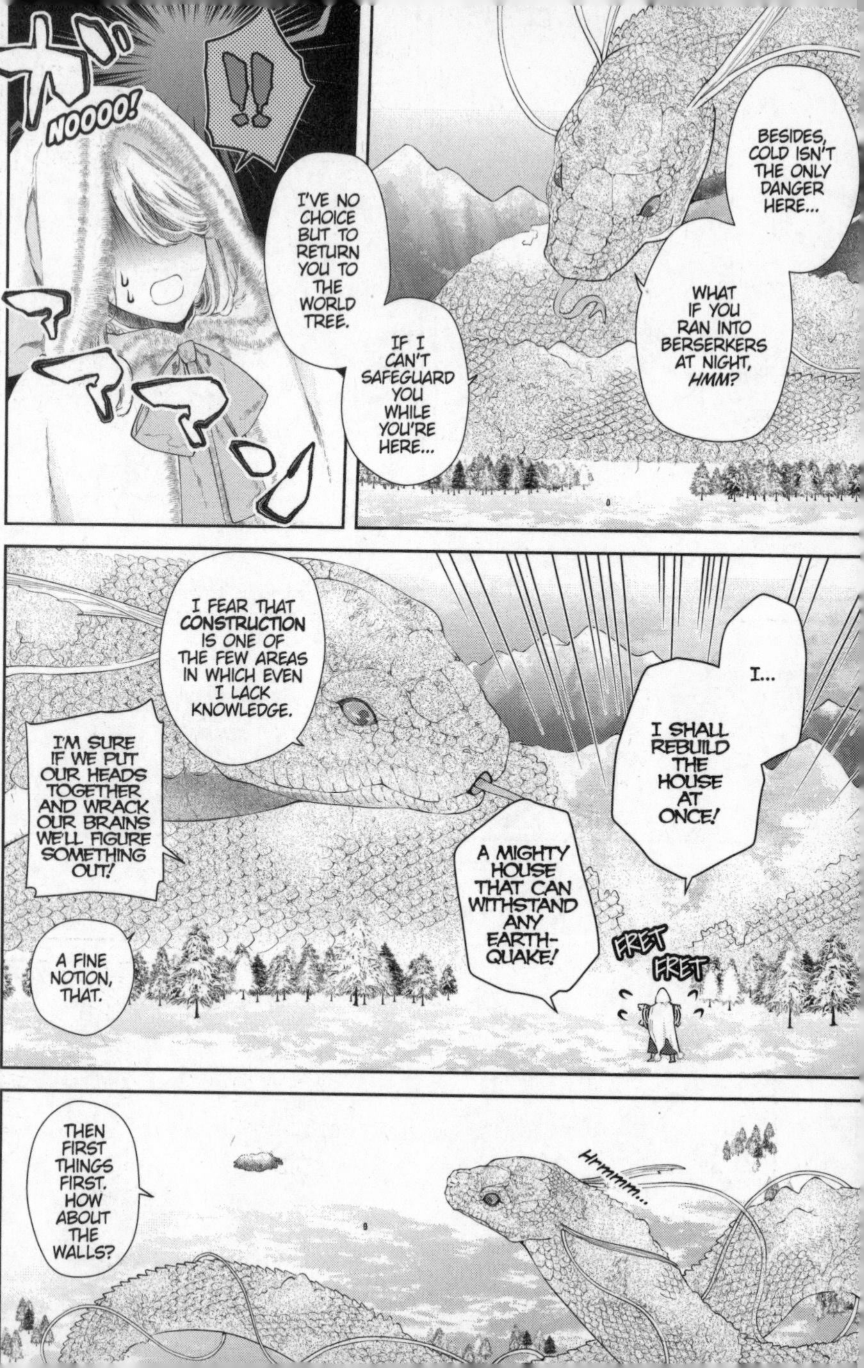
BESIDES, COLD ISN'T THE ONLY DANGER HERE...
WHAT IF YOU RAN INTO BERSERKERS AT NIGHT, *HMM?*
IF I CAN'T SAFEGUARD YOU WHILE YOU'RE HERE...
I'VE NO CHOICE BUT TO RETURN YOU TO THE WORLD TREE.
!!
NOOOO!
I...
I SHALL REBUILD THE HOUSE AT ONCE!
A MIGHTY HOUSE THAT CAN WITHSTAND ANY EARTHQUAKE!
FRET FRET
I FEAR THAT **CONSTRUCTION** IS ONE OF THE FEW AREAS IN WHICH EVEN I LACK KNOWLEDGE.
I'M SURE IF WE PUT OUR HEADS TOGETHER AND WRACK OUR BRAINS WE'LL FIGURE SOMETHING OUT!
A FINE NOTION, THAT.
Hrmmm...
THEN FIRST THINGS FIRST. HOW ABOUT THE WALLS?

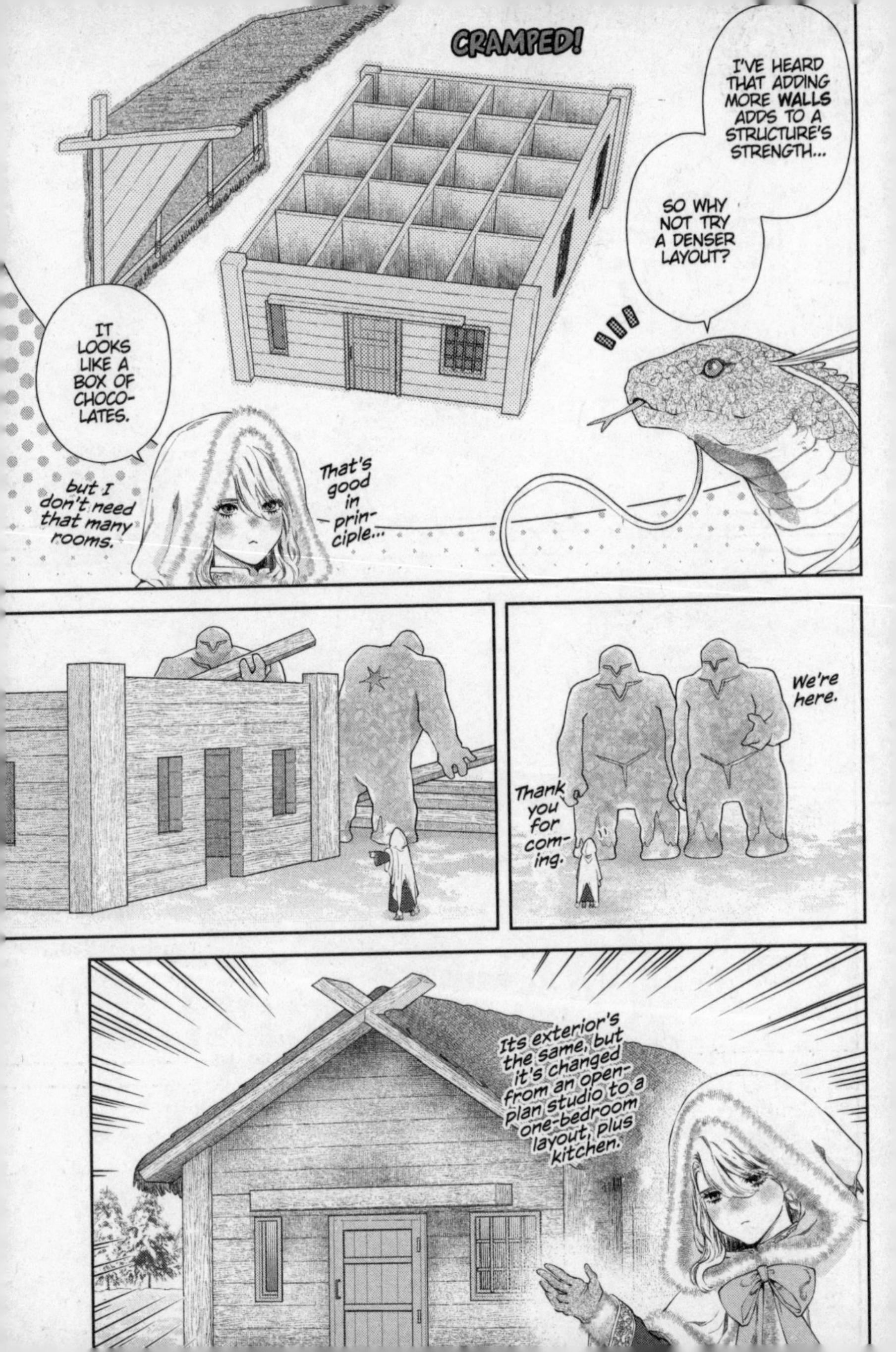
CRAMPED!
I'VE HEARD THAT ADDING MORE WALLS ADDS TO A STRUCTURE'S STRENGTH...
SO WHY NOT TRY A DENSER LAYOUT?
That's good in prin-ciple...
but I don't need that many rooms.
IT LOOKS LIKE A BOX OF CHOCO-LATES.
We're here.
Thank you for com-ing.
Its exterior's the same, but it's changed from an open-plan studio to a one-bedroom layout, plus kitchen.

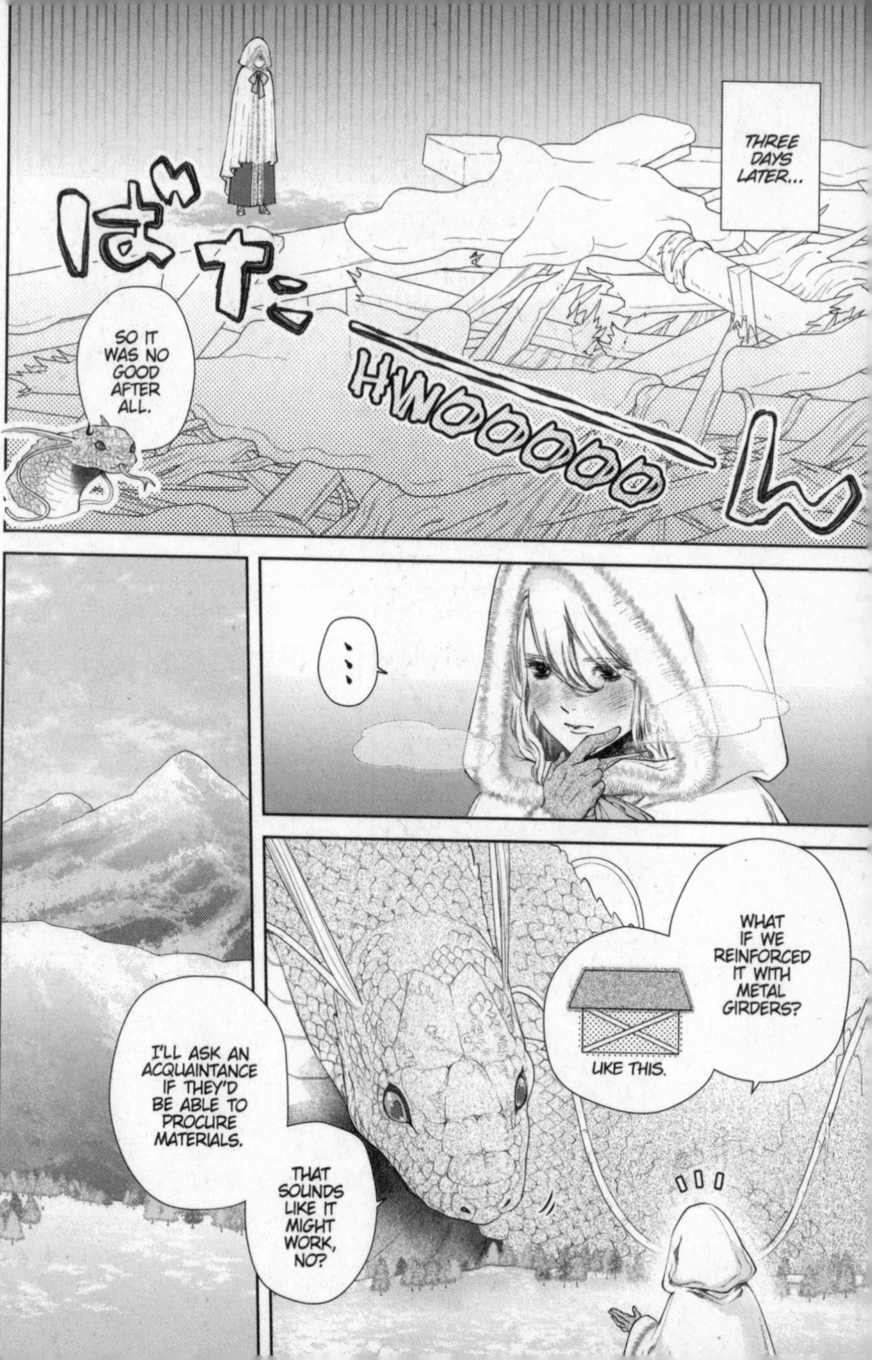
THREE DAYS LATER...
ばっ
HWOOOOOO
SO IT WAS NO GOOD AFTER ALL.
...
WHAT IF WE REINFORCED IT WITH METAL GIRDERS?
LIKE THIS.
I'LL ASK AN ACQUAINTANCE IF THEY'D BE ABLE TO PROCURE MATERIALS.
THAT SOUNDS LIKE IT MIGHT WORK, NO?

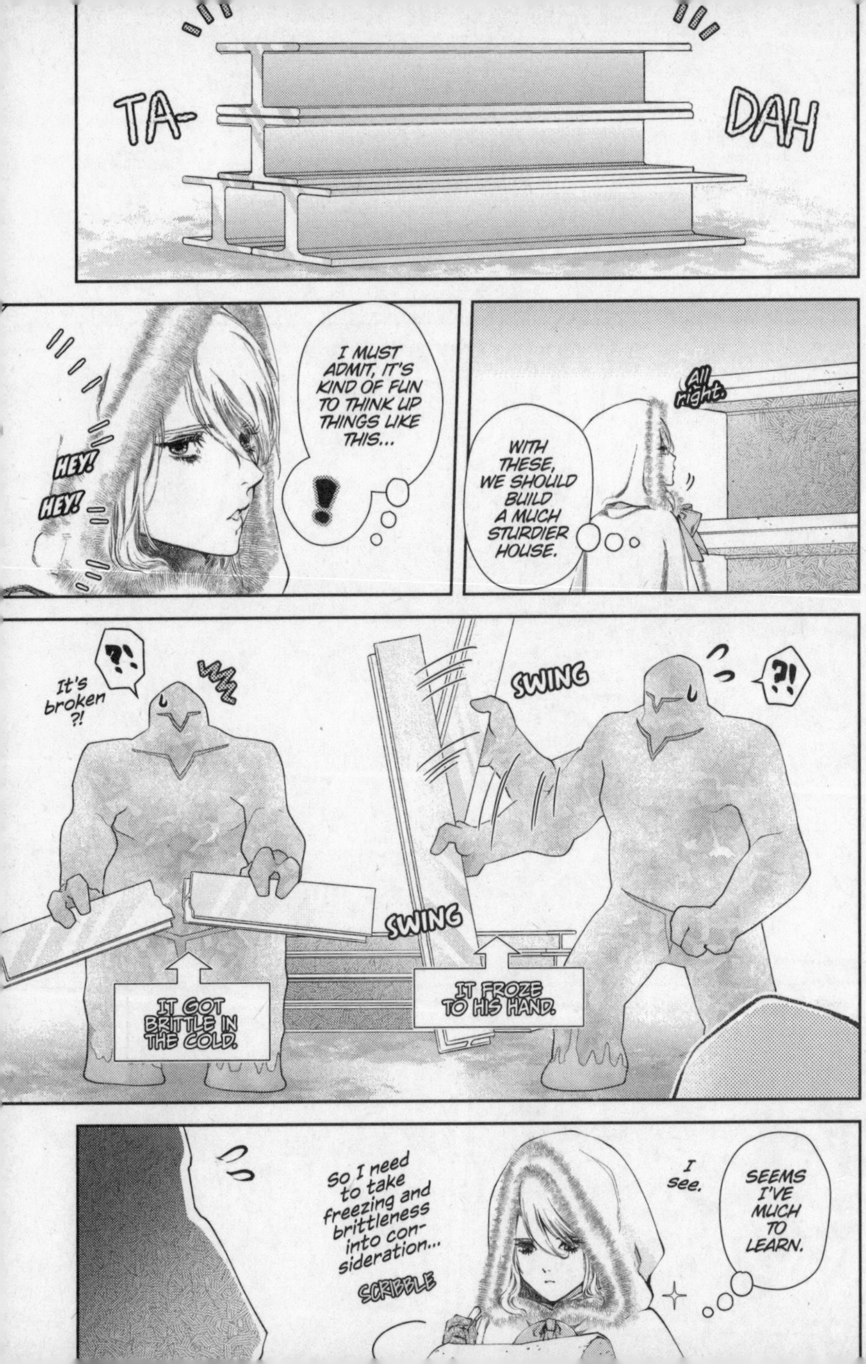
TA-
DAH
All right.
WITH THESE, WE SHOULD BUILD A MUCH STURDIER HOUSE.
I MUST ADMIT, IT'S KIND OF FUN TO THINK UP THINGS LIKE THIS...
!
HEY!
HEY!
?!
SWING
SWING
IT FROZE TO HIS HAND.
?!
It's broken ?!
IT GOT BRITTLE IN THE COLD.
SEEMS I'VE MUCH TO LEARN.
I see.
So I need to take freezing and brittleness into con-sideration...
SCRIBBLE

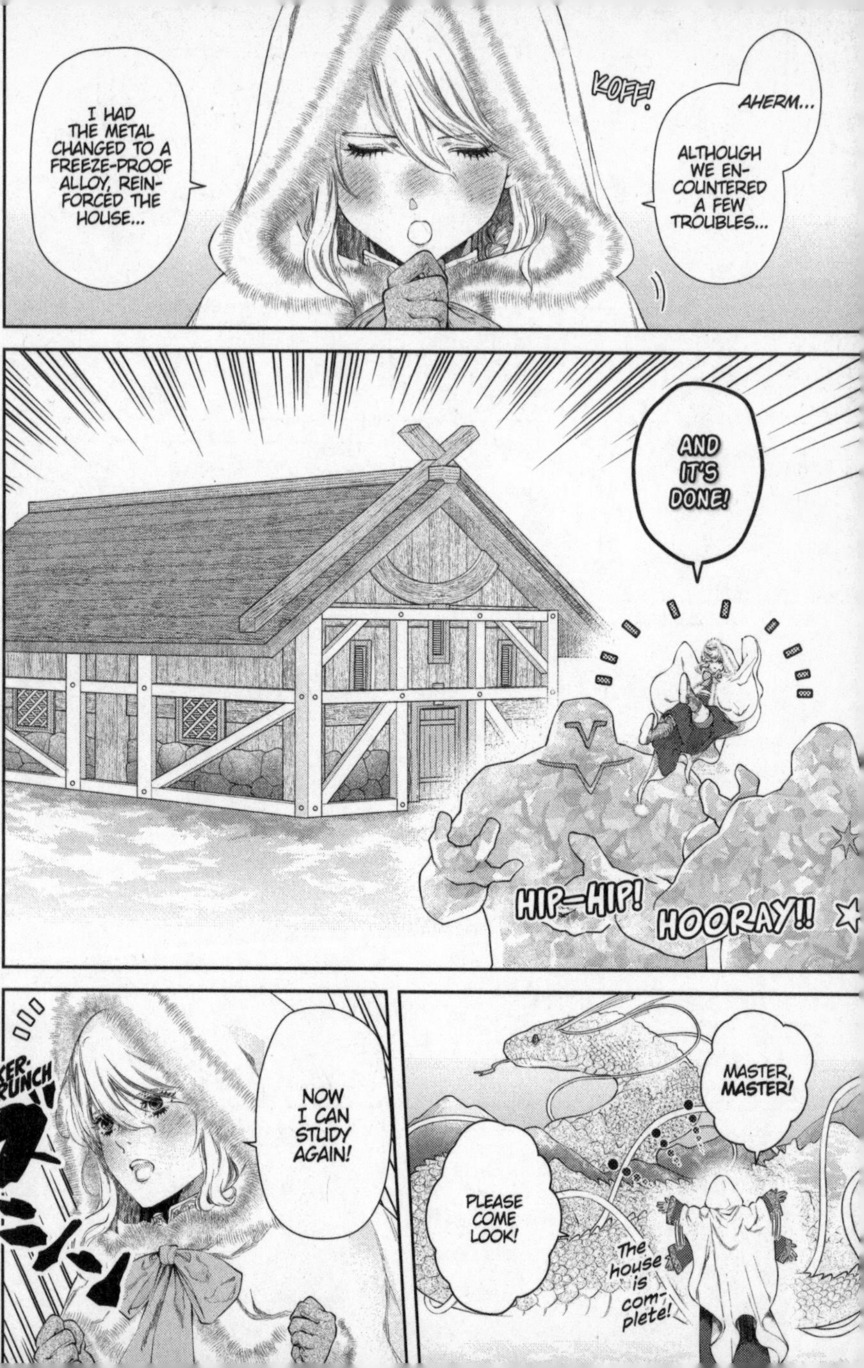
KOFF!
AHERM...
ALTHOUGH WE EN-COUNTERED A FEW TROUBLES...
I HAD THE METAL CHANGED TO A FREEZE-PROOF ALLOY, REIN-FORCED THE HOUSE...
AND IT'S DONE!
HIP-HIP!
HOORAY!!
MASTER, MASTER!
PLEASE COME LOOK!
The house is com-plete!
NOW I CAN STUDY AGAIN!
KER-CRUNCH

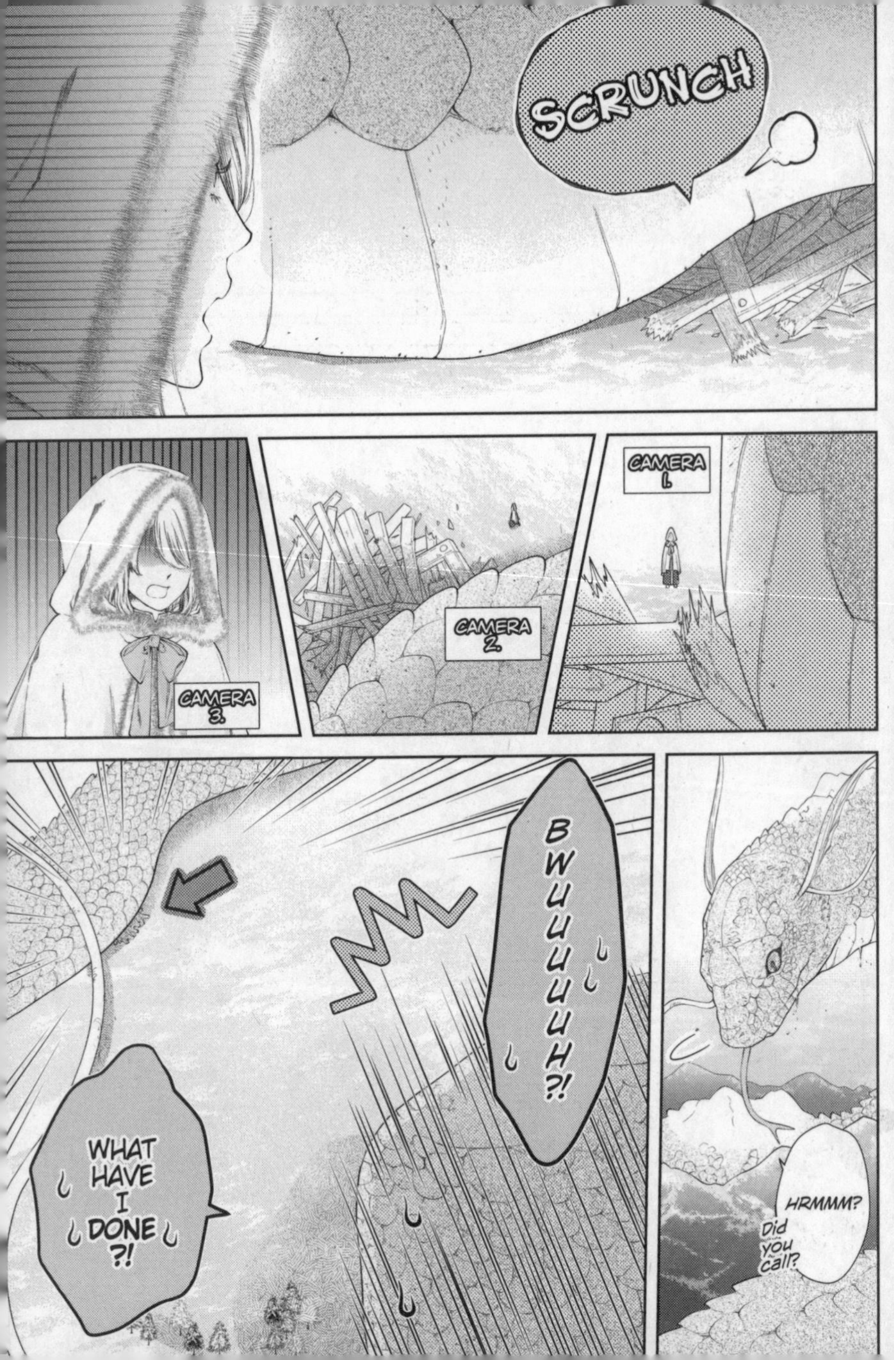
SCRUNCH
CAMERA 1.
CAMERA 2.
CAMERA 3.
BWUUUUUUH?!
WHAT HAVE I DONE?!
HRMMM?
Did you call?

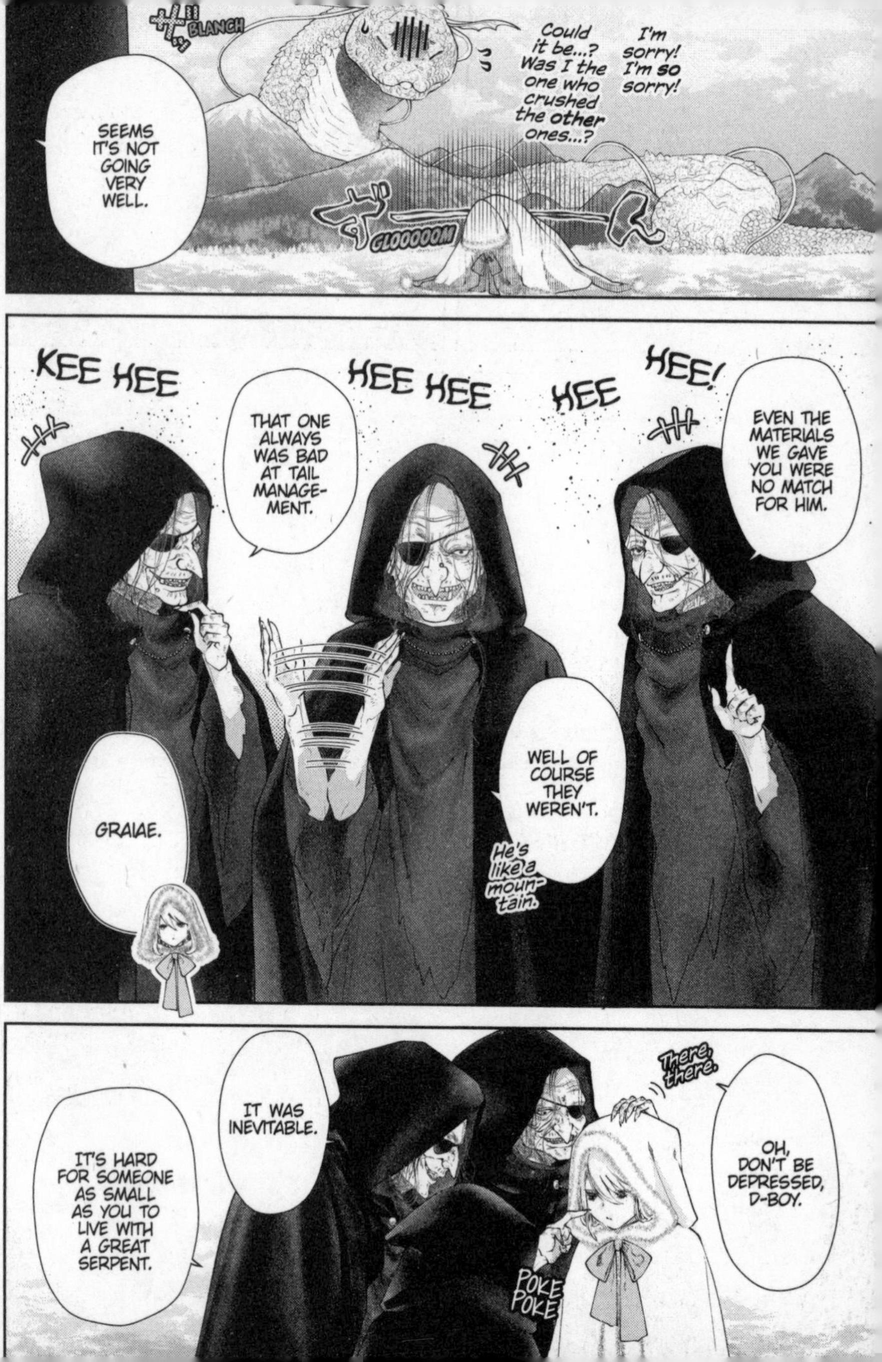

BLANCH
Could it be...? Was I the one who crushed the other ones...?
I'm sorry! I'm so sorry!
SEEMS IT'S NOT GOING VERY WELL.
GLOOOOOM
KEE HEE
HEE HEE
HEE
HEE!
THAT ONE ALWAYS WAS BAD AT TAIL MANAGE-MENT.
EVEN THE MATERIALS WE GAVE YOU WERE NO MATCH FOR HIM.
WELL OF COURSE THEY WEREN'T.
He's like a moun-tain.
GRAIAE.
IT'S HARD FOR SOMEONE AS SMALL AS YOU TO LIVE WITH A GREAT SERPENT.
IT WAS INEVITABLE.
There, there.
OH, DON'T BE DEPRESSED, D-BOY.
POKE POKE

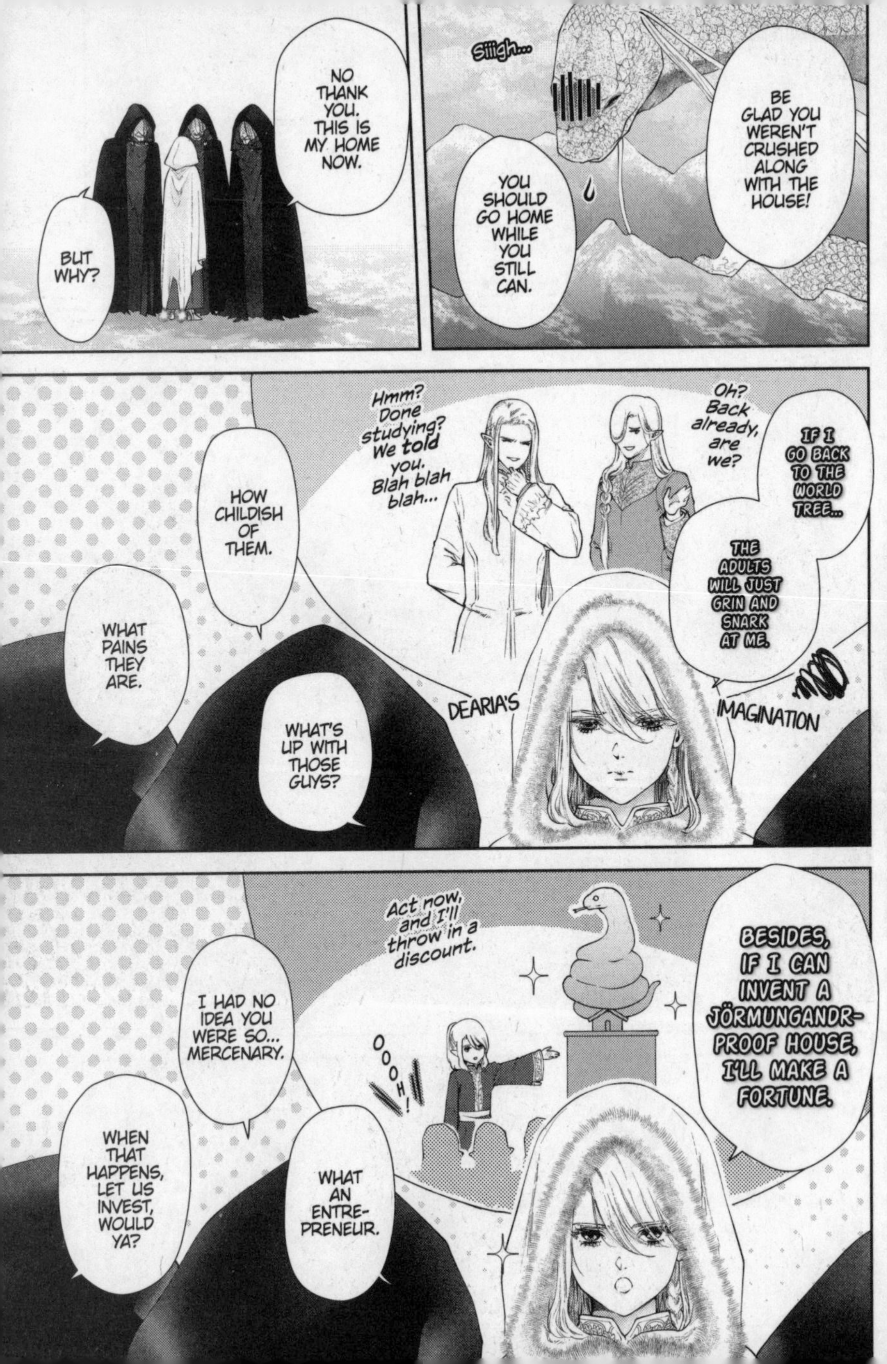
Siiigh...
BE GLAD YOU WEREN'T CRUSHED ALONG WITH THE HOUSE!
YOU SHOULD GO HOME WHILE YOU STILL CAN.
NO THANK YOU. THIS IS MY HOME NOW.
BUT WHY?
IF I GO BACK TO THE WORLD TREE...
THE ADULTS WILL JUST GRIN AND SNARK AT ME.
Oh? Back already, are we?
Hmm? Done studying? We told you. Blah blah blah...
DEARIA'S IMAGINATION
HOW CHILDISH OF THEM.
WHAT'S UP WITH THOSE GUYS?
WHAT PAINS THEY ARE.
BESIDES, IF I CAN INVENT A JÖRMUNGANDR-PROOF HOUSE, I'LL MAKE A FORTUNE.
Act now, and I'll throw in a discount.
OOOH!
I HAD NO IDEA YOU WERE SO... MERCENARY.
WHAT AN ENTRE-PRENEUR.
WHEN THAT HAPPENS, LET US INVEST, WOULD YA?

NO MATTER WHAT...

I...

AT ANY RATE...

DON'T WANT TO LEAVE.

I WANT TO STAY WITH MY MASTER.

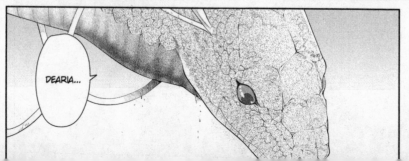

DEARIA...

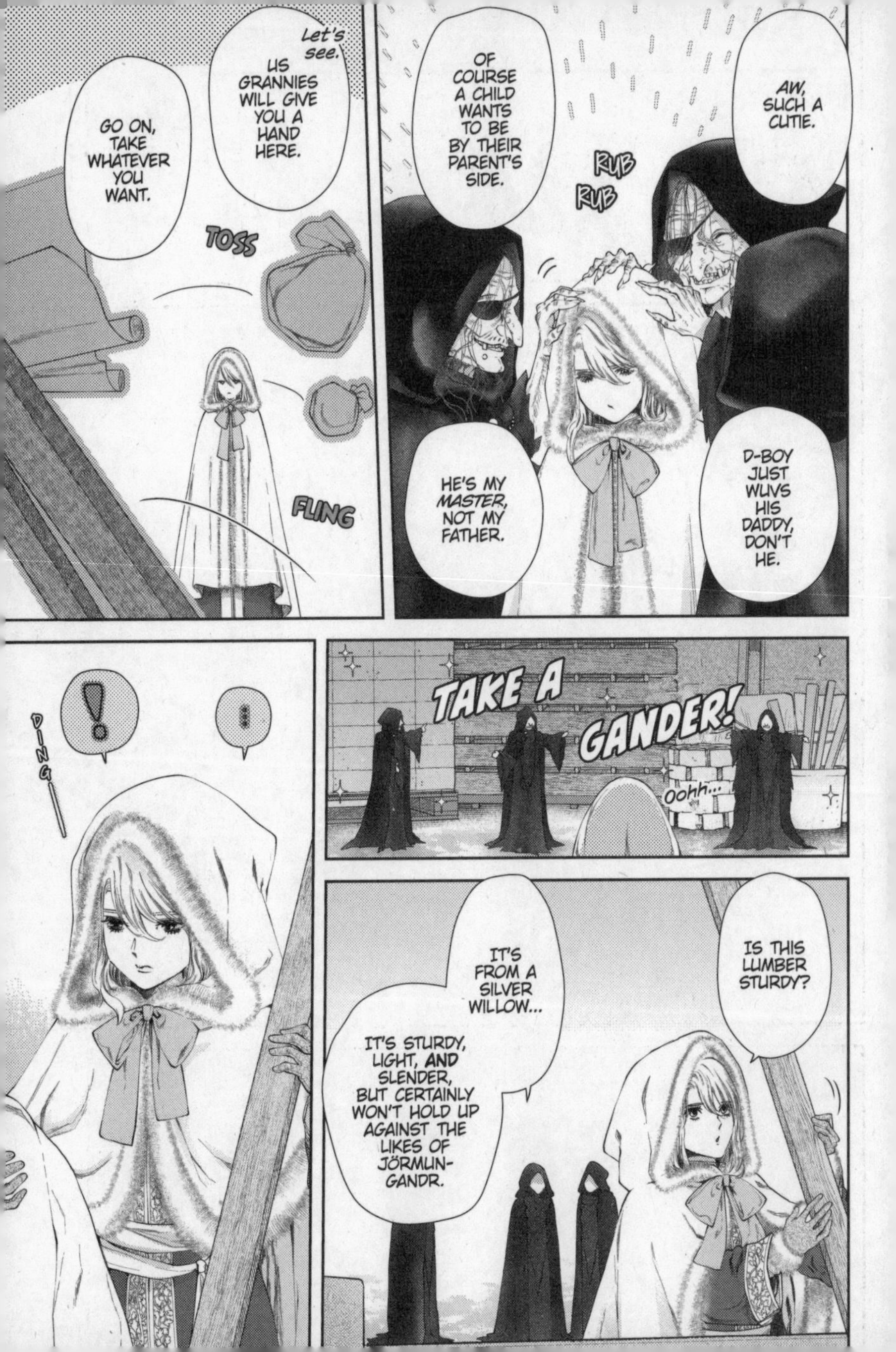
AW, SUCH A CUTIE.
RUB
RUB
OF COURSE A CHILD WANTS TO BE BY THEIR PARENT'S SIDE.
D-BOY JUST WUVS HIS DADDY, DON'T HE.
HE'S MY *MASTER*, NOT MY FATHER.
Let's see.
US GRANNIES WILL GIVE YOU A HAND HERE.
GO ON, TAKE WHATEVER YOU WANT.
TOSS
FLING
TAKE A GANDER!
Oohh...
IS THIS LUMBER STURDY?
IT'S FROM A SILVER WILLOW...
IT'S STURDY, LIGHT, AND SLENDER, BUT CERTAINLY WON'T HOLD UP AGAINST THE LIKES OF JÖRMUN-GANDR.
DING
!
...

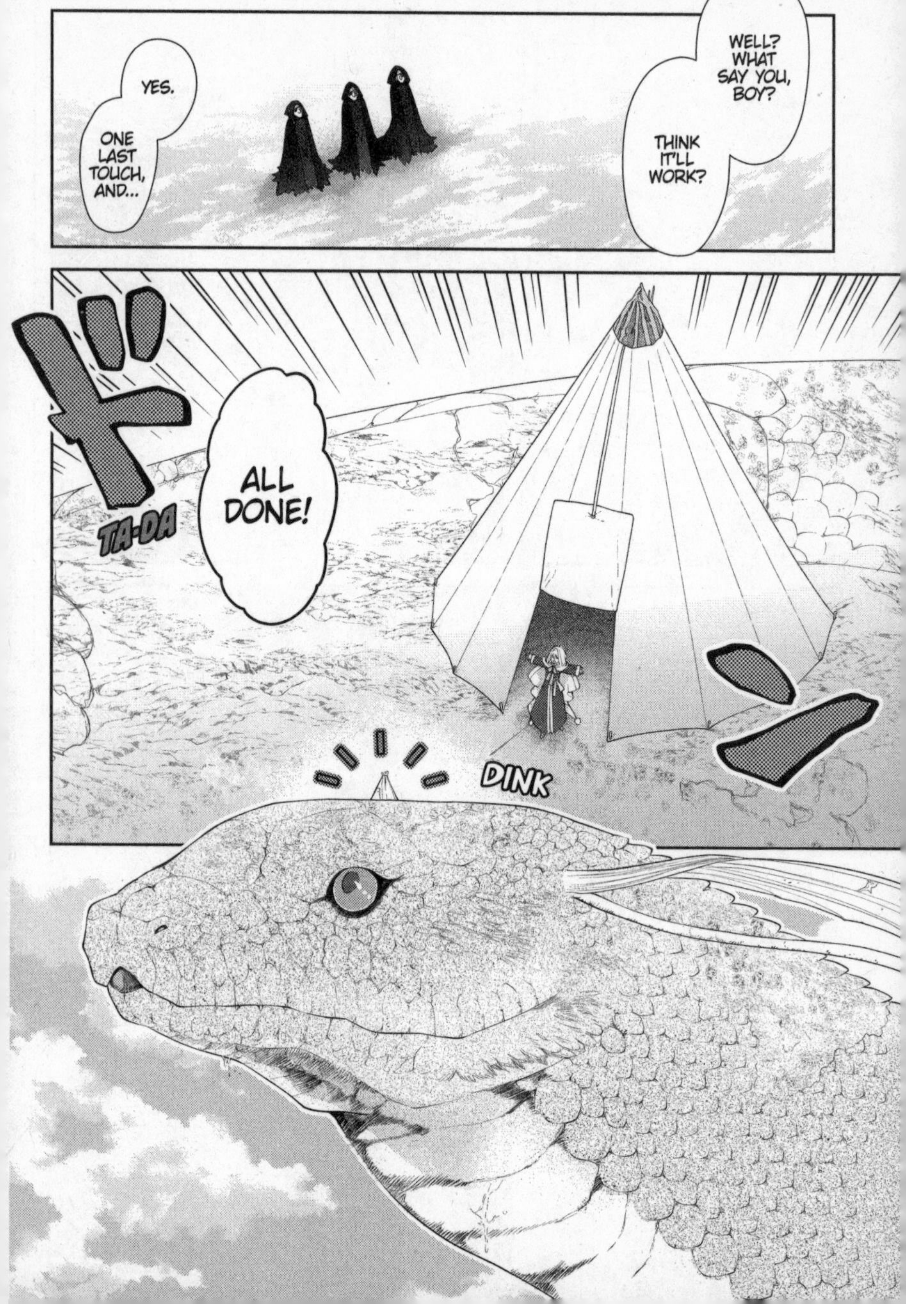
WELL? WHAT SAY YOU, BOY?
THINK IT'LL WORK?
YES.
ONE LAST TOUCH, AND...
ド
TA-DA
ALL DONE!
DINK

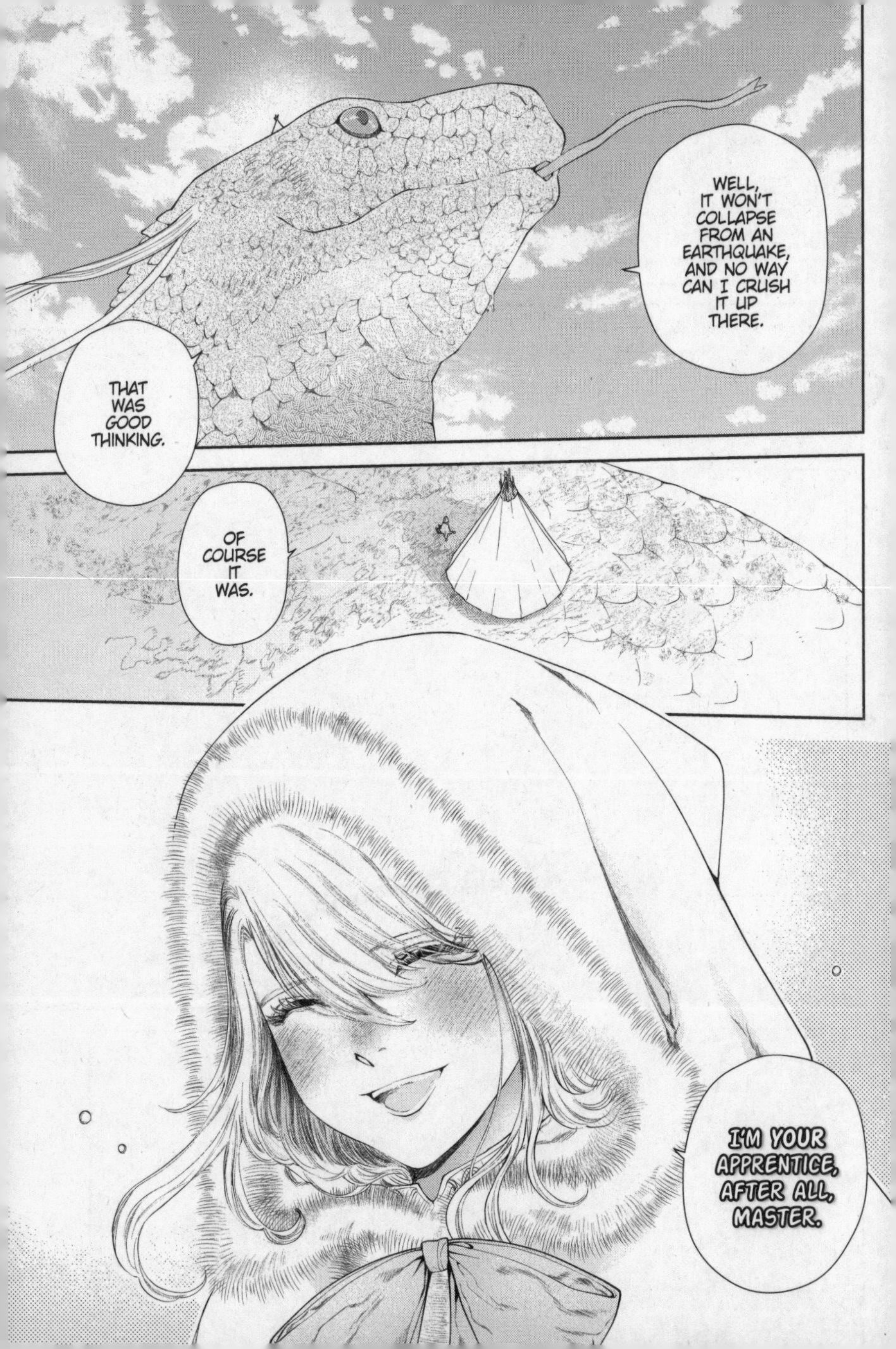
WELL, IT WON'T COLLAPSE FROM AN EARTHQUAKE, AND NO WAY CAN I CRUSH IT UP THERE.
THAT WAS GOOD THINKING.
OF COURSE IT WAS.
I'M YOUR APPRENTICE, AFTER ALL, MASTER.

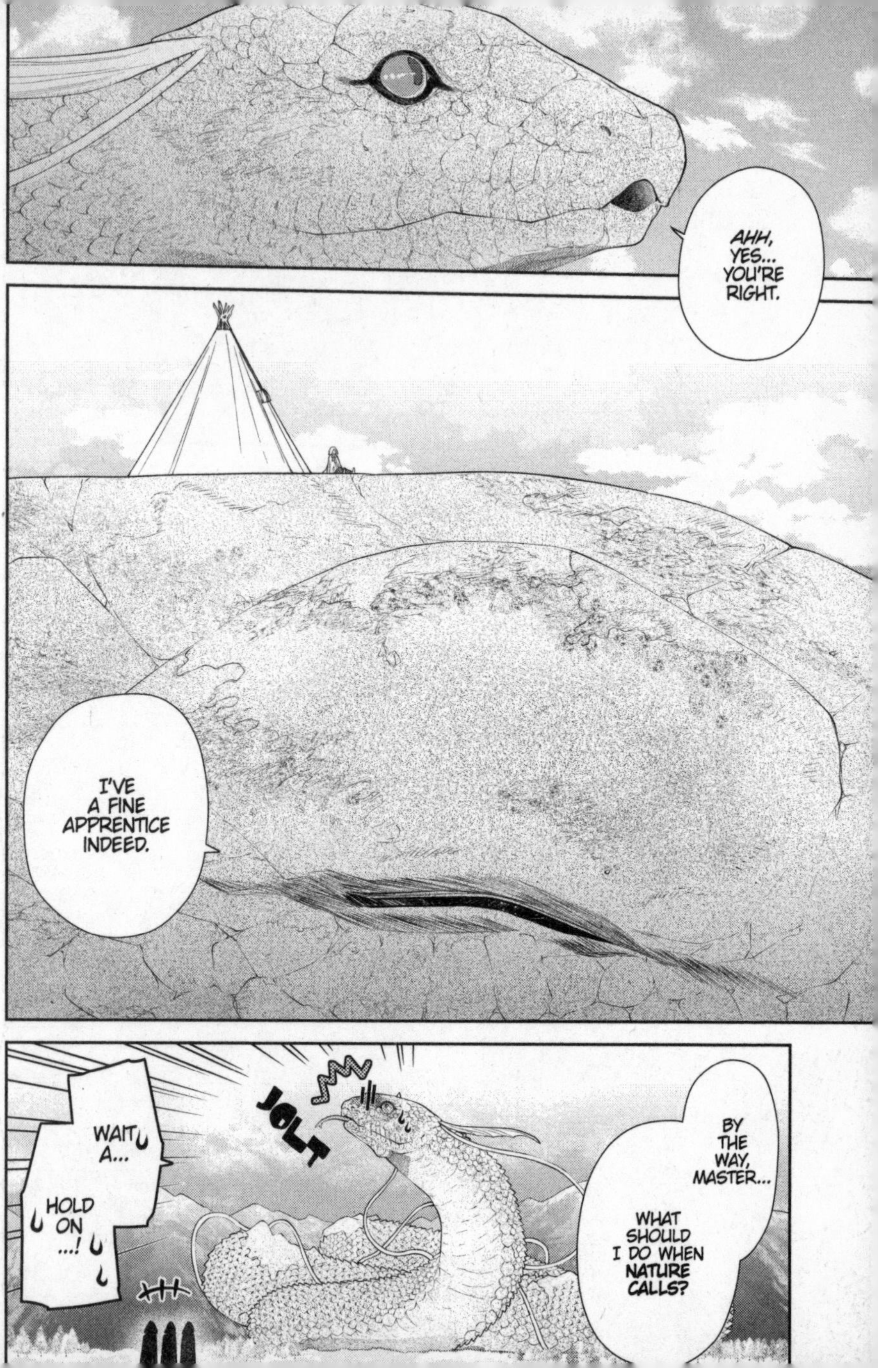
AHH, YES... YOU'RE RIGHT.
I'VE A FINE APPRENTICE INDEED.
BY THE WAY, MASTER...
WHAT SHOULD I DO WHEN NATURE CALLS?
JOLT
WAIT A...
HOLD ON ...!

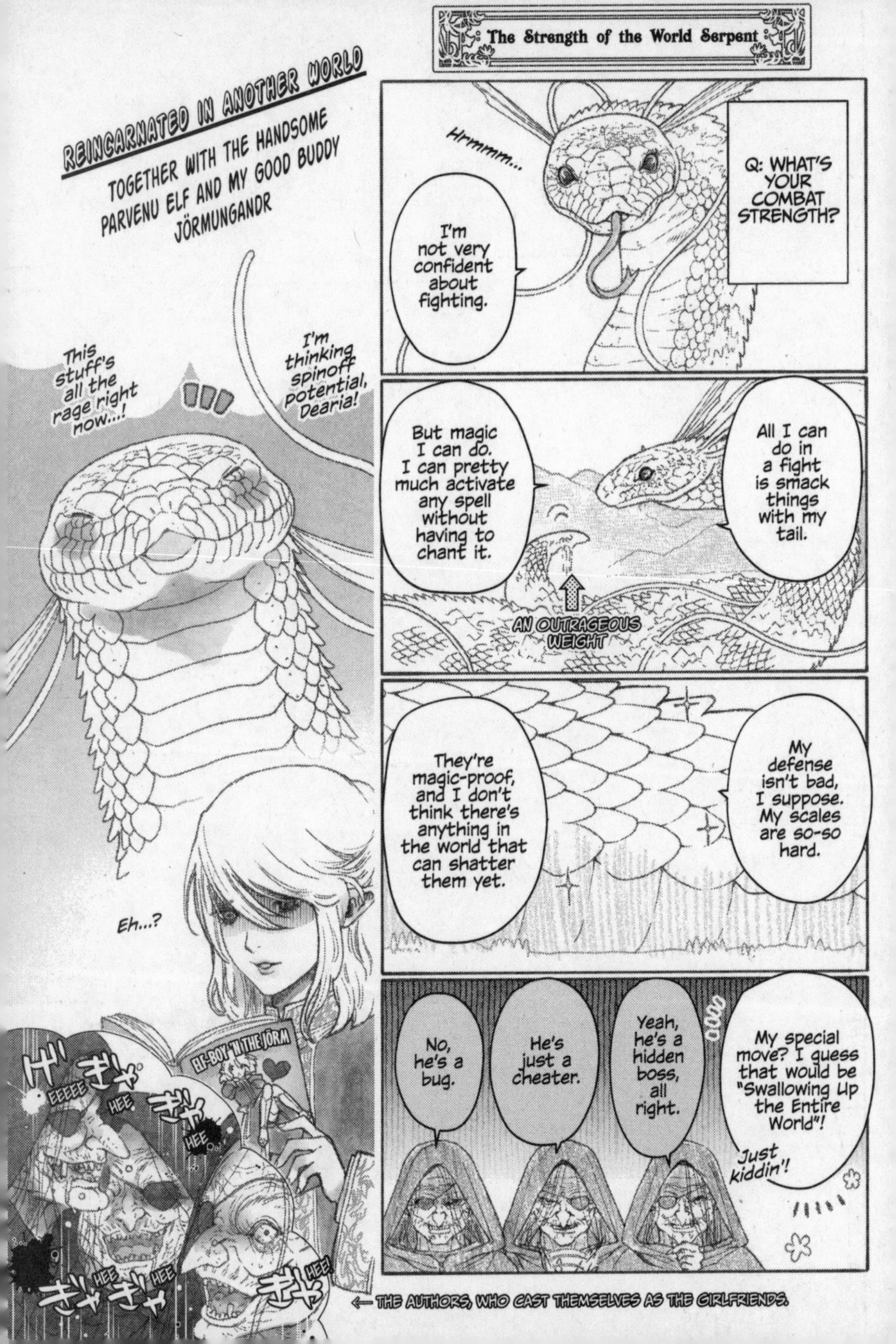

The Strength of the World Serpent
Q: WHAT'S YOUR COMBAT STRENGTH?
Hrmmmm...
I'm not very confident about fighting.
All I can do in a fight is smack things with my tail.
But magic I can do. I can pretty much activate any spell without having to chant it.
AN OUTRAGEOUS WEIGHT
My defense isn't bad, I suppose. My scales are so-so hard.
They're magic-proof, and I don't think there's anything in the world that can shatter them yet.
My special move? I guess that would be "Swallowing Up the Entire World"!
Just kiddin'!
Yeah, he's a hidden boss, all right.
He's just a cheater.
No, he's a bug.
← THE AUTHORS, WHO CAST THEMSELVES AS THE GIRLFRIENDS.
REINCARNATED IN ANOTHER WORLD
TOGETHER WITH THE HANDSOME PARVENU ELF AND MY GOOD BUDDY JÖRMUNGANDR
This stuff's all the rage right now...!
I'm thinking spinoff potential, Dearia!
Eh...?
ELF-BOY 'N THE JÖRM
EEEEE
HEE
HEE
HEE
HEE
HEE!

Dragon
Goes
House-
Hunting

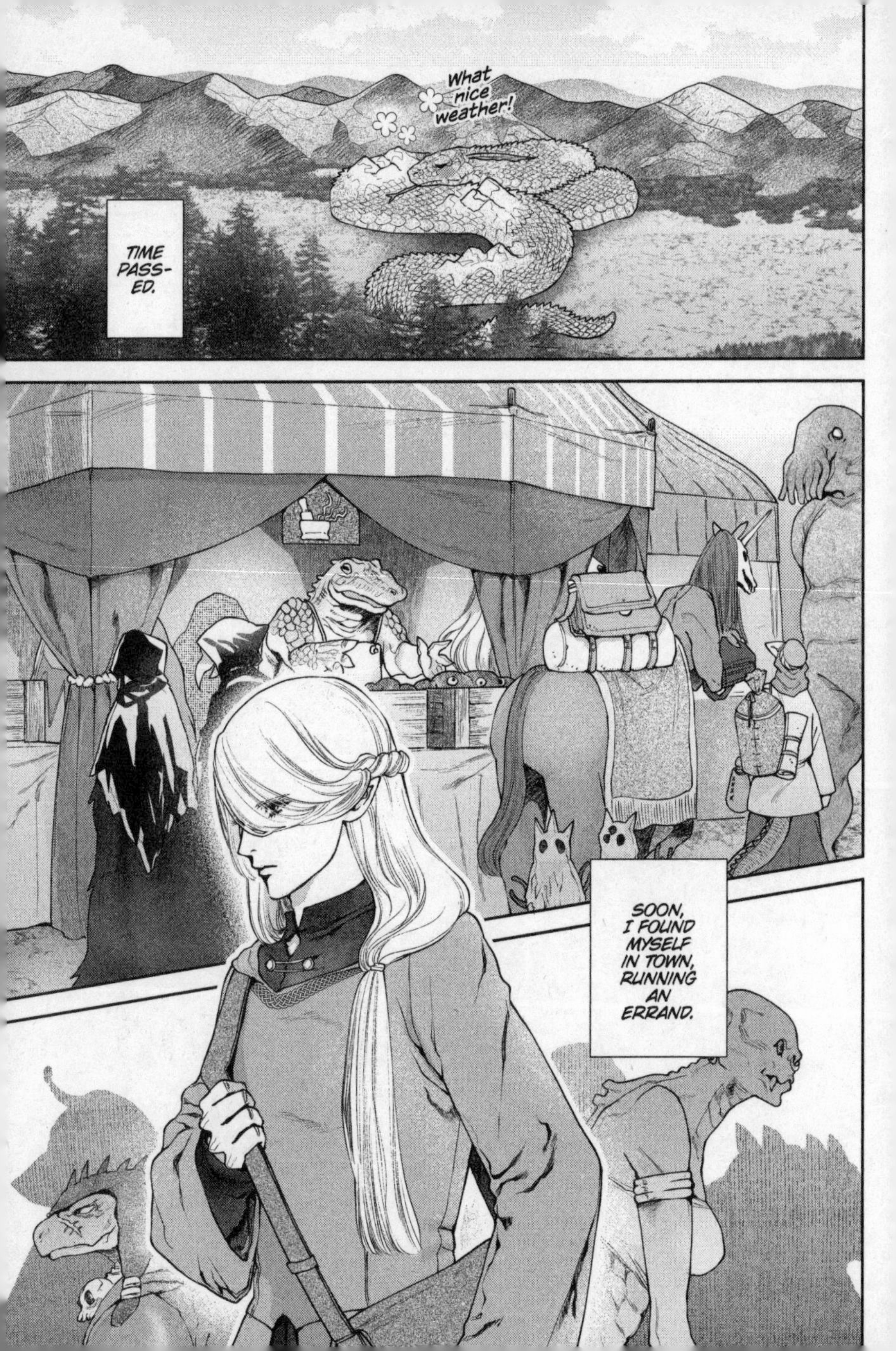
What nice weather!
TIME PASSED.
SOON, I FOUND MYSELF IN TOWN, RUNNING AN ERRAND.

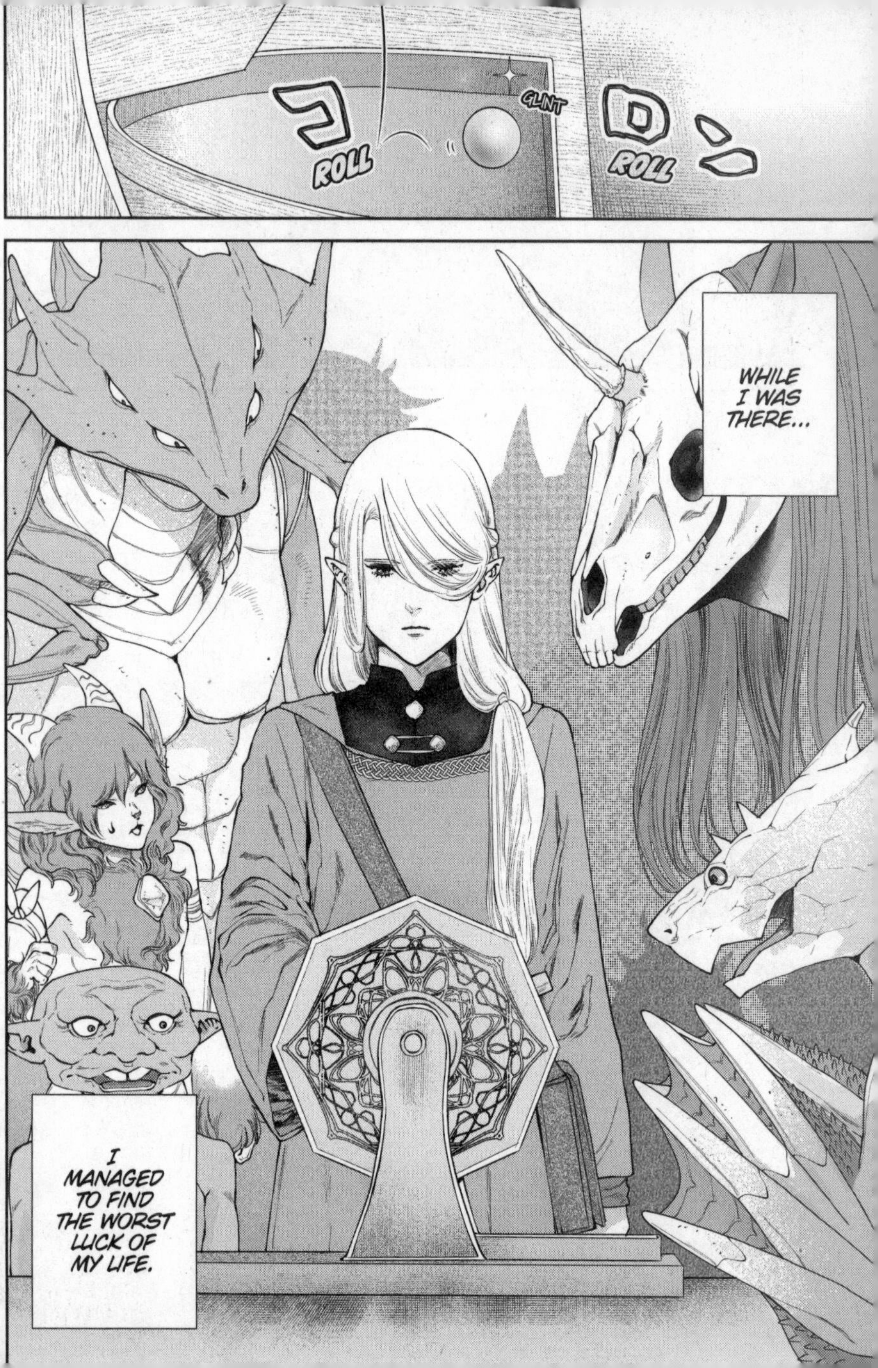
GLINT
ROLL
ROLL
WHILE I WAS THERE...
I MANAGED TO FIND THE WORST LUCK OF MY LIFE.

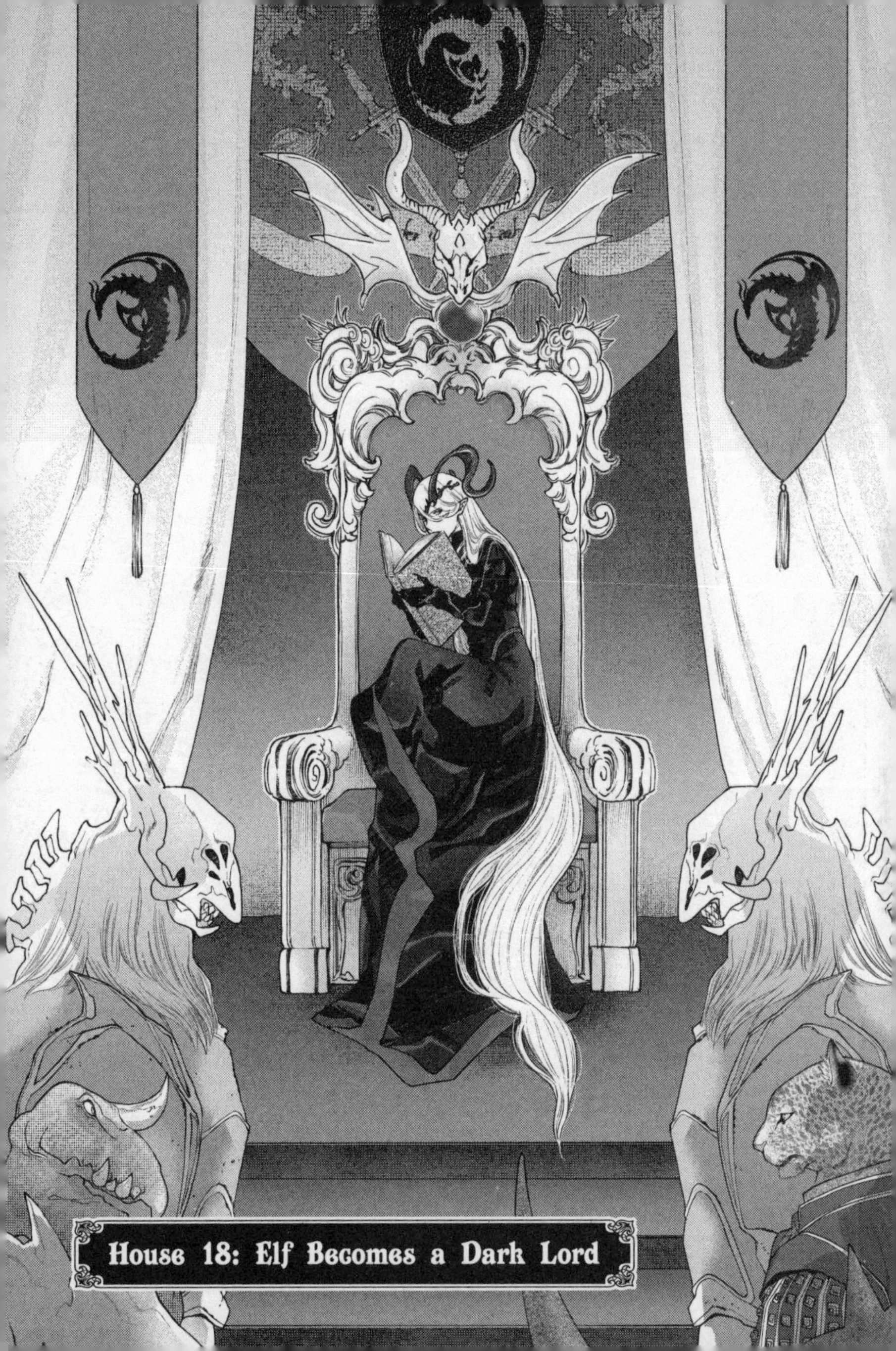
House 18: Elf Becomes a Dark Lord

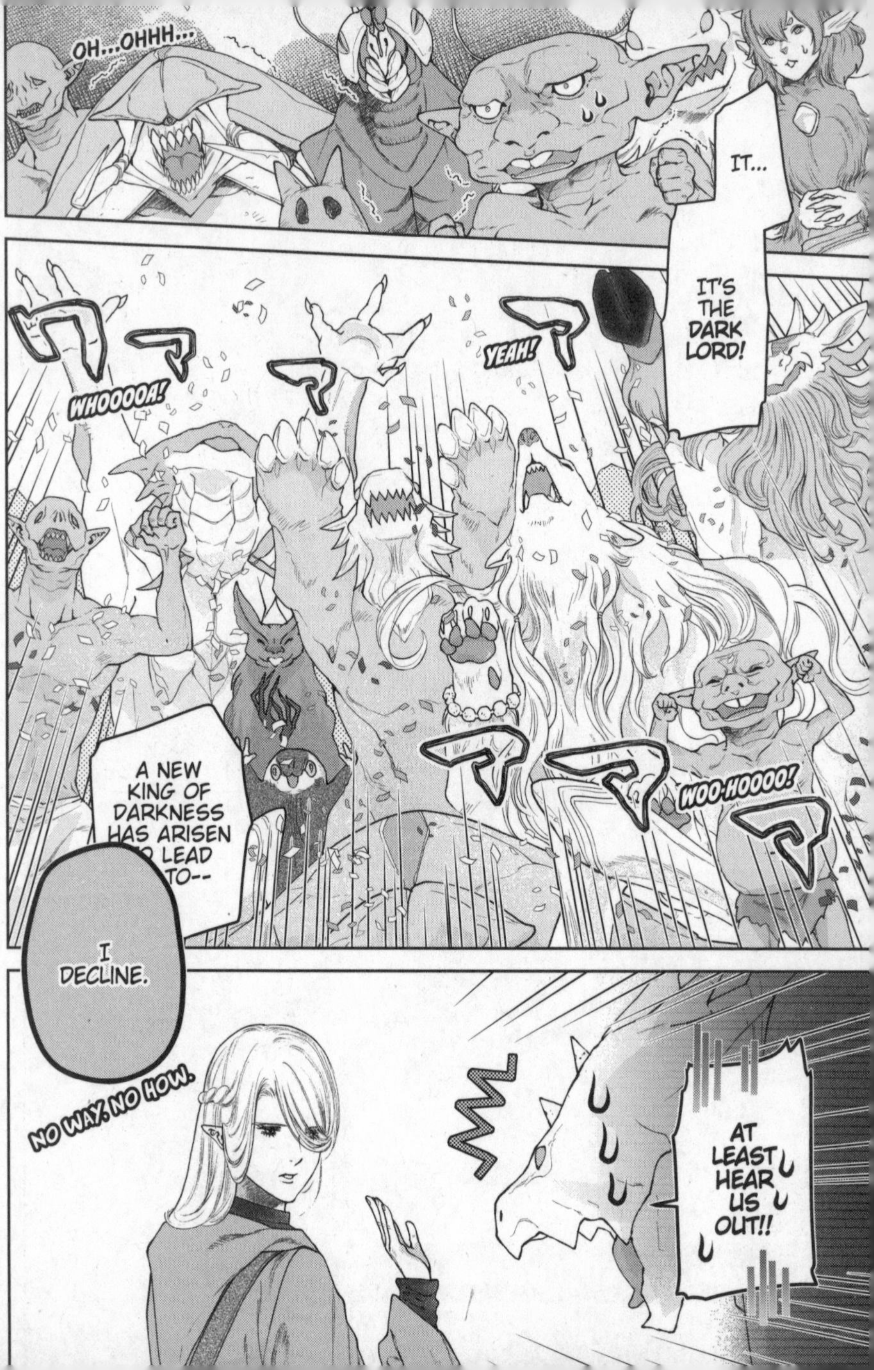
IT...
OH...OHHH...
IT'S THE DARK LORD!
YEAH!
WHOOOOA!
WOO-HOOOO!
A NEW KING OF DARKNESS HAS ARISEN
LEAD
TO--
I DECLINE.
NO WAY. NO HOW.
AT LEAST HEAR US OUT!!

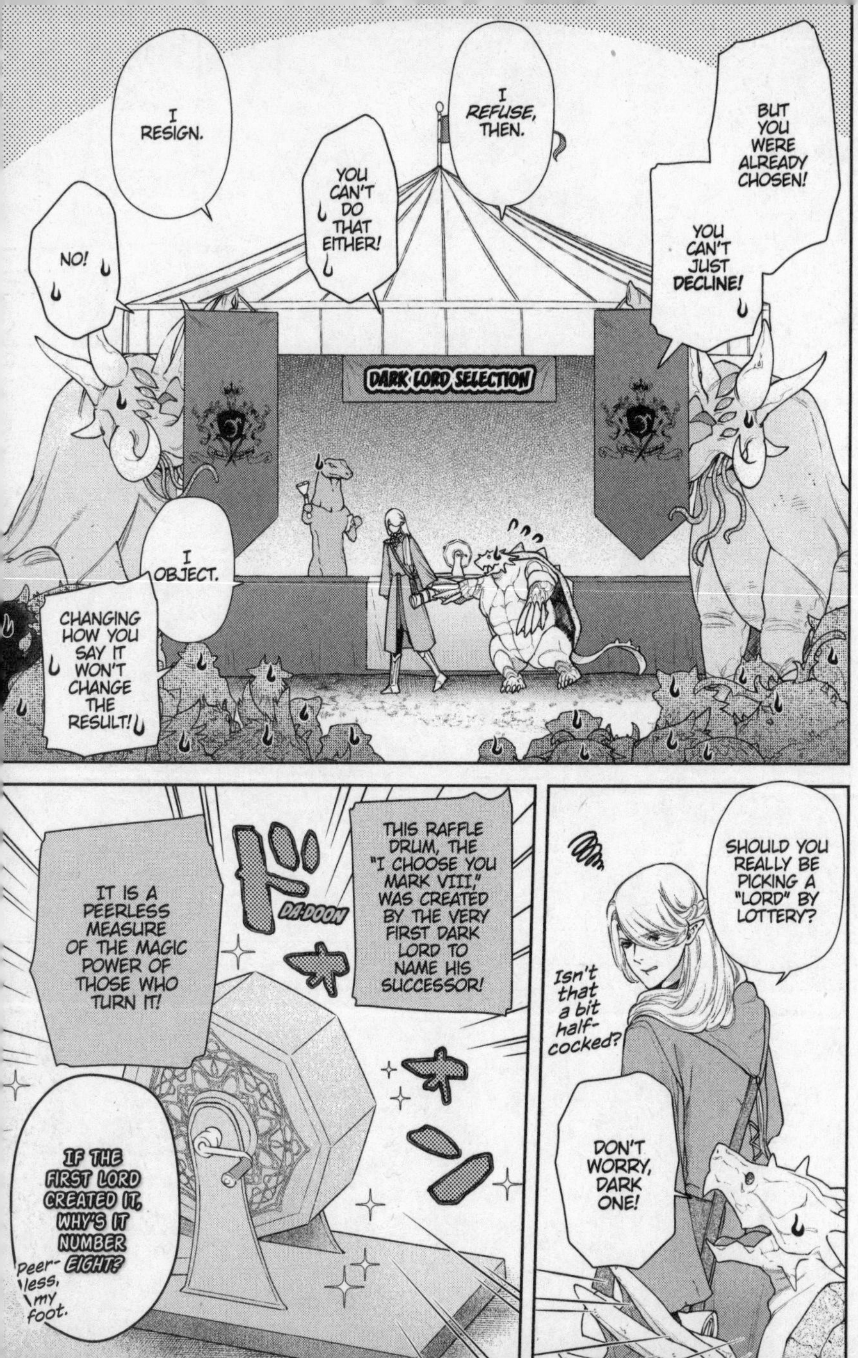
BUT YOU WERE ALREADY CHOSEN!
YOU CAN'T JUST DECLINE!
I REFUSE, THEN.
YOU CAN'T DO THAT EITHER!
I RESIGN.
NO!
DARK LORD SELECTION
I OBJECT.
CHANGING HOW YOU SAY IT WON'T CHANGE THE RESULT!
SHOULD YOU REALLY BE PICKING A "LORD" BY LOTTERY?
Isn't that a bit half-cocked?
DON'T WORRY, DARK ONE!
THIS RAFFLE DRUM, THE "I CHOOSE YOU MARK VIII," WAS CREATED BY THE VERY FIRST DARK LORD TO NAME HIS SUCCESSOR!
DA-DOON
IT IS A PEERLESS MEASURE OF THE MAGIC POWER OF THOSE WHO TURN IT!
IF THE FIRST LORD CREATED IT, WHY'S IT NUMBER EIGHT?
Peer-less, my foot.

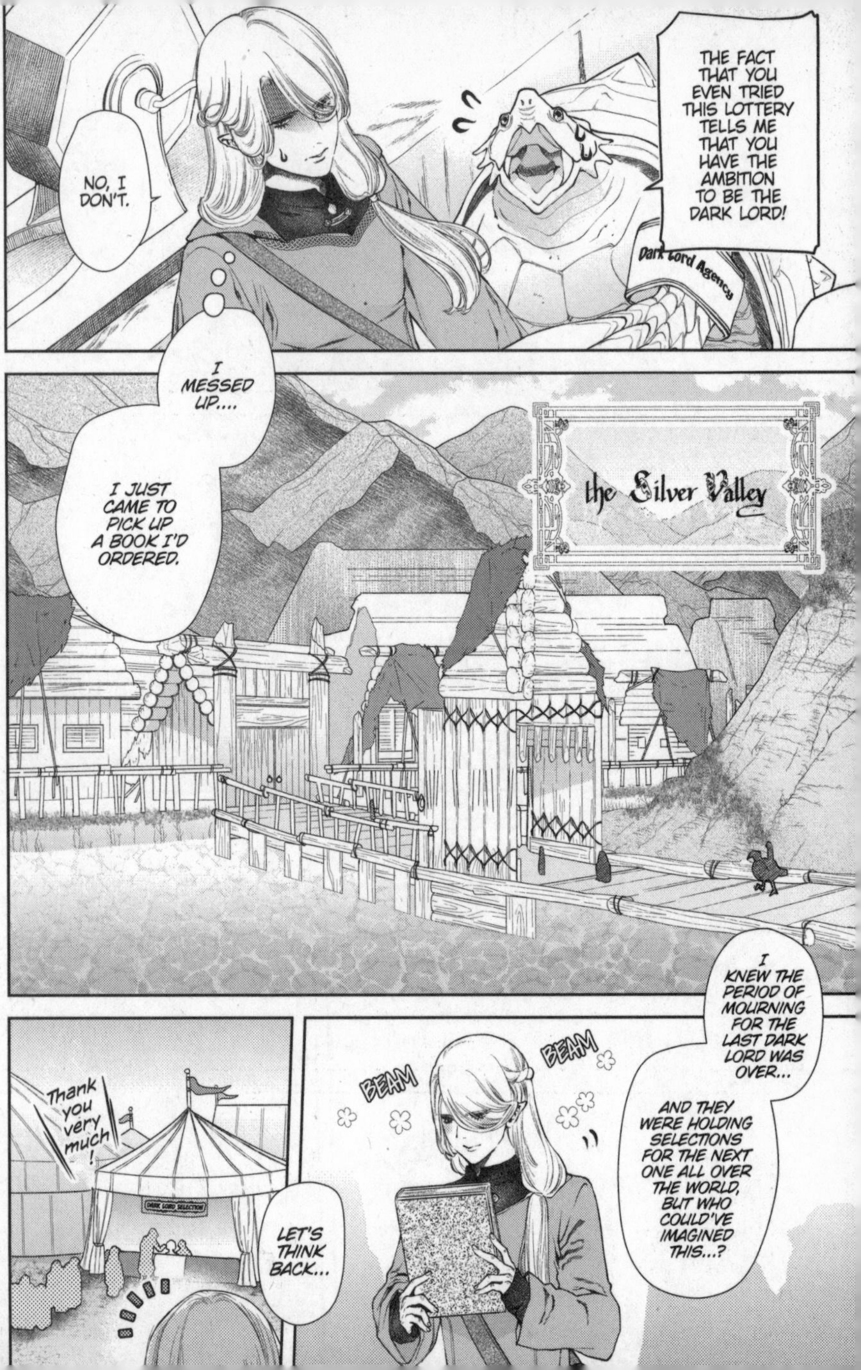
THE FACT THAT YOU EVEN TRIED THIS LOTTERY TELLS ME THAT YOU HAVE THE AMBITION TO BE THE DARK LORD!
Dark Lord Agency
NO, I DON'T.
I MESSED UP....
the Silver Valley
I JUST CAME TO PICK UP A BOOK I'D ORDERED.
I KNEW THE PERIOD OF MOURNING FOR THE LAST DARK LORD WAS OVER...
BEAM
BEAM
AND THEY WERE HOLDING SELECTIONS FOR THE NEXT ONE ALL OVER THE WORLD, BUT WHO COULD'VE IMAGINED THIS...?
LET'S THINK BACK...
Thank you very much!
DARK LORD SELECTION

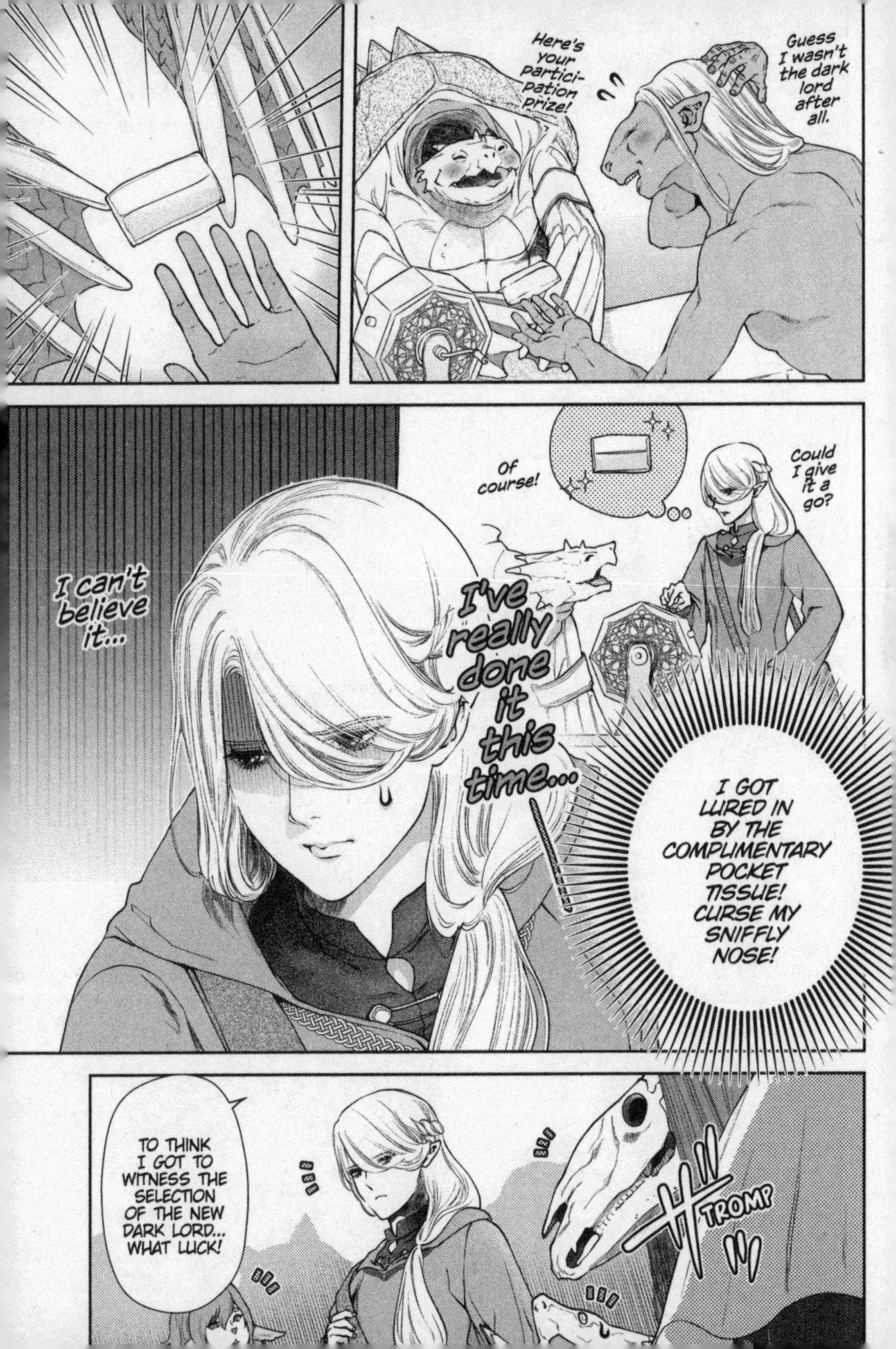
Guess I wasn't the dark lord after all.
Here's your partici-pation prize!
Could I give it a go?
Of course!
I can't believe it...
I've really done it this time...
I GOT LURED IN BY THE COMPLIMENTARY POCKET TISSUE! CURSE MY SNIFFLY NOSE!
TROMP
TO THINK I GOT TO WITNESS THE SELECTION OF THE NEW DARK LORD... WHAT LUCK!

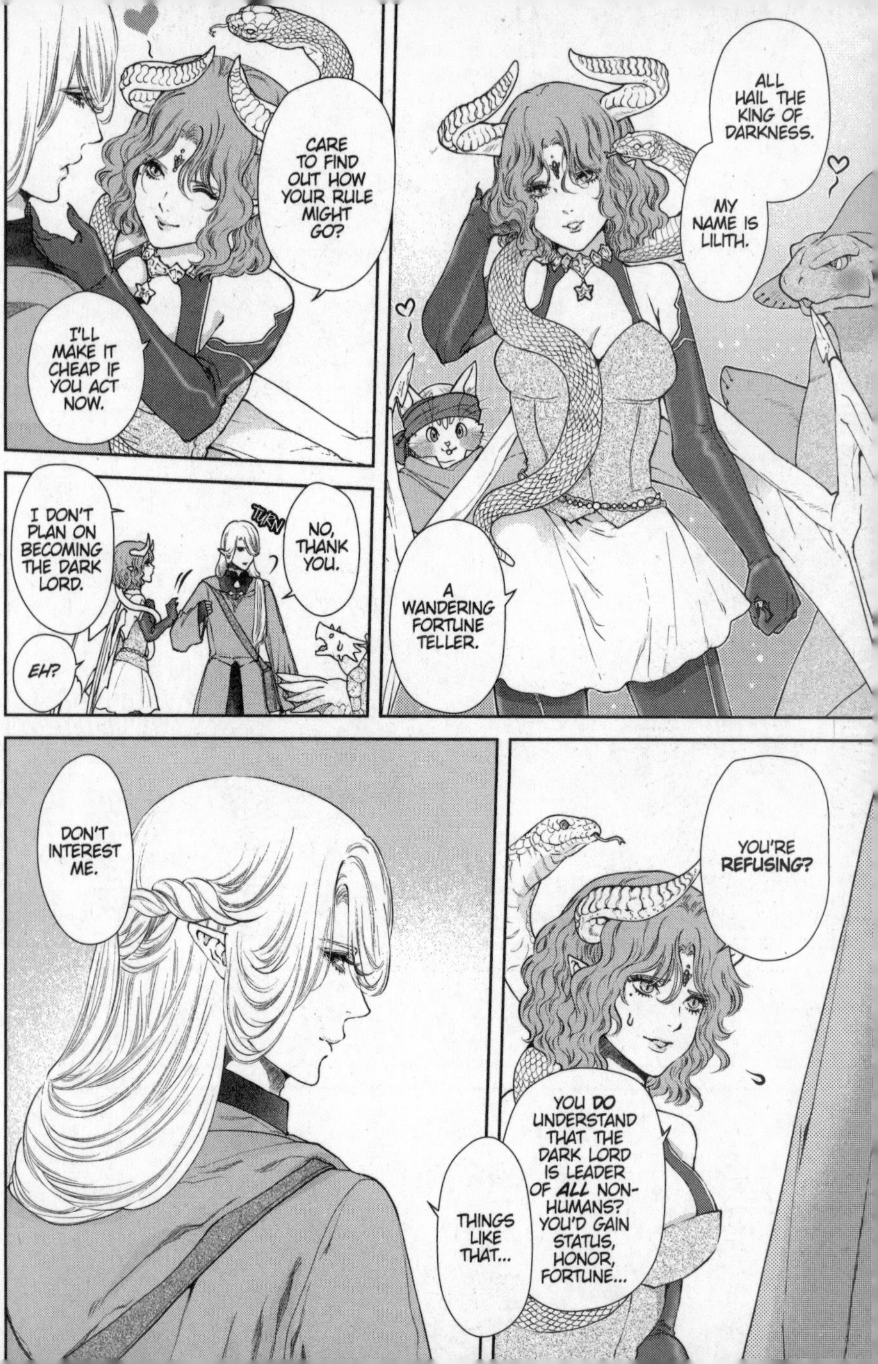
ALL HAIL THE KING OF DARKNESS.
MY NAME IS LILITH.
A WANDERING FORTUNE TELLER.
CARE TO FIND OUT HOW YOUR RULE MIGHT GO?
I'LL MAKE IT CHEAP IF YOU ACT NOW.
TURN
NO, THANK YOU.
I DON'T PLAN ON BECOMING THE DARK LORD.
EH?
YOU'RE REFUSING?
YOU DO UNDERSTAND THAT THE DARK LORD IS LEADER OF ALL NON-HUMANS? YOU'D GAIN STATUS, HONOR, FORTUNE...
THINGS LIKE THAT...
DON'T INTEREST ME.

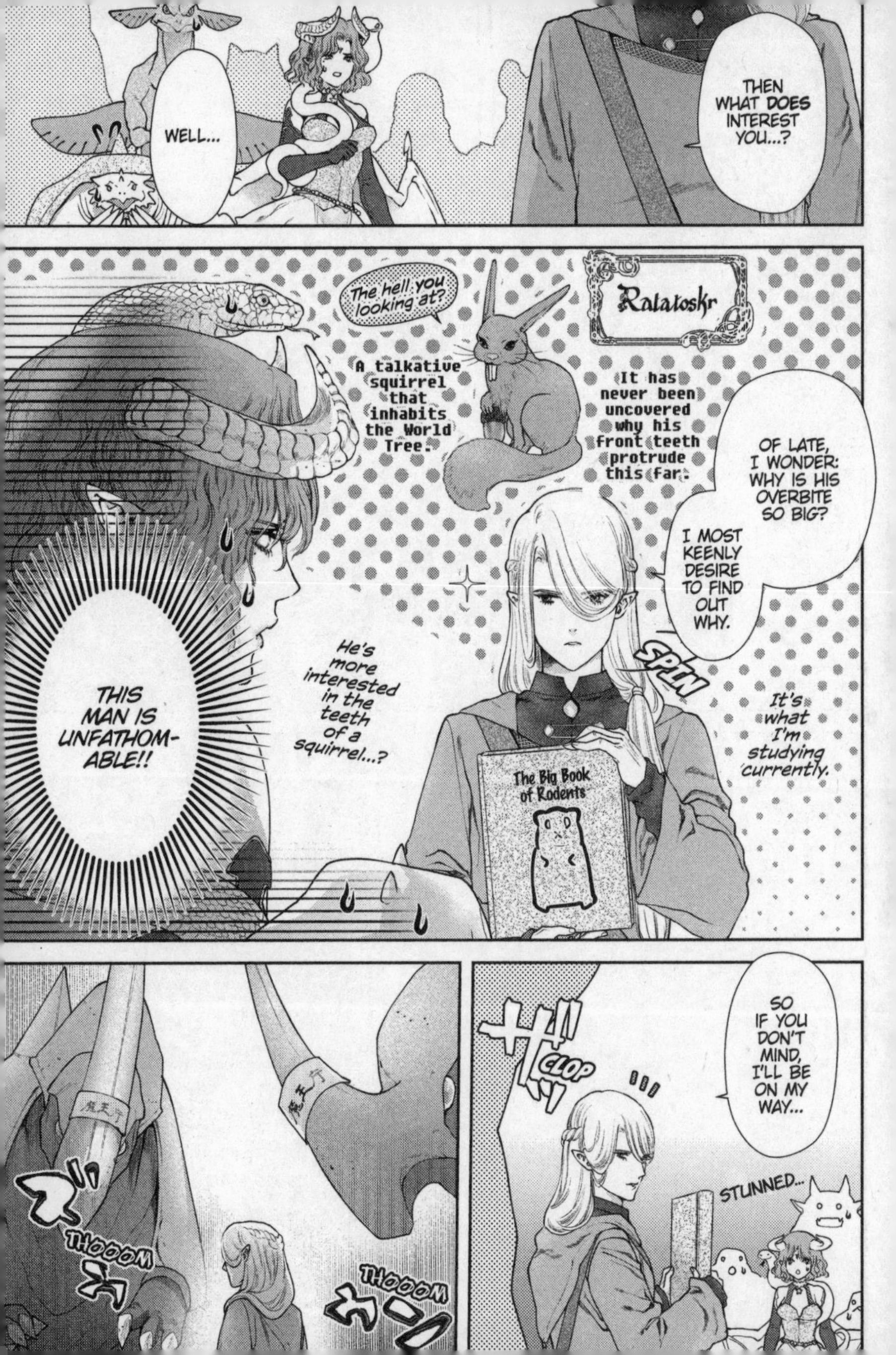
THEN WHAT DOES INTEREST YOU...?
WELL...
Ratatoskr
The hell you looking at?
A talkative squirrel that inhabits the World Tree.
It has never been uncovered why his front teeth protrude this far.
OF LATE, I WONDER: WHY IS HIS OVERBITE SO BIG?
I MOST KEENLY DESIRE TO FIND OUT WHY.
SPIN
It's what I'm studying currently.
The Big Book of Rodents
He's more interested in the teeth of a squirrel...?
THIS MAN IS UNFATHOM-ABLE!!
SO IF YOU DON'T MIND, I'LL BE ON MY WAY...
CLOP
STUNNED...
THOOOM
THOOOM

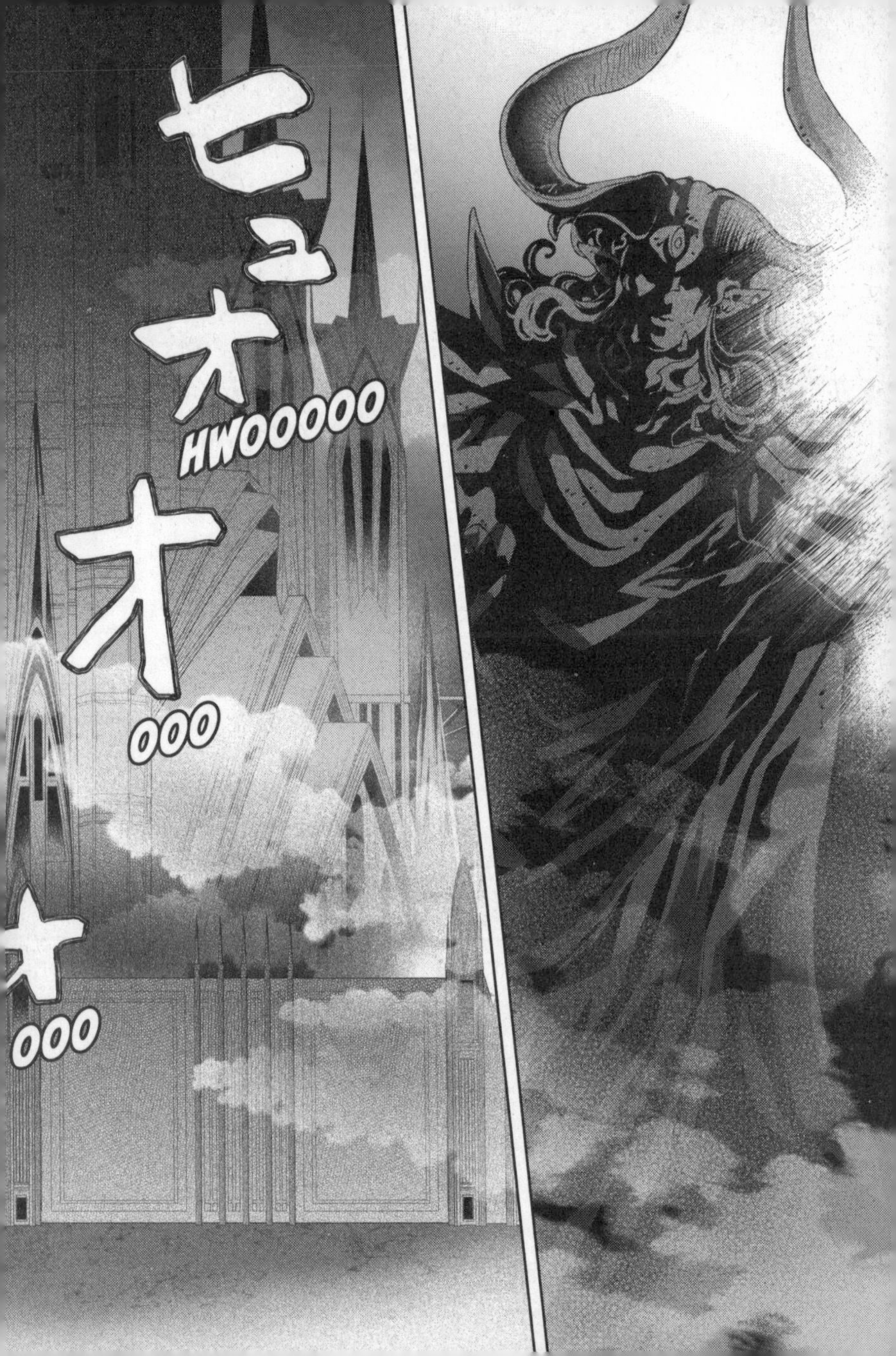
ヒュオオオ
HWOOOOOO
オ
OOO
OOO

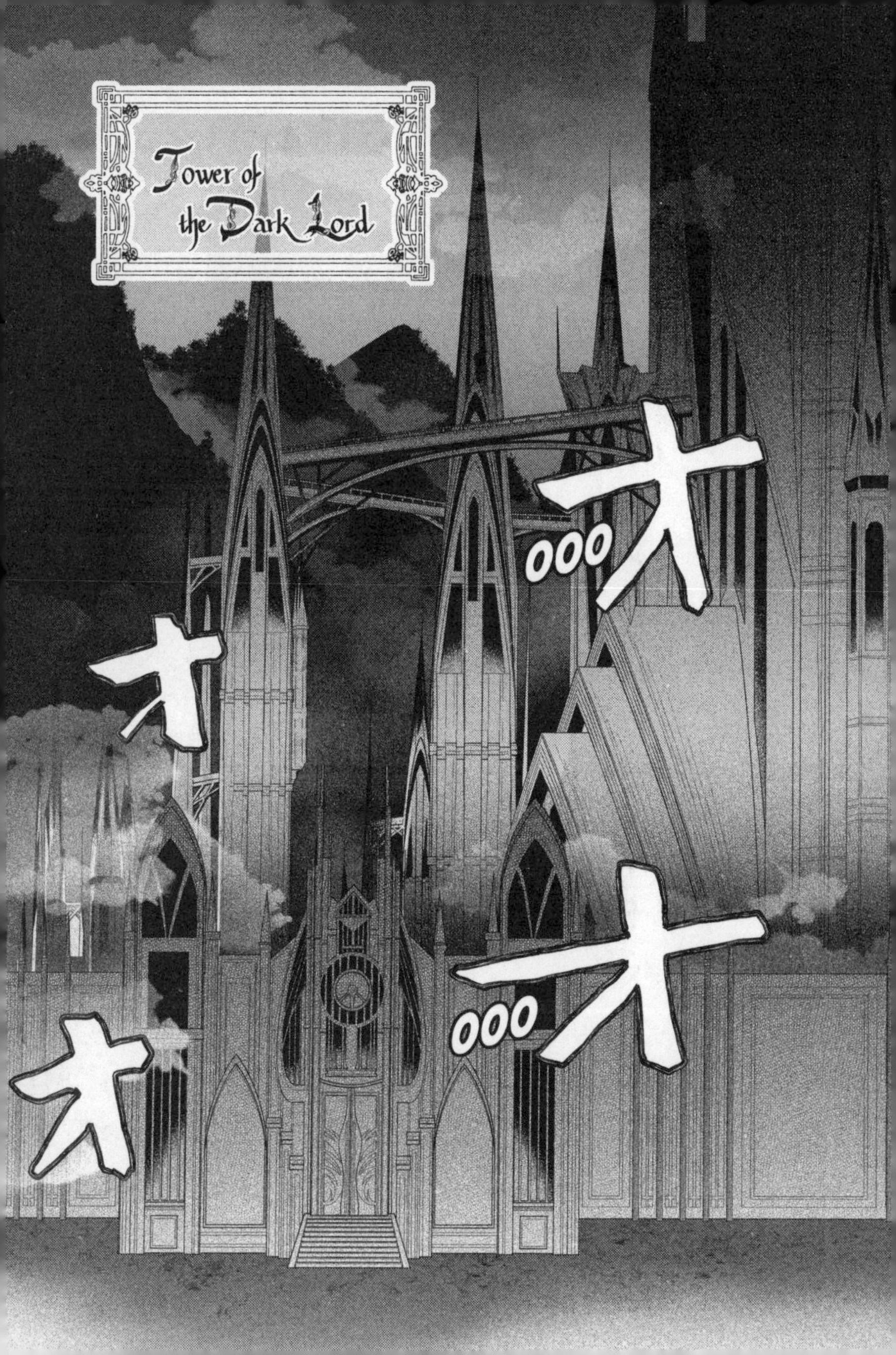
Tower of the Dark Lord
oooオ
オ
oooオ
オ

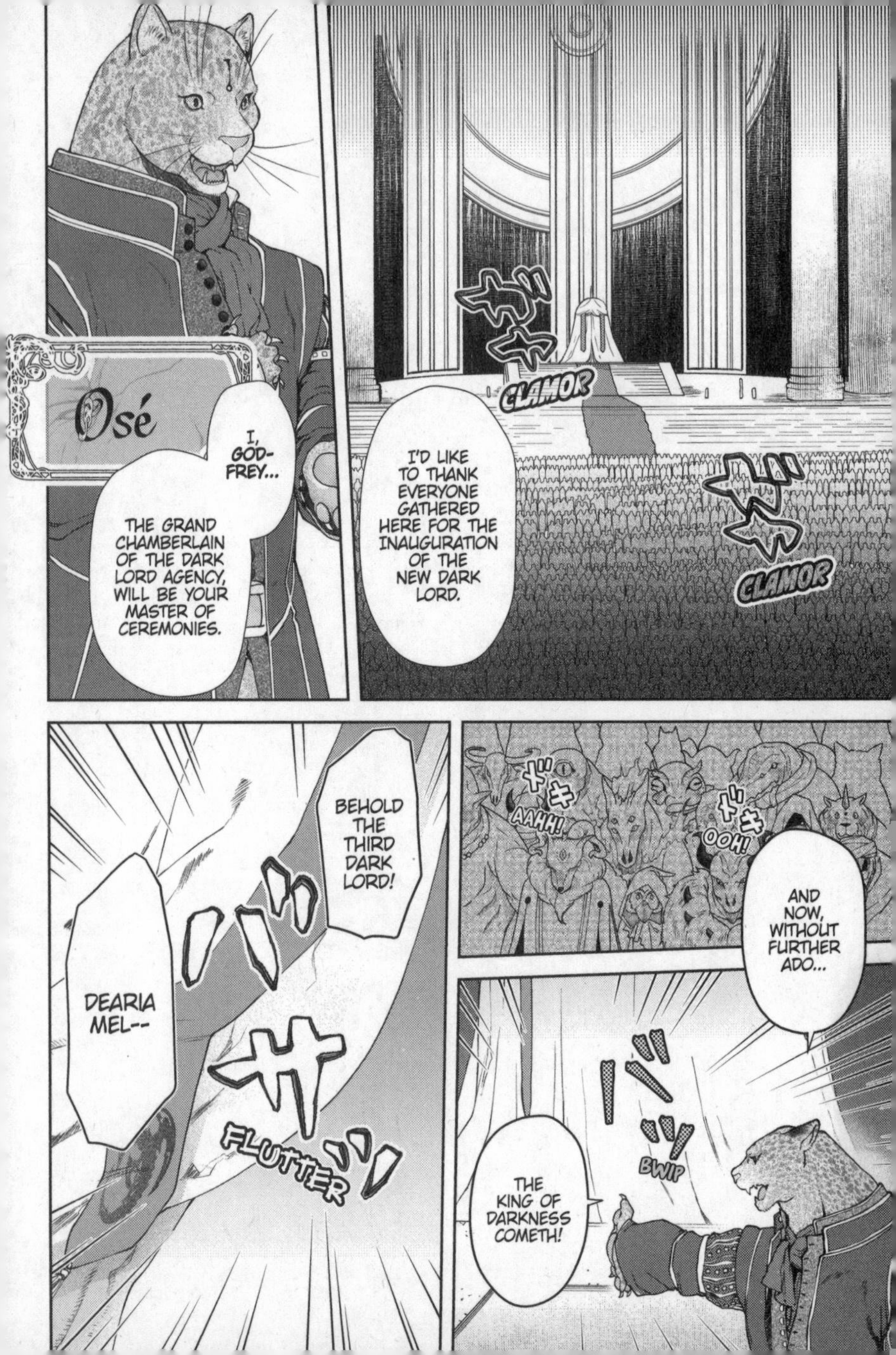
CLAMOR
CLAMOR
I'D LIKE TO THANK EVERYONE GATHERED HERE FOR THE INAUGURATION OF THE NEW DARK LORD.
Osé
I, GOD-FREY...
THE GRAND CHAMBERLAIN OF THE DARK LORD AGENCY, WILL BE YOUR MASTER OF CEREMONIES.
AAHH!
OOH!
AND NOW, WITHOUT FURTHER ADO...
BWIP
THE KING OF DARKNESS COMETH!
BEHOLD THE THIRD DARK LORD!
DEARIA MEL--
FLUTTER

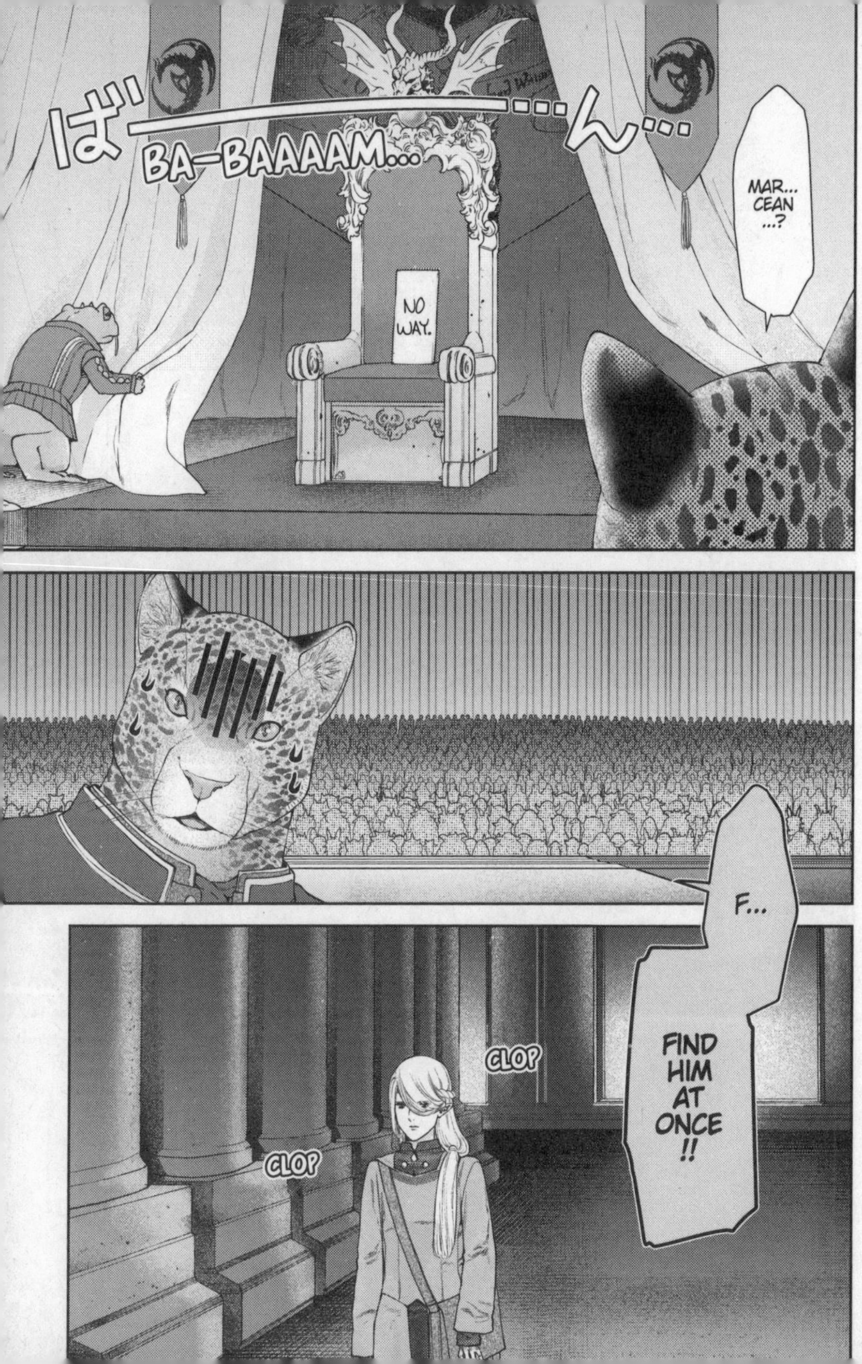
ばーーーーーん…
BA-BAAAAM...
MAR... CEAN ...?
NO WAY.
F...
FIND HIM AT ONCE !!
CLOP
CLOP

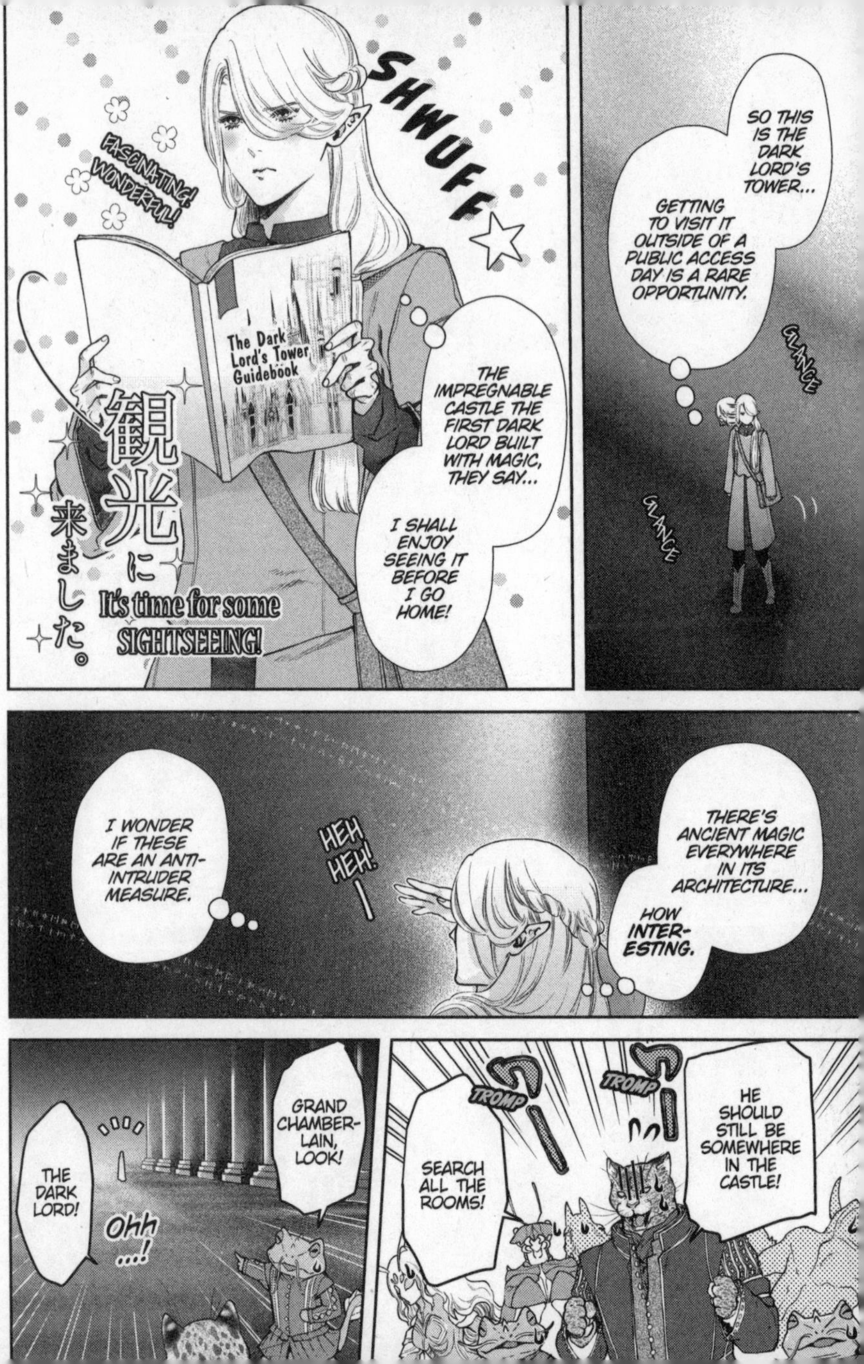
SO THIS IS THE DARK LORD'S TOWER...
GETTING TO VISIT IT OUTSIDE OF A PUBLIC ACCESS DAY IS A RARE OPPORTUNITY.
GLANCE
GLANCE
SHWUFF
The Dark Lord's Tower Guidebook
THE IMPREGNABLE CASTLE THE FIRST DARK LORD BUILT WITH MAGIC, THEY SAY...
I SHALL ENJOY SEEING IT BEFORE I GO HOME!
FASCINATING! WONDERFUL!
観光に来ました。
It's time for some SIGHTSEEING!
THERE'S ANCIENT MAGIC EVERYWHERE IN ITS ARCHITECTURE...
HOW INTER-ESTING.
HEH HEH!
I WONDER IF THESE ARE AN ANTI-INTRUDER MEASURE.
TROMP
TROMP
HE SHOULD STILL BE SOMEWHERE IN THE CASTLE!
SEARCH ALL THE ROOMS!
GRAND CHAMBER-LAIN, LOOK!
THE DARK LORD!
Ohh ...!

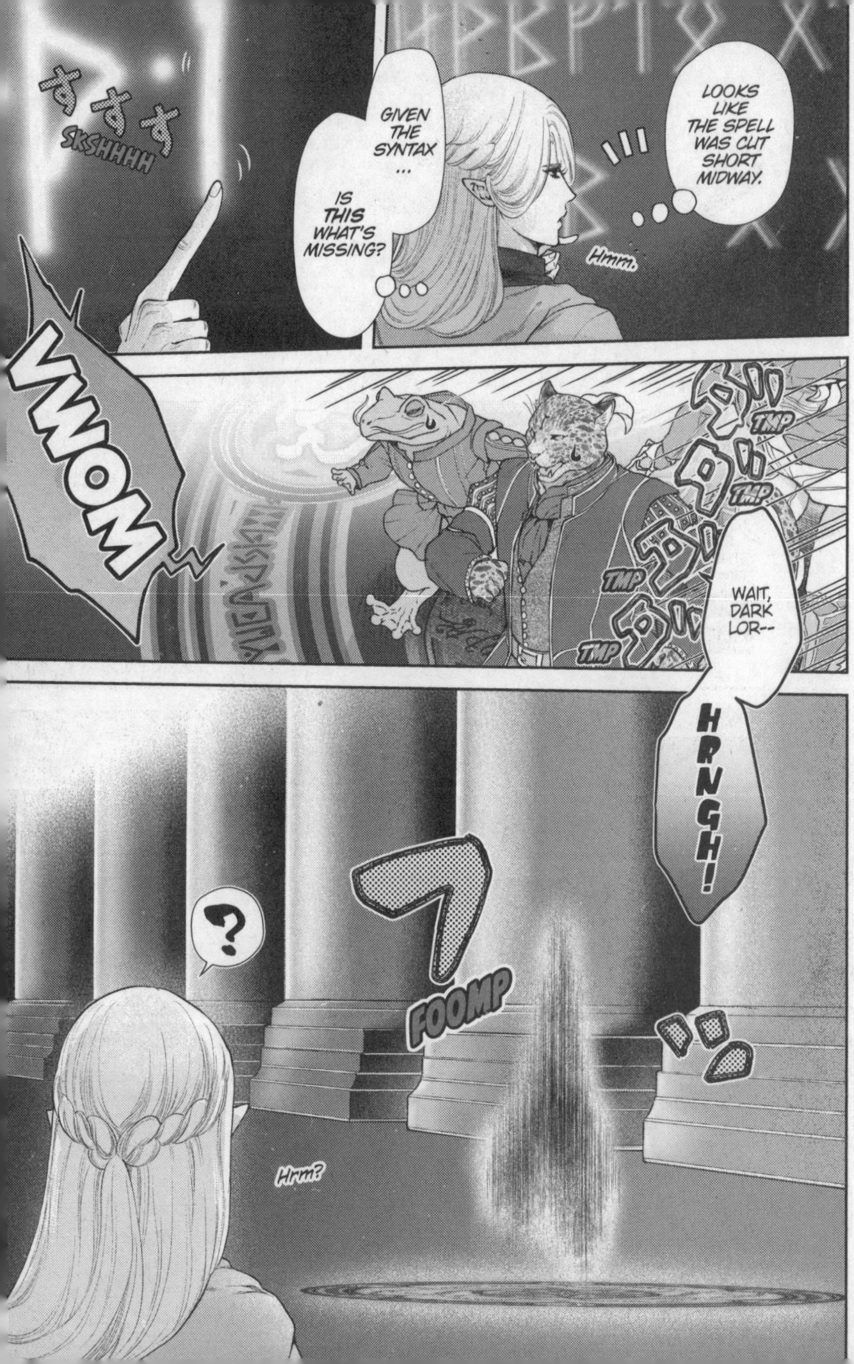

LOOKS LIKE THE SPELL WAS CUT SHORT MIDWAY.
Hmm.
GIVEN THE SYNTAX ... IS THIS WHAT'S MISSING?
すすす
SKSHHHH
WAIT, DARK LOR--
TMP
TMP
TMP
TMP
VWOM
HRNGH!
FOOMP
?
Hrm?

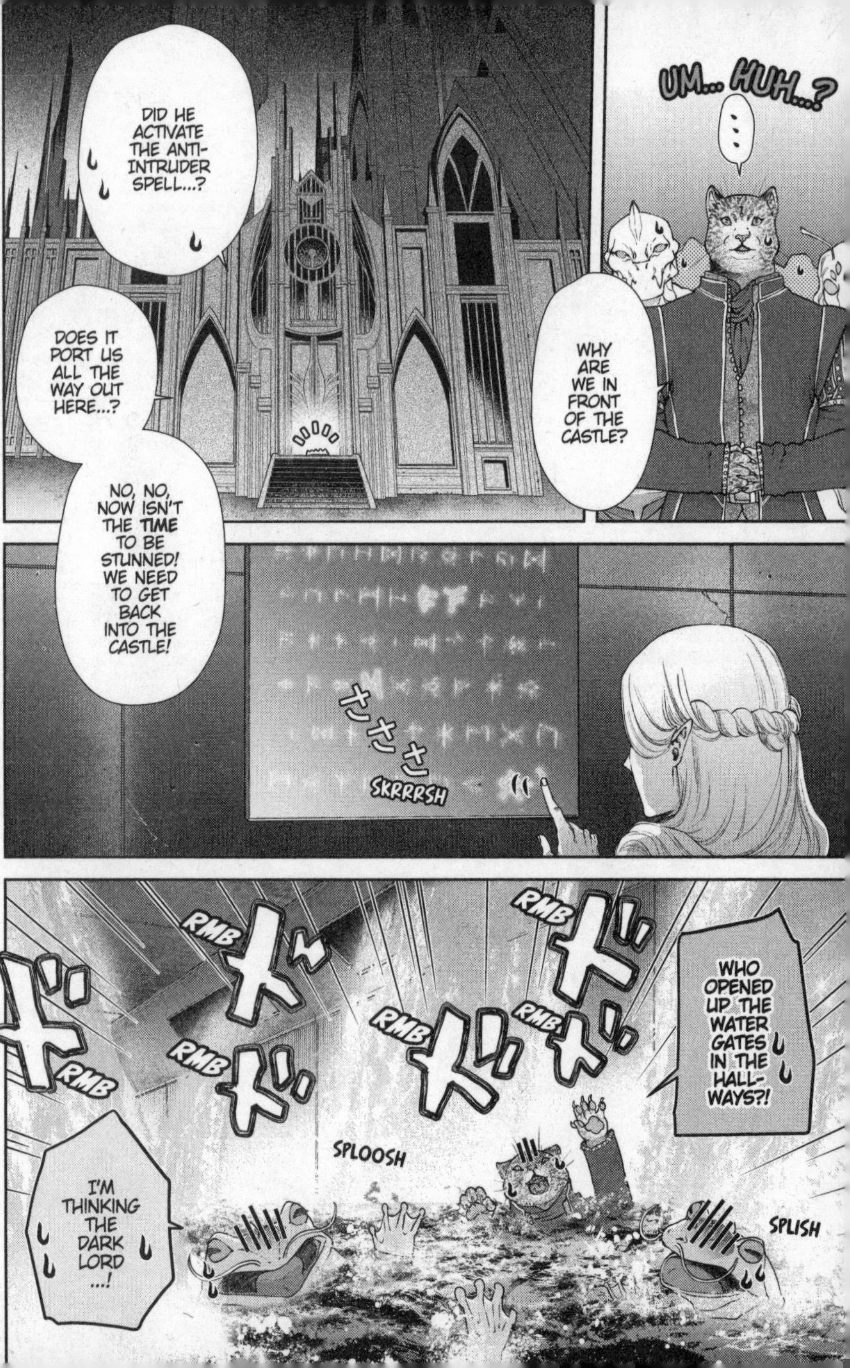
UM... HUH...?
...
WHY ARE WE IN FRONT OF THE CASTLE?
DID HE ACTIVATE THE ANTI-INTRUDER SPELL...?
DOES IT PORT US ALL THE WAY OUT HERE...?
NO, NO, NOW ISN'T THE TIME TO BE STUNNED! WE NEED TO GET BACK INTO THE CASTLE!
SKRRRSH
WHO OPENED UP THE WATER GATES IN THE HALLWAYS?!
RMB
RMB
RMB
RMB
RMB
RMB
SPLOOSH
SPLISH
I'M THINKING THE DARK LORD ...!

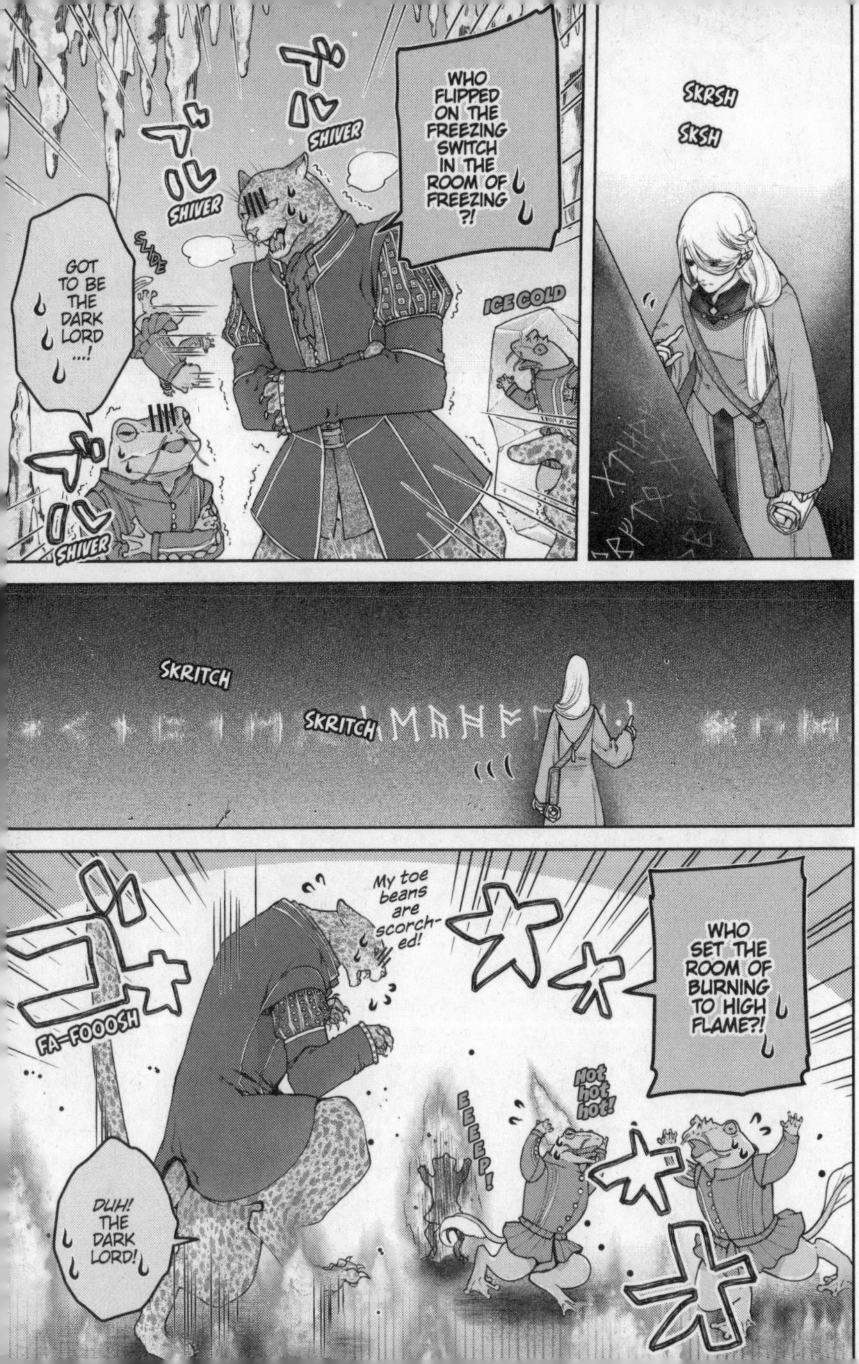
SKRSH
SKSH
WHO FLIPPED ON THE FREEZING SWITCH IN THE ROOM OF FREEZING?!
SHIVER
SHIVER
ICE COLD
SLIDE
GOT TO BE THE DARK LORD...!
SHIVER
SKRITCH
SKRITCH
WHO SET THE ROOM OF BURNING TO HIGH FLAME?!
My toe beans are scorched!
FA-FOOOSH
Hot hot hot!
EEEEP!
DUH! THE DARK LORD!

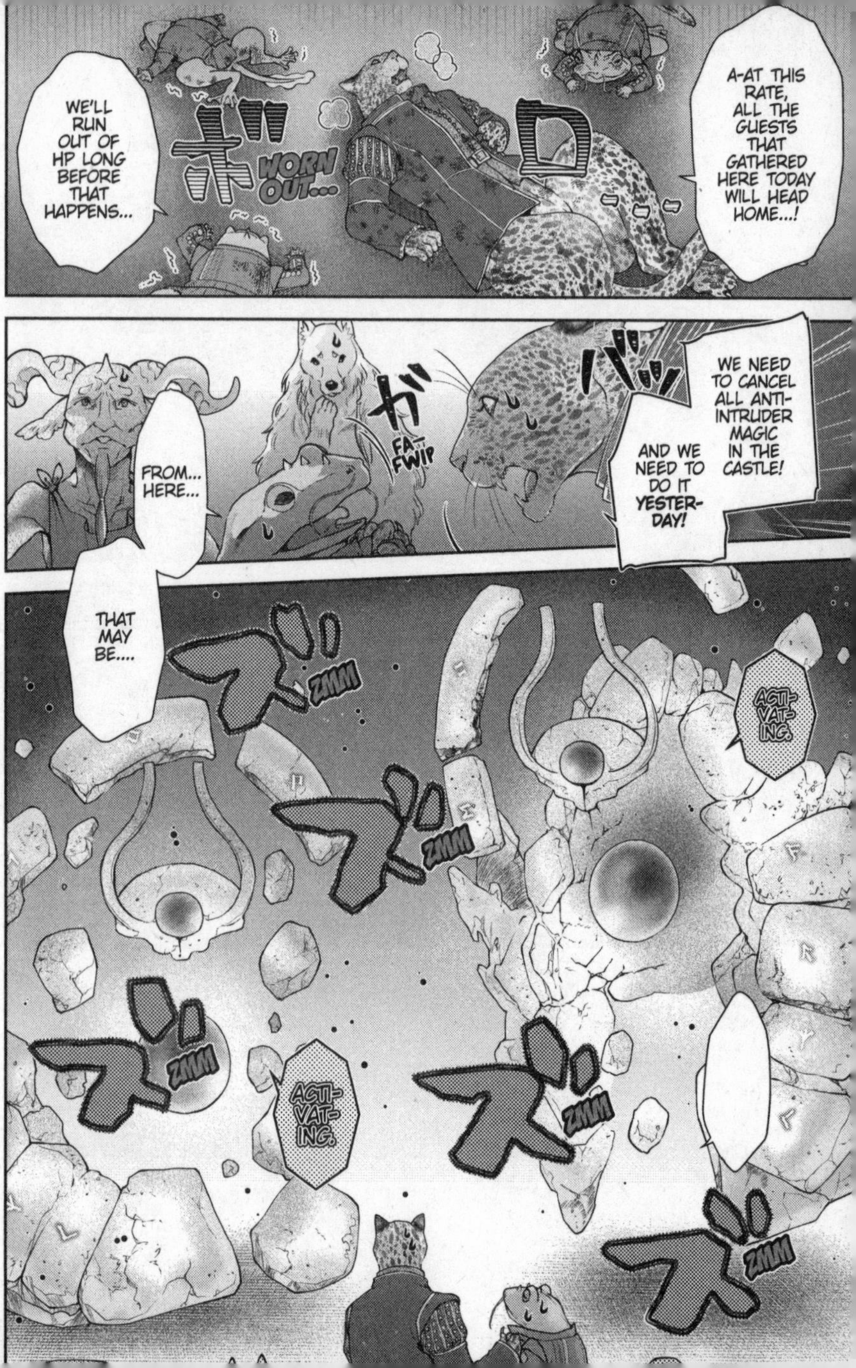
A-AT THIS RATE, ALL THE GUESTS THAT GATHERED HERE TODAY WILL HEAD HOME...!
WORN OUT...
WE'LL RUN OUT OF HP LONG BEFORE THAT HAPPENS...
WE NEED TO CANCEL ALL ANTI-INTRUDER MAGIC IN THE CASTLE!
AND WE NEED TO DO IT YESTER-DAY!
FA-FWIP
FROM... HERE...
THAT MAY BE....
ZMM
ACTI-VAT-ING.
ZMM
ZMM
ACTI-VAT-ING.
ZMM
ZMM

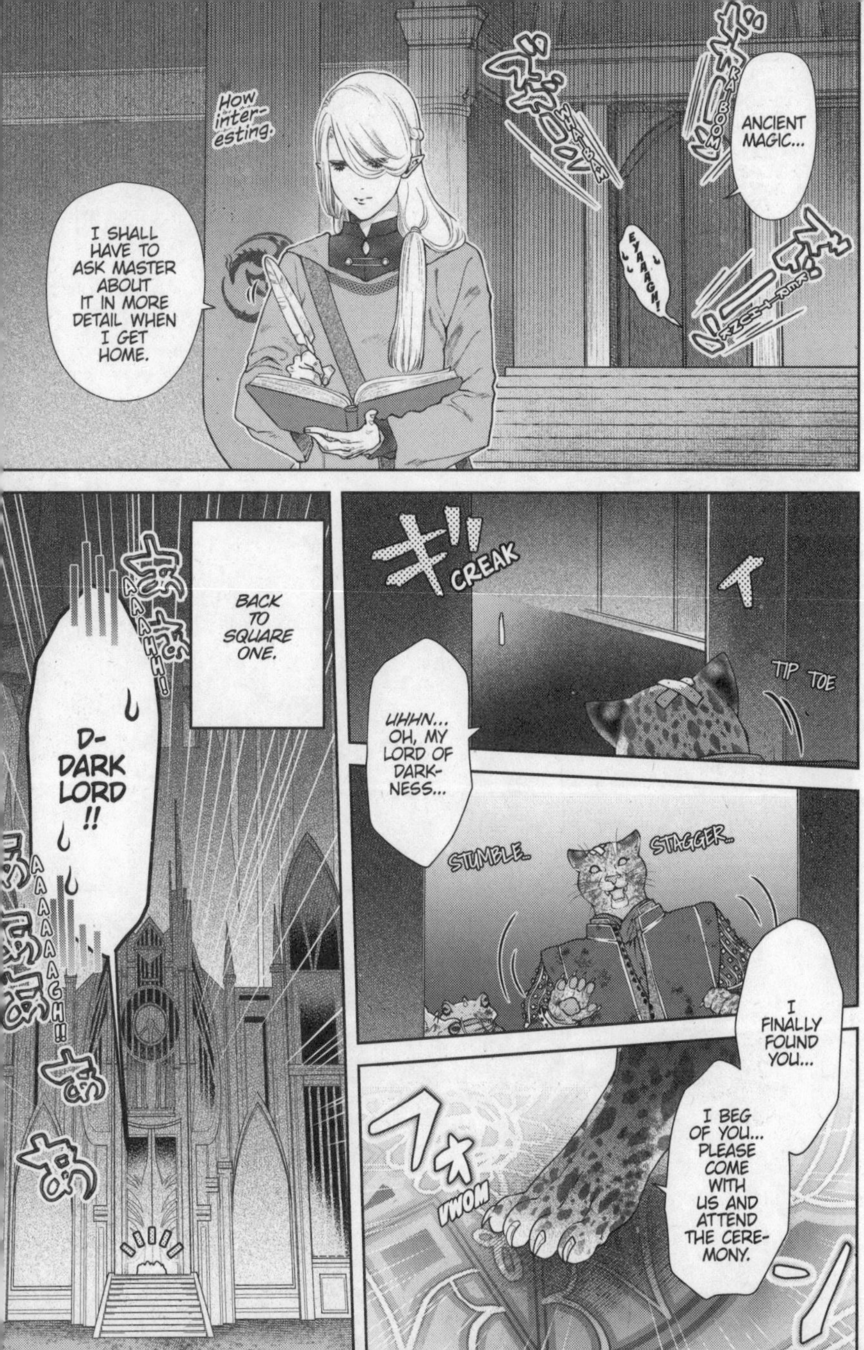
ANCIENT MAGIC...
KAIBOOM
WHA-BAM
EYAAARGH!
How interesting.
I SHALL HAVE TO ASK MASTER ABOUT IT IN MORE DETAIL WHEN I GET HOME.
CREAK
TIP TOE
UHHN... OH, MY LORD OF DARKNESS...
STAGGER...
STUMBLE...
I FINALLY FOUND YOU...
I BEG OF YOU... PLEASE COME WITH US AND ATTEND THE CEREMONY.
VWOM
BACK TO SQUARE ONE.
AAAAHH!
D-DARK LORD!!
AAAAAAAAGH!!

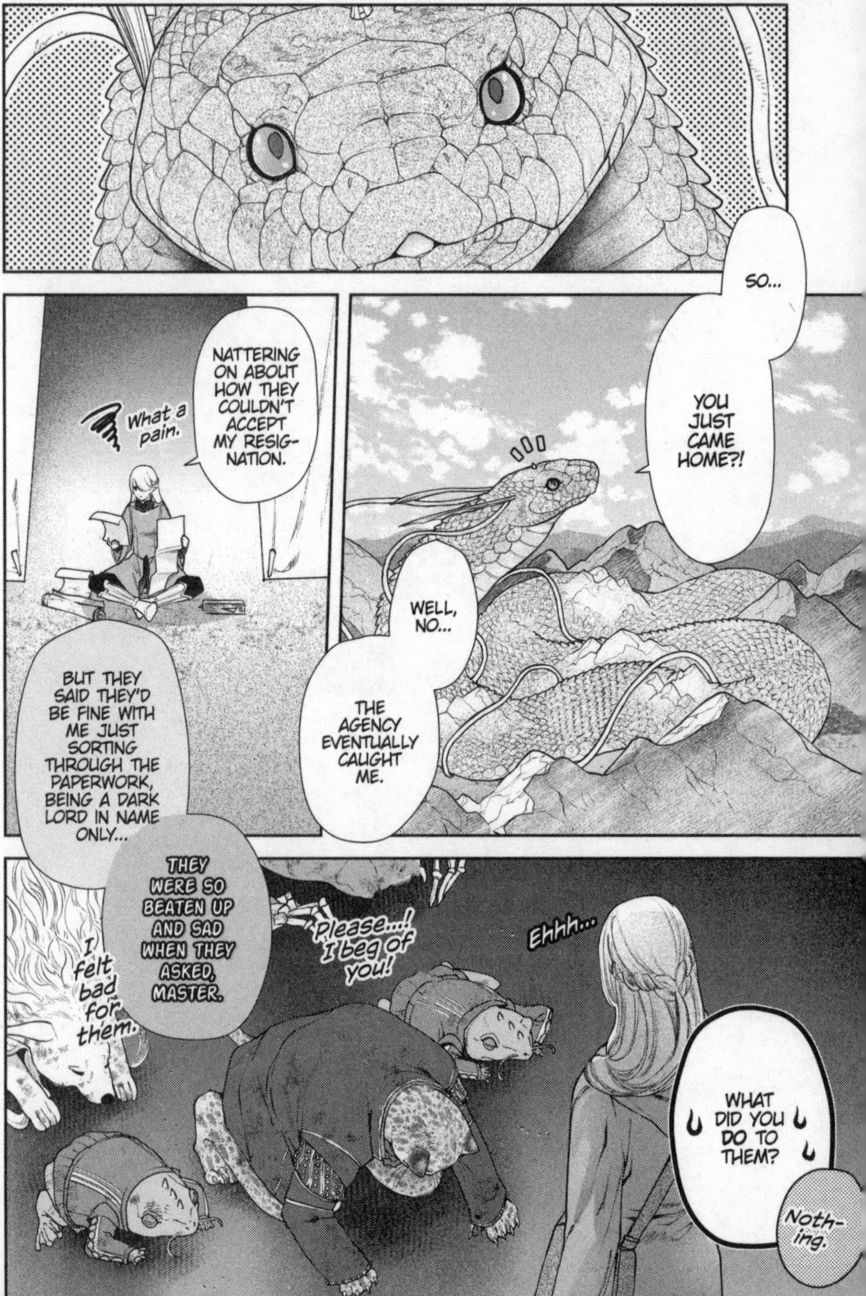
SO...
YOU JUST CAME HOME?!
WELL, NO...
THE AGENCY EVENTUALLY CAUGHT ME.
NATTERING ON ABOUT HOW THEY COULDN'T ACCEPT MY RESIGNATION.
What a pain.
BUT THEY SAID THEY'D BE FINE WITH ME JUST SORTING THROUGH THE PAPERWORK, BEING A DARK LORD IN NAME ONLY...
Please...! I beg of you!
Ehhh...
WHAT DID YOU DO TO THEM?
Nothing.
THEY WERE SO BEATEN UP AND SAD WHEN THEY ASKED, MASTER.
I felt bad for them.

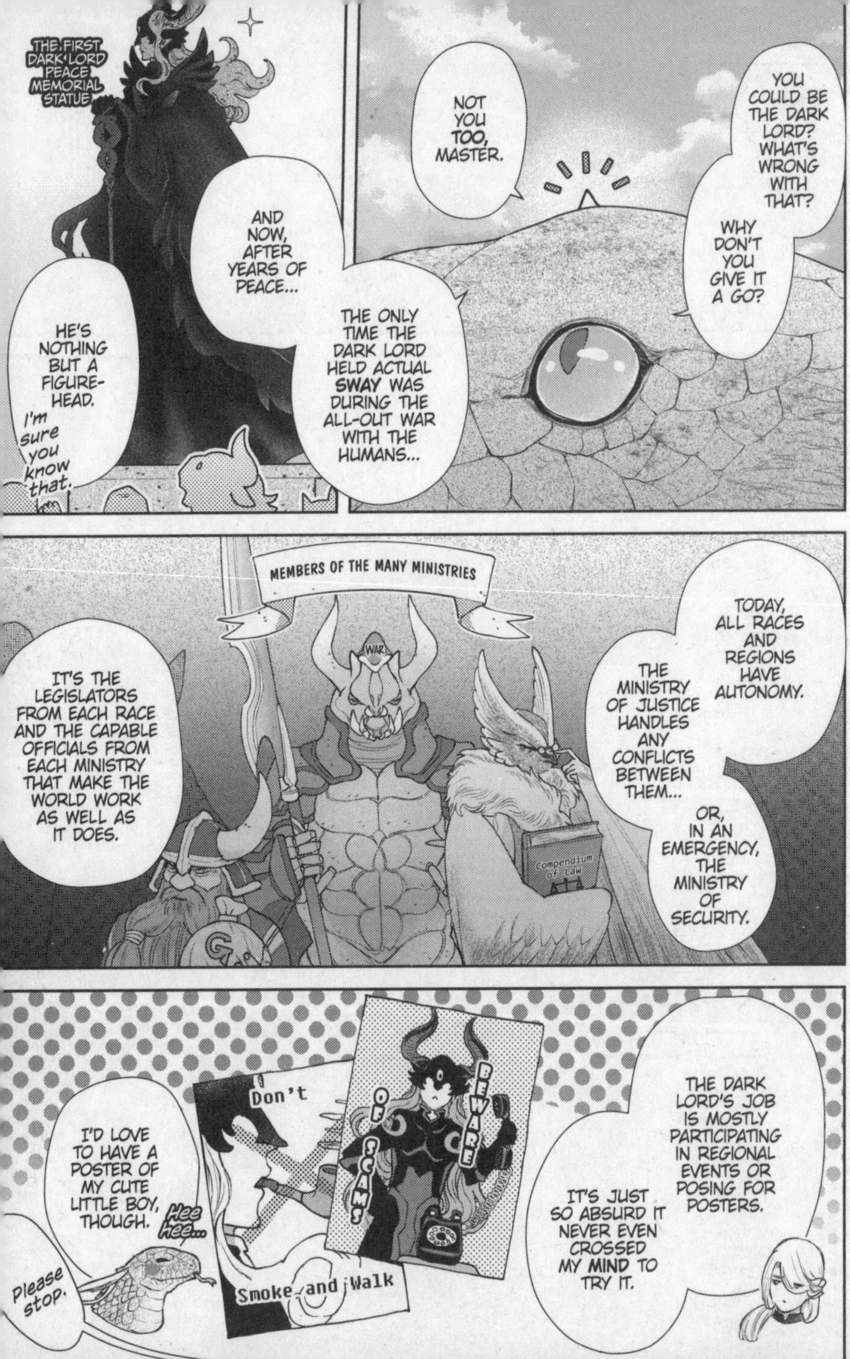
YOU COULD BE THE DARK LORD? WHAT'S WRONG WITH THAT?
WHY DON'T YOU GIVE IT A GO?
NOT YOU TOO, MASTER.
THE FIRST DARK LORD PEACE MEMORIAL STATUE
AND NOW, AFTER YEARS OF PEACE...
THE ONLY TIME THE DARK LORD HELD ACTUAL SWAY WAS DURING THE ALL-OUT WAR WITH THE HUMANS...
HE'S NOTHING BUT A FIGUREHEAD.
I'm sure you know that.
MEMBERS OF THE MANY MINISTRIES
TODAY, ALL RACES AND REGIONS HAVE AUTONOMY.
THE MINISTRY OF JUSTICE HANDLES ANY CONFLICTS BETWEEN THEM...
OR, IN AN EMERGENCY, THE MINISTRY OF SECURITY.
WAR
Compendium of Law
IT'S THE LEGISLATORS FROM EACH RACE AND THE CAPABLE OFFICIALS FROM EACH MINISTRY THAT MAKE THE WORLD WORK AS WELL AS IT DOES.
THE DARK LORD'S JOB IS MOSTLY PARTICIPATING IN REGIONAL EVENTS OR POSING FOR POSTERS.
IT'S JUST SO ABSURD IT NEVER EVEN CROSSED MY MIND TO TRY IT.
BEWARE OF SCAMS
Don't
Smoke and Walk
I'D LOVE TO HAVE A POSTER OF MY CUTE LITTLE BOY, THOUGH.
Hee hee...
Please stop.

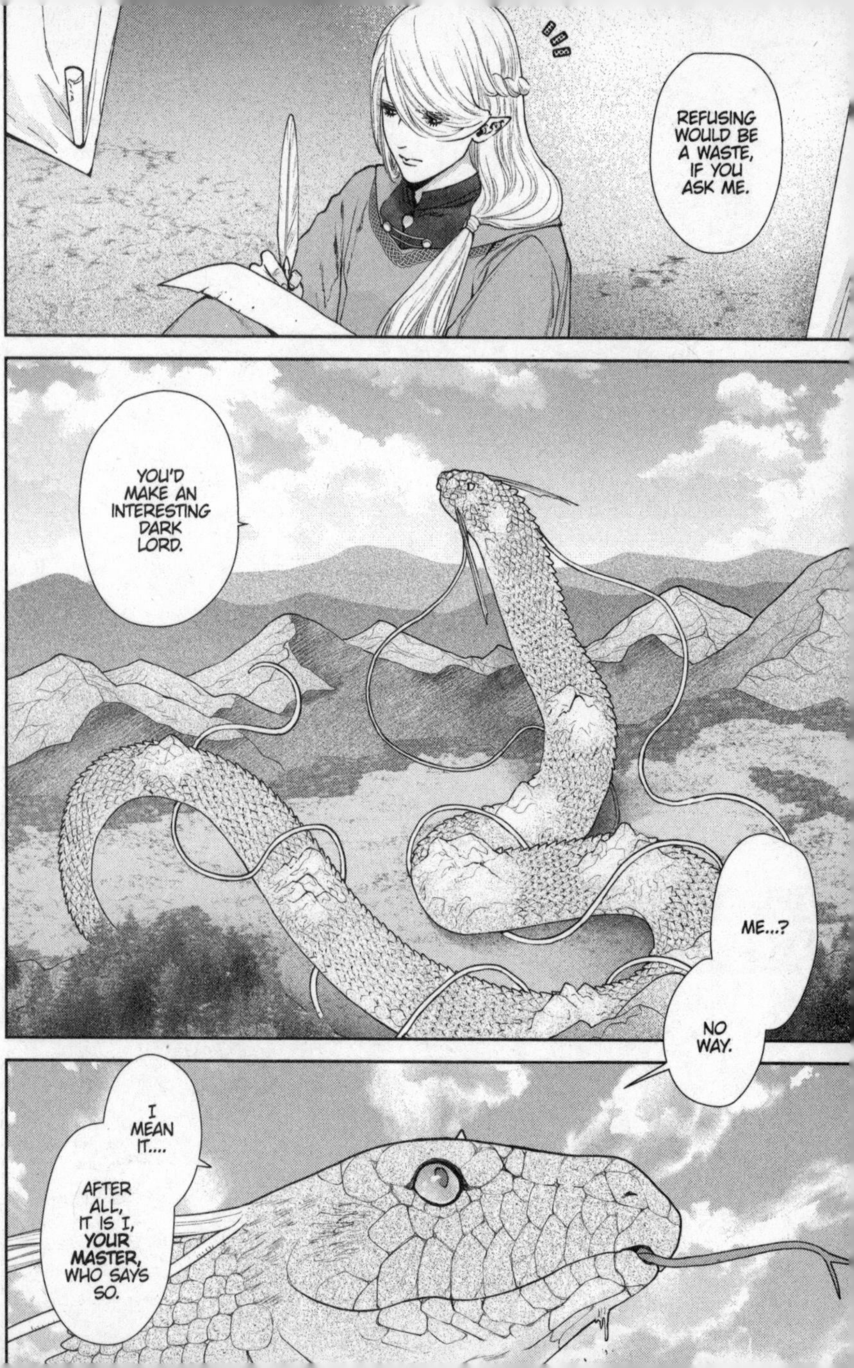
REFUSING WOULD BE A WASTE, IF YOU ASK ME.
YOU'D MAKE AN INTERESTING DARK LORD.
ME...?
NO WAY.
I MEAN IT....
AFTER ALL, IT IS I, **YOUR MASTER,** WHO SAYS SO.

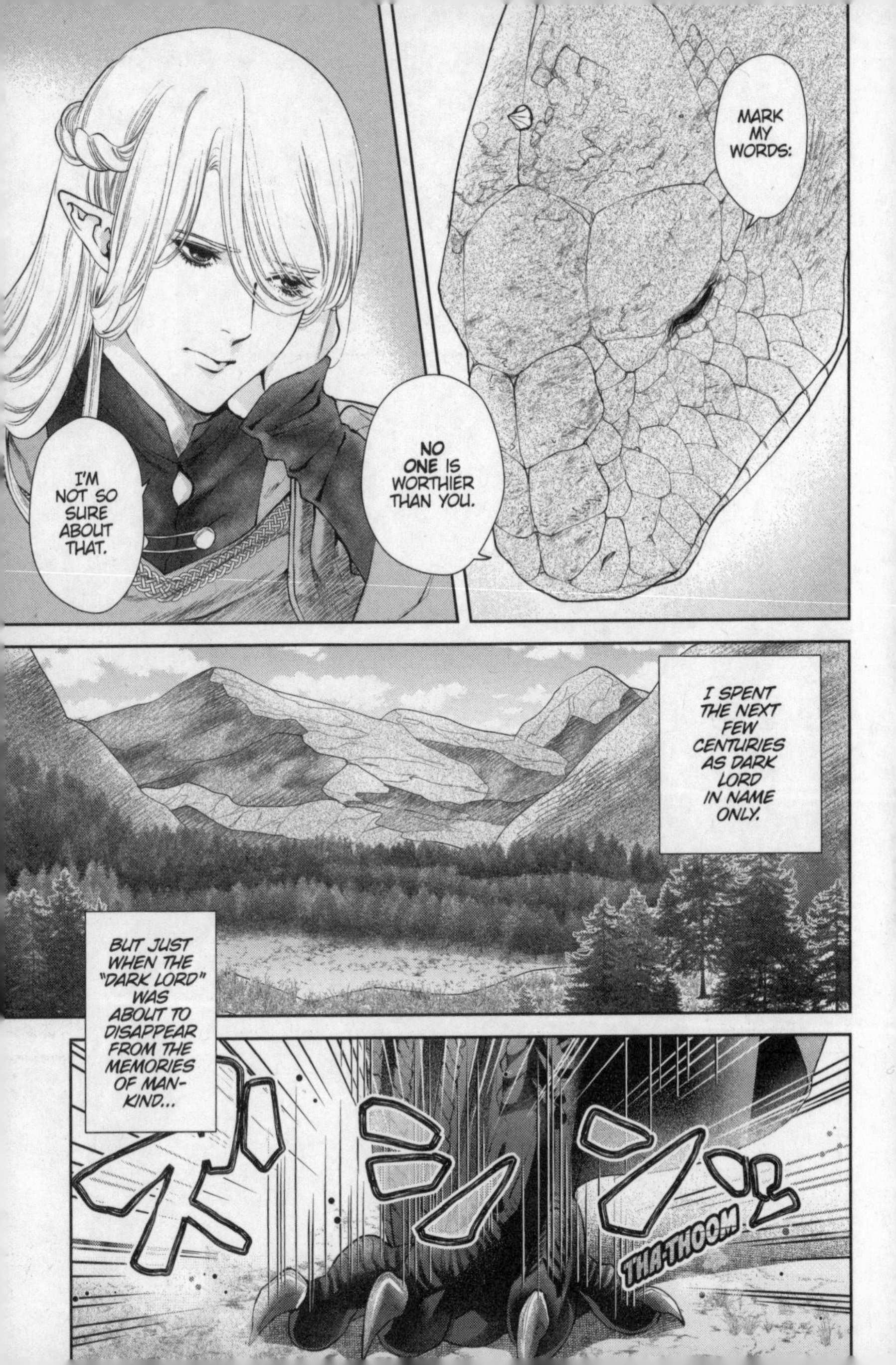
MARK MY WORDS:
NO ONE IS WORTHIER THAN YOU.
I'M NOT SO SURE ABOUT THAT.
I SPENT THE NEXT FEW CENTURIES AS DARK LORD IN NAME ONLY.
BUT JUST WHEN THE "DARK LORD" WAS ABOUT TO DISAPPEAR FROM THE MEMORIES OF MAN-KIND...
THA-THOOM

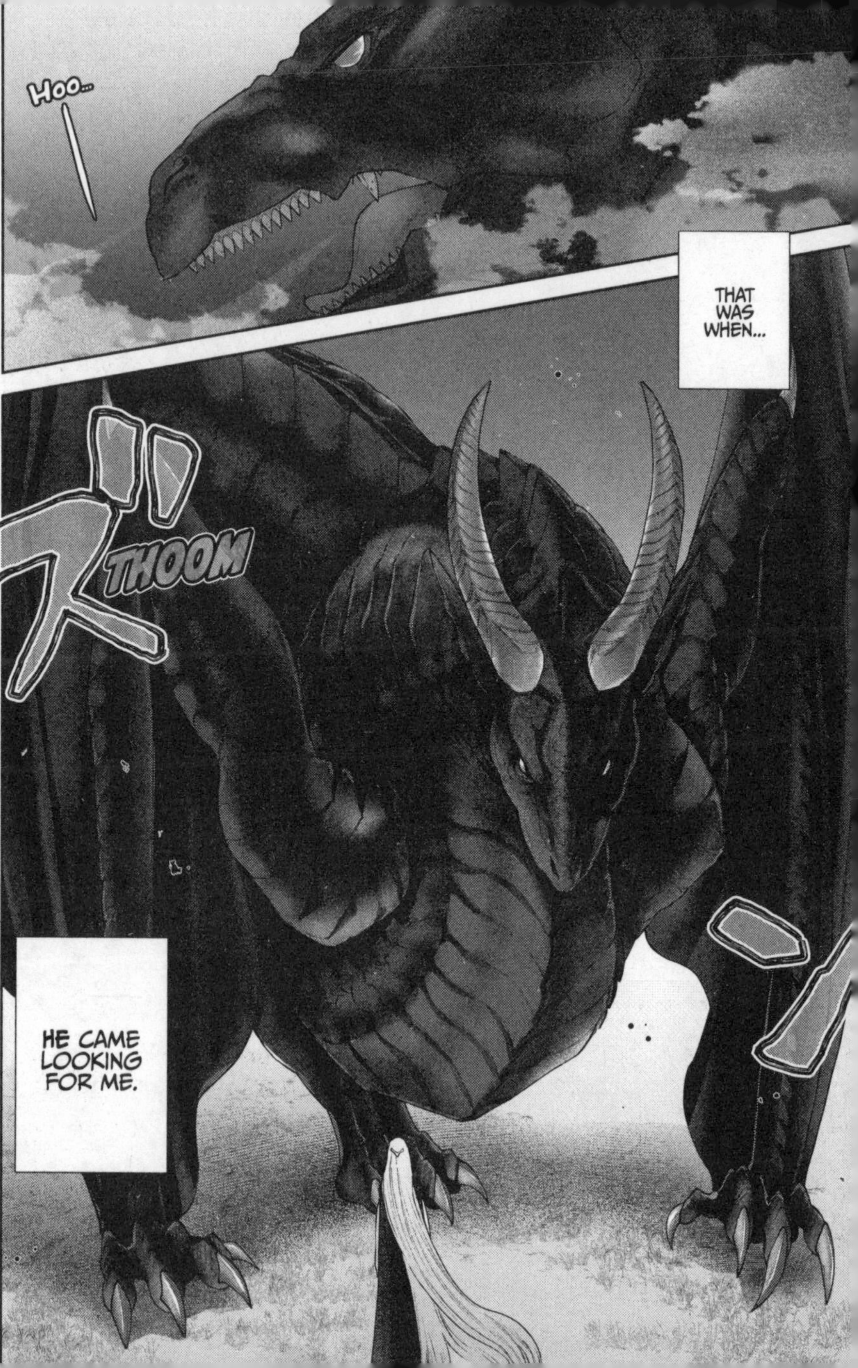
Hoo...
THAT WAS WHEN...
THOOM
HE CAME LOOKING FOR ME.

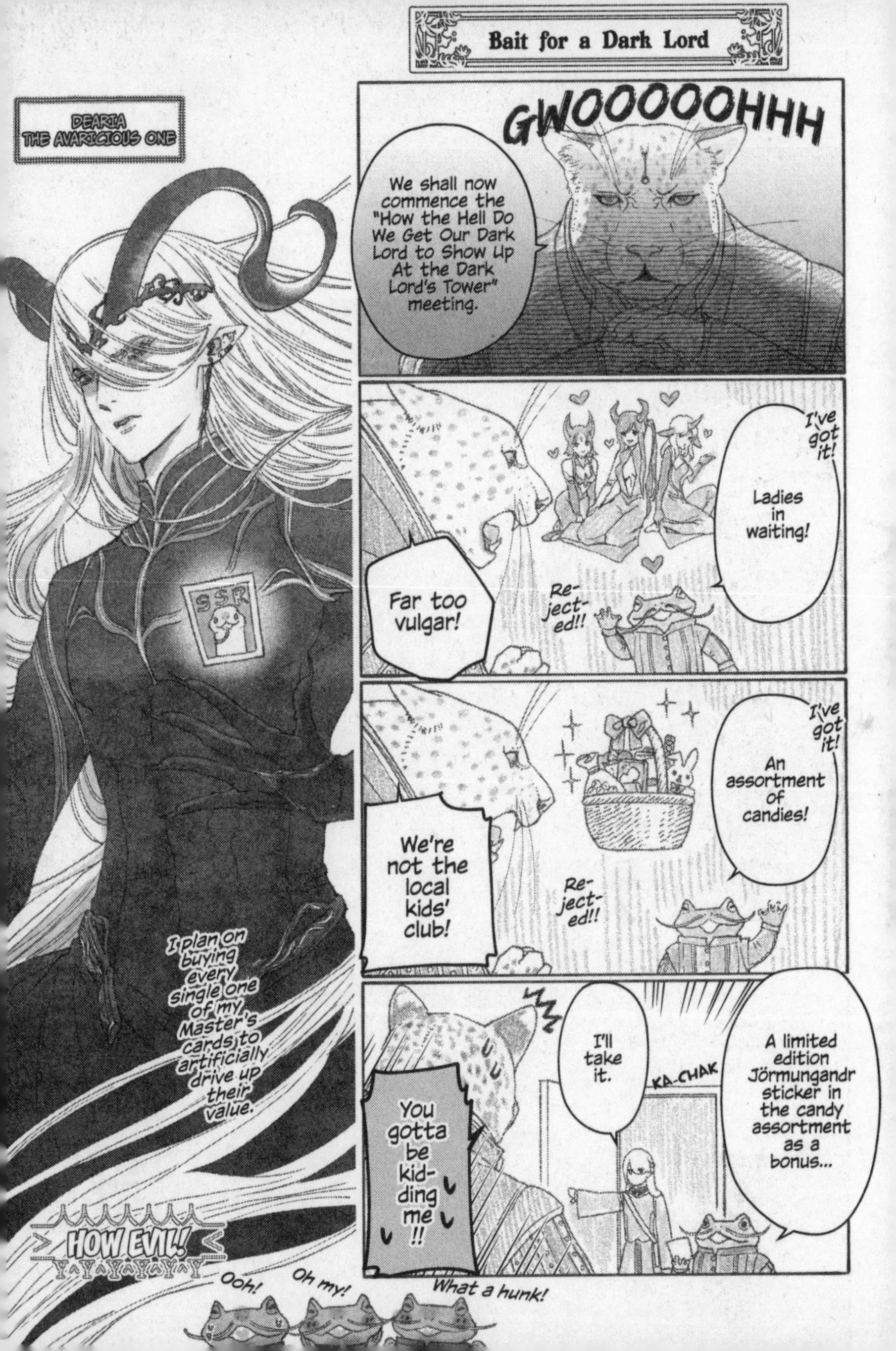
Bait for a Dark Lord
GWOOOOOHHH
We shall now commence the "How the Hell Do We Get Our Dark Lord to Show Up At the Dark Lord's Tower" meeting.
I've got it!
Ladies in waiting!
Far too vulgar!
Re-ject-ed!!
I've got it!
An assortment of candies!
We're not the local kids' club!
Re-ject-ed!!
A limited edition Jörmungandr sticker in the candy assortment as a bonus...
I'll take it.
KA-CHAK
You gotta be kid-ding me!!
DEARIA THE AVARICIOUS ONE
SSR
I plan on buying every single one of my Master's cards to artificially drive up their value.
HOW EVIL!
Ooh!
Oh my!
What a hunk!

Dragon
Goes
House-
Hunting

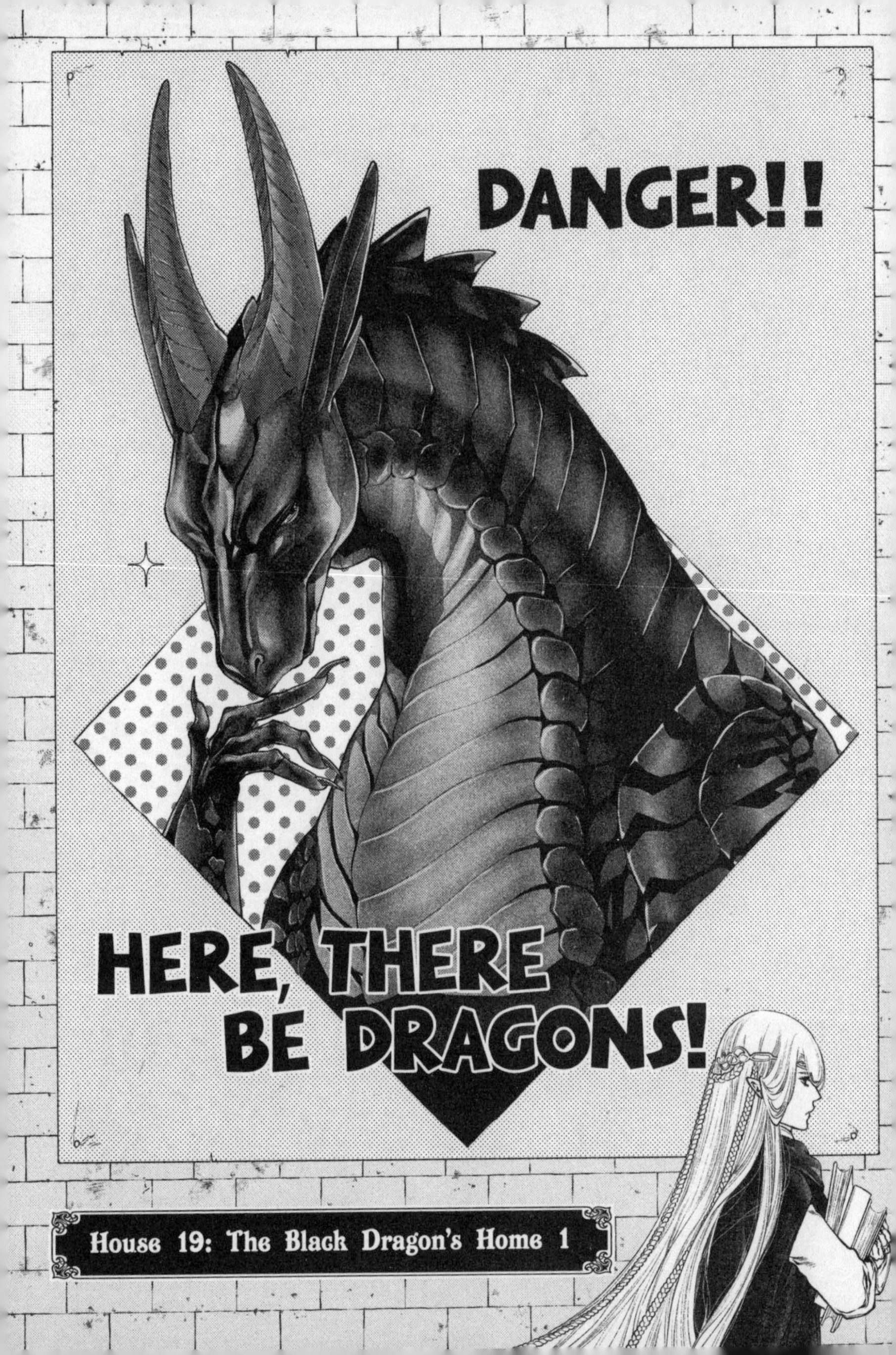
DANGER!!
HERE, THERE BE DRAGONS!
House 19: The Black Dragon's Home 1

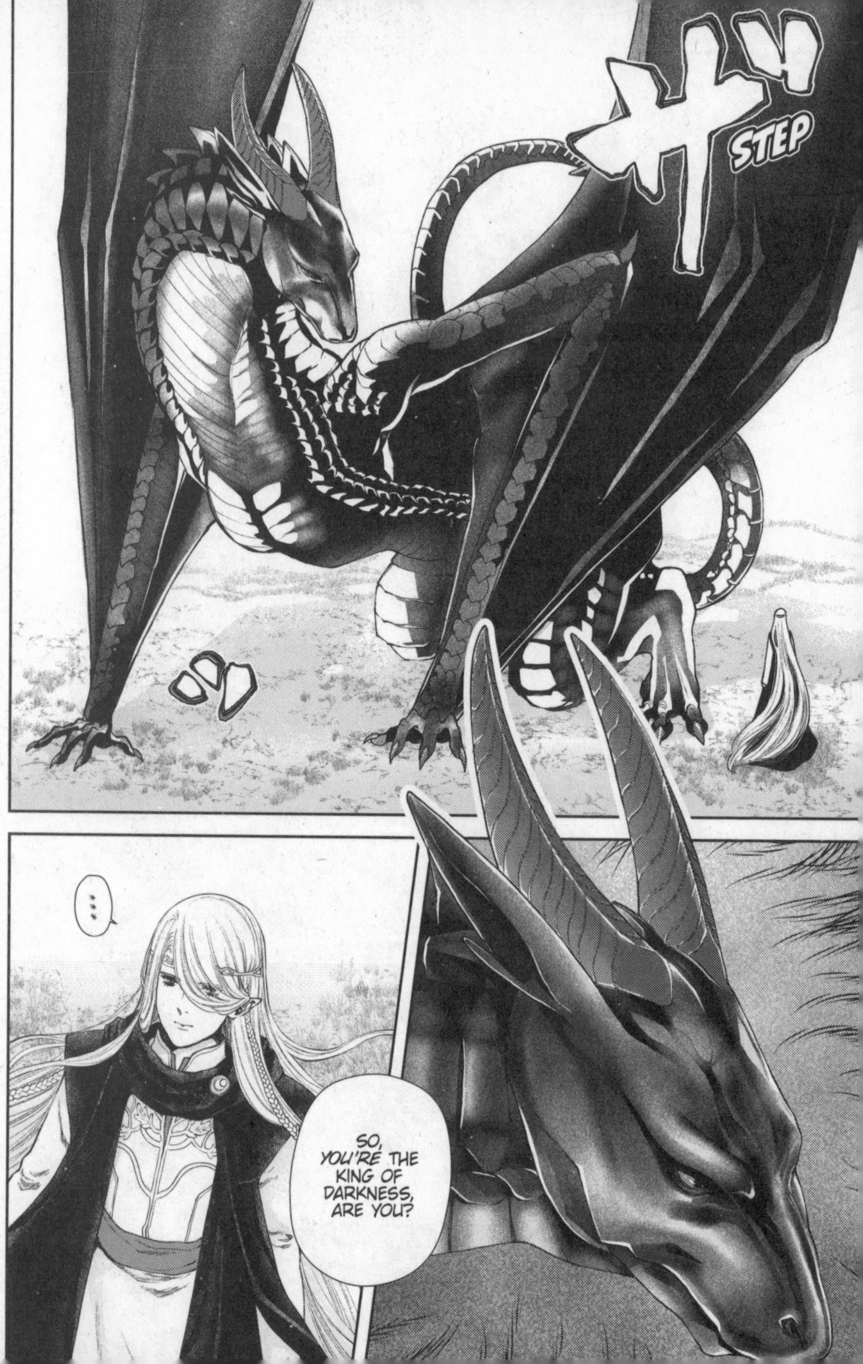
STEP
...
SO, YOU'RE THE KING OF DARKNESS, ARE YOU?

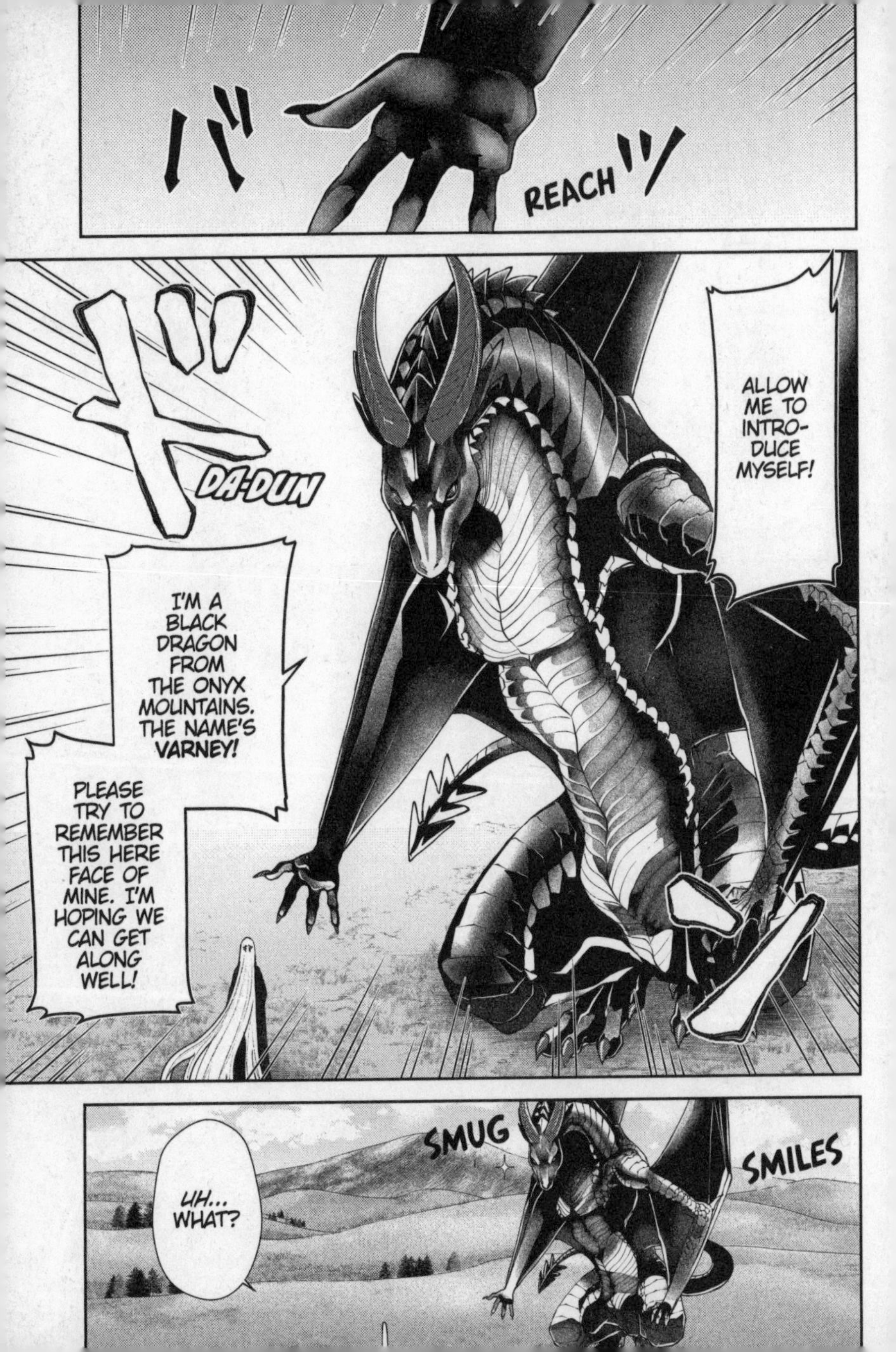
バッ
REACH
ALLOW ME TO INTRO-DUCE MYSELF!
DA-DUN
I'M A BLACK DRAGON FROM THE ONYX MOUNTAINS. THE NAME'S VARNEY!
PLEASE TRY TO REMEMBER THIS HERE FACE OF MINE. I'M HOPING WE CAN GET ALONG WELL!
SMUG
SMILES
UH... WHAT?

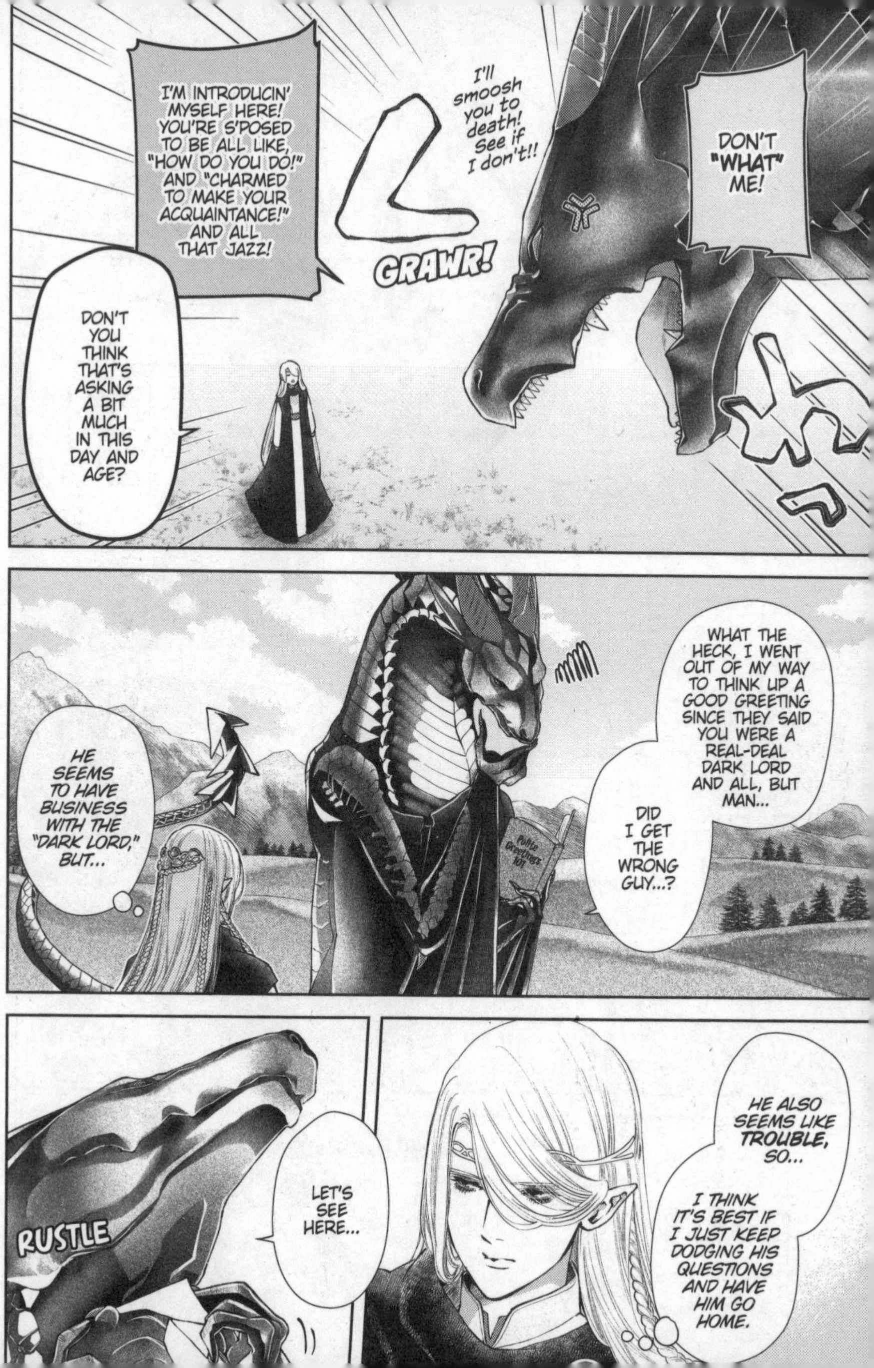
DON'T "WHAT" ME!
I'll smoosh you to death! See if I don't!!
I'M INTRODUCIN' MYSELF HERE! YOU'RE S'POSED TO BE ALL LIKE, "HOW DO YOU DO!" AND "CHARMED TO MAKE YOUR ACQUAINTANCE!" AND ALL THAT JAZZ!
GRAWR!
DON'T YOU THINK THAT'S ASKING A BIT MUCH IN THIS DAY AND AGE?
WHAT THE HECK, I WENT OUT OF MY WAY TO THINK UP A GOOD GREETING SINCE THEY SAID YOU WERE A REAL-DEAL DARK LORD AND ALL, BUT MAN...
DID I GET THE WRONG GUY...?
HE SEEMS TO HAVE BUSINESS WITH THE "DARK LORD," BUT...
HE ALSO SEEMS LIKE TROUBLE, SO...
I THINK IT'S BEST IF I JUST KEEP DODGING HIS QUESTIONS AND HAVE HIM GO HOME.
LET'S SEE HERE...
RUSTLE

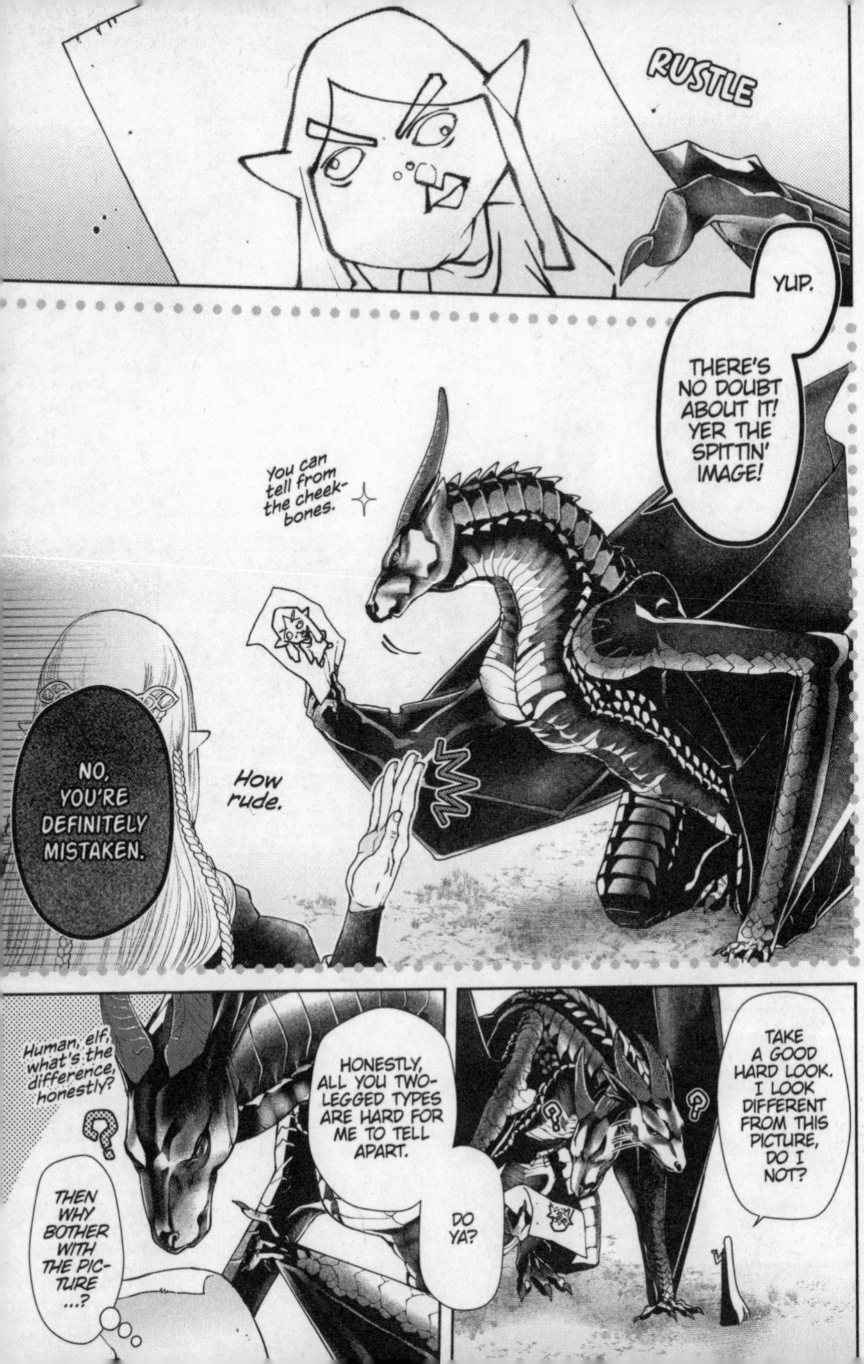
RUSTLE
YUP.
THERE'S NO DOUBT ABOUT IT! YER THE SPITTIN' IMAGE!
You can tell from the cheek-bones.
How rude.
NO, YOU'RE DEFINITELY MISTAKEN.
TAKE A GOOD HARD LOOK. I LOOK DIFFERENT FROM THIS PICTURE, DO I NOT?
DO YA?
HONESTLY, ALL YOU TWO-LEGGED TYPES ARE HARD FOR ME TO TELL APART.
Human, elf, what's the difference, honestly?
THEN WHY BOTHER WITH THE PIC-TURE ...?

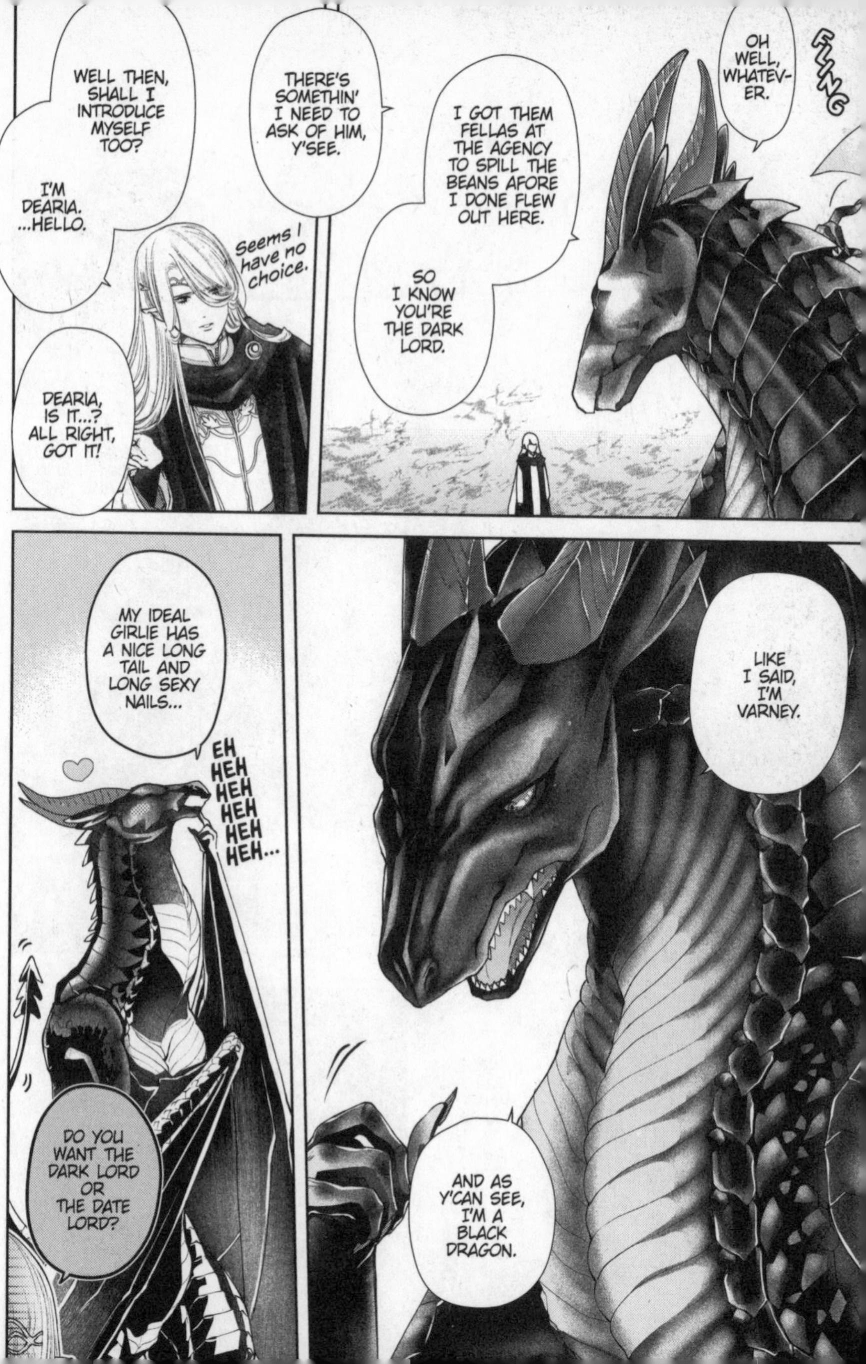
OH WELL, WHATEVER.
FLING
I GOT THEM FELLAS AT THE AGENCY TO SPILL THE BEANS AFORE I DONE FLEW OUT HERE.
SO I KNOW YOU'RE THE DARK LORD.
THERE'S SOMETHIN' I NEED TO ASK OF HIM, Y'SEE.
WELL THEN, SHALL I INTRODUCE MYSELF TOO?
I'M DEARIA. ...HELLO.
Seems I have no choice.
DEARIA, IS IT...? ALL RIGHT, GOT IT!
LIKE I SAID, I'M VARNEY.
AND AS Y'CAN SEE, I'M A BLACK DRAGON.
MY IDEAL GIRLIE HAS A NICE LONG TAIL AND LONG SEXY NAILS...
EH HEH HEH HEH HEH HEH...
DO YOU WANT THE DARK LORD OR THE DATE LORD?

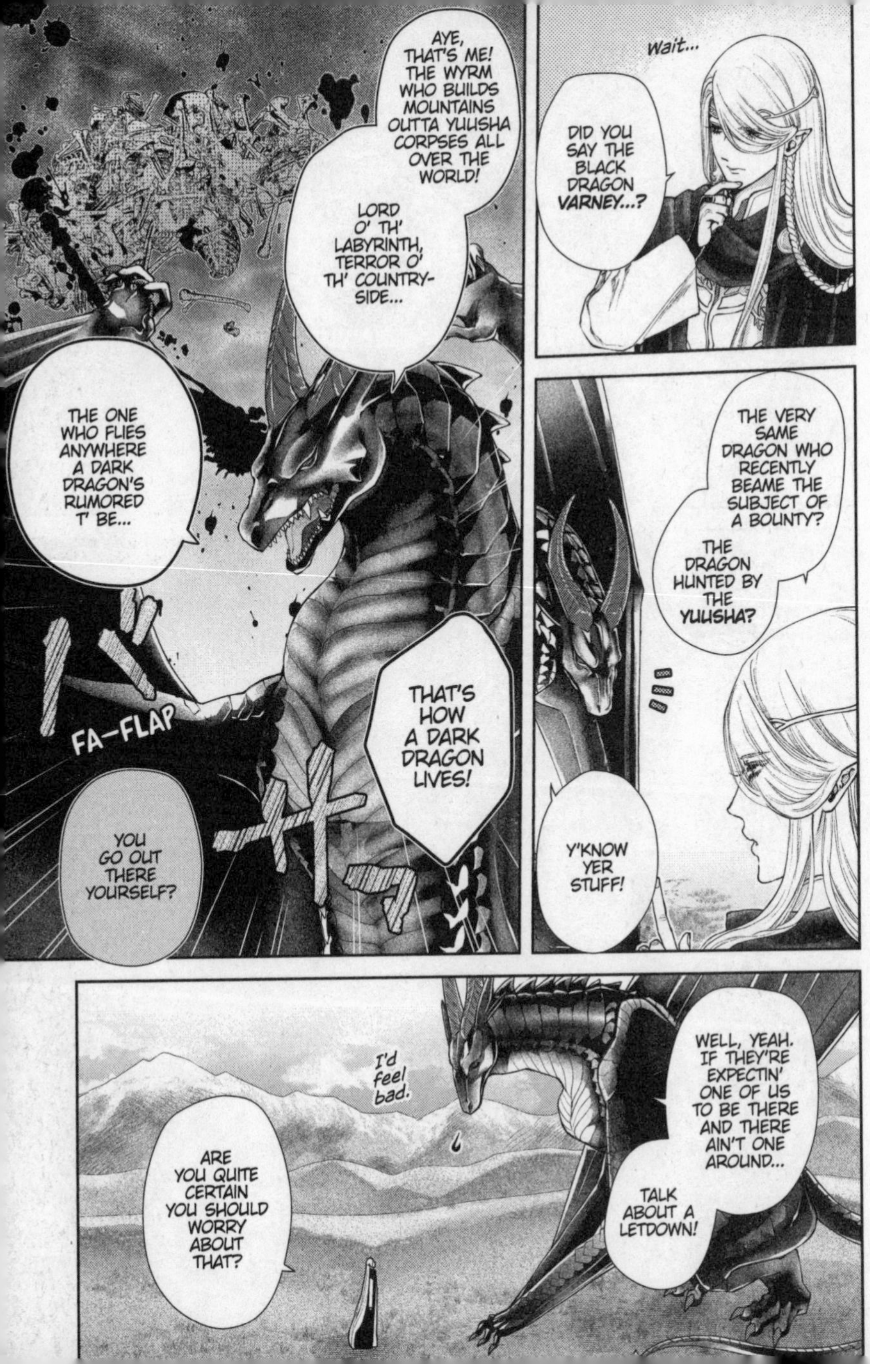
Wait...
DID YOU SAY THE BLACK DRAGON VARNEY...?
AYE, THAT'S ME! THE WYRM WHO BUILDS MOUNTAINS OUTTA YUUSHA CORPSES ALL OVER THE WORLD!
LORD O' TH' LABYRINTH, TERROR O' TH' COUNTRY-SIDE...
THE VERY SAME DRAGON WHO RECENTLY BEAME THE SUBJECT OF A BOUNTY?
THE DRAGON HUNTED BY THE YUUSHA?
Y'KNOW YER STUFF!
THE ONE WHO FLIES ANYWHERE A DARK DRAGON'S RUMORED T' BE...
FA-FLAP
THAT'S HOW A DARK DRAGON LIVES!
YOU GO OUT THERE YOURSELF?
WELL, YEAH. IF THEY'RE EXPECTIN' ONE OF US TO BE THERE AND THERE AIN'T ONE AROUND...
TALK ABOUT A LETDOWN!
I'd feel bad.
ARE YOU QUITE CERTAIN YOU SHOULD WORRY ABOUT THAT?

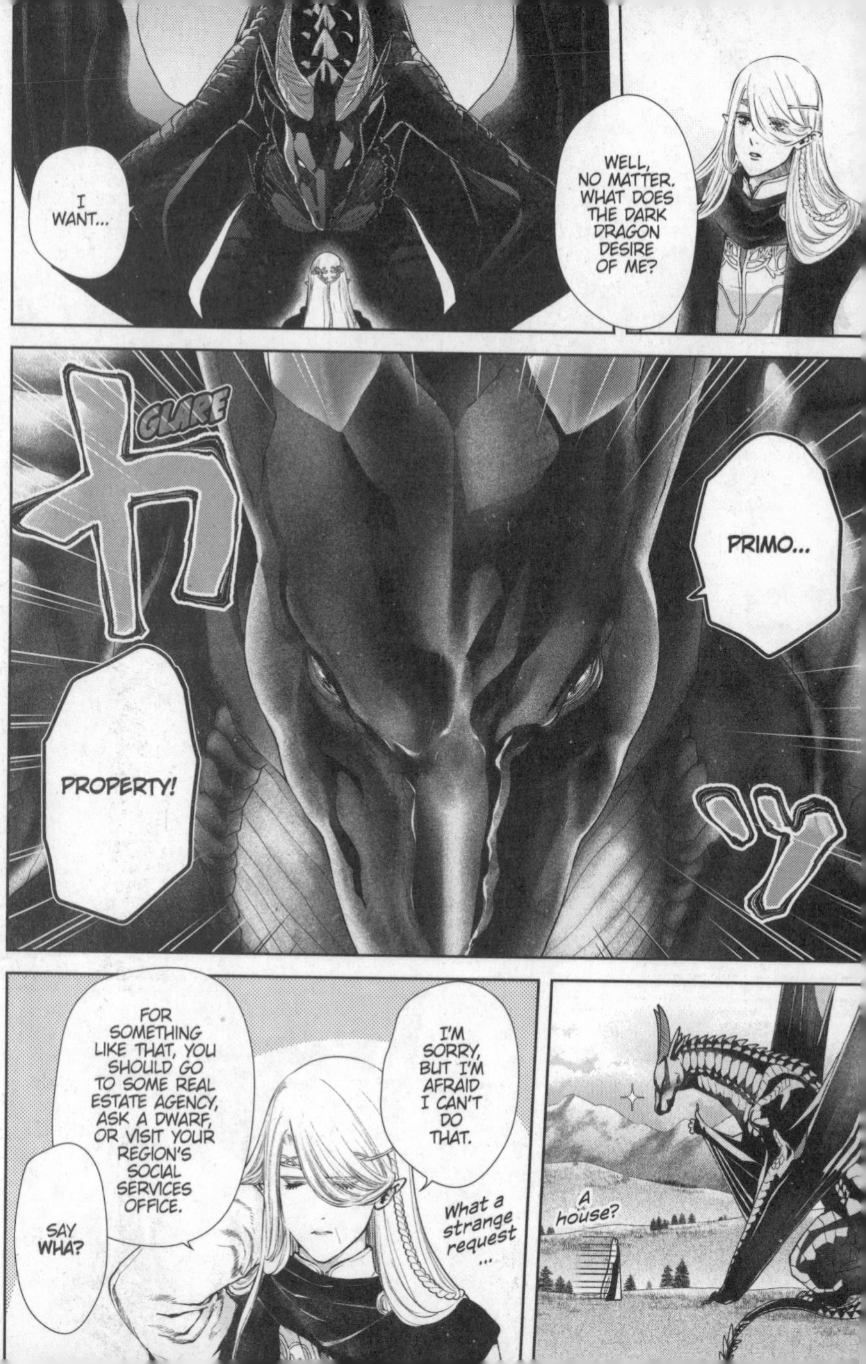
WELL, NO MATTER. WHAT DOES THE DARK DRAGON DESIRE OF ME?
I WANT...
PRIMO...
GLARE
PROPERTY!
A house?
I'M SORRY, BUT I'M AFRAID I CAN'T DO THAT.
What a strange request ...
FOR SOMETHING LIKE THAT, YOU SHOULD GO TO SOME REAL ESTATE AGENCY, ASK A DWARF, OR VISIT YOUR REGION'S SOCIAL SERVICES OFFICE.
SAY WHA?

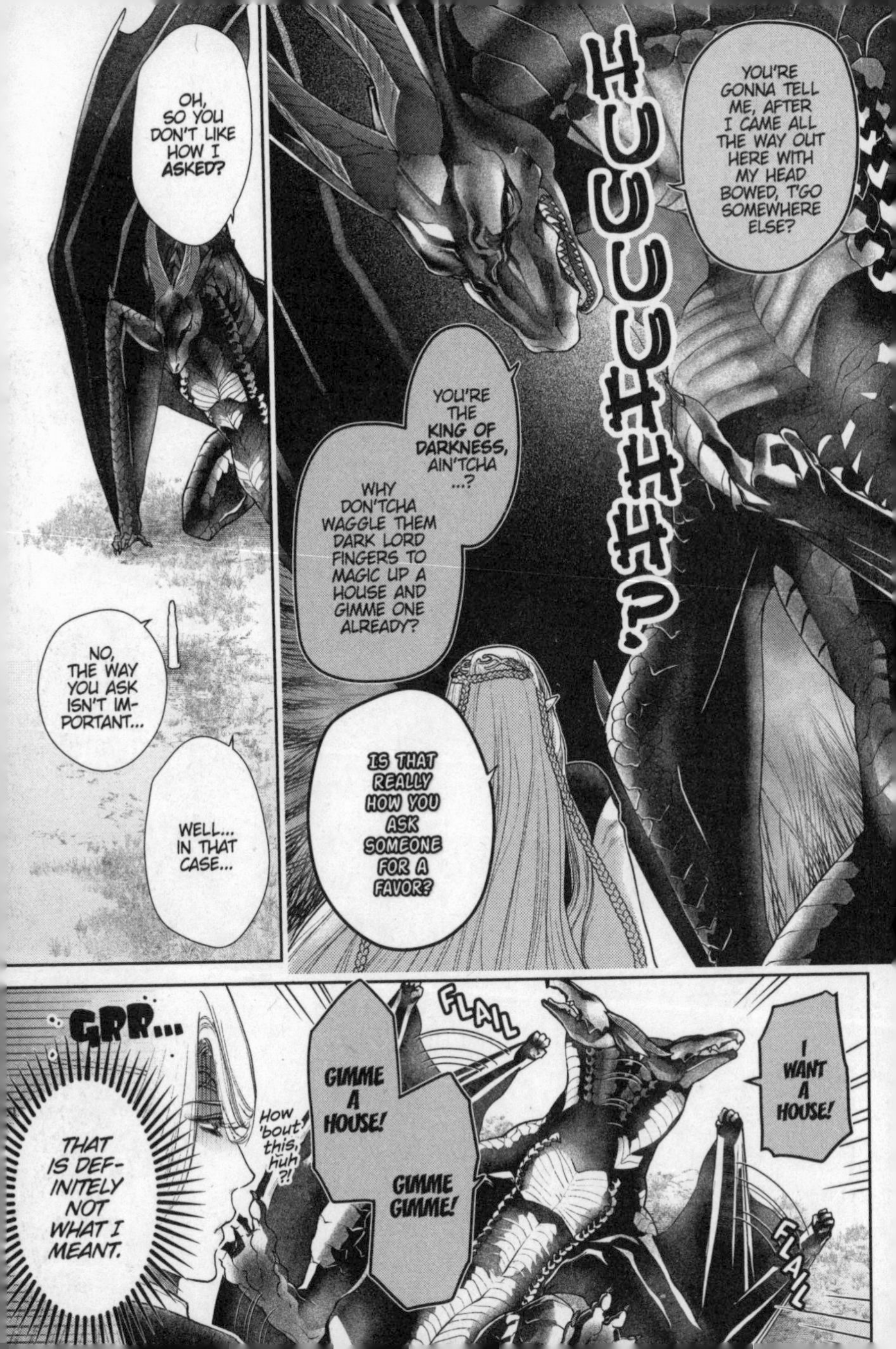
YOU'RE GONNA TELL ME, AFTER I CAME ALL THE WAY OUT HERE WITH MY HEAD BOWED, T'GO SOMEWHERE ELSE?
YOU'RE THE KING OF DARKNESS, AIN'TCHA ...?
WHY DON'TCHA WAGGLE THEM DARK LORD FINGERS TO MAGIC UP A HOUSE AND GIMME ONE ALREADY?
IS THAT REALLY HOW YOU ASK SOMEONE FOR A FAVOR?
OH, SO YOU DON'T LIKE HOW I ASKED?
NO, THE WAY YOU ASK ISN'T IM-PORTANT...
WELL... IN THAT CASE...
I WANT A HOUSE!
FLAIL
FLAIL
GIMME A HOUSE!
GIMME GIMME!
How 'bout this, huh?!
GRR...
THAT IS DEF-INITELY NOT WHAT I MEANT.

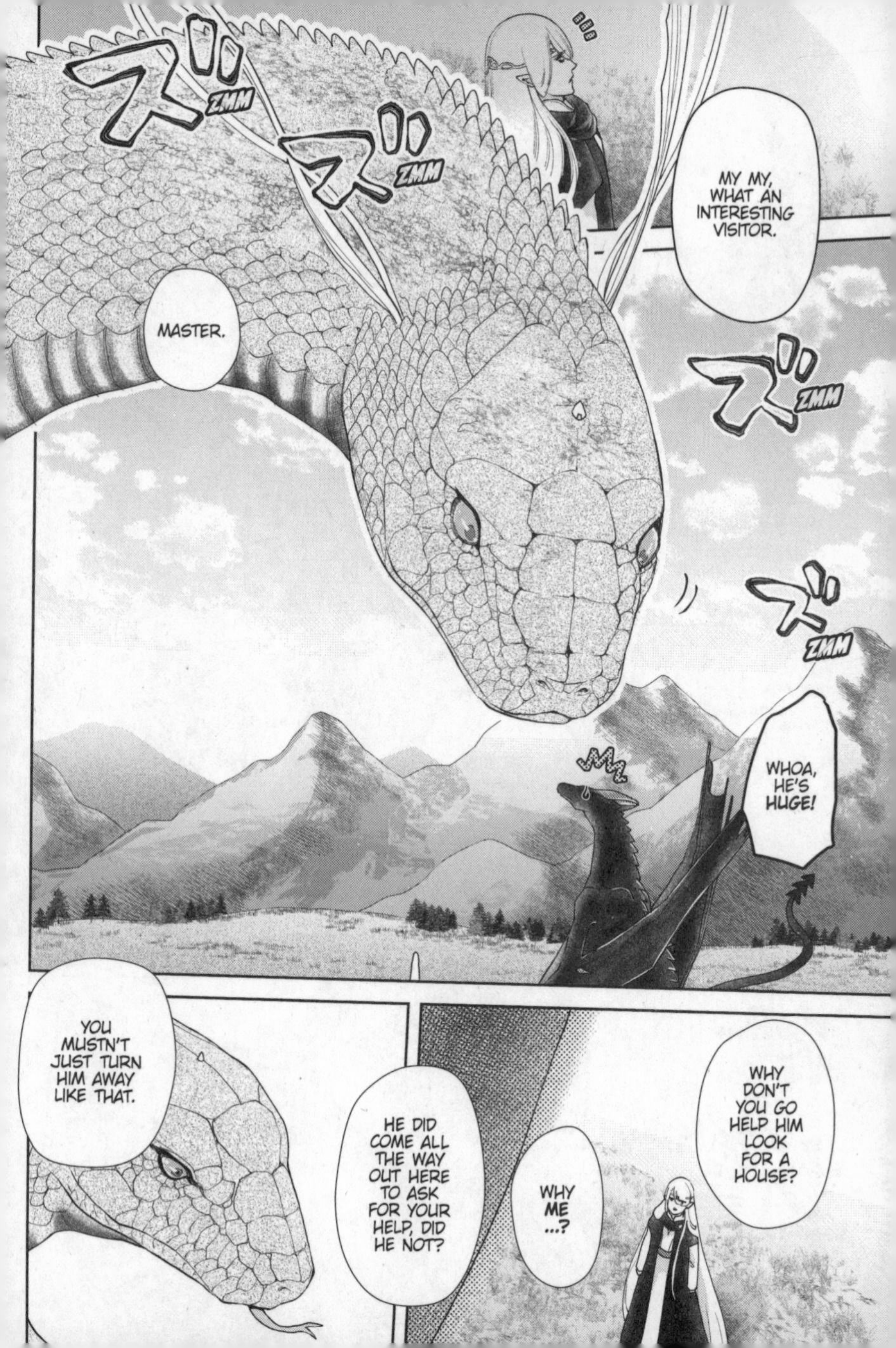
ZMM
ZMM
MY MY, WHAT AN INTERESTING VISITOR.
MASTER.
ZMM
ZMM
WHOA, HE'S HUGE!
WHY DON'T YOU GO HELP HIM LOOK FOR A HOUSE?
WHY ME ...?
HE DID COME ALL THE WAY OUT HERE TO ASK FOR YOUR HELP, DID HE NOT?
YOU MUSTN'T JUST TURN HIM AWAY LIKE THAT.

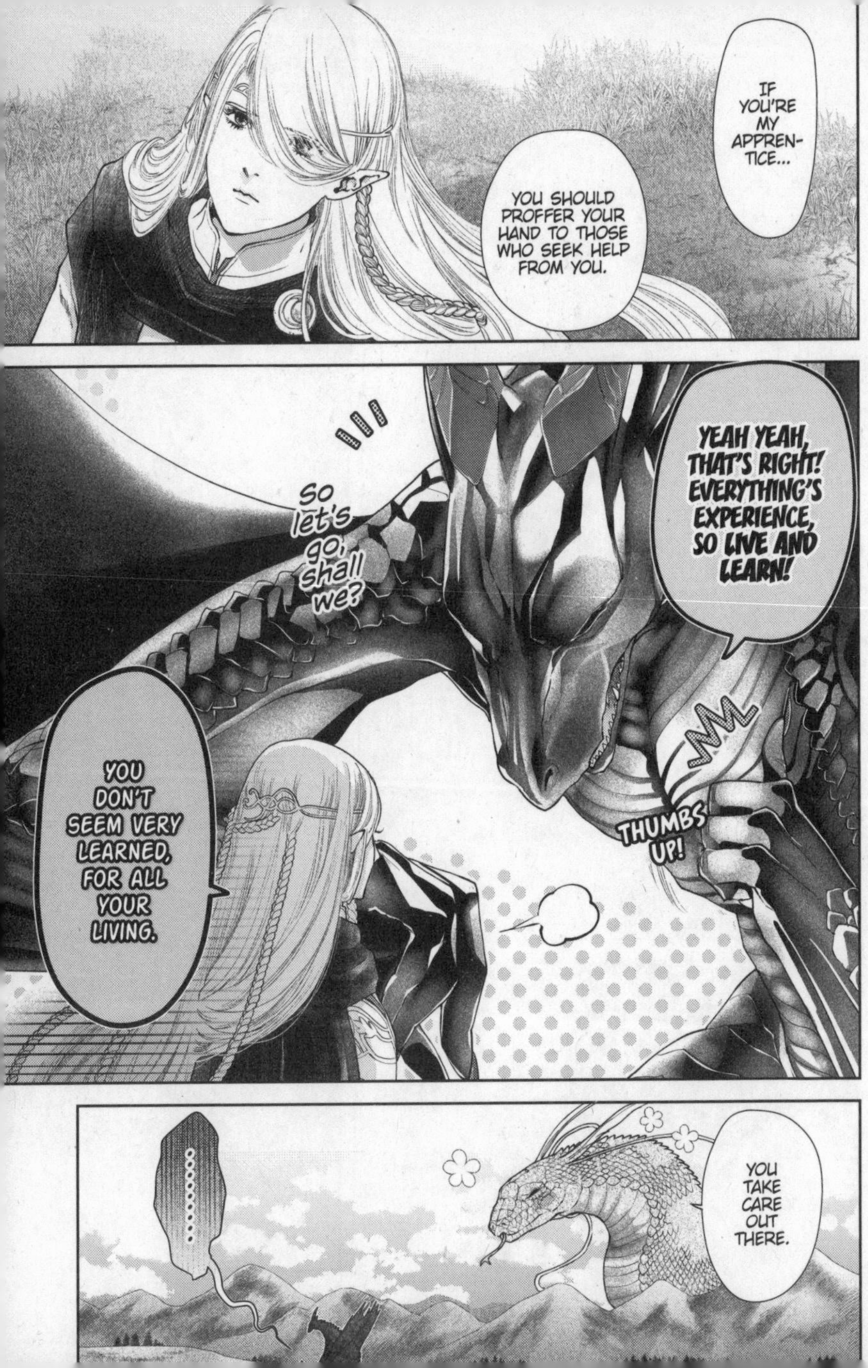
IF YOU'RE MY APPRENTICE...
YOU SHOULD PROFFER YOUR HAND TO THOSE WHO SEEK HELP FROM YOU.
YEAH YEAH, THAT'S RIGHT! EVERYTHING'S EXPERIENCE, SO LIVE AND LEARN!
THUMBS UP!
So let's go, shall we?
YOU DON'T SEEM VERY LEARNED, FOR ALL YOUR LIVING.
YOU TAKE CARE OUT THERE.

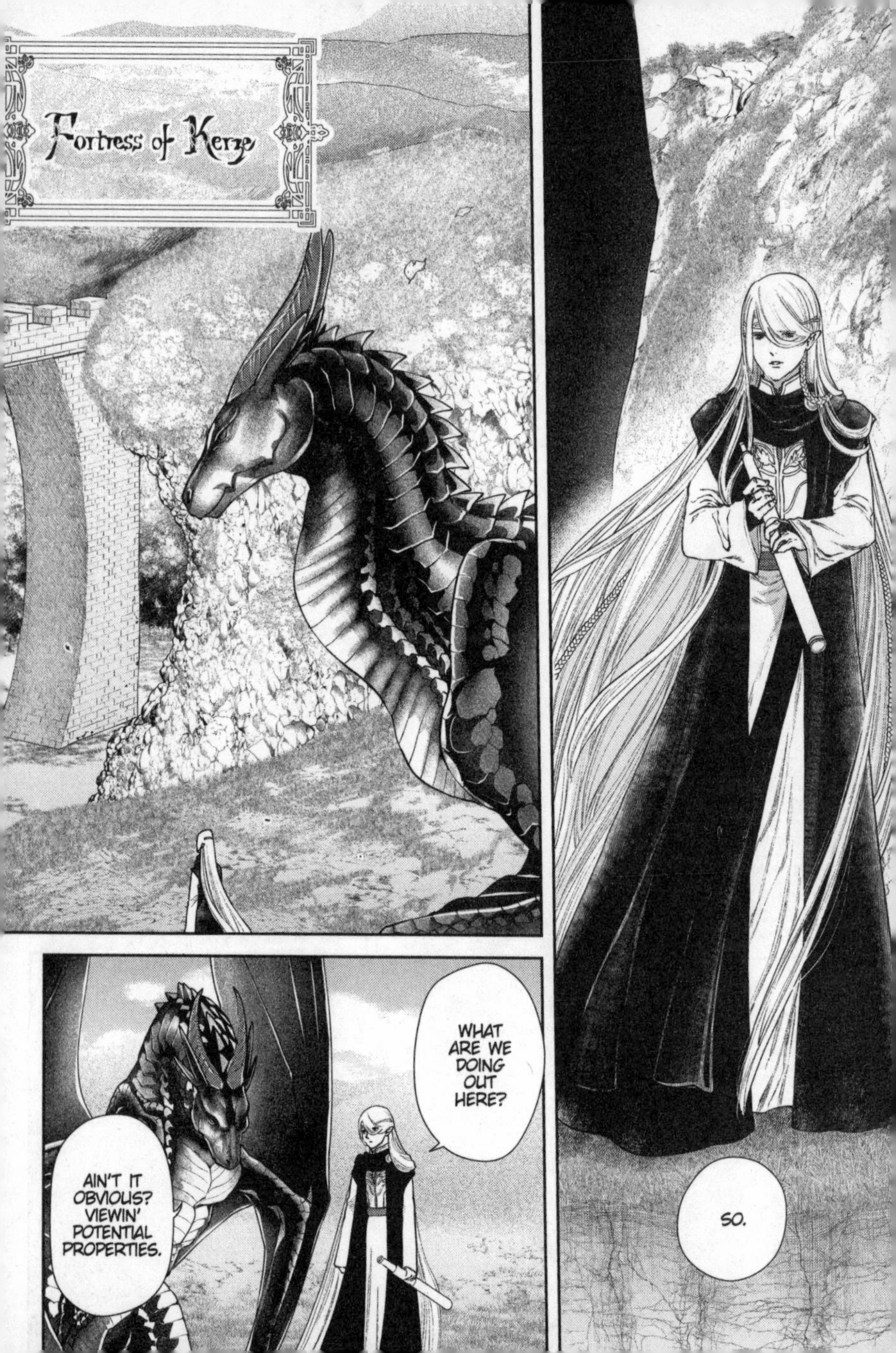
SO.
Fortress of Kerze
WHAT ARE WE DOING OUT HERE?
AIN'T IT OBVIOUS? VIEWIN' POTENTIAL PROPERTIES.

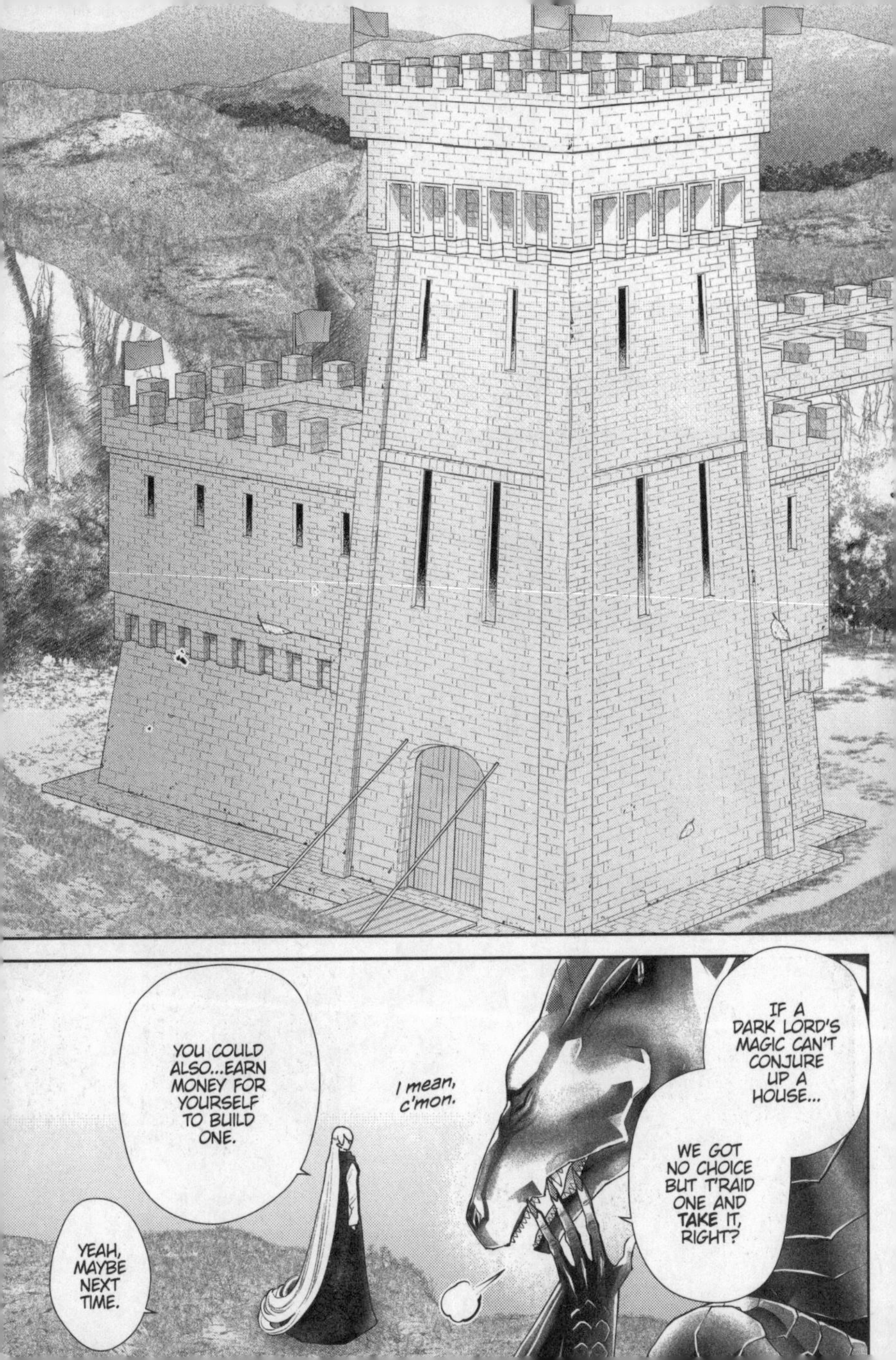
IF A DARK LORD'S MAGIC CAN'T CONJURE UP A HOUSE...
WE GOT NO CHOICE BUT T'RAID ONE AND TAKE IT, RIGHT?
I mean, c'mon.
YOU COULD ALSO...EARN MONEY FOR YOURSELF TO BUILD ONE.
YEAH, MAYBE NEXT TIME.

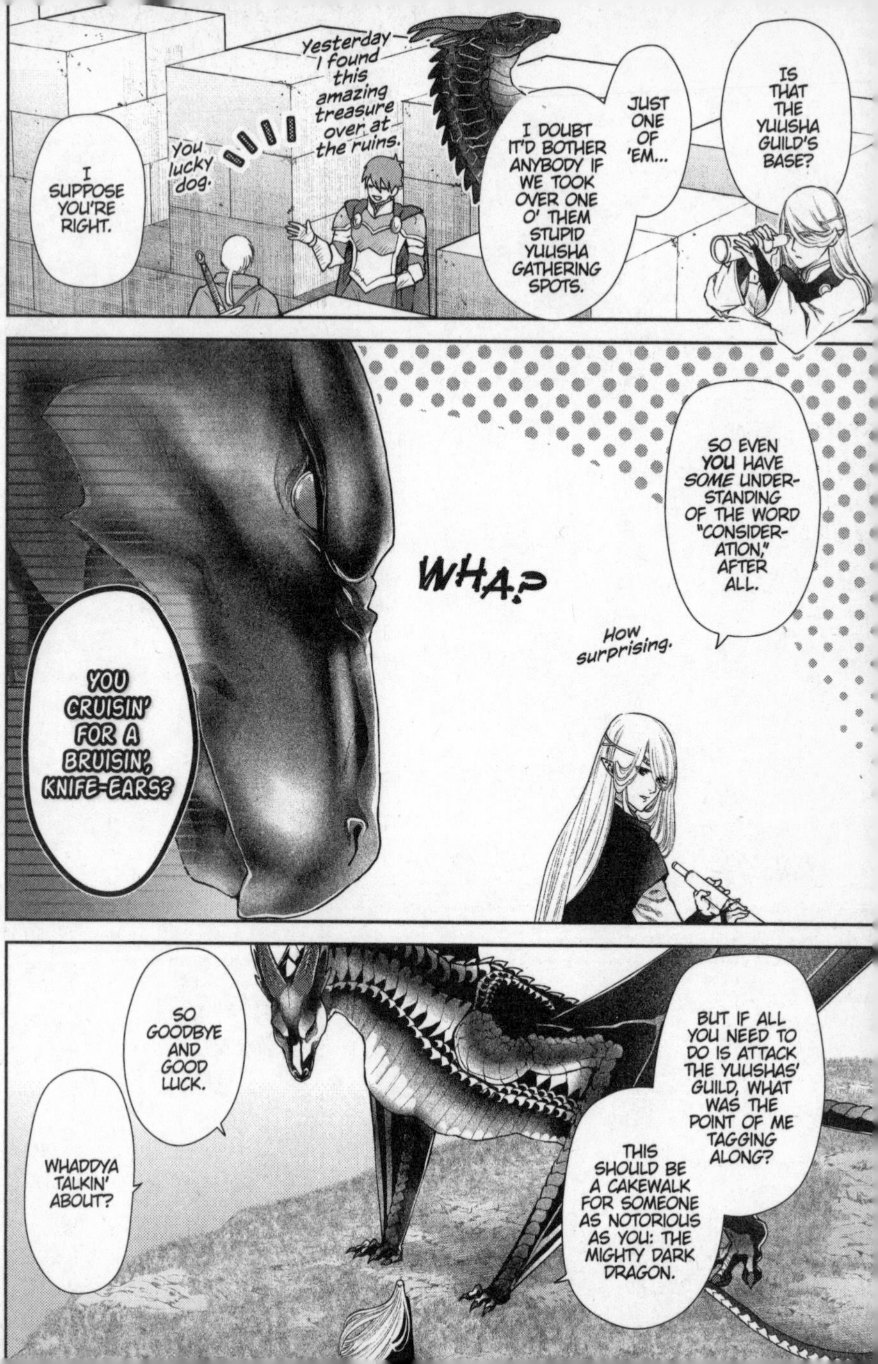
IS THAT THE YUUSHA GUILD'S BASE?
JUST ONE OF 'EM...
I DOUBT IT'D BOTHER ANYBODY IF WE TOOK OVER ONE O' THEM STUPID YUUSHA GATHERING SPOTS.
Yesterday— I found this amazing treasure over at the ruins.
!!!
You lucky dog.
I SUPPOSE YOU'RE RIGHT.
SO EVEN YOU HAVE SOME UNDERSTANDING OF THE WORD "CONSIDERATION," AFTER ALL.
How surprising.
WHA?
YOU CRUISIN' FOR A BRUISIN', KNIFE-EARS?
BUT IF ALL YOU NEED TO DO IS ATTACK THE YUUSHAS' GUILD, WHAT WAS THE POINT OF ME TAGGING ALONG?
THIS SHOULD BE A CAKEWALK FOR SOMEONE AS NOTORIOUS AS YOU: THE MIGHTY DARK DRAGON.
SO GOODBYE AND GOOD LUCK.
WHADDYA TALKIN' ABOUT?

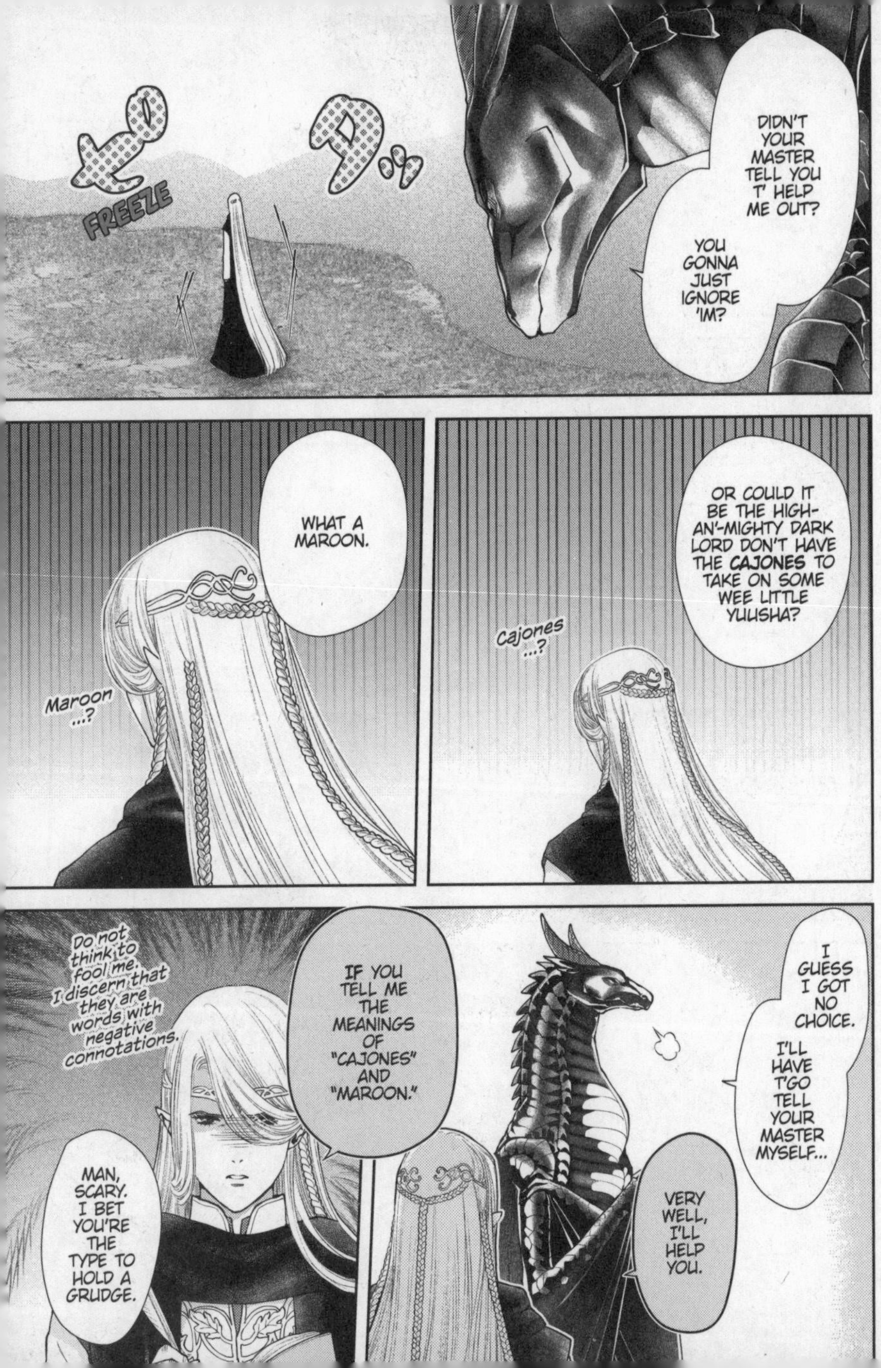

DIDN'T YOUR MASTER TELL YOU T' HELP ME OUT?
YOU GONNA JUST IGNORE 'IM?
FREEZE
OR COULD IT BE THE HIGH-AN'-MIGHTY DARK LORD DON'T HAVE THE **CAJONES** TO TAKE ON SOME WEE LITTLE YUUSHA?
Cajones ...?
WHAT A MAROON.
Maroon ...?
I GUESS I GOT NO CHOICE.
I'LL HAVE T'GO TELL YOUR MASTER MYSELF...
VERY WELL, I'LL HELP YOU.
IF YOU TELL ME THE MEANINGS OF "CAJONES" AND "MAROON."
Do not think to fool me. I discern that they are words with negative connotations.
MAN, SCARY. I BET YOU'RE THE TYPE TO HOLD A GRUDGE.

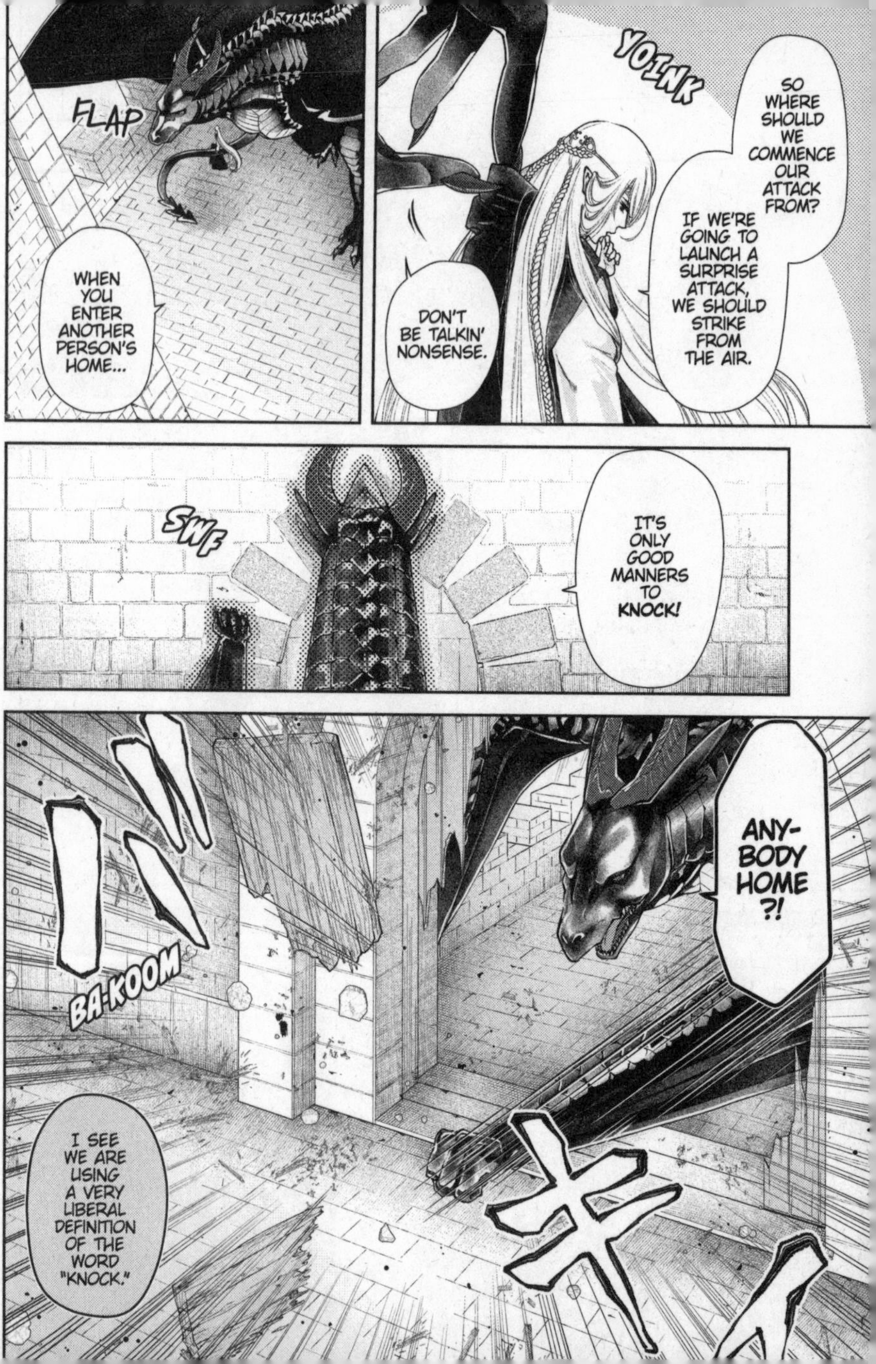
YOINK
SO WHERE SHOULD WE COMMENCE OUR ATTACK FROM?
IF WE'RE GOING TO LAUNCH A SURPRISE ATTACK, WE SHOULD STRIKE FROM THE AIR.
DON'T BE TALKIN' NONSENSE.
FLAP
WHEN YOU ENTER ANOTHER PERSON'S HOME...
IT'S ONLY GOOD MANNERS TO KNOCK!
SWF
ANY-BODY HOME?!
BA-KOOM
I SEE WE ARE USING A VERY LIBERAL DEFINITION OF THE WORD "KNOCK."

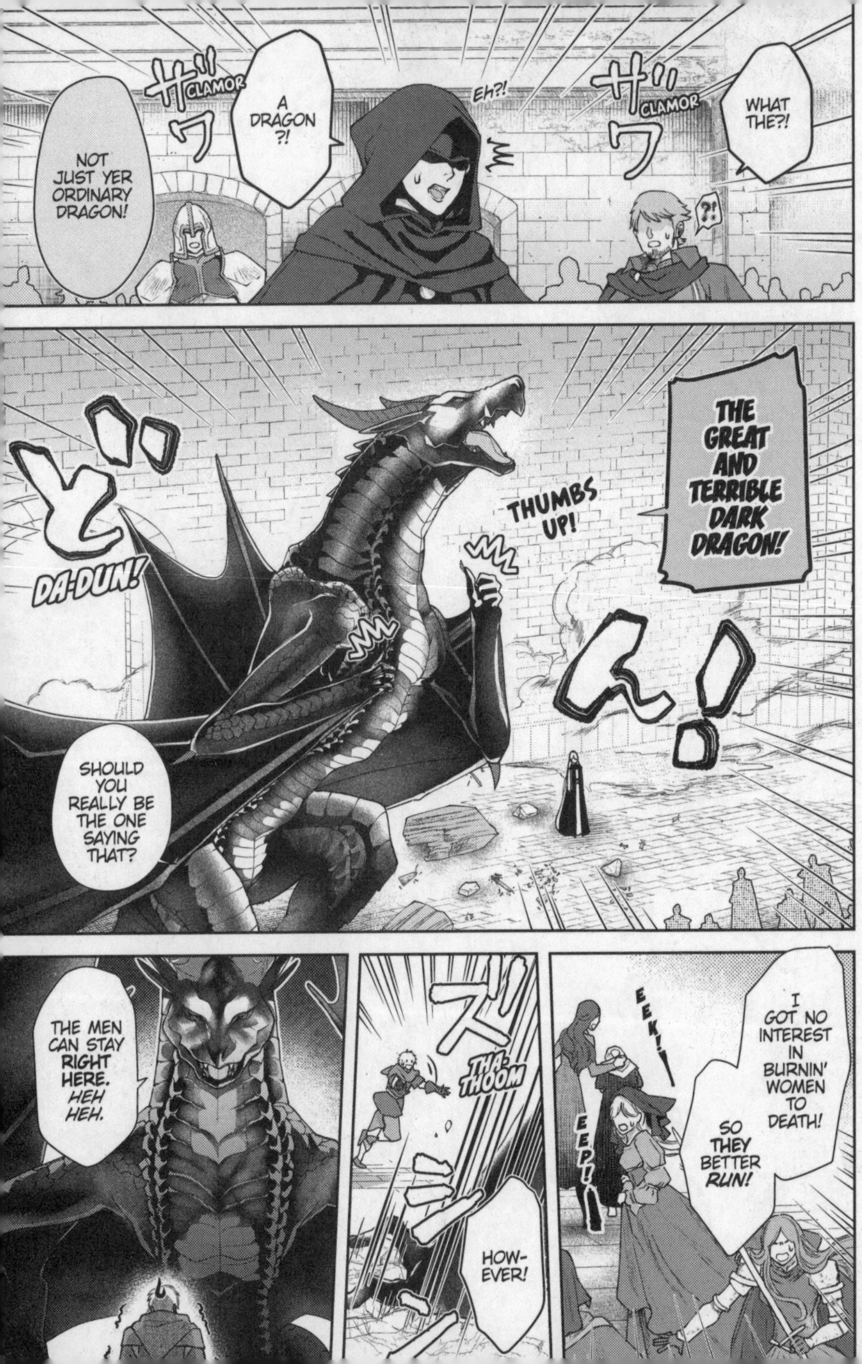
WHAT THE?!
?!
CLAMOR
Eh?!
A DRAGON ?!
CLAMOR
NOT JUST YER ORDINARY DRAGON!
THE GREAT AND TERRIBLE DARK DRAGON!
THUMBS UP!
DA-DUN!
SHOULD YOU REALLY BE THE ONE SAYING THAT?
I GOT NO INTEREST IN BURNIN' WOMEN TO DEATH!
SO THEY BETTER RUN!
EEK!
EEP!
THA-THOOM
HOW-EVER!
THE MEN CAN STAY RIGHT HERE. HEH HEH.

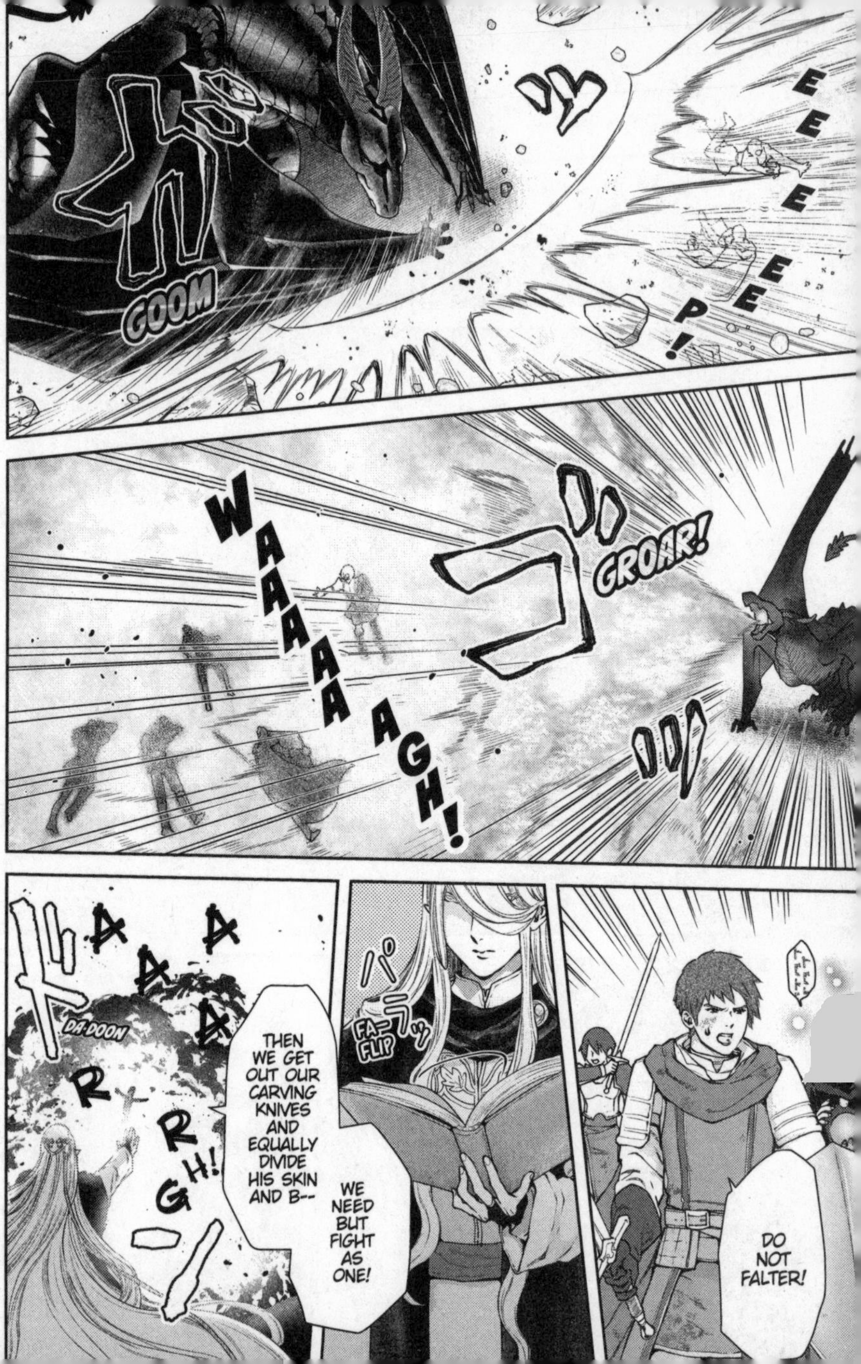
EEEEEP!
GOOM
GROAR!
WAAAAAAGH!
DO NOT FALTER!
FA-FLIP
WE NEED BUT FIGHT AS ONE!
THEN WE GET OUT OUR CARVING KNIVES AND EQUALLY DIVIDE HIS SKIN AND B--
DA-DOON
AAAARRGH!

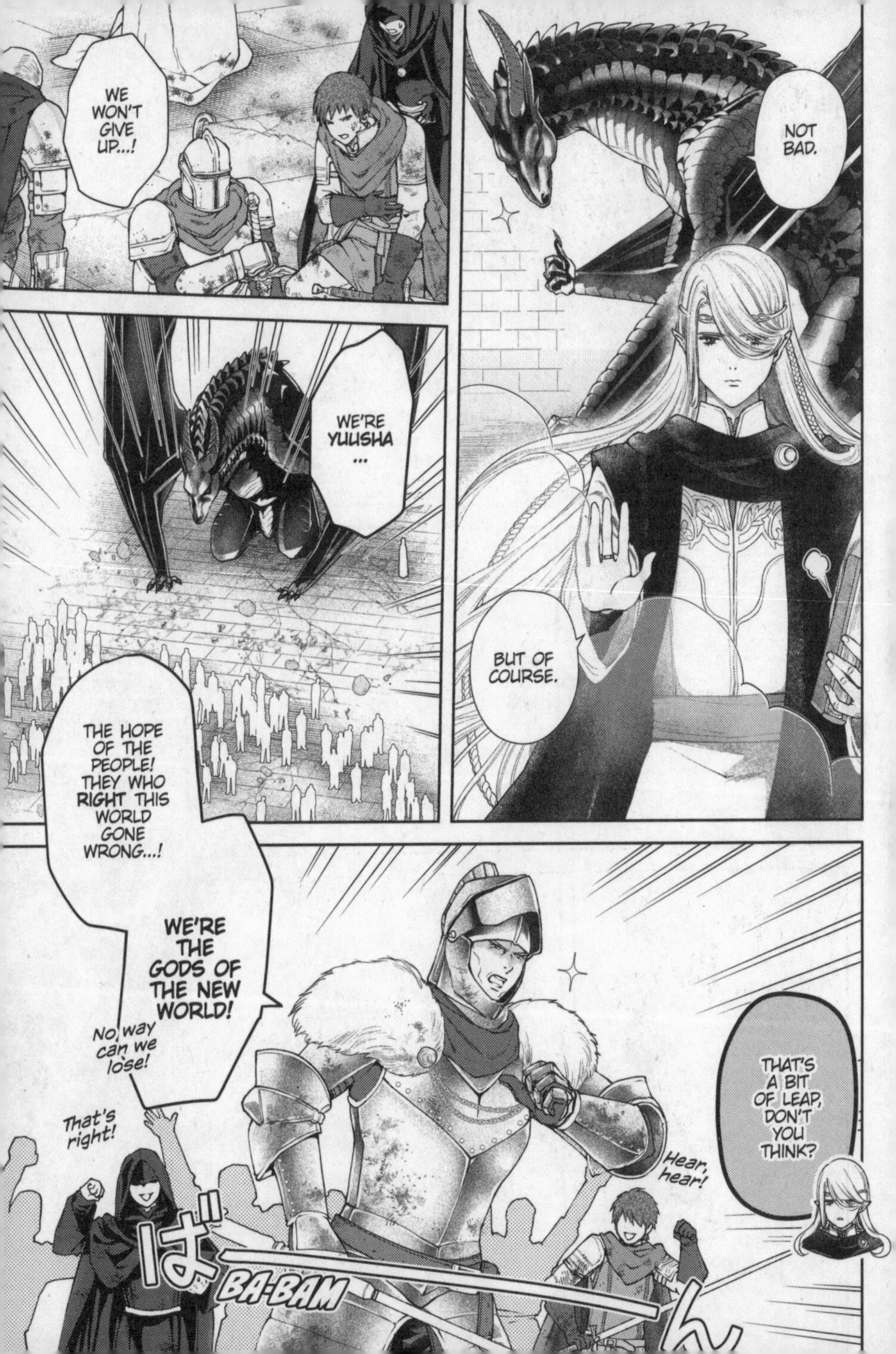
NOT BAD.
WE WON'T GIVE UP...!
WE'RE YUUSHA ...
BUT OF COURSE.
THE HOPE OF THE PEOPLE! THEY WHO RIGHT THIS WORLD GONE WRONG...!
THAT'S A BIT OF LEAP, DON'T YOU THINK?
Hear, hear!
WE'RE THE GODS OF THE NEW WORLD!
No way can we lose!
That's right!
ば
BA-BAM
ん

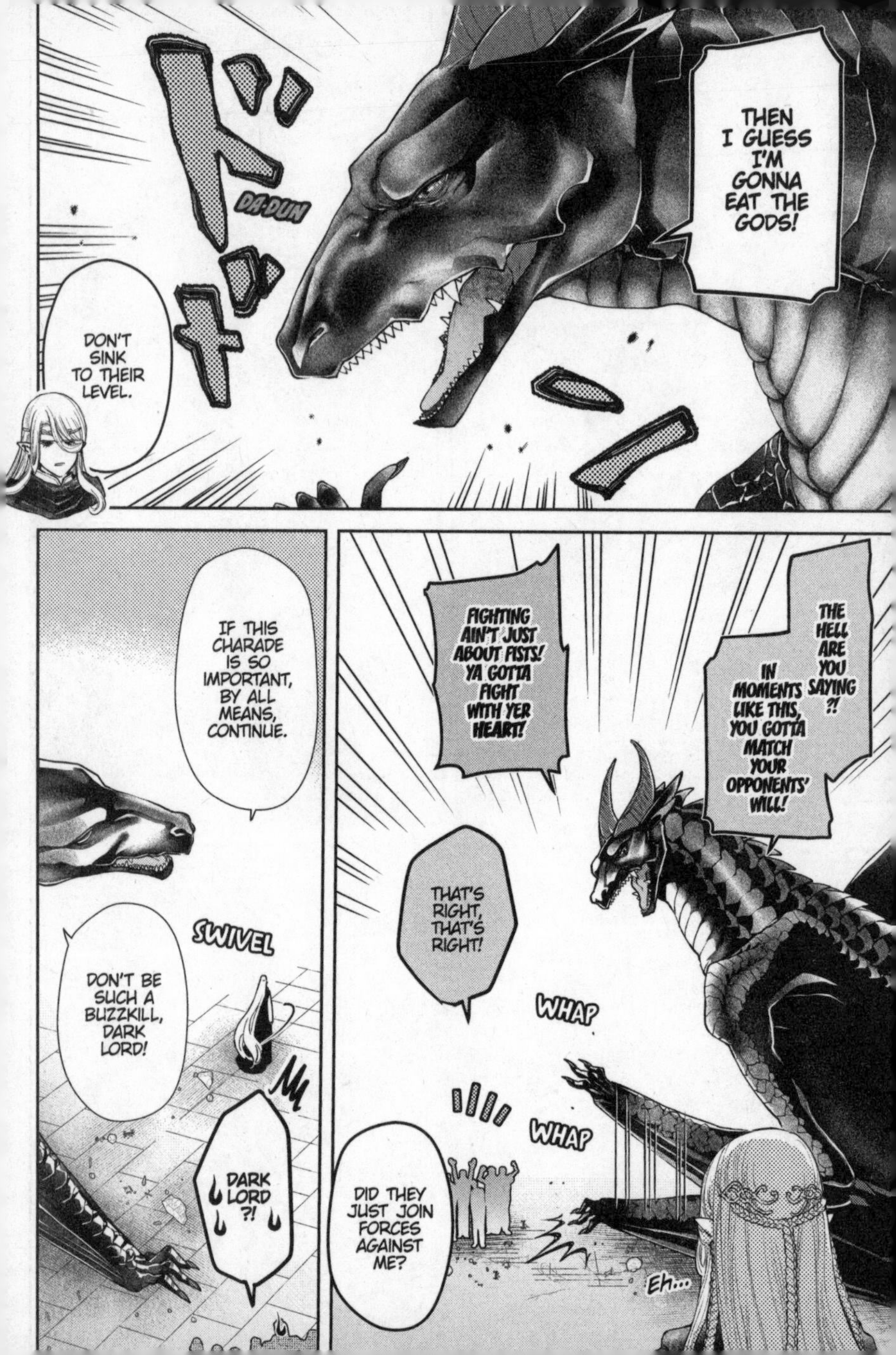
THEN I GUESS I'M GONNA EAT THE GODS!
DA-DUN
DON'T SINK TO THEIR LEVEL.
THE HELL ARE YOU SAYING?!
IN MOMENTS LIKE THIS, YOU GOTTA MATCH YOUR OPPONENTS' WILL!
FIGHTING AIN'T JUST ABOUT FISTS! YA GOTTA FIGHT WITH YER HEART!
THAT'S RIGHT, THAT'S RIGHT!
WHAP
WHAP
DID THEY JUST JOIN FORCES AGAINST ME?
Eh...
IF THIS CHARADE IS SO IMPORTANT, BY ALL MEANS, CONTINUE.
SWIVEL
DON'T BE SUCH A BUZZKILL, DARK LORD!
DARK LORD?!

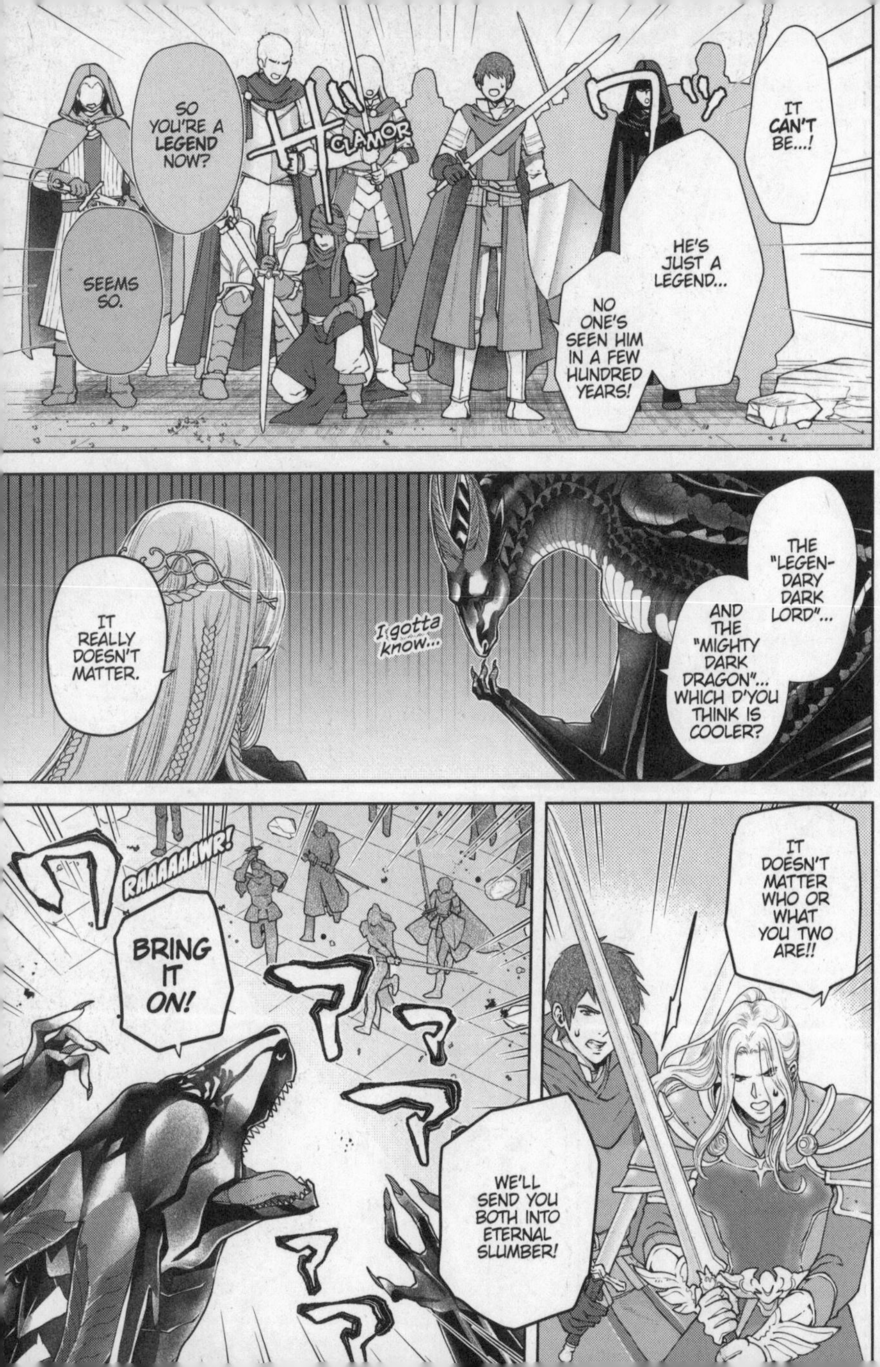
SO YOU'RE A LEGEND NOW?
SEEMS SO.
CLAMOR
IT CAN'T BE...!
HE'S JUST A LEGEND...
NO ONE'S SEEN HIM IN A FEW HUNDRED YEARS!
I gotta know...
THE "LEGENDARY DARK LORD"...
AND THE "MIGHTY DARK DRAGON"... WHICH D'YOU THINK IS COOLER?
IT REALLY DOESN'T MATTER.
RAAAAAAWR!
BRING IT ON!
IT DOESN'T MATTER WHO OR WHAT YOU TWO ARE!!
WE'LL SEND YOU BOTH INTO ETERNAL SLUMBER!

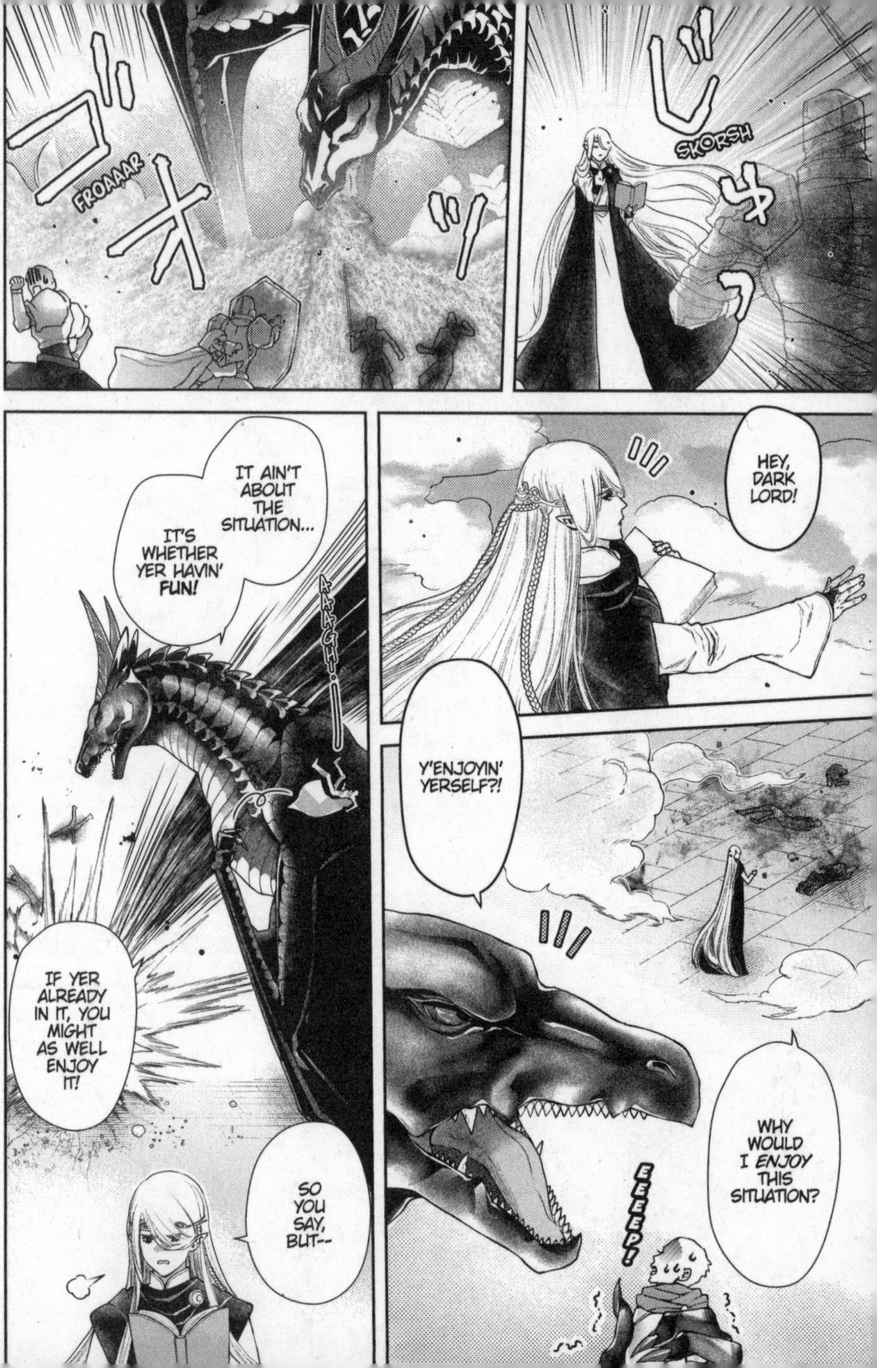
SKORSH
FROAAAR
HEY, DARK LORD!
Y'ENJOYIN' YERSELF?!
WHY WOULD I ENJOY THIS SITUATION?
EEEEP!
IT AIN'T ABOUT THE SITUATION...
IT'S WHETHER YER HAVIN' FUN!
AAAGH!
IF YER ALREADY IN IT, YOU MIGHT AS WELL ENJOY IT!
SO YOU SAY, BUT--

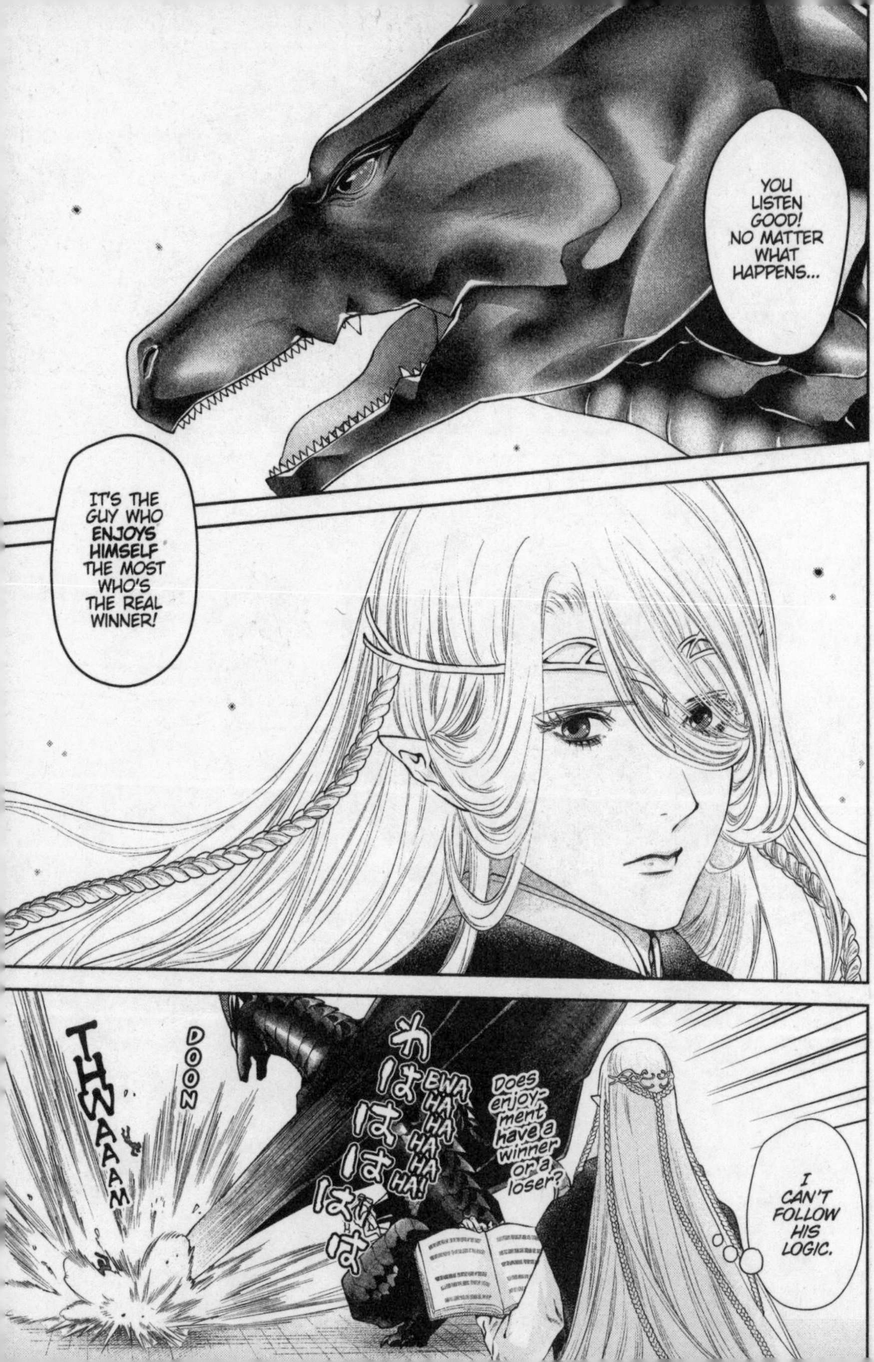
YOU LISTEN GOOD! NO MATTER WHAT HAPPENS...
IT'S THE GUY WHO ENJOYS HIMSELF THE MOST WHO'S THE REAL WINNER!
I CAN'T FOLLOW HIS LOGIC.
Does enjoyment have a winner or a loser?
BWA HA HA HA HA HA!
DOOON
THWAAAM

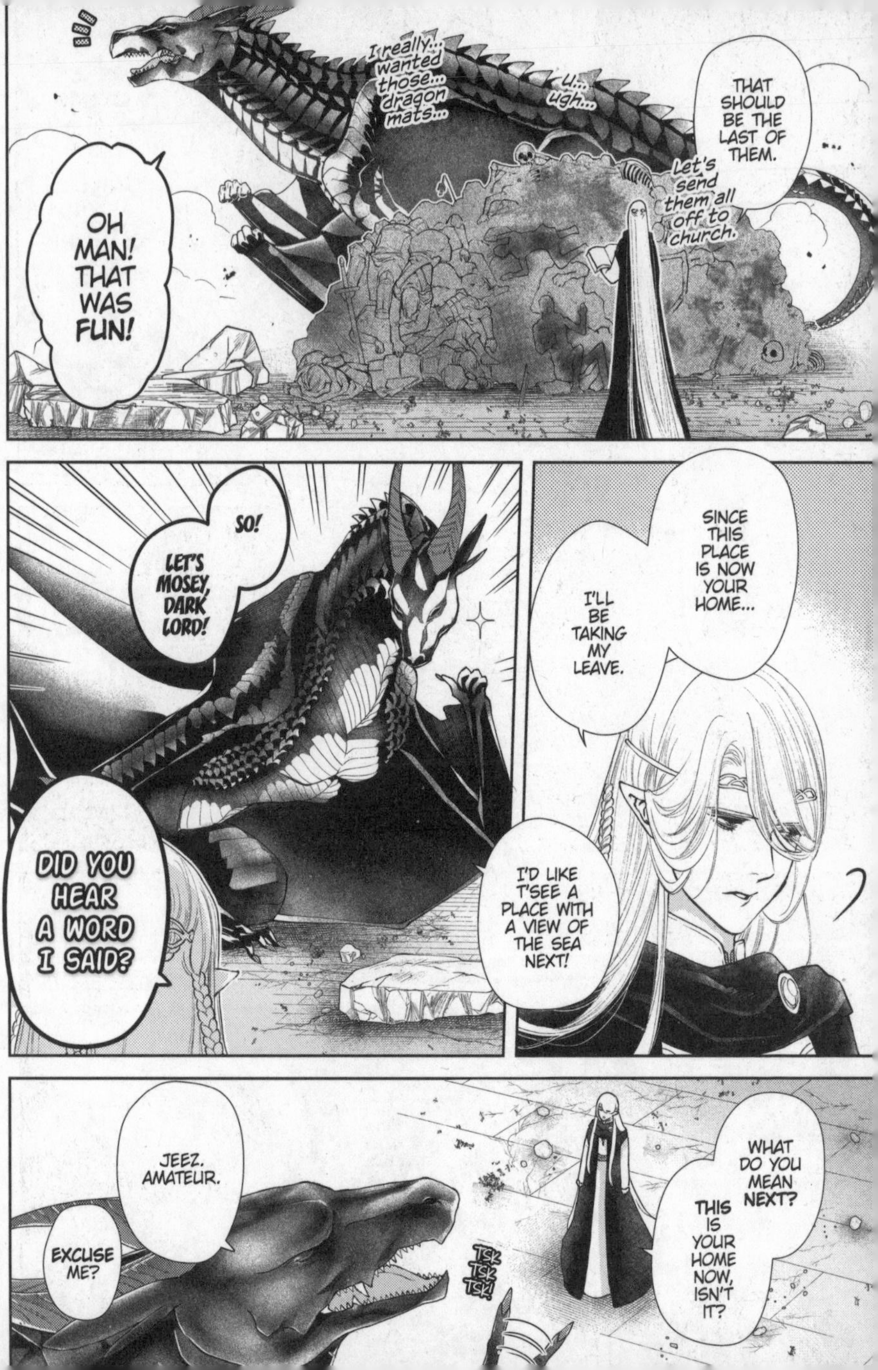
THAT SHOULD BE THE LAST OF THEM.
Let's send them all off to church.
U... ugh...
I really... wanted those... dragon mats...
OH MAN! THAT WAS FUN!
SINCE THIS PLACE IS NOW YOUR HOME...
I'LL BE TAKING MY LEAVE.
I'D LIKE T'SEE A PLACE WITH A VIEW OF THE SEA NEXT!
SO!
LET'S MOSEY, DARK LORD!
DID YOU HEAR A WORD I SAID?
WHAT DO YOU MEAN NEXT?
THIS IS YOUR HOME NOW, ISN'T IT?
TSK TSK TSK!
JEEZ. AMATEUR.
EXCUSE ME?

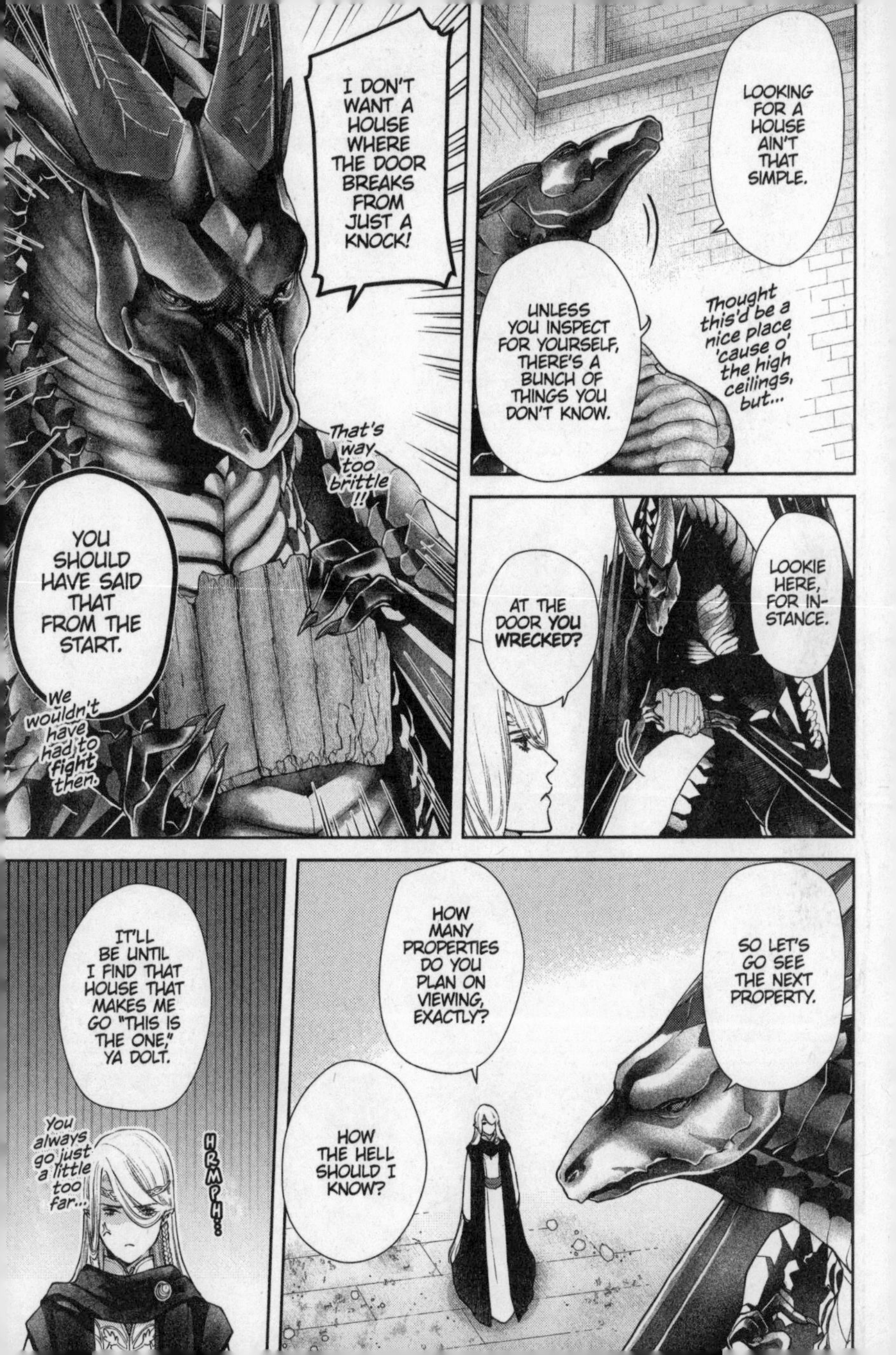
LOOKING FOR A HOUSE AIN'T THAT SIMPLE.
Thought this'd be a nice place 'cause o' the high ceilings, but...
UNLESS YOU INSPECT FOR YOURSELF, THERE'S A BUNCH OF THINGS YOU DON'T KNOW.
LOOKIE HERE, FOR IN-STANCE.
AT THE DOOR YOU WRECKED?
I DON'T WANT A HOUSE WHERE THE DOOR BREAKS FROM JUST A KNOCK!
That's way too brittle!!
YOU SHOULD HAVE SAID THAT FROM THE START.
We wouldn't have had to fight then.
SO LET'S GO SEE THE NEXT PROPERTY.
HOW MANY PROPERTIES DO YOU PLAN ON VIEWING, EXACTLY?
HOW THE HELL SHOULD I KNOW?
IT'LL BE UNTIL I FIND THAT HOUSE THAT MAKES ME GO "THIS IS THE ONE," YA DOLT.
HRMPH...
You always go just a little too far...

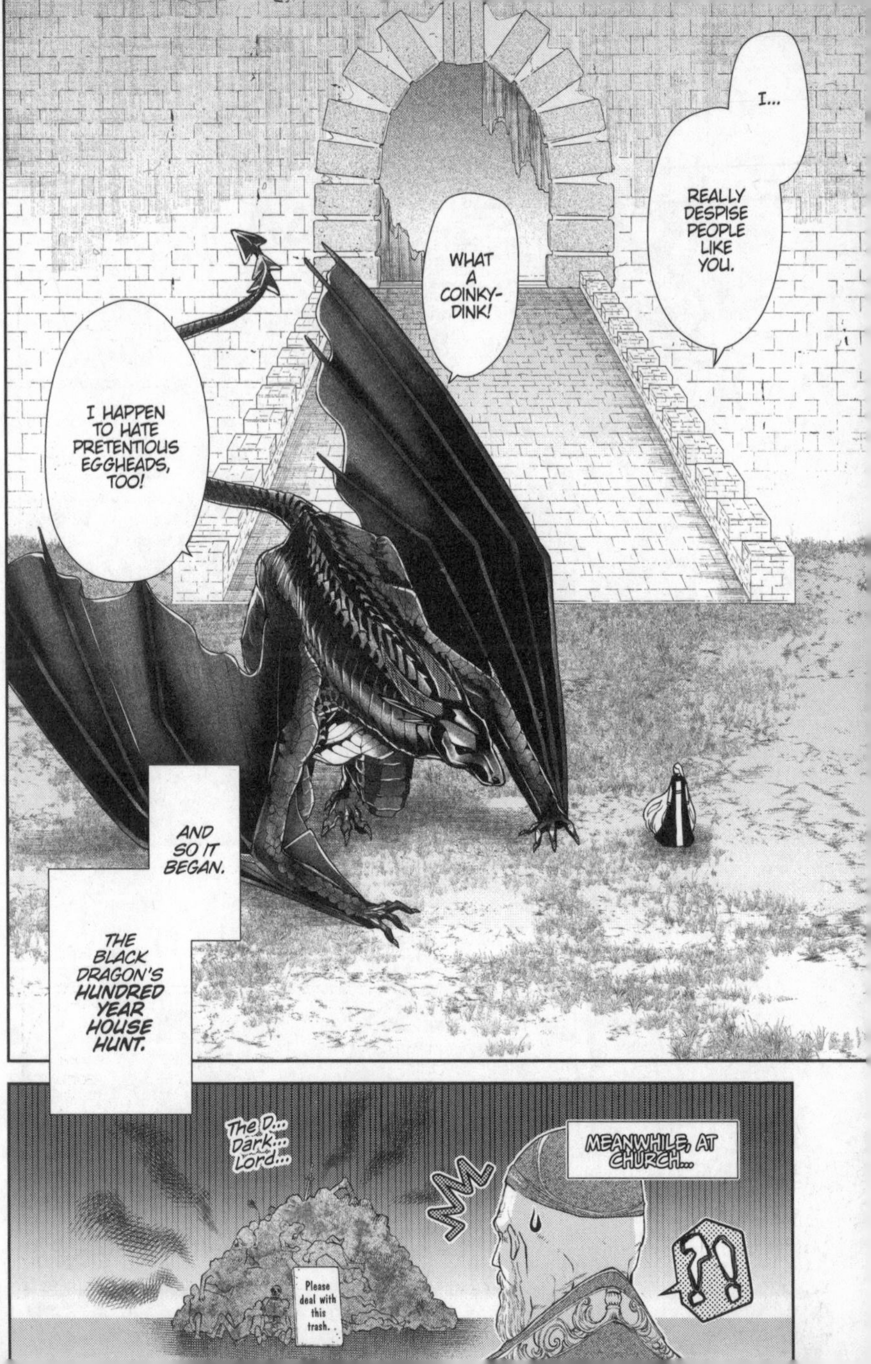
I...
REALLY DESPISE PEOPLE LIKE YOU.
WHAT A COINKY-DINK!
I HAPPEN TO HATE PRETENTIOUS EGGHEADS, TOO!
AND SO IT BEGAN.
THE BLACK DRAGON'S HUNDRED YEAR HOUSE HUNT.
MEANWHILE, AT CHURCH...
The D... Dark... Lord...
Please deal with this trash.
?!

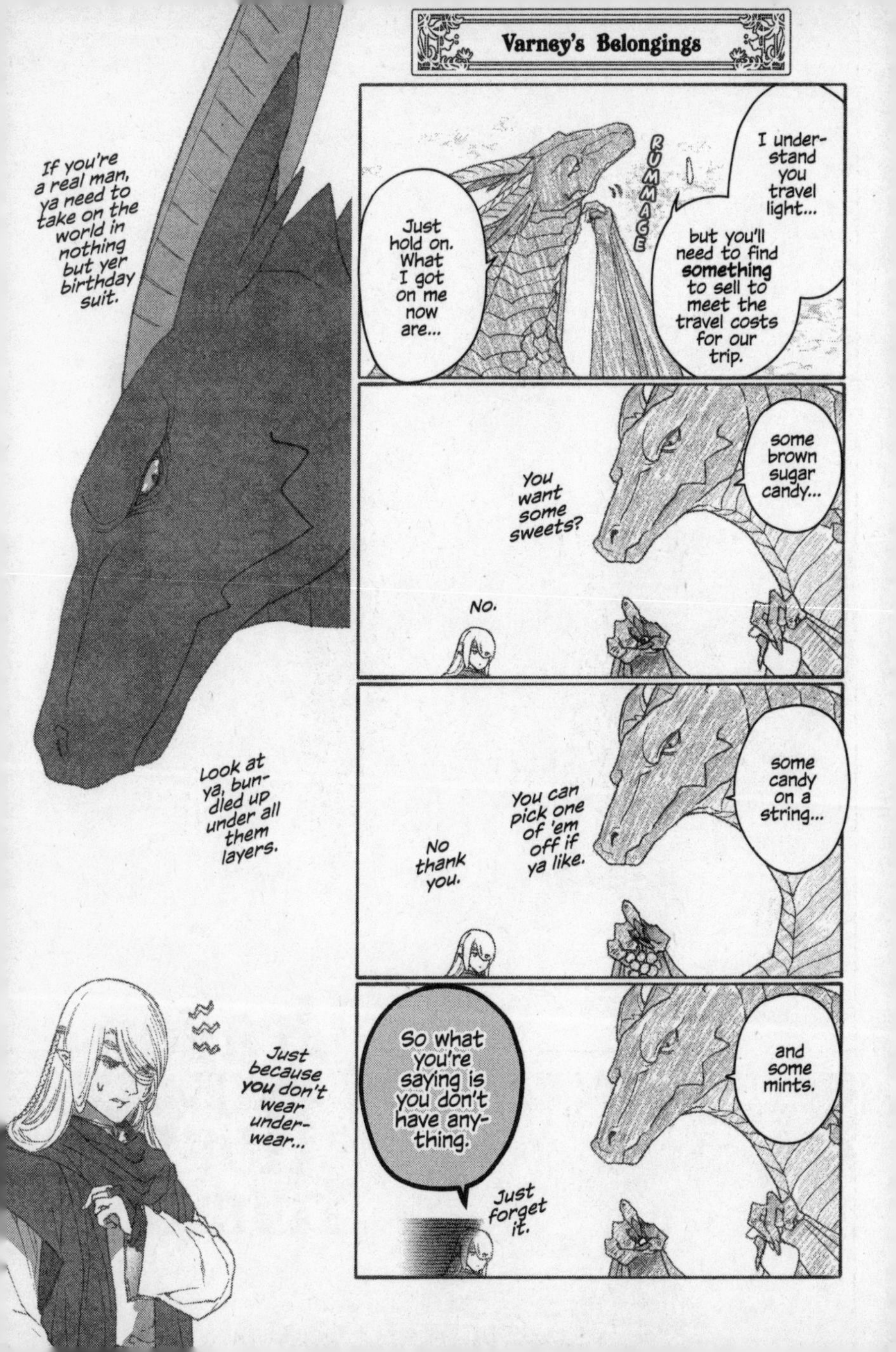

Varney's Belongings
I understand you travel light... but you'll need to find something to sell to meet the travel costs for our trip.
RUMMAGE
Just hold on. What I got on me now are...
some brown sugar candy...
You want some sweets?
No.
some candy on a string...
You can pick one of 'em off if ya like.
No thank you.
and some mints.
So what you're saying is you don't have anything.
Just forget it.
If you're a real man, ya need to take on the world in nothing but yer birthday suit.
Look at ya, bundled up under all them layers.
Just because you don't wear underwear...

Dragon
Goes
House-
Hunting

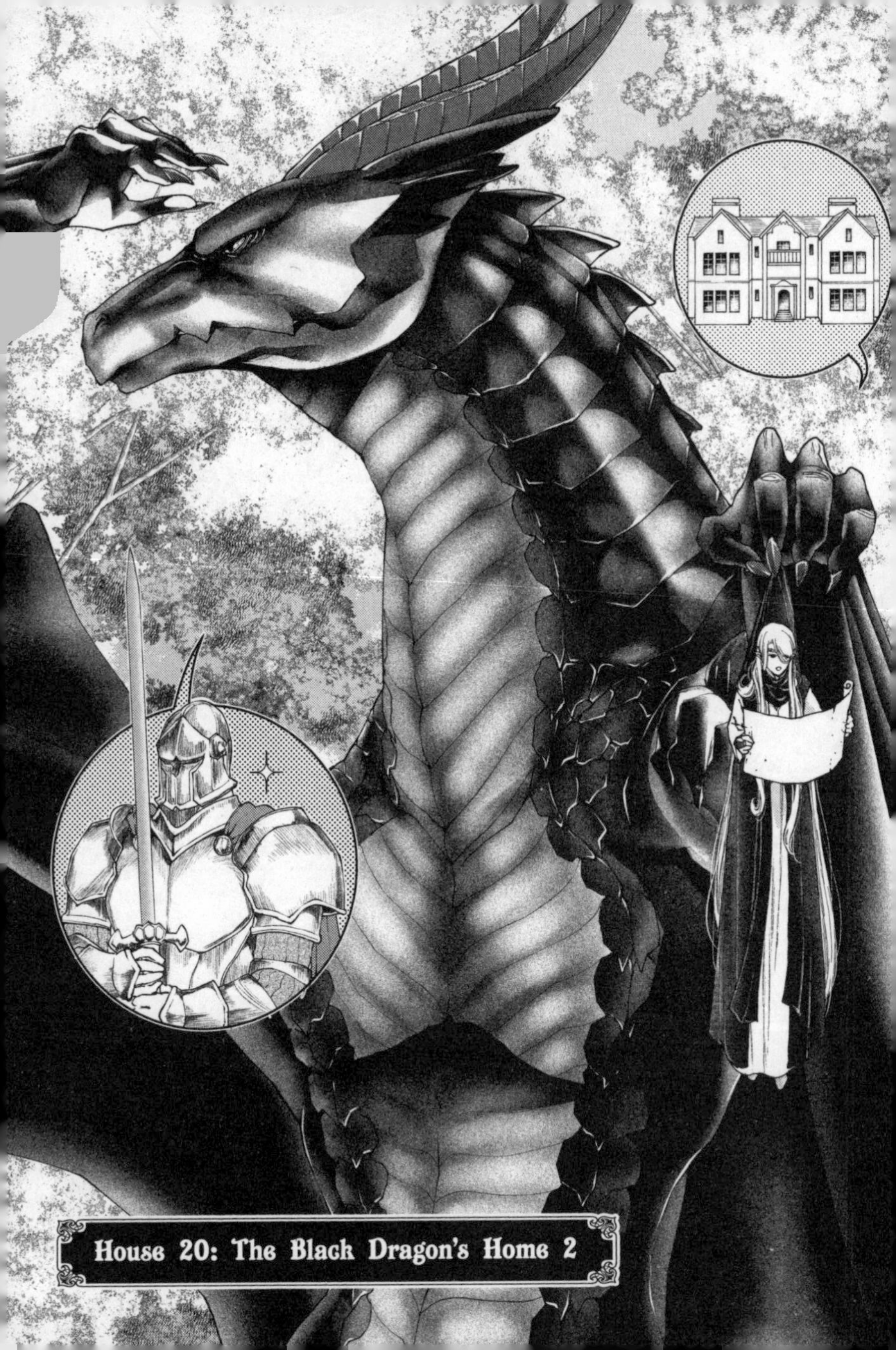
House 20: The Black Dragon's Home 2

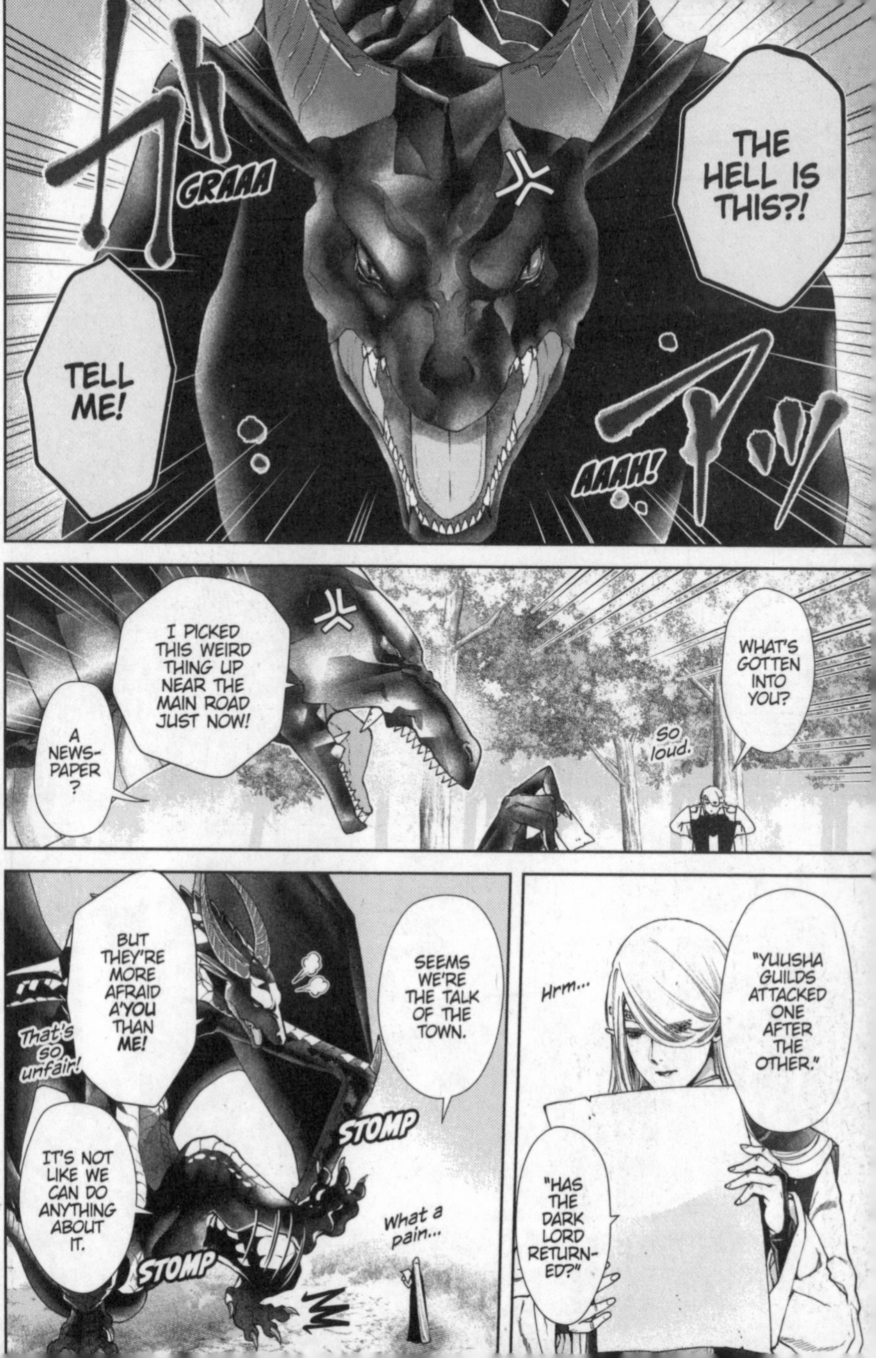
THE HELL IS THIS?!
AAAH!
GRAAA
TELL ME!
WHAT'S GOTTEN INTO YOU?
So loud.
I PICKED THIS WEIRD THING UP NEAR THE MAIN ROAD JUST NOW!
A NEWSPAPER?
"YUUSHA GUILDS ATTACKED ONE AFTER THE OTHER."
Hrm...
"HAS THE DARK LORD RETURNED?"
SEEMS WE'RE THE TALK OF THE TOWN.
BUT THEY'RE MORE AFRAID A'YOU THAN ME!
That's so unfair!
STOMP
IT'S NOT LIKE WE CAN DO ANYTHING ABOUT IT.
What a pain...
STOMP

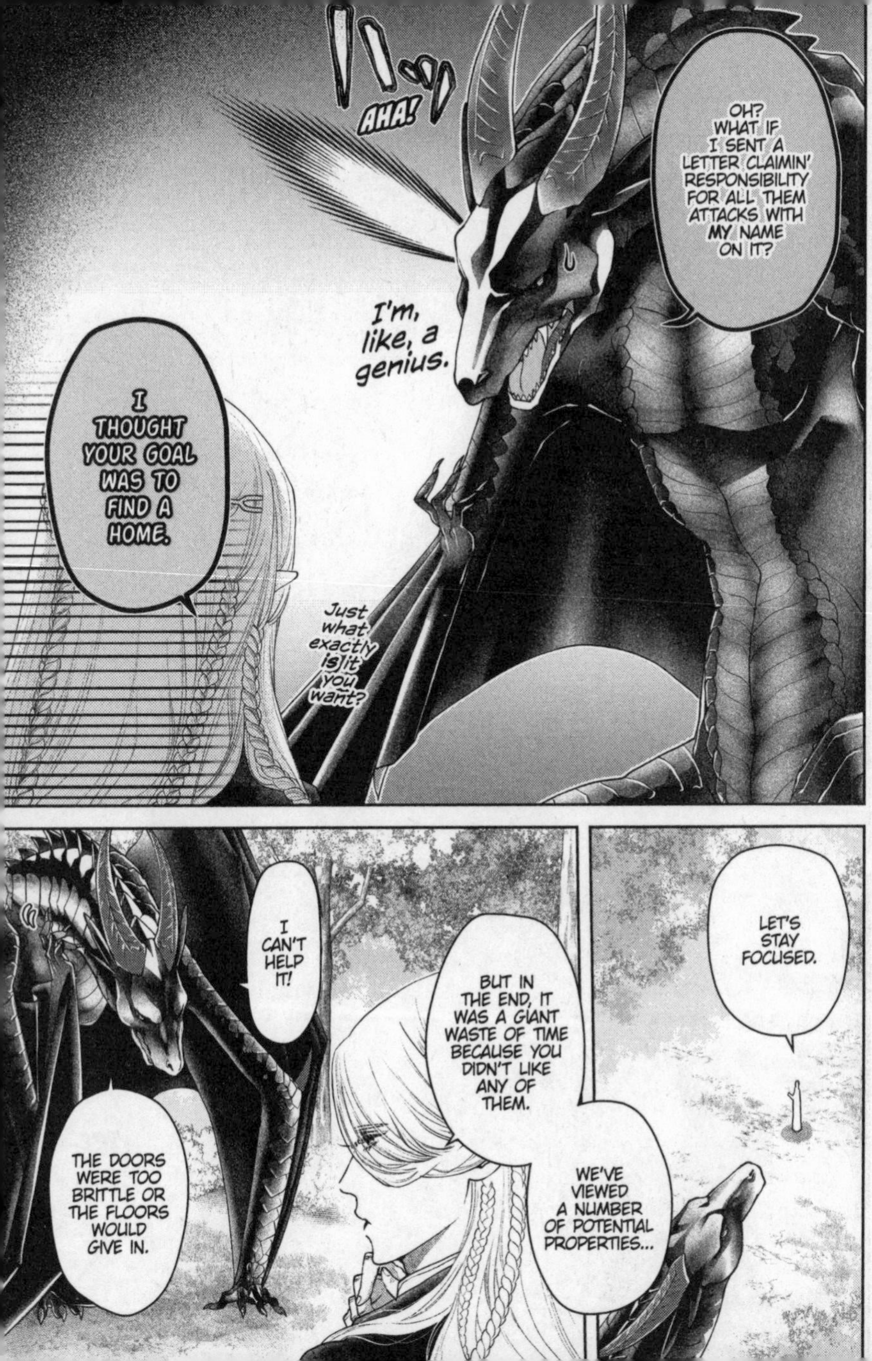
ハッ
AHA!
OH? WHAT IF I SENT A LETTER CLAIMIN' RESPONSIBILITY FOR ALL THEM ATTACKS WITH MY NAME ON IT?
I'm, like, a genius.
I THOUGHT YOUR GOAL WAS TO FIND A HOME.
Just what exactly is it you want?
LET'S STAY FOCUSED.
WE'VE VIEWED A NUMBER OF POTENTIAL PROPERTIES...
BUT IN THE END, IT WAS A GIANT WASTE OF TIME BECAUSE YOU DIDN'T LIKE ANY OF THEM.
I CAN'T HELP IT!
THE DOORS WERE TOO BRITTLE OR THE FLOORS WOULD GIVE IN.

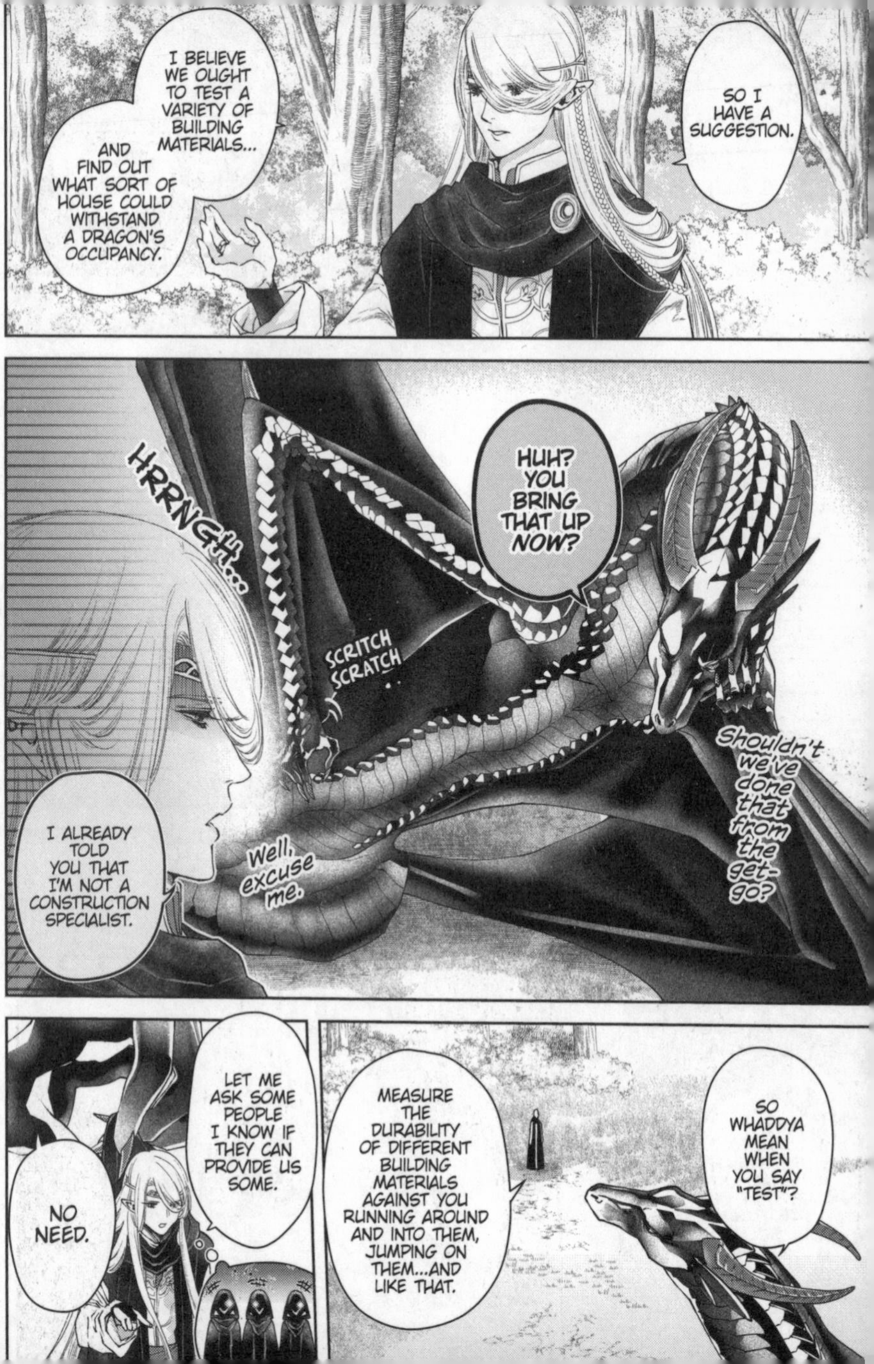
SO I HAVE A SUGGESTION.
I BELIEVE WE OUGHT TO TEST A VARIETY OF BUILDING MATERIALS...
AND FIND OUT WHAT SORT OF HOUSE COULD WITHSTAND A DRAGON'S OCCUPANCY.
HUH? YOU BRING THAT UP NOW?
Shouldn't we've done that from the get-go?
HRRNGH...
SCRITCH SCRATCH
Well, excuse me.
I ALREADY TOLD YOU THAT I'M NOT A CONSTRUCTION SPECIALIST.
SO WHADDYA MEAN WHEN YOU SAY "TEST"?
MEASURE THE DURABILITY OF DIFFERENT BUILDING MATERIALS AGAINST YOU RUNNING AROUND AND INTO THEM, JUMPING ON THEM...AND LIKE THAT.
LET ME ASK SOME PEOPLE I KNOW IF THEY CAN PROVIDE US SOME.
NO NEED.

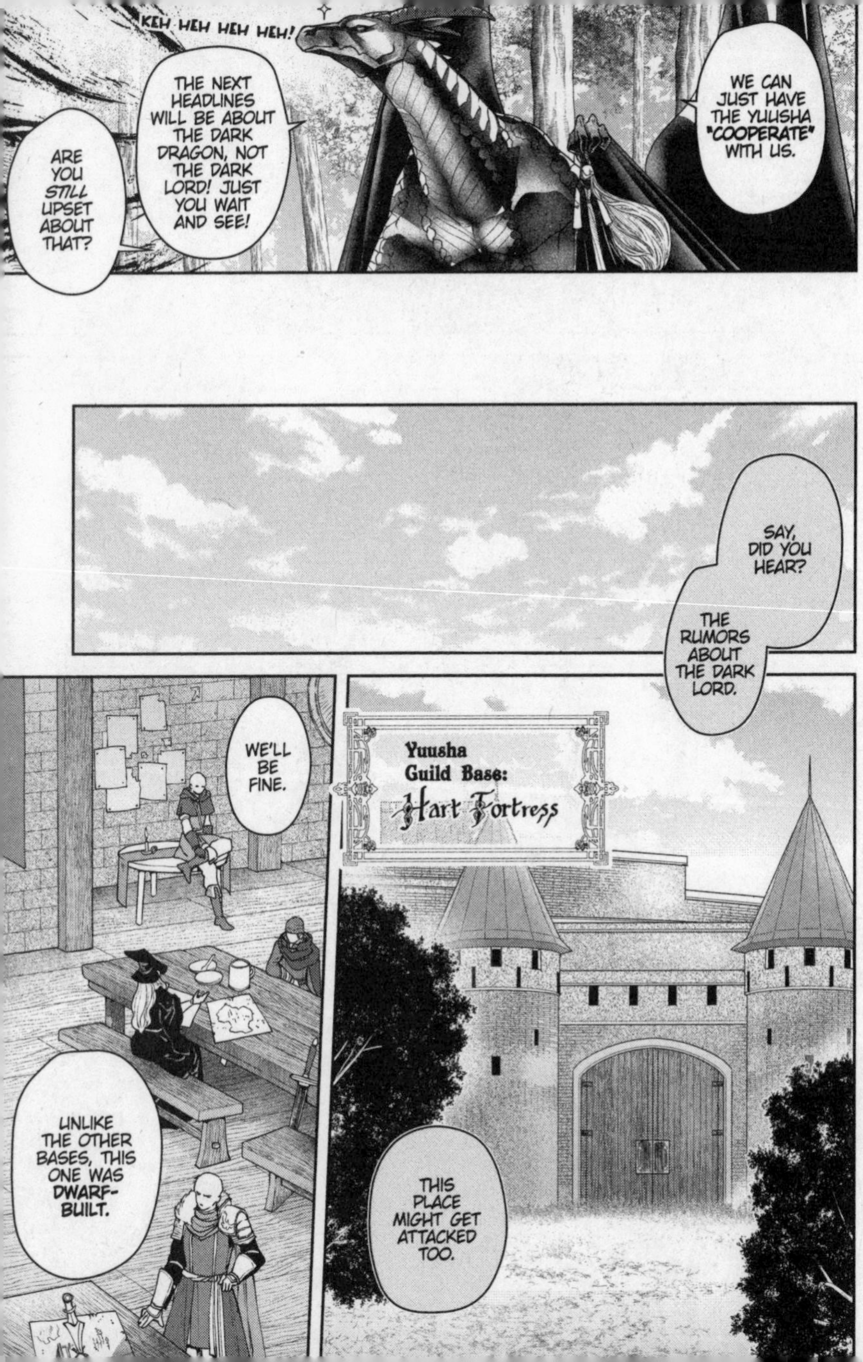
WE CAN JUST HAVE THE YUUSHA "COOPERATE" WITH US.
KEH HEH HEH HEH!
THE NEXT HEADLINES WILL BE ABOUT THE DARK DRAGON, NOT THE DARK LORD! JUST YOU WAIT AND SEE!
ARE YOU STILL UPSET ABOUT THAT?
SAY, DID YOU HEAR?
THE RUMORS ABOUT THE DARK LORD.
Yuusha Guild Base: Hart Fortress
THIS PLACE MIGHT GET ATTACKED TOO.
WE'LL BE FINE.
UNLIKE THE OTHER BASES, THIS ONE WAS DWARF-BUILT.

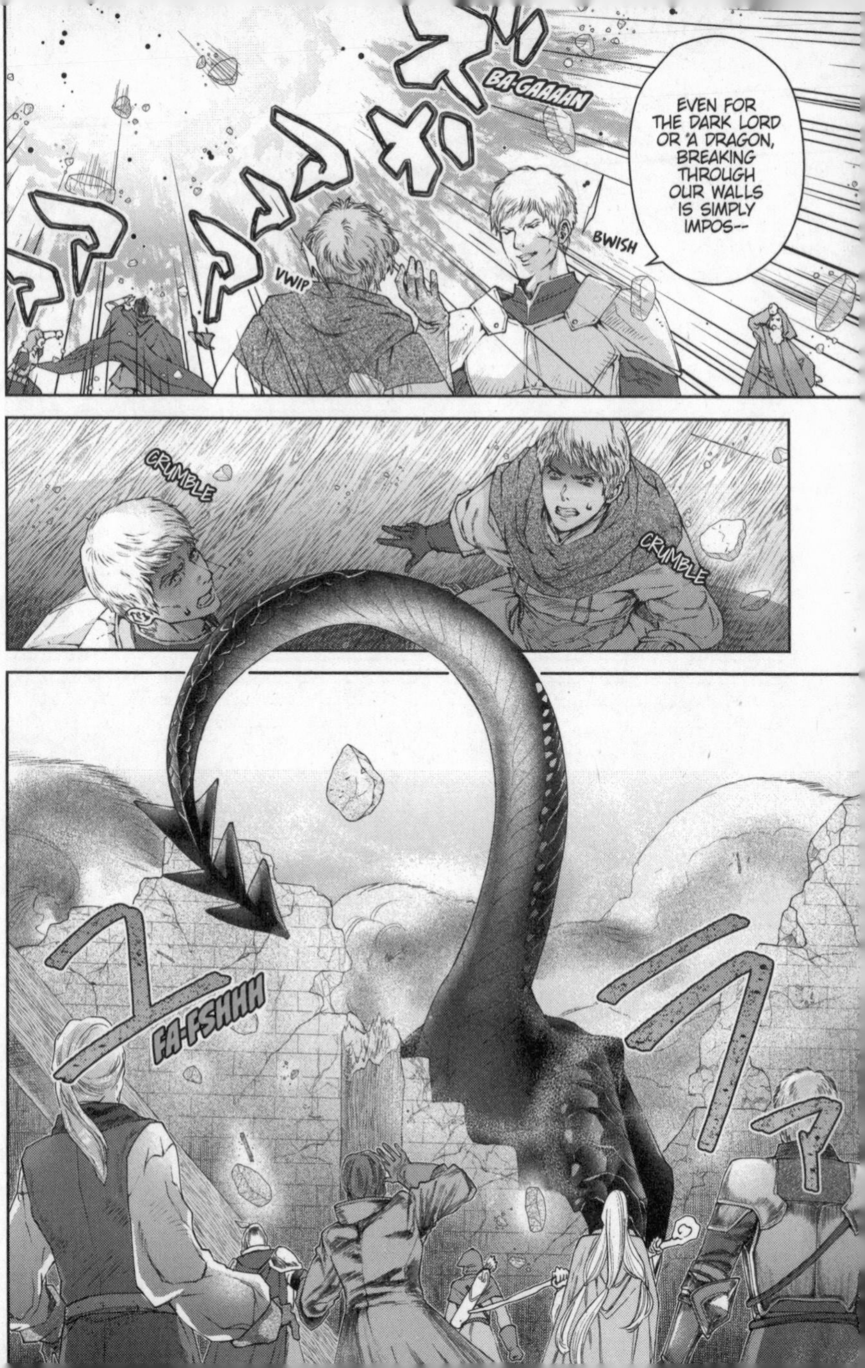
EVEN FOR THE DARK LORD OR A DRAGON, BREAKING THROUGH OUR WALLS IS SIMPLY IMPOS--
BA-GAAAAN
BWISH
VWIP
CRUMBLE
CRUMBLE
FA-FSHHH

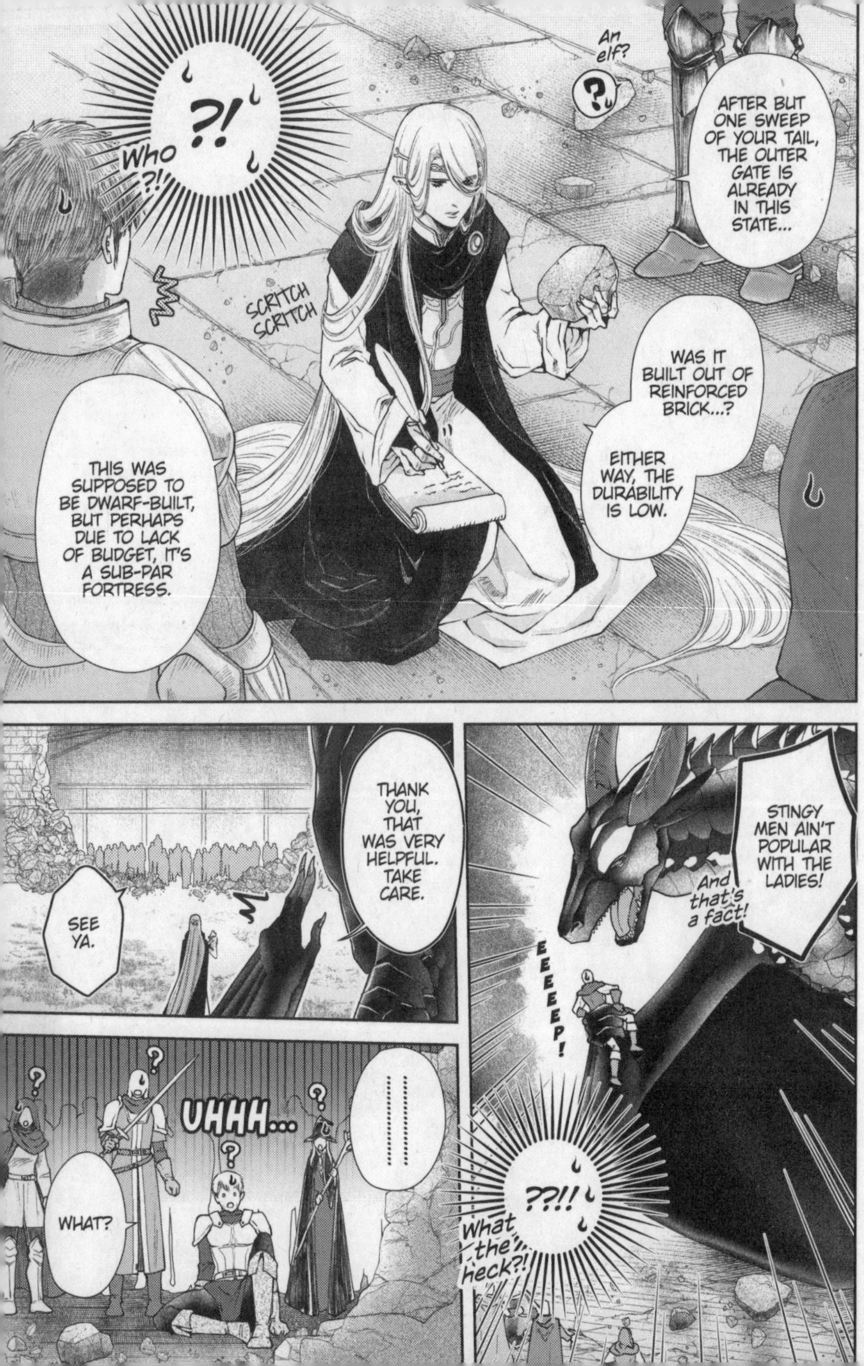
AFTER BUT ONE SWEEP OF YOUR TAIL, THE OUTER GATE IS ALREADY IN THIS STATE...
An elf?
?
?!
Who?!
SCRITCH SCRITCH
WAS IT BUILT OUT OF REINFORCED BRICK...?
EITHER WAY, THE DURABILITY IS LOW.
THIS WAS SUPPOSED TO BE DWARF-BUILT, BUT PERHAPS DUE TO LACK OF BUDGET, IT'S A SUB-PAR FORTRESS.
STINGY MEN AIN'T POPULAR WITH THE LADIES!
And that's a fact!
EEEEEP!
??!!
What the heck?!
THANK YOU, THAT WAS VERY HELPFUL. TAKE CARE.
SEE YA.
......
UHHH...
WHAT?

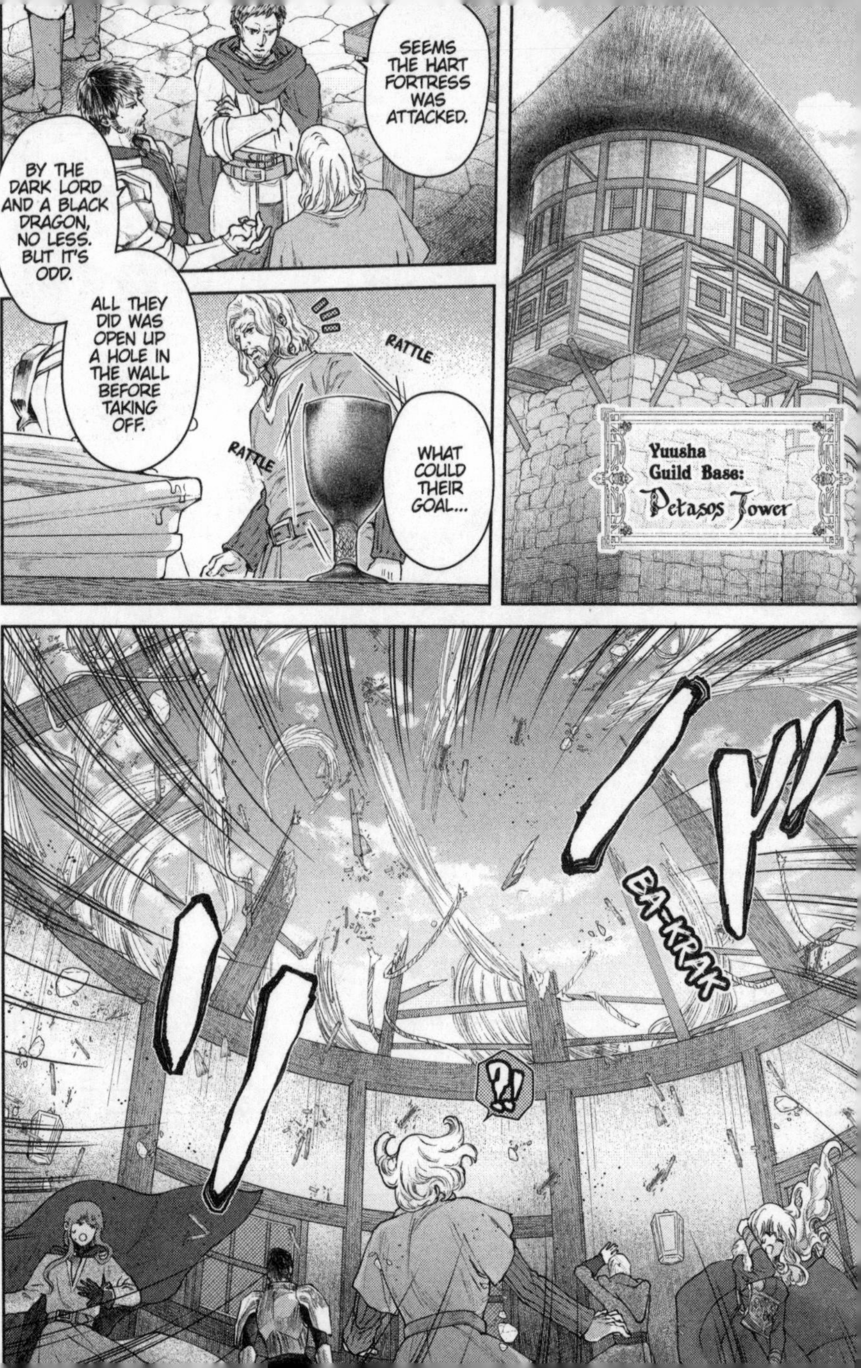
Yuusha Guild Base:
Petasos Tower
SEEMS THE HART FORTRESS WAS ATTACKED.
BY THE DARK LORD AND A BLACK DRAGON, NO LESS. BUT IT'S ODD.
ALL THEY DID WAS OPEN UP A HOLE IN THE WALL BEFORE TAKING OFF.
RATTLE
RATTLE
WHAT COULD THEIR GOAL...
BA-KRAK
?!

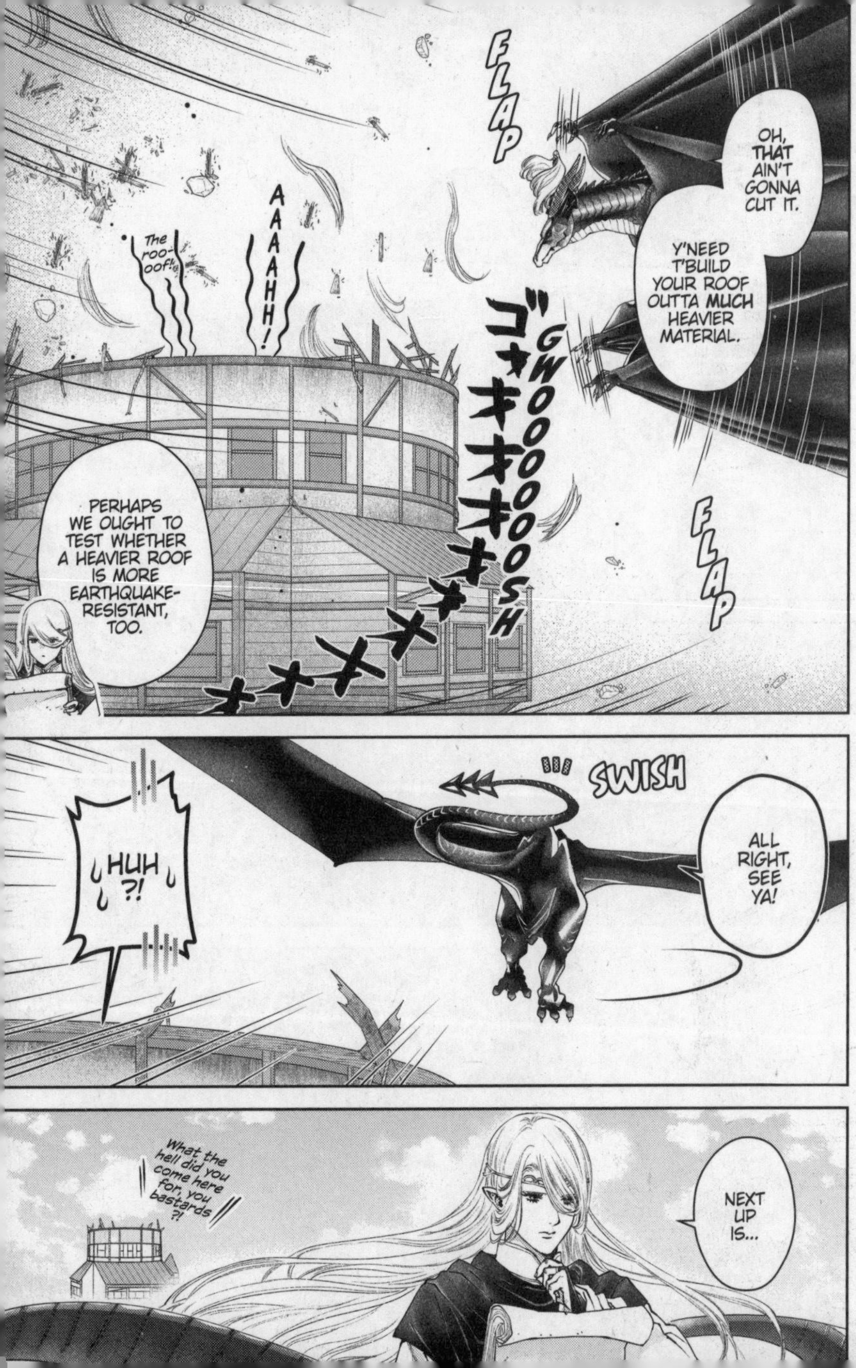
FLAP
OH, THAT AIN'T GONNA CUT IT.
Y'NEED T'BUILD YOUR ROOF OUTTA MUCH HEAVIER MATERIAL.
AAAAAHH!
The rooo-oof!!
ゴォォォォォォォォ
GWOOOOOOOOSH
FLAP
PERHAPS WE OUGHT TO TEST WHETHER A HEAVIER ROOF IS MORE EARTHQUAKE-RESISTANT, TOO.
SWISH
ALL RIGHT, SEE YA!
HUH?!
NEXT UP IS...
What the hell did you come here for, you bastards?!

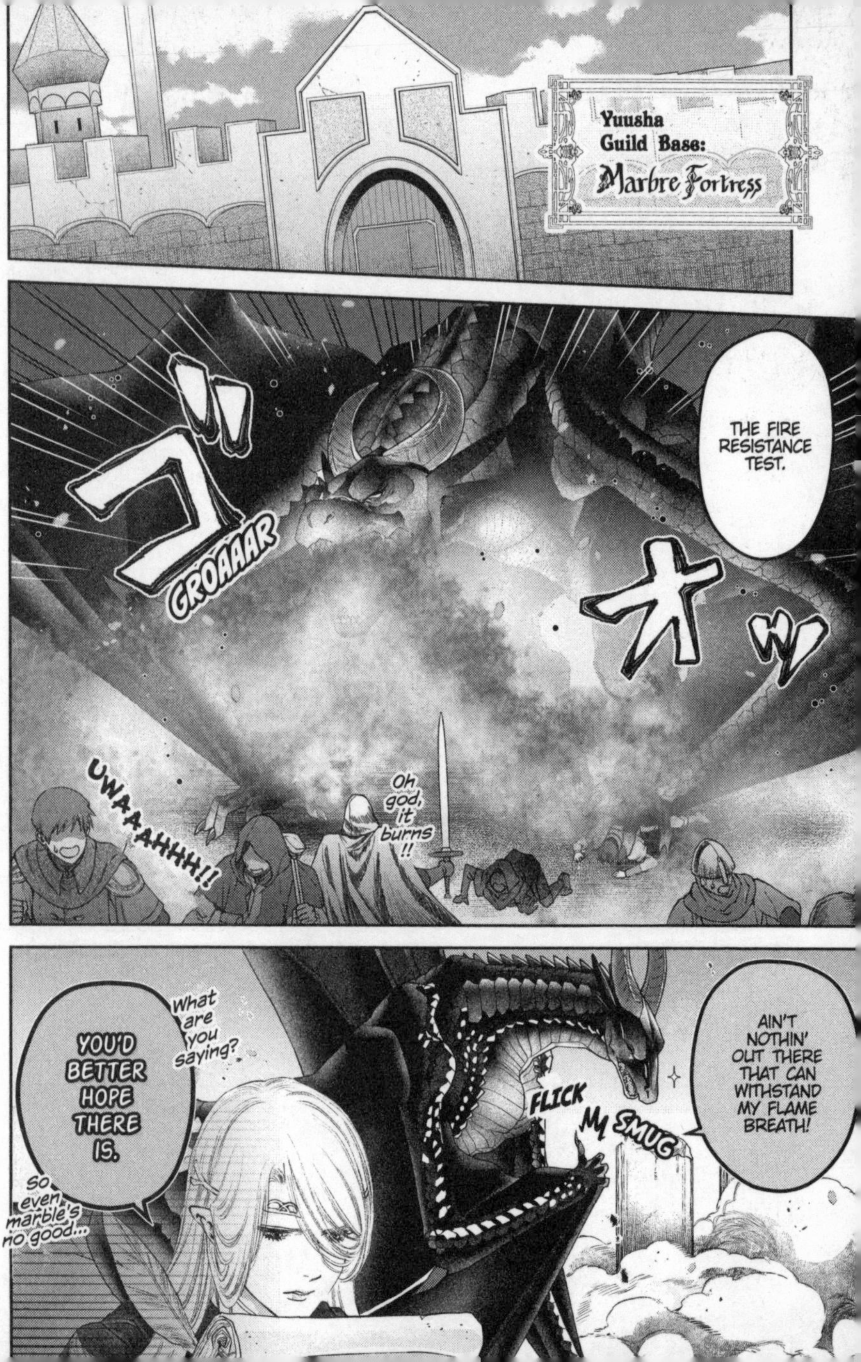

Yuusha Guild Base:
Marbre Fortress
THE FIRE RESISTANCE TEST.
ゴ
GROAAAR
オ
ッ
Oh god, it burns!!
UWAAAAHHH!!
AIN'T NOTHIN' OUT THERE THAT CAN WITHSTAND MY FLAME BREATH!
FLICK
SMUG
What are you saying?
YOU'D BETTER HOPE THERE IS.
So even marble's no good...

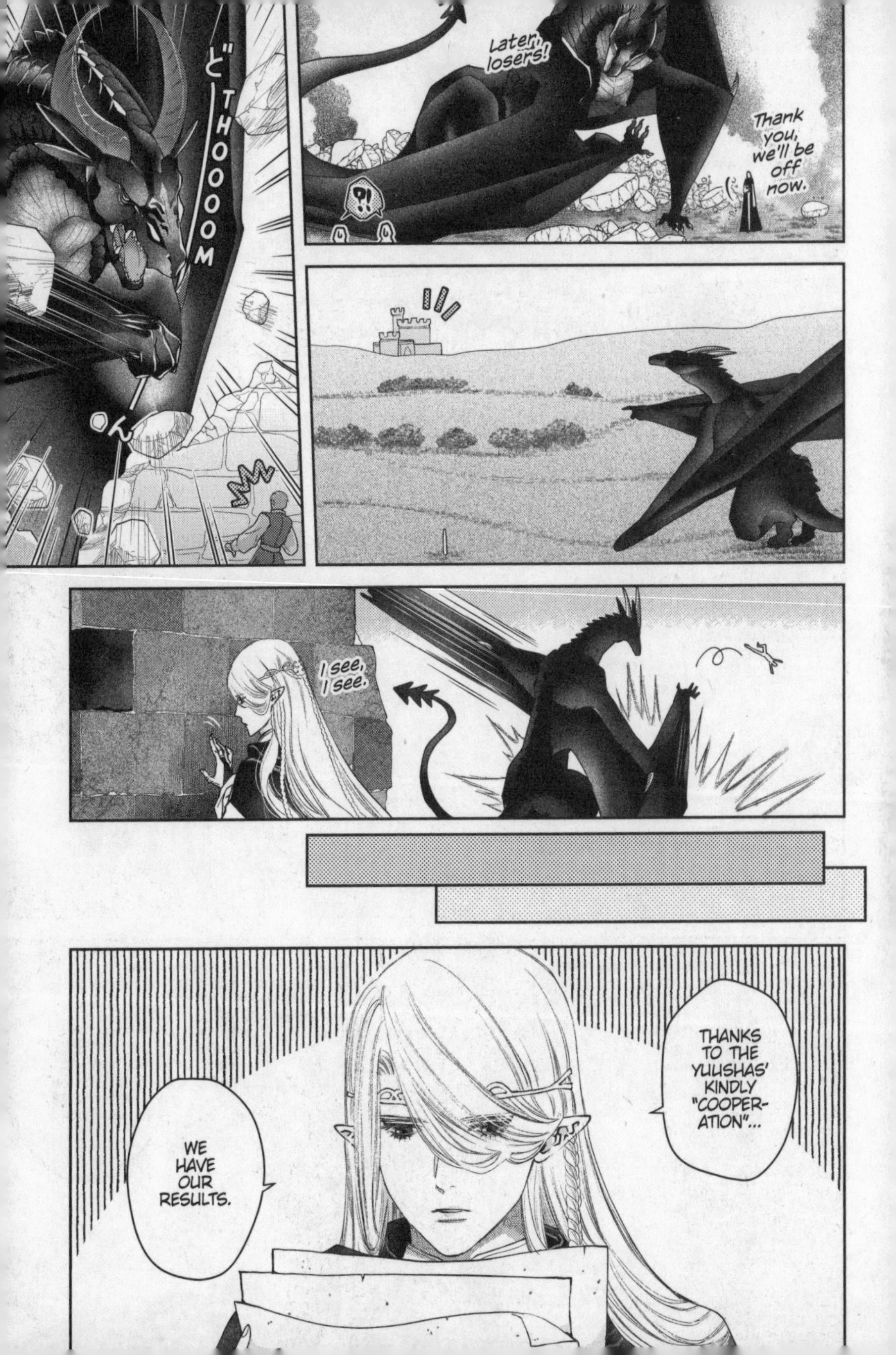
Later, losers!
?!
Thank you, we'll be off now.
どーん
THOOOOOM
I see, I see.
THANKS TO THE YUUSHAS' KINDLY "COOPERATION"...
WE HAVE OUR RESULTS.

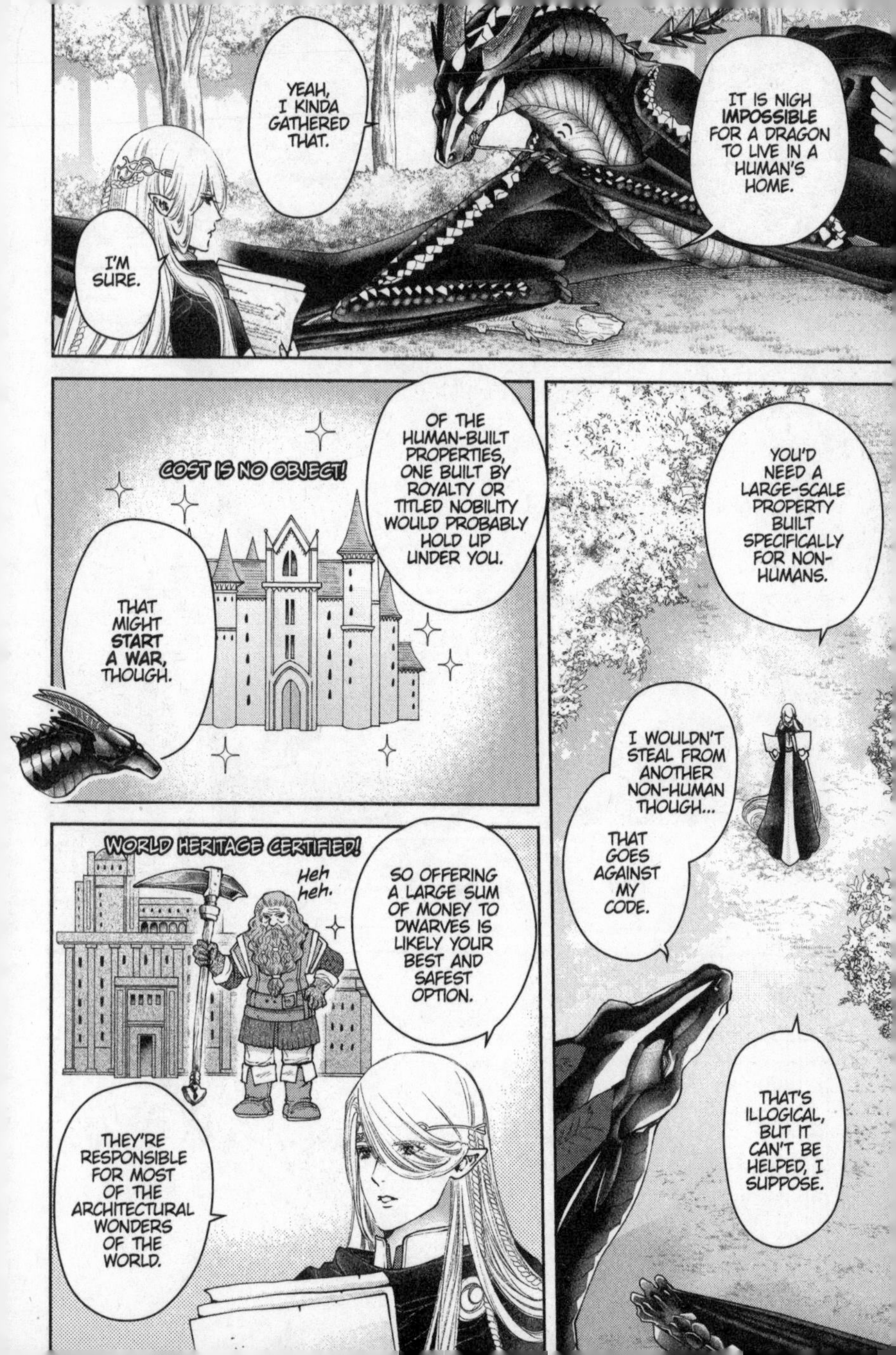

IT IS NIGH IMPOSSIBLE FOR A DRAGON TO LIVE IN A HUMAN'S HOME.
YEAH, I KINDA GATHERED THAT.
I'M SURE.
YOU'D NEED A LARGE-SCALE PROPERTY BUILT SPECIFICALLY FOR NON-HUMANS.
I WOULDN'T STEAL FROM ANOTHER NON-HUMAN THOUGH...
THAT GOES AGAINST MY CODE.
OF THE HUMAN-BUILT PROPERTIES, ONE BUILT BY ROYALTY OR TITLED NOBILITY WOULD PROBABLY HOLD UP UNDER YOU.
COST IS NO OBJECT!
THAT MIGHT START A WAR, THOUGH.
SO OFFERING A LARGE SUM OF MONEY TO DWARVES IS LIKELY YOUR BEST AND SAFEST OPTION.
WORLD HERITAGE CERTIFIED!
Heh heh.
THEY'RE RESPONSIBLE FOR MOST OF THE ARCHITECTURAL WONDERS OF THE WORLD.
THAT'S ILLOGICAL, BUT IT CAN'T BE HELPED, I SUPPOSE.

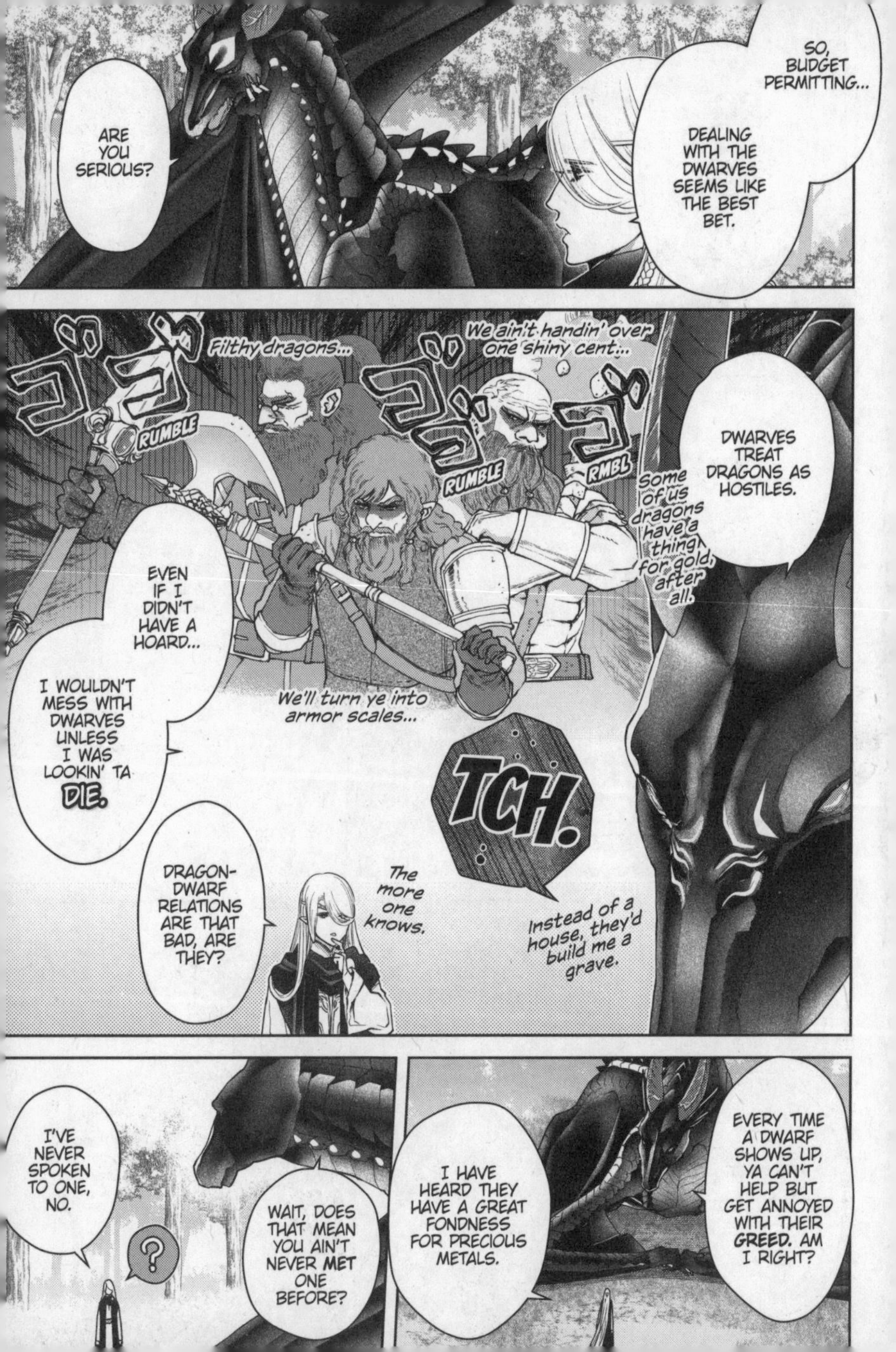
SO, BUDGET PERMITTING...
DEALING WITH THE DWARVES SEEMS LIKE THE BEST BET.
ARE YOU SERIOUS?
DWARVES TREAT DRAGONS AS HOSTILES.
Some of us dragons have a thing for gold, after all.
We ain't handin' over one shiny cent...
RMBL
RUMBLE
Filthy dragons...
RUMBLE
EVEN IF I DIDN'T HAVE A HOARD...
I WOULDN'T MESS WITH DWARVES UNLESS I WAS LOOKIN' TA **DIE.**
We'll turn ye into armor scales...
TCH.
Instead of a house, they'd build me a grave.
The more one knows.
DRAGON-DWARF RELATIONS ARE THAT BAD, ARE THEY?
EVERY TIME A DWARF SHOWS UP, YA CAN'T HELP BUT GET ANNOYED WITH THEIR **GREED.** AM I RIGHT?
I HAVE HEARD THEY HAVE A GREAT FONDNESS FOR PRECIOUS METALS.
WAIT, DOES THAT MEAN YOU AIN'T NEVER **MET** ONE BEFORE?
?
I'VE NEVER SPOKEN TO ONE, NO.

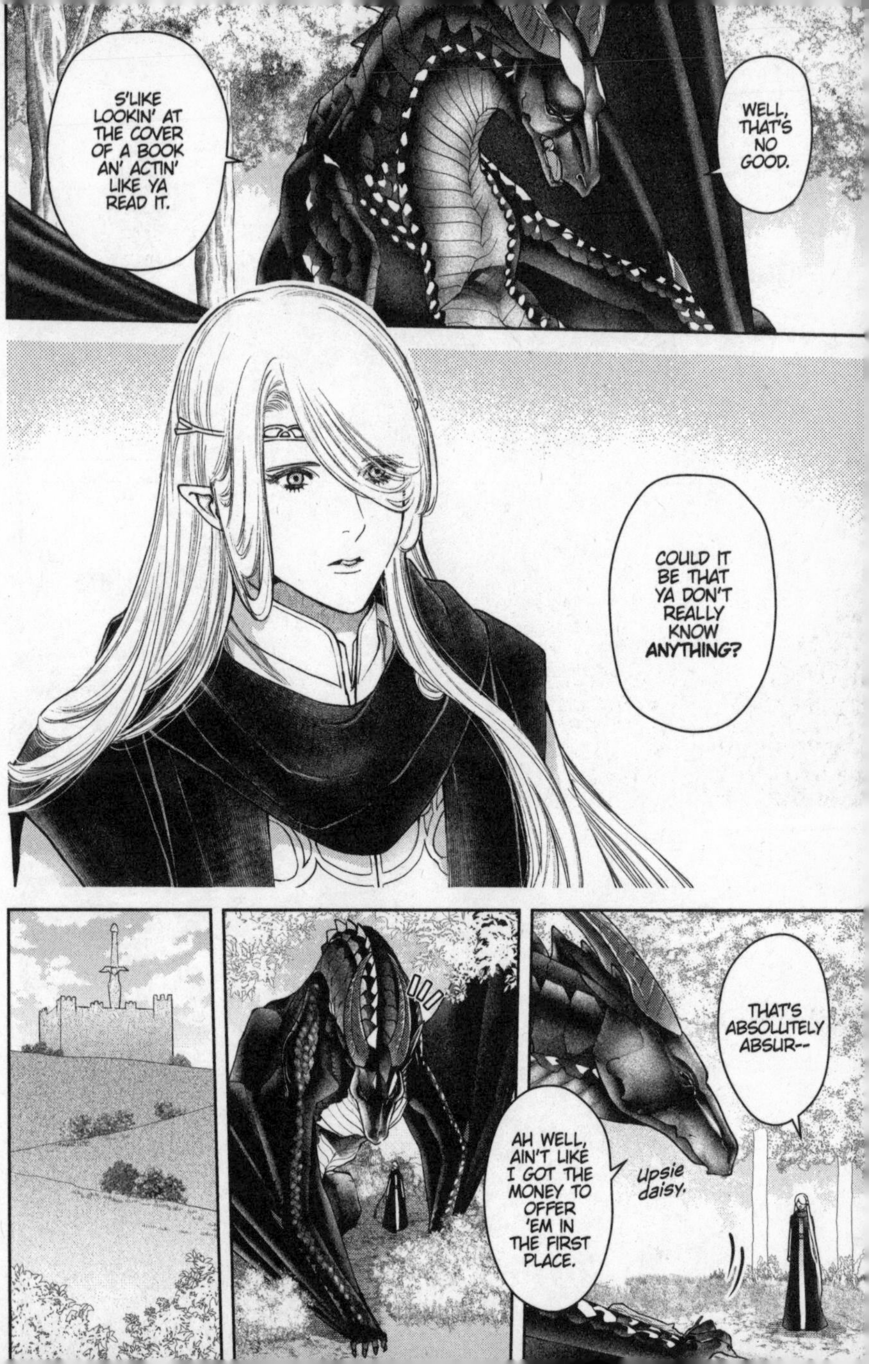
WELL, THAT'S NO GOOD.
S'LIKE LOOKIN' AT THE COVER OF A BOOK AN' ACTIN' LIKE YA READ IT.
COULD IT BE THAT YA DON'T REALLY KNOW ANYTHING?
THAT'S ABSOLUTELY ABSUR--
upsie daisy.
AH WELL, AIN'T LIKE I GOT THE MONEY TO OFFER 'EM IN THE FIRST PLACE.

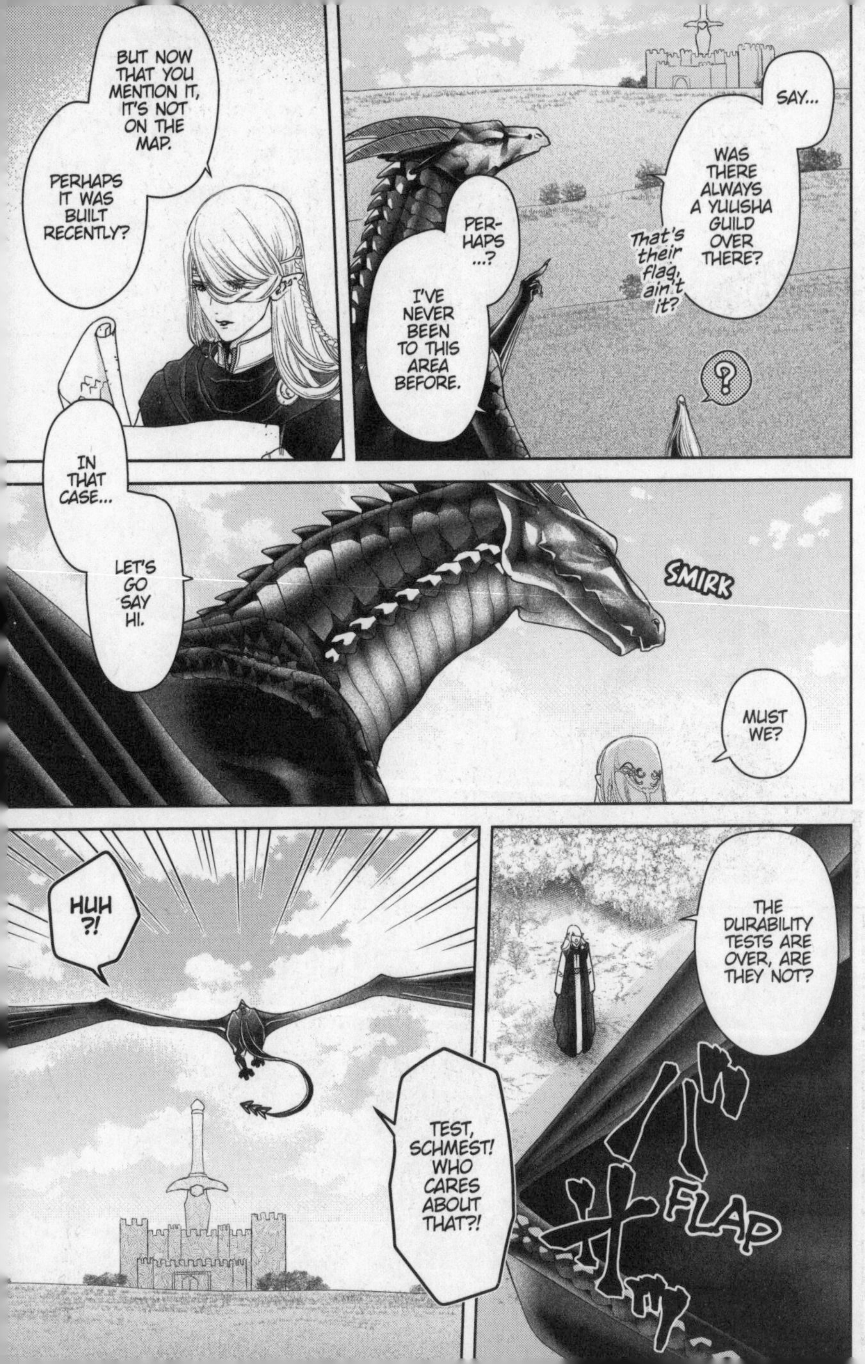
SAY...
WAS THERE ALWAYS A YUUSHA GUILD OVER THERE?
That's their flag, ain't it?
?
PER-HAPS ...?
I'VE NEVER BEEN TO THIS AREA BEFORE.
BUT NOW THAT YOU MENTION IT, IT'S NOT ON THE MAP.
PERHAPS IT WAS BUILT RECENTLY?
SMIRK
IN THAT CASE...
LET'S GO SAY HI.
MUST WE?
THE DURABILITY TESTS ARE OVER, ARE THEY NOT?
FLAP
HUH ?!
TEST, SCHMEST! WHO CARES ABOUT THAT?!

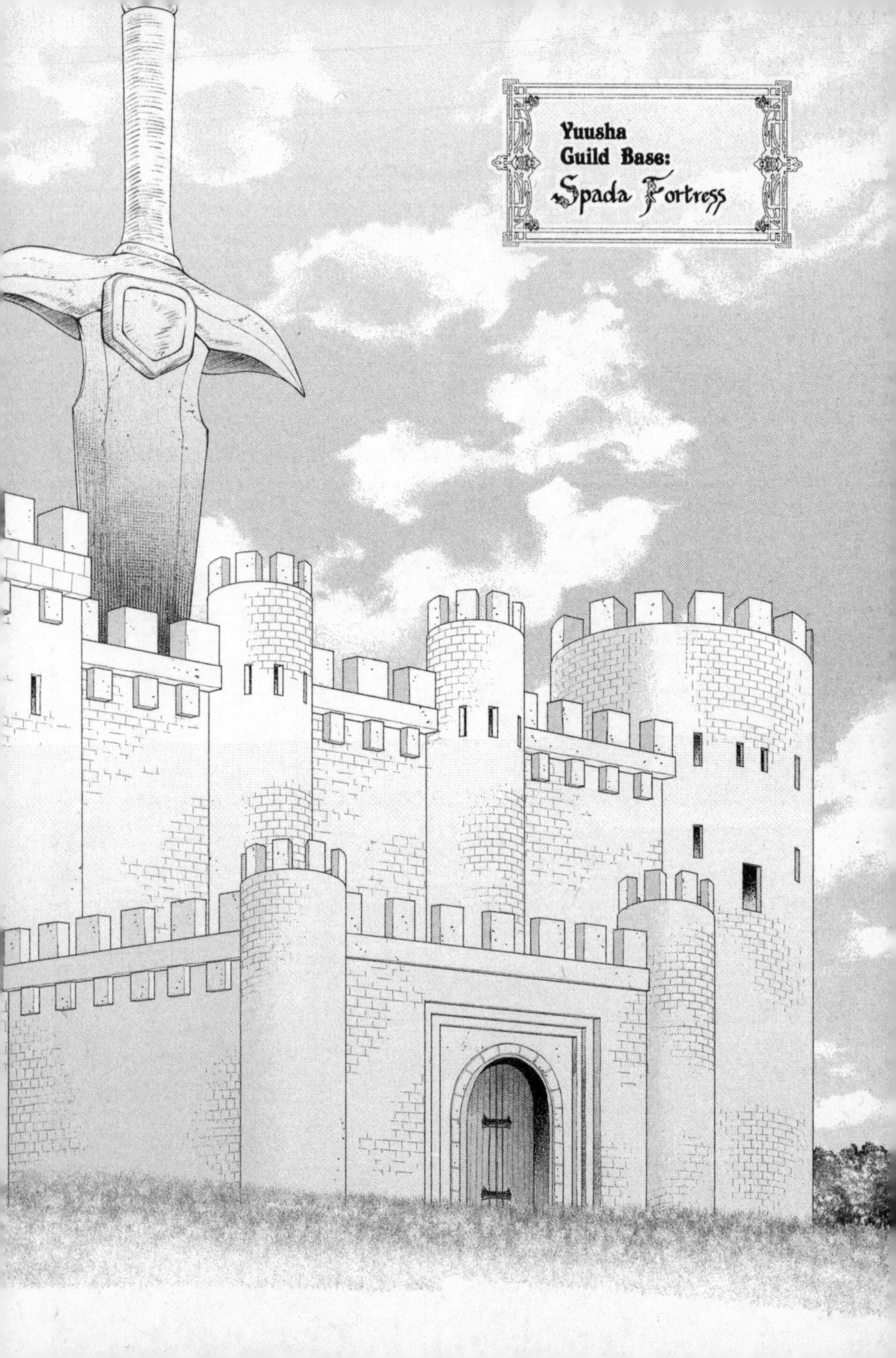
Yuusha
Guild Base:
Spada Fortress

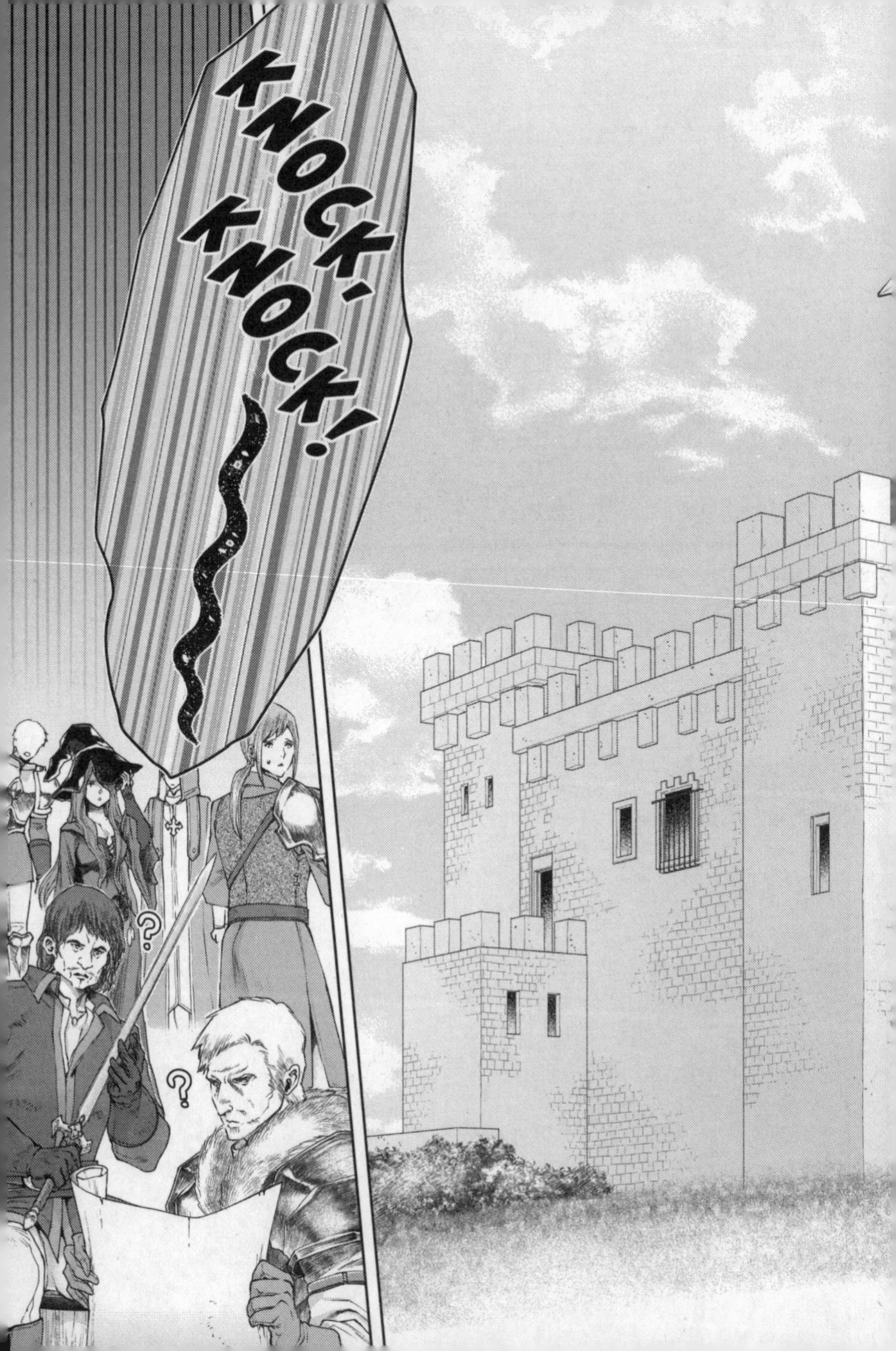
KNOCK, KNOCK, KNOCK!

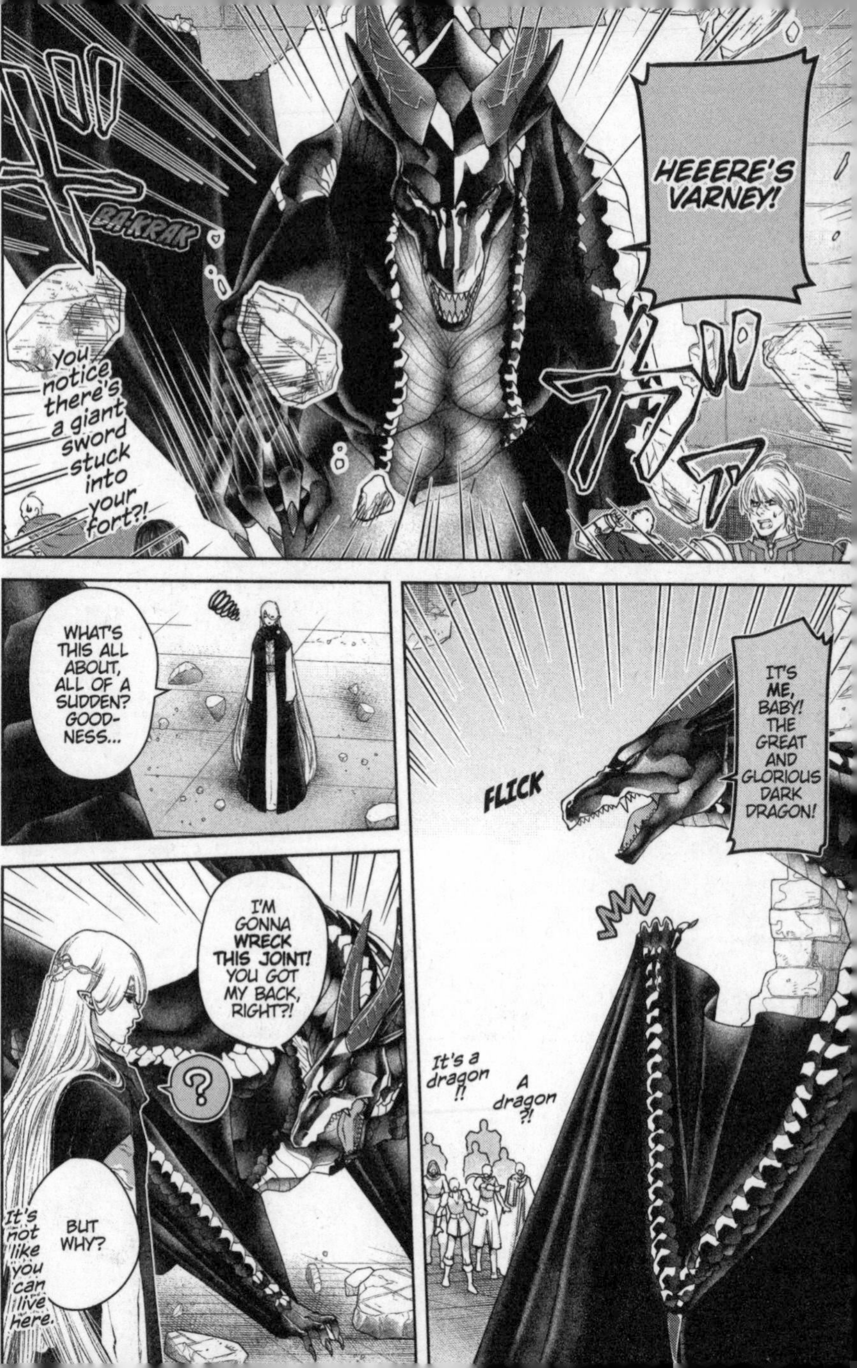
HEEERE'S VARNEY!
BA-KRAK
You notice there's a giant sword stuck into your fort?!
IT'S ME, BABY! THE GREAT AND GLORIOUS DARK DRAGON!
FLICK
WHAT'S THIS ALL ABOUT, ALL OF A SUDDEN? GOODNESS...
It's a dragon!!
A dragon?!
I'M GONNA WRECK THIS JOINT! YOU GOT MY BACK, RIGHT?!
?
BUT WHY?
It's not like you can live here.

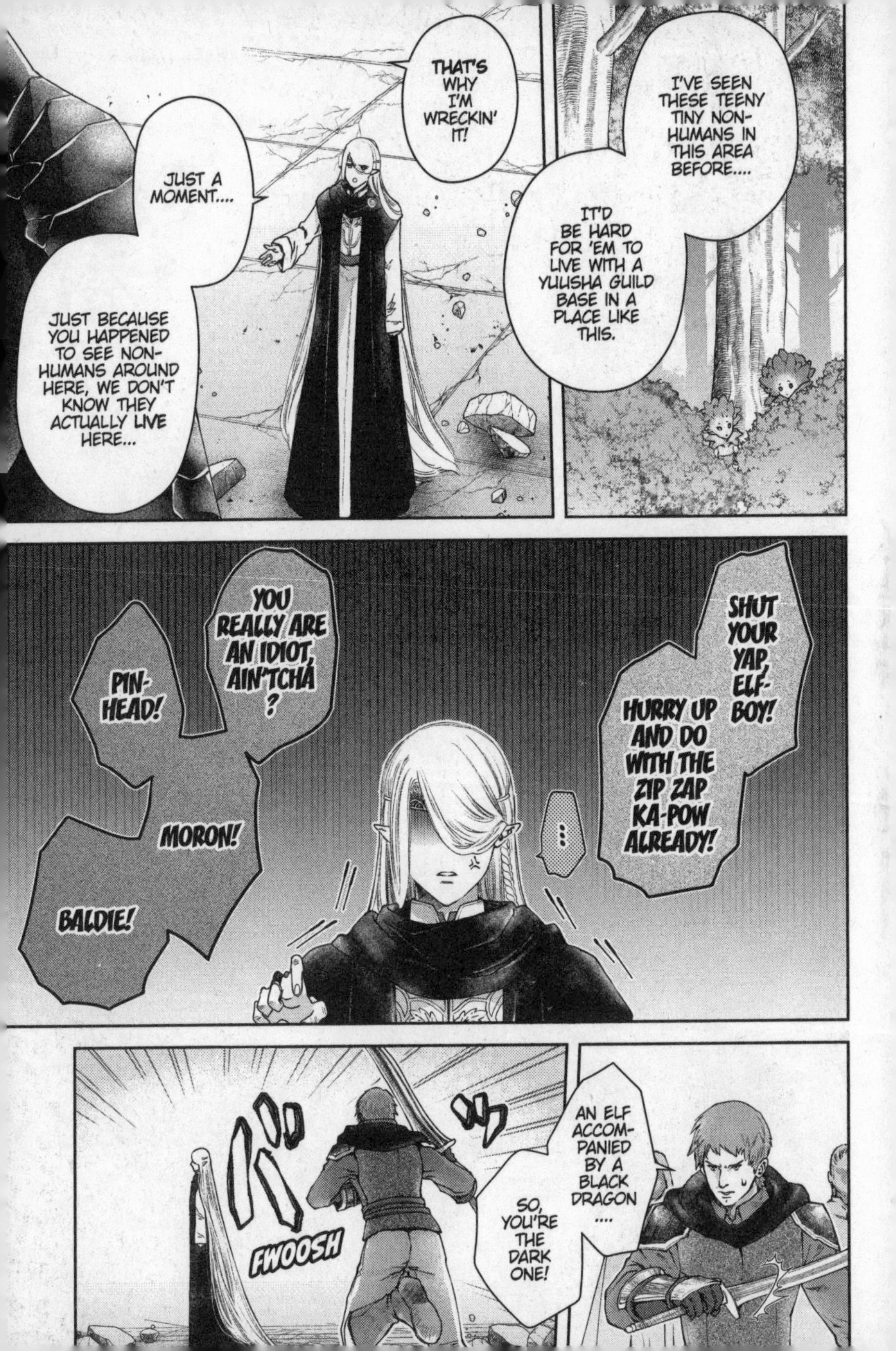
I'VE SEEN THESE TEENY TINY NON-HUMANS IN THIS AREA BEFORE....
IT'D BE HARD FOR 'EM TO LIVE WITH A YUUSHA GUILD BASE IN A PLACE LIKE THIS.
THAT'S WHY I'M WRECKIN' IT!
JUST A MOMENT....
JUST BECAUSE YOU HAPPENED TO SEE NON-HUMANS AROUND HERE, WE DON'T KNOW THEY ACTUALLY LIVE HERE...
SHUT YOUR YAP, ELF-BOY!
HURRY UP AND DO WITH THE ZIP ZAP KA-POW ALREADY!
...
YOU REALLY ARE AN IDIOT, AIN'TCHA?
PIN-HEAD!
MORON!
BALDIE!
AN ELF ACCOMPANIED BY A BLACK DRAGON....
SO, YOU'RE THE DARK ONE!
FWOOSH

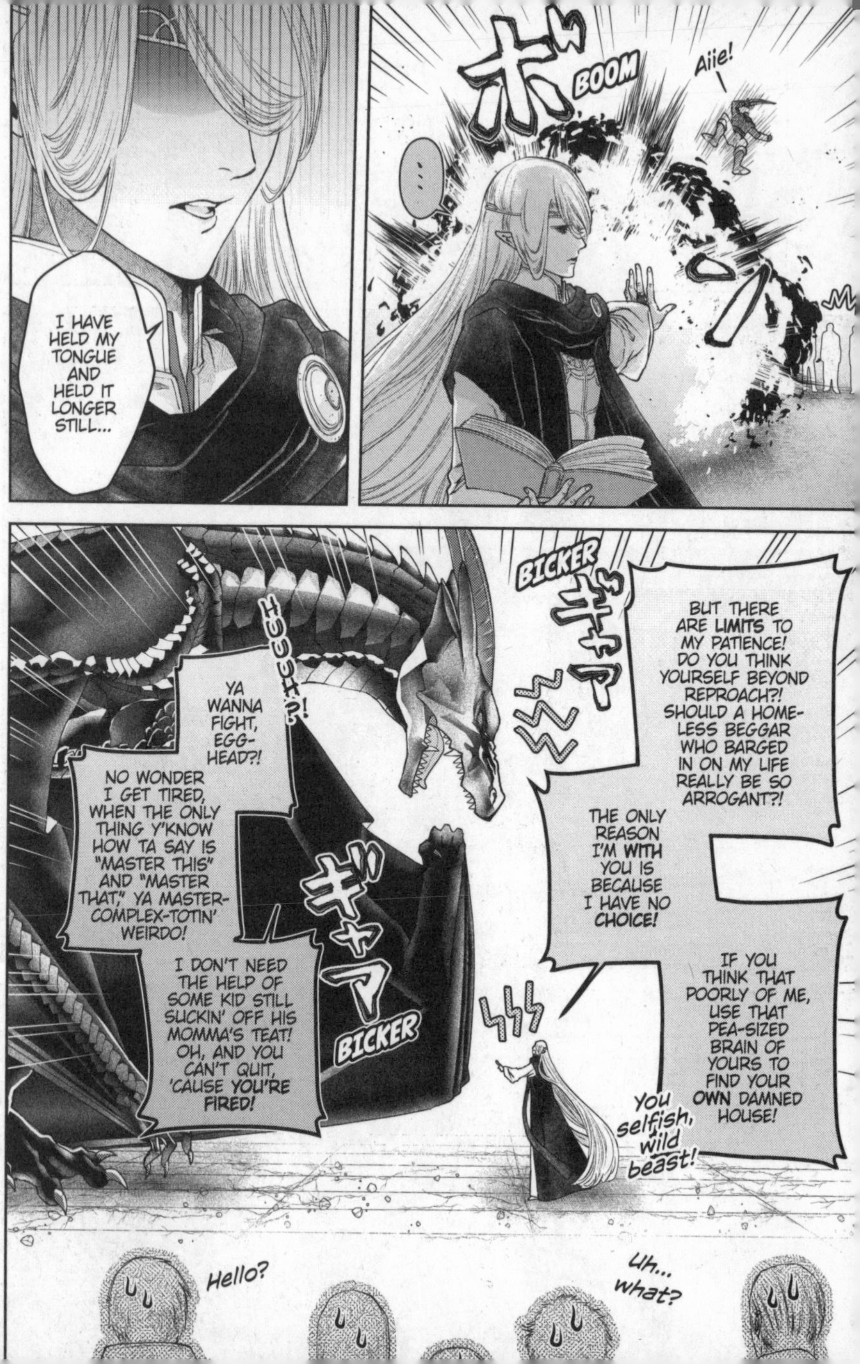
BOOM
Aiie!
...
I HAVE HELD MY TONGUE AND HELD IT LONGER STILL...
BICKER
BUT THERE ARE LIMITS TO MY PATIENCE! DO YOU THINK YOURSELF BEYOND REPROACH?! SHOULD A HOME-LESS BEGGAR WHO BARGED IN ON MY LIFE REALLY BE SO ARROGANT?!
THE ONLY REASON I'M WITH YOU IS BECAUSE I HAVE NO CHOICE!
IF YOU THINK THAT POORLY OF ME, USE THAT PEA-SIZED BRAIN OF YOURS TO FIND YOUR OWN DAMNED HOUSE!
You selfish, wild beast!
HUUUHH?!
YA WANNA FIGHT, EGG-HEAD?!
NO WONDER I GET TIRED, WHEN THE ONLY THING Y'KNOW HOW TA SAY IS "MASTER THIS" AND "MASTER THAT," YA MASTER-COMPLEX-TOTIN' WEIRDO!
I DON'T NEED THE HELP OF SOME KID STILL SUCKIN' OFF HIS MOMMA'S TEAT! OH, AND YOU CAN'T QUIT, 'CAUSE YOU'RE FIRED!
BICKER
Uh... what?
Hello?

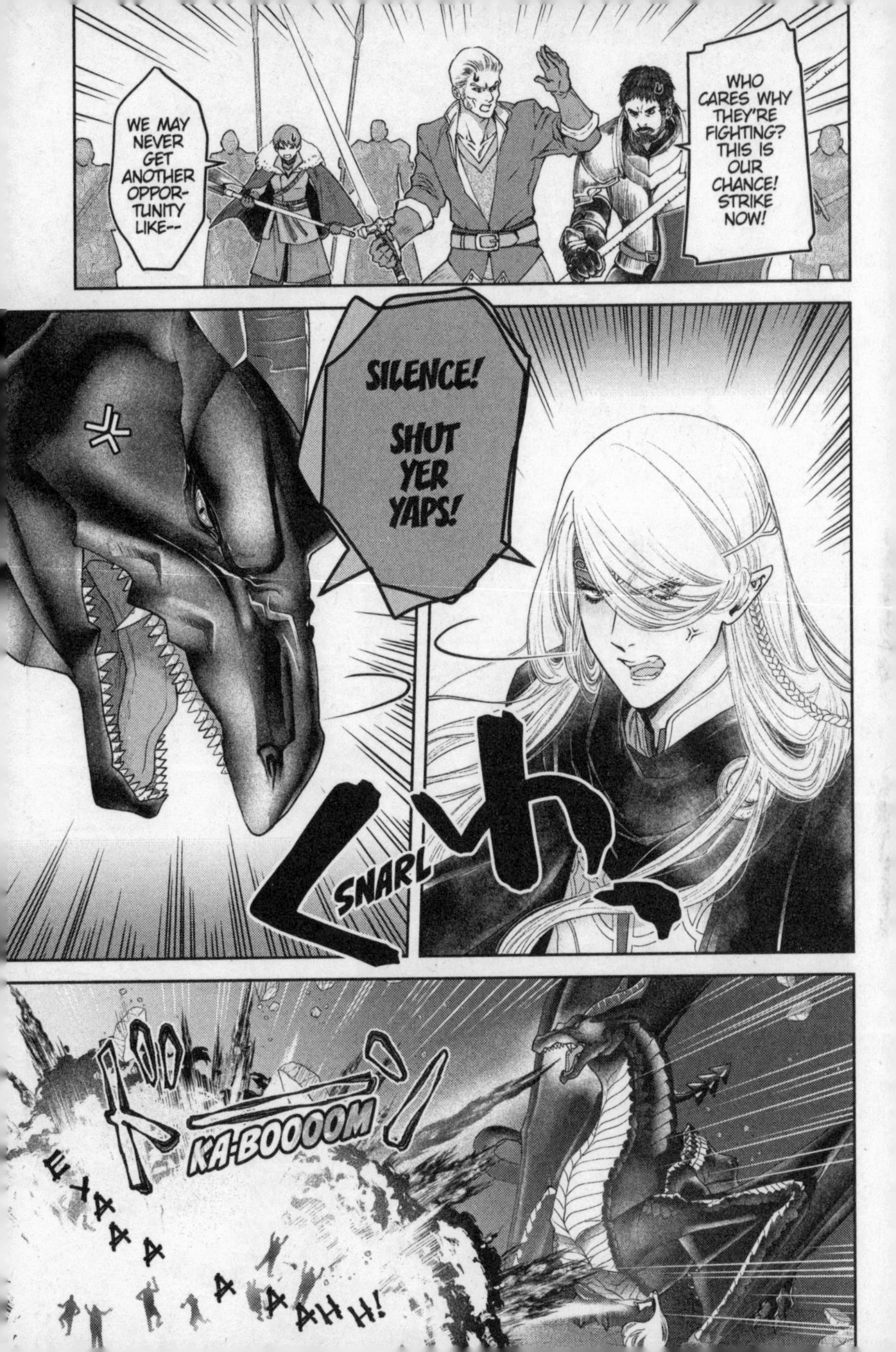
WHO CARES WHY THEY'RE FIGHTING? THIS IS OUR CHANCE! STRIKE NOW!
WE MAY NEVER GET ANOTHER OPPORTUNITY LIKE--
SILENCE!
SHUT YER YAPS!
SNARL
KA-BOOOOM
EYAAAA AAAHH!

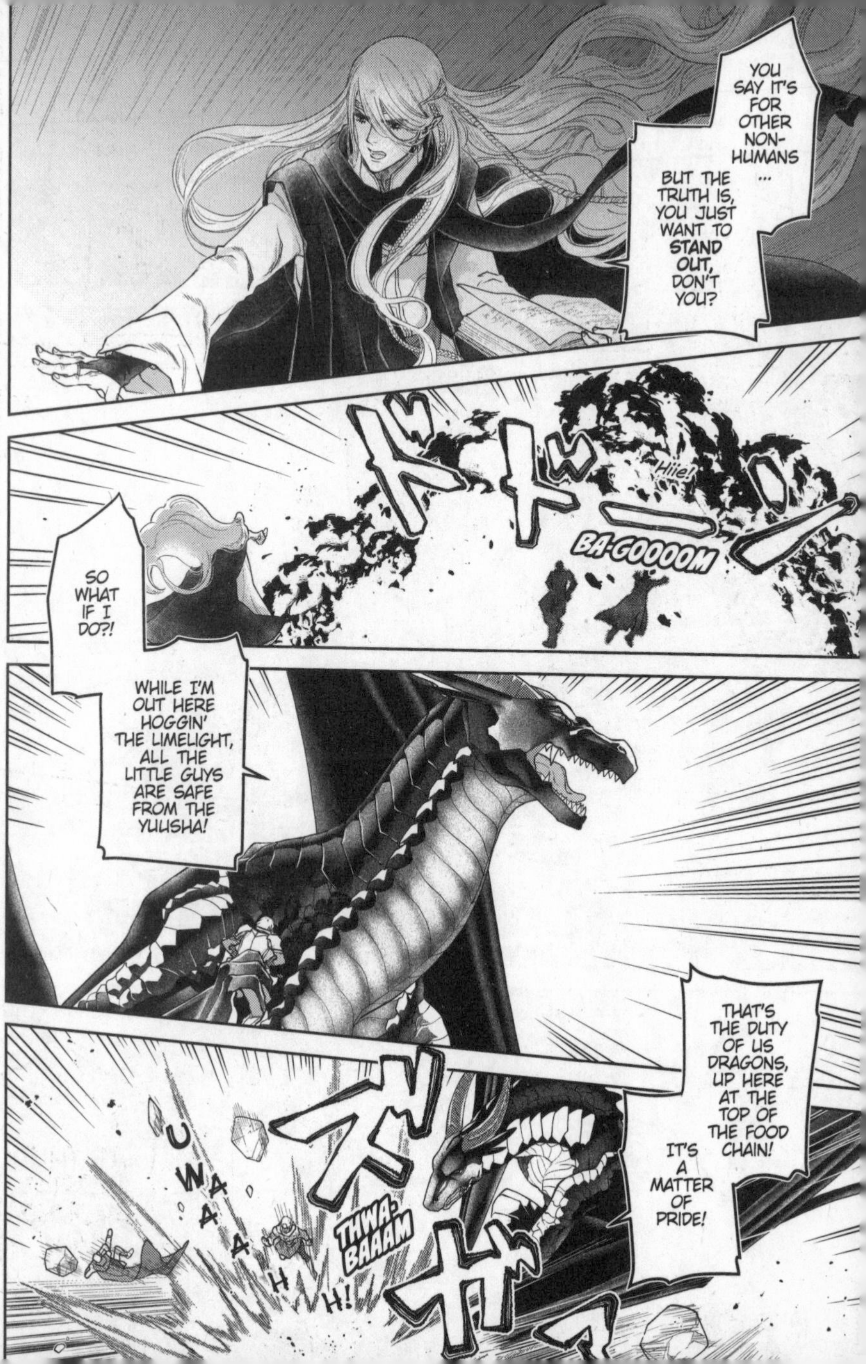
YOU SAY IT'S FOR OTHER NON-HUMANS...
BUT THE TRUTH IS, YOU JUST WANT TO STAND OUT, DON'T YOU?
Hiie!
BA-GOOOOM
SO WHAT IF I DO?!
WHILE I'M OUT HERE HOGGIN' THE LIMELIGHT, ALL THE LITTLE GUYS ARE SAFE FROM THE YUUSHA!
THAT'S THE DUTY OF US DRAGONS, UP HERE AT THE TOP OF THE FOOD CHAIN!
IT'S A MATTER OF PRIDE!
THWA-BAAAM
UWAAAHH!

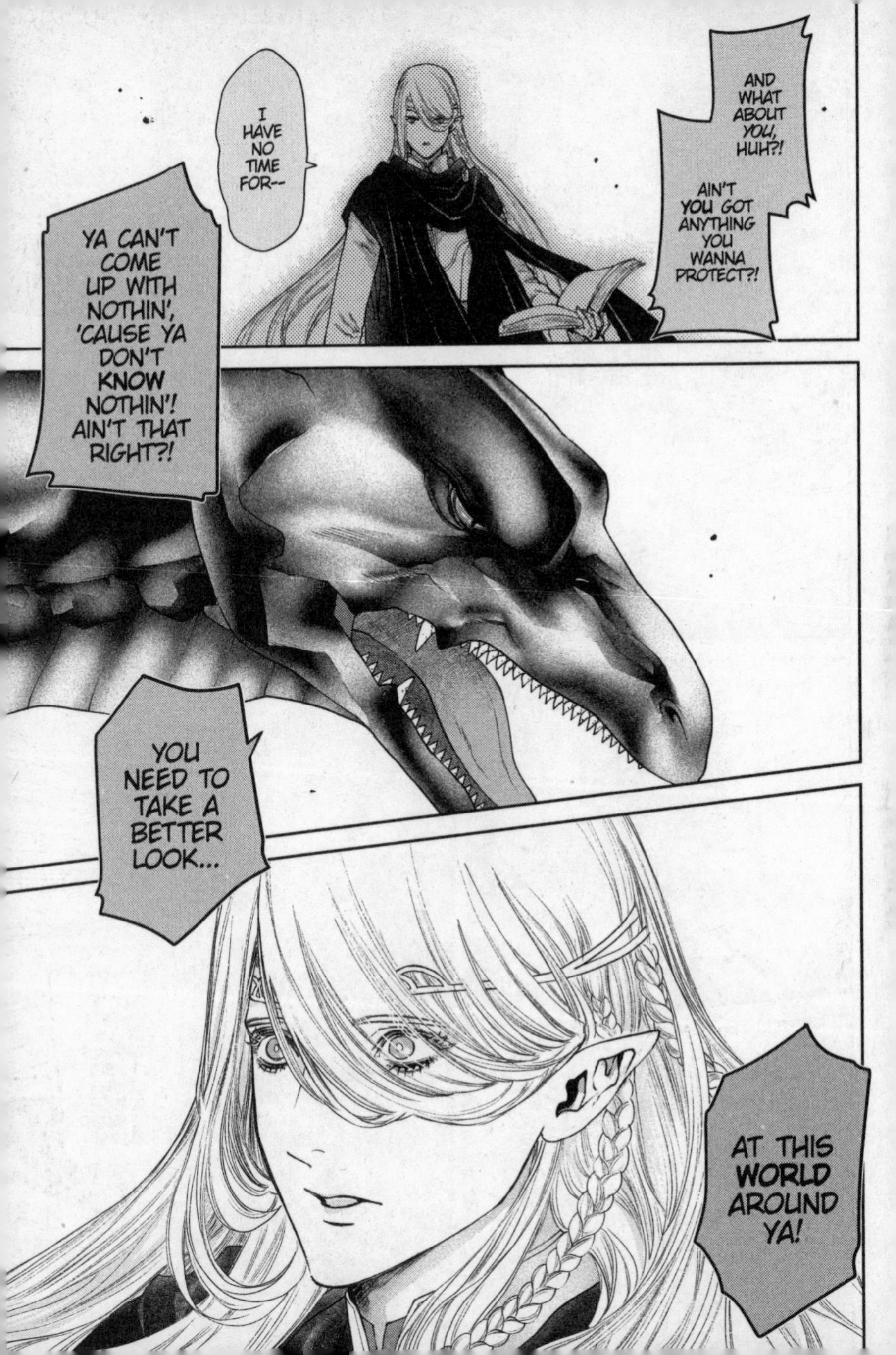
AND WHAT ABOUT YOU, HUH?!
AIN'T YOU GOT ANYTHING YOU WANNA PROTECT?!
I HAVE NO TIME FOR--
YA CAN'T COME UP WITH NOTHIN', 'CAUSE YA DON'T KNOW NOTHIN'! AIN'T THAT RIGHT?!
YOU NEED TO TAKE A BETTER LOOK...
AT THIS WORLD AROUND YA!

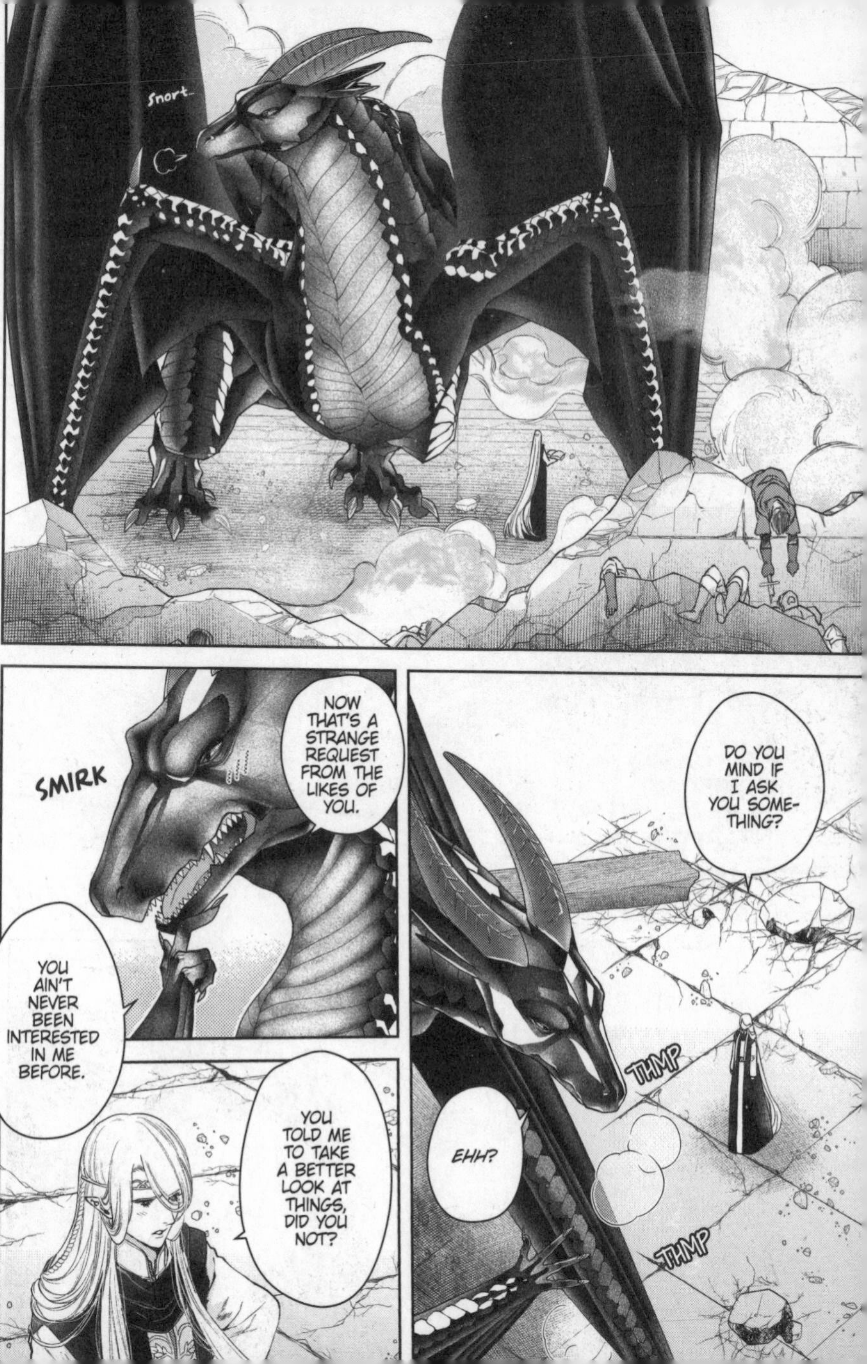
Snort
DO YOU MIND IF I ASK YOU SOME-THING?
THMP
THMP
EHH?
SMIRK
NOW THAT'S A STRANGE REQUEST FROM THE LIKES OF YOU.
YOU AIN'T NEVER BEEN INTERESTED IN ME BEFORE.
YOU TOLD ME TO TAKE A BETTER LOOK AT THINGS, DID YOU NOT?

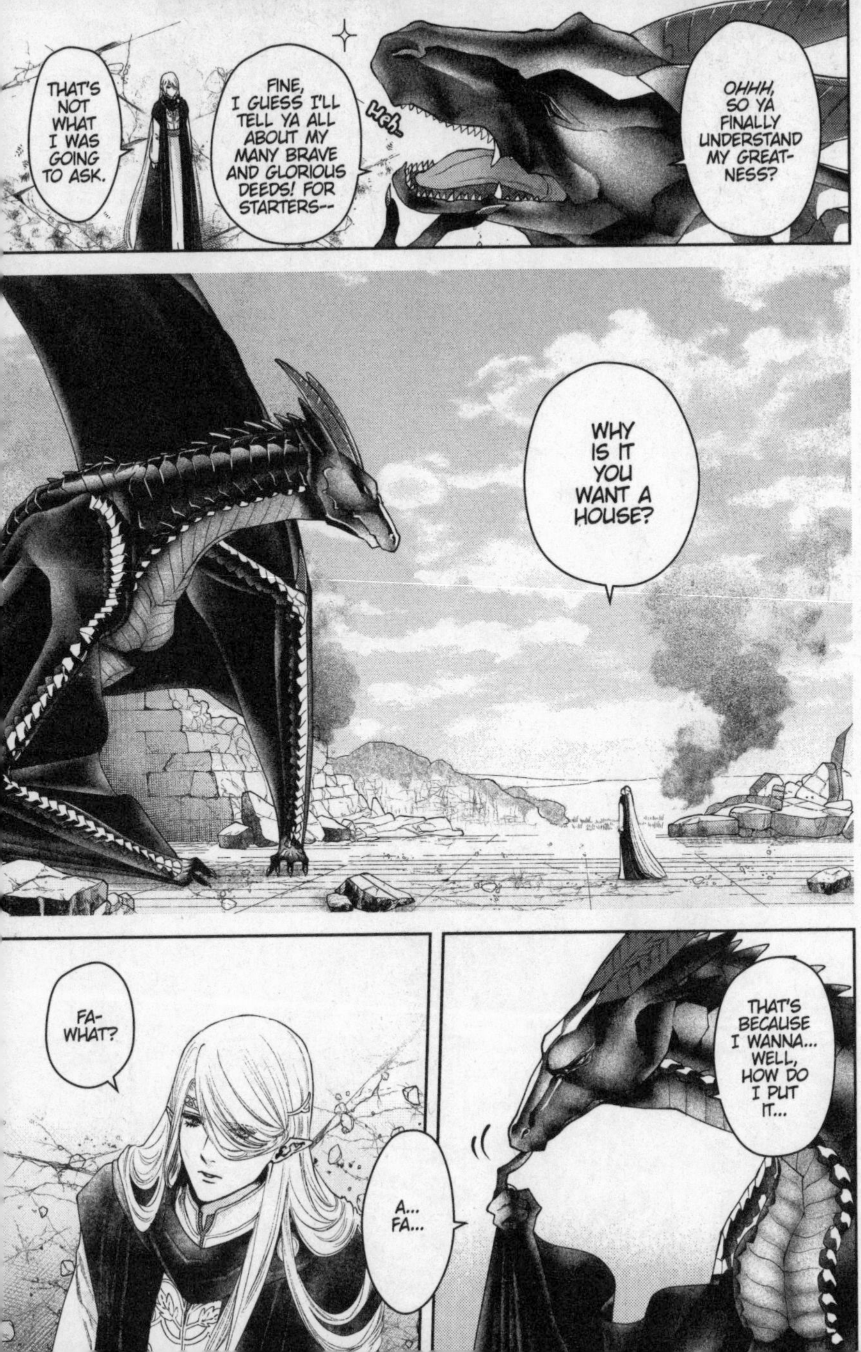
OHHH, SO YA FINALLY UNDERSTAND MY GREAT-NESS?
Heh
FINE, I GUESS I'LL TELL YA ALL ABOUT MY MANY BRAVE AND GLORIOUS DEEDS! FOR STARTERS--
THAT'S NOT WHAT I WAS GOING TO ASK.
WHY IS IT YOU WANT A HOUSE?
THAT'S BECAUSE I WANNA... WELL, HOW DO I PUT IT...
A... FA...
FA-WHAT?

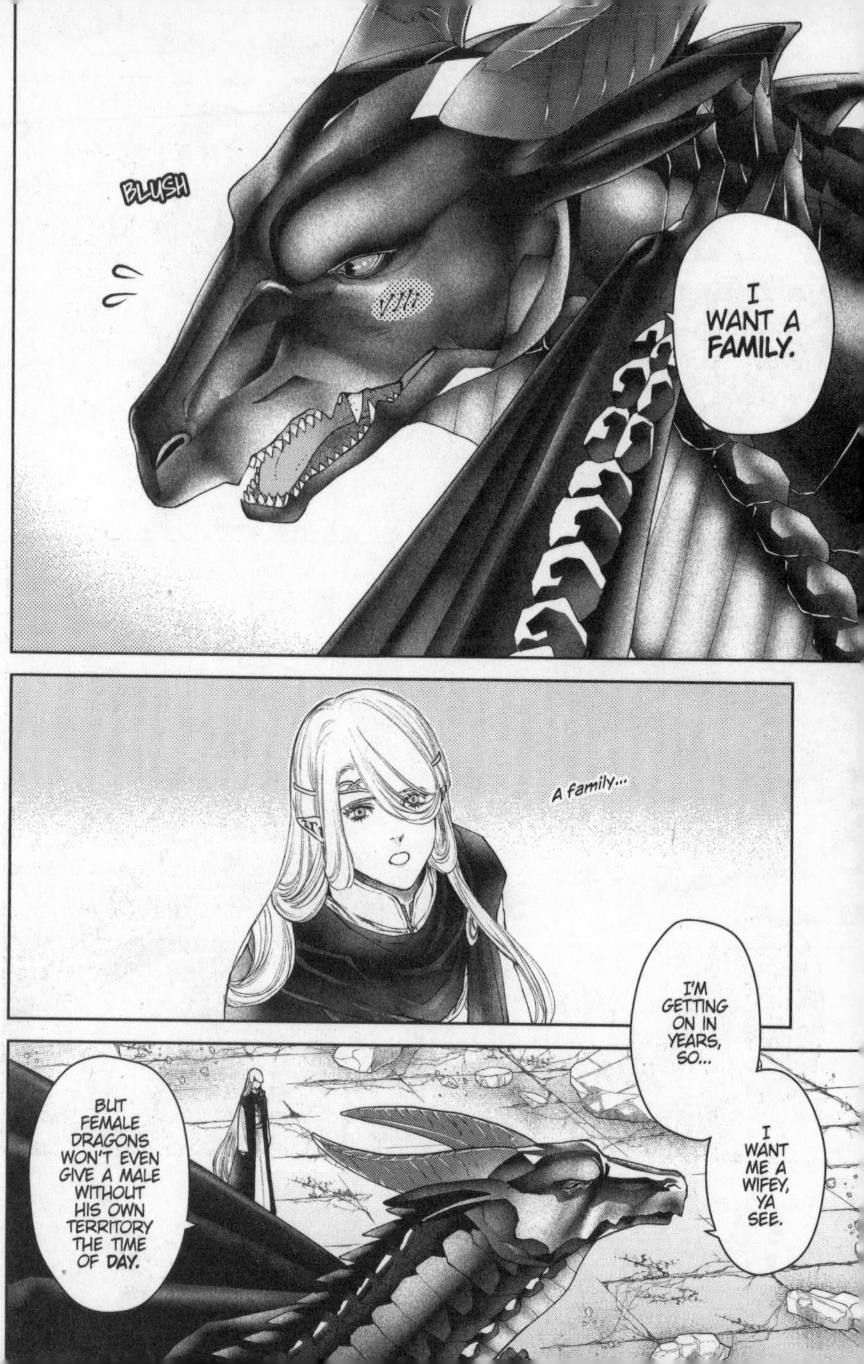
I WANT A FAMILY.
BLUSH
A family...
I'M GETTING ON IN YEARS, SO...
I WANT ME A WIFEY, YA SEE.
BUT FEMALE DRAGONS WON'T EVEN GIVE A MALE WITHOUT HIS OWN TERRITORY THE TIME OF DAY.

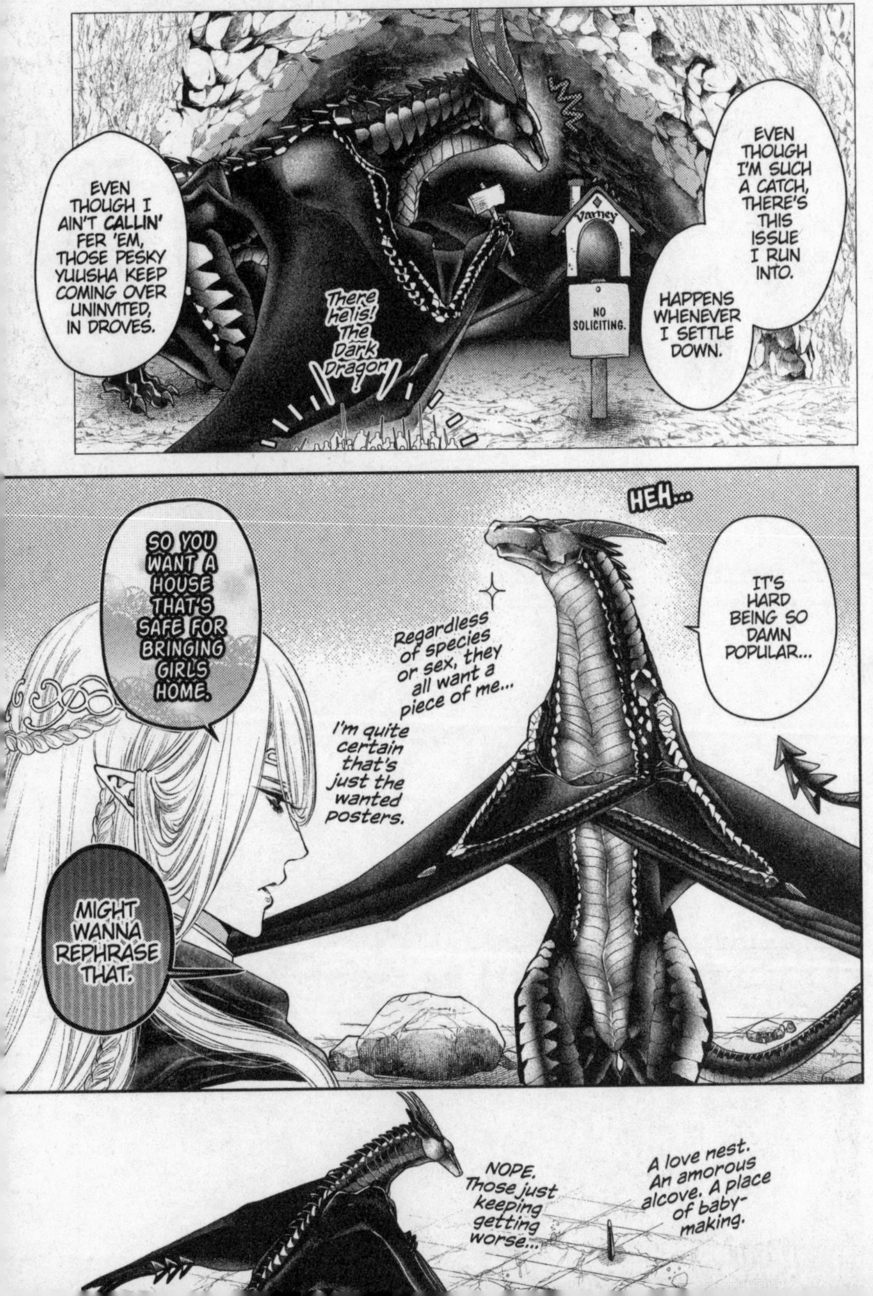
EVEN THOUGH I'M SUCH A CATCH, THERE'S THIS ISSUE I RUN INTO.
HAPPENS WHENEVER I SETTLE DOWN.
Varney
NO SOLICITING.
There he is! The Dark Dragon!
EVEN THOUGH I AIN'T CALLIN' FER 'EM, THOSE PESKY YUUSHA KEEP COMING OVER UNINVITED, IN DROVES.
HEH...
IT'S HARD BEING SO DAMN POPULAR...
Regardless of species or sex, they all want a piece of me...
I'm quite certain that's just the wanted posters.
SO YOU WANT A HOUSE THAT'S SAFE FOR BRINGING GIRLS HOME.
MIGHT WANNA REPHRASE THAT.
A love nest. An amorous alcove. A place of baby-making.
NOPE. Those just keeping getting worse...

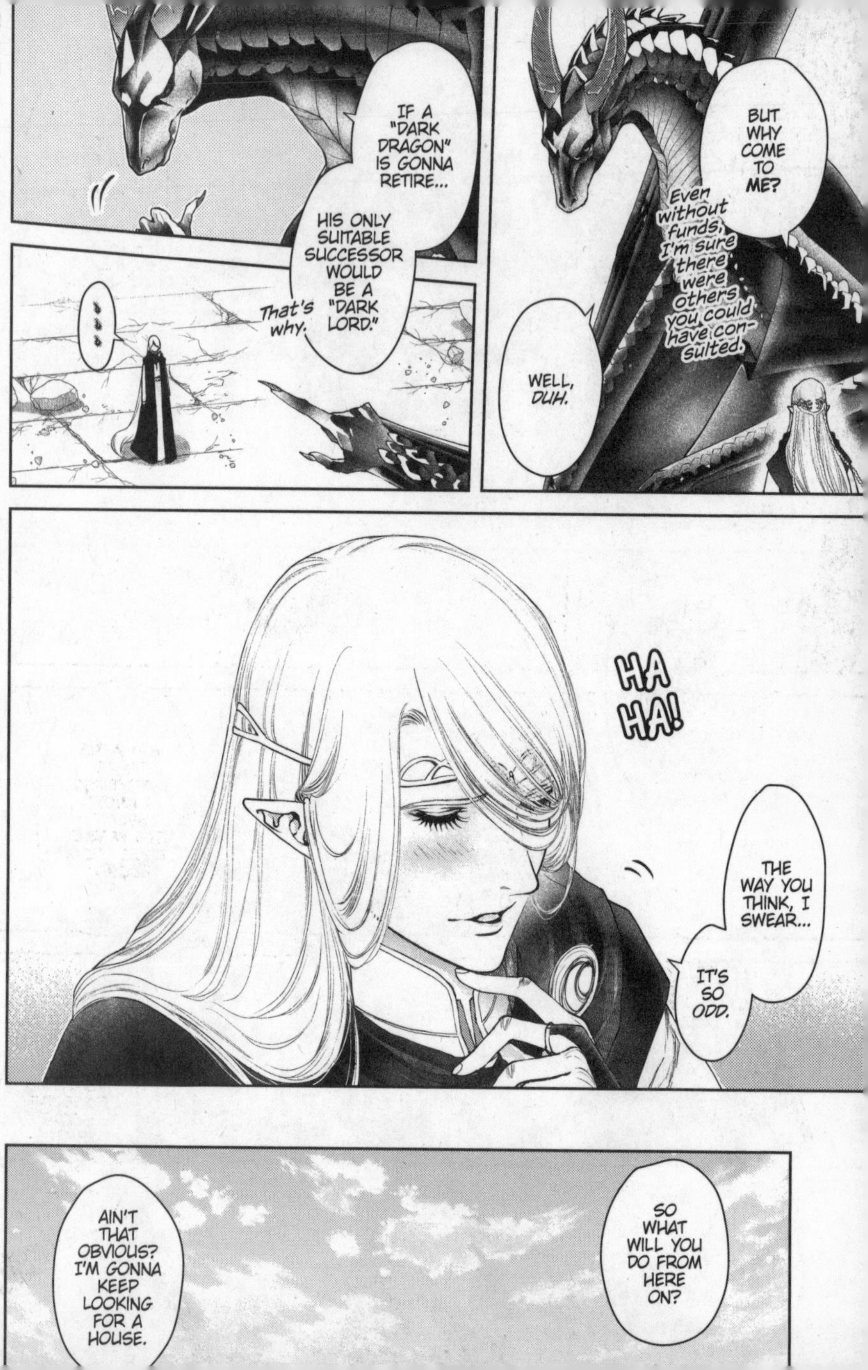
BUT WHY COME TO ME?
Even without funds, I'm sure there were others you could have consulted.
WELL, DUH.
IF A "DARK DRAGON" IS GONNA RETIRE...
HIS ONLY SUITABLE SUCCESSOR WOULD BE A "DARK LORD."
That's why.
...
HA HA!
THE WAY YOU THINK, I SWEAR...
IT'S SO ODD.
SO WHAT WILL YOU DO FROM HERE ON?
AIN'T THAT OBVIOUS? I'M GONNA KEEP LOOKING FOR A HOUSE.

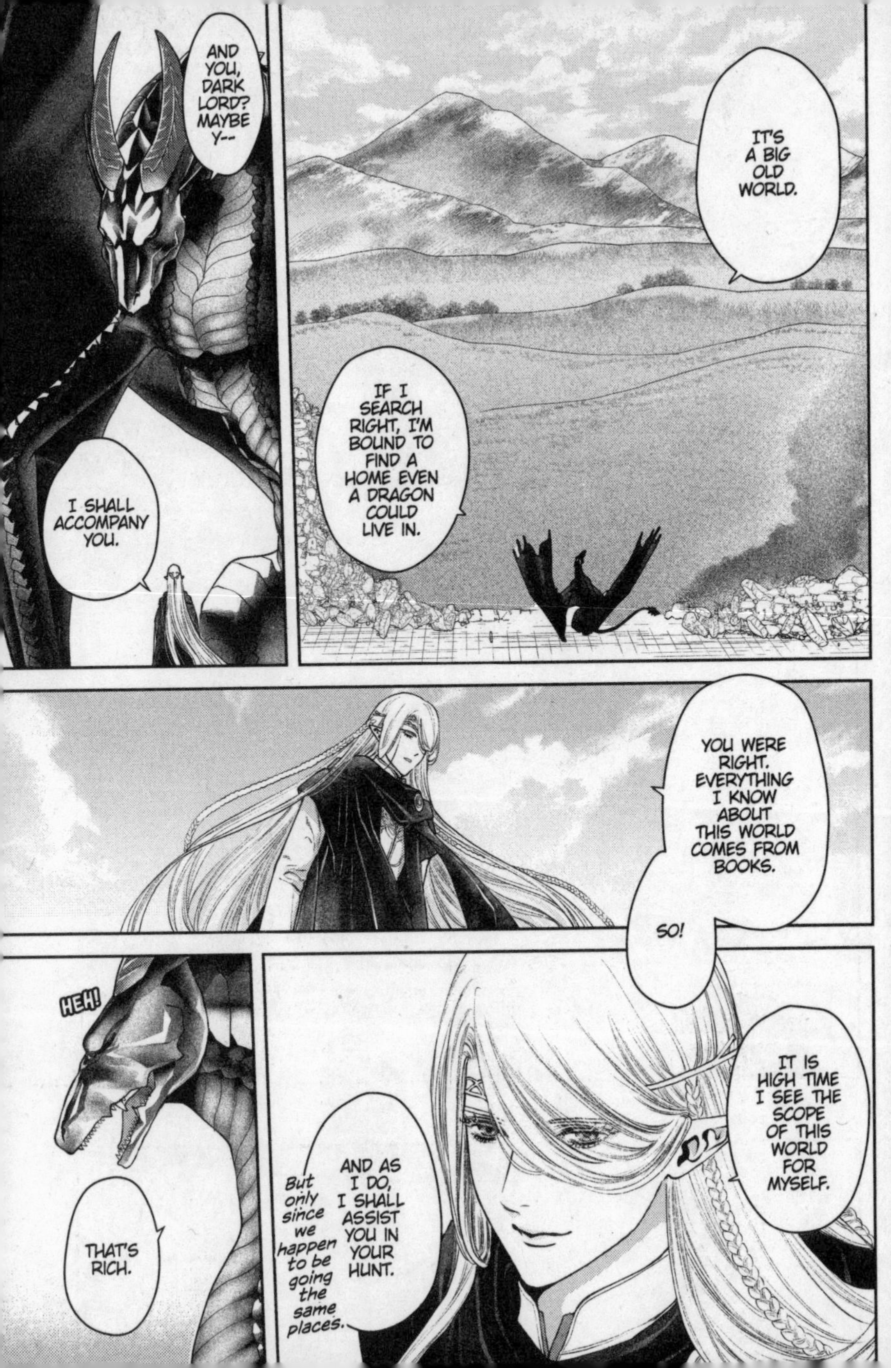
IT'S A BIG OLD WORLD.
IF I SEARCH RIGHT, I'M BOUND TO FIND A HOME EVEN A DRAGON COULD LIVE IN.
AND YOU, DARK LORD? MAYBE Y--
I SHALL ACCOMPANY YOU.
YOU WERE RIGHT. EVERYTHING I KNOW ABOUT THIS WORLD COMES FROM BOOKS.
SO!
IT IS HIGH TIME I SEE THE SCOPE OF THIS WORLD FOR MYSELF.
AND AS I DO, I SHALL ASSIST YOU IN YOUR HUNT.
But only since we happen to be going the same places.
HEH!
THAT'S RICH.

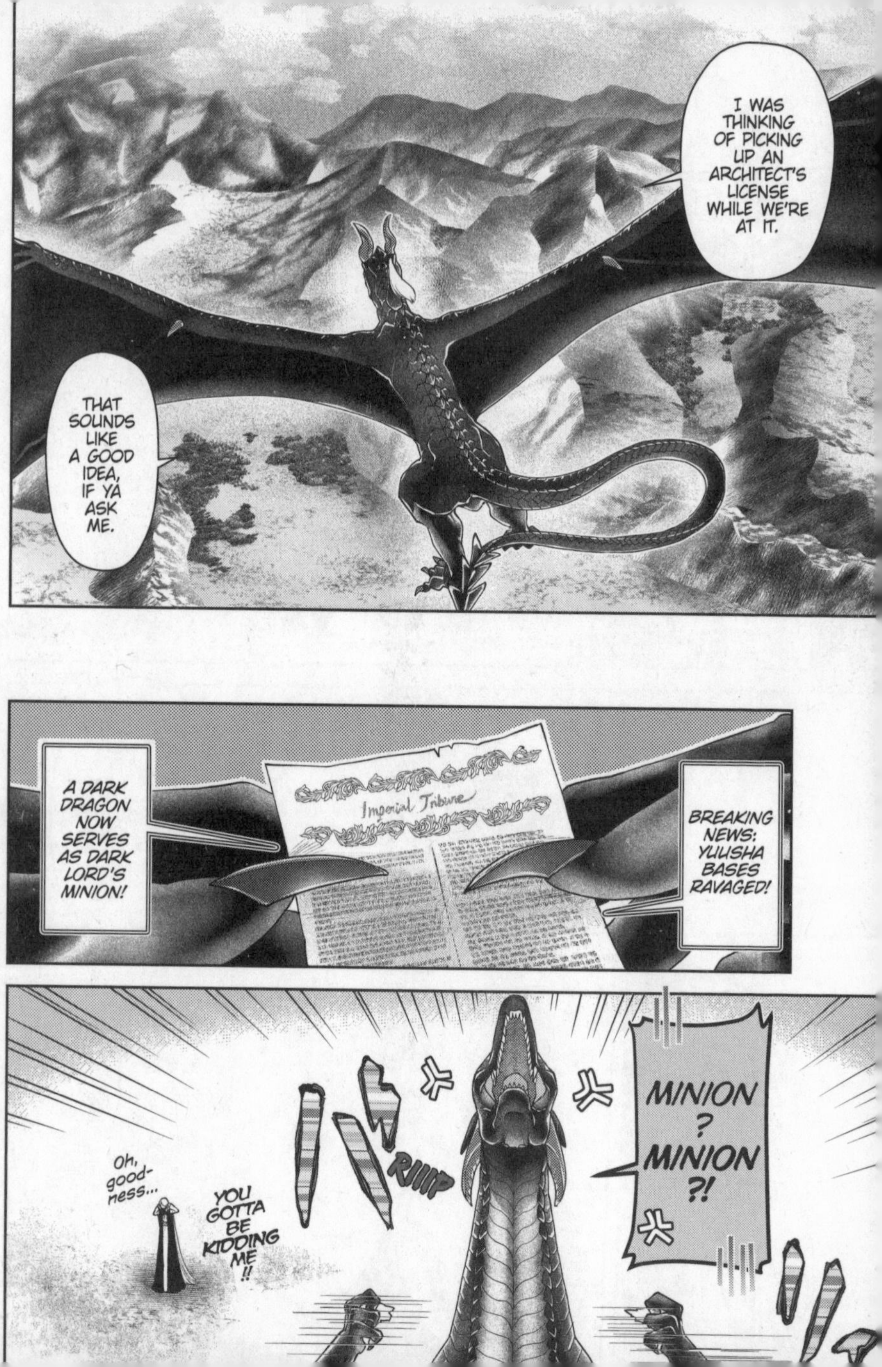
I WAS THINKING OF PICKING UP AN ARCHITECT'S LICENSE WHILE WE'RE AT IT.
THAT SOUNDS LIKE A GOOD IDEA, IF YA ASK ME.
BREAKING NEWS: YUUSHA BASES RAVAGED!
Imperial Tribune
A DARK DRAGON NOW SERVES AS DARK LORD'S MINION!
MINION? MINION?!
RIIIP
YOU GOTTA BE KIDDING ME!!
Oh, goodness...

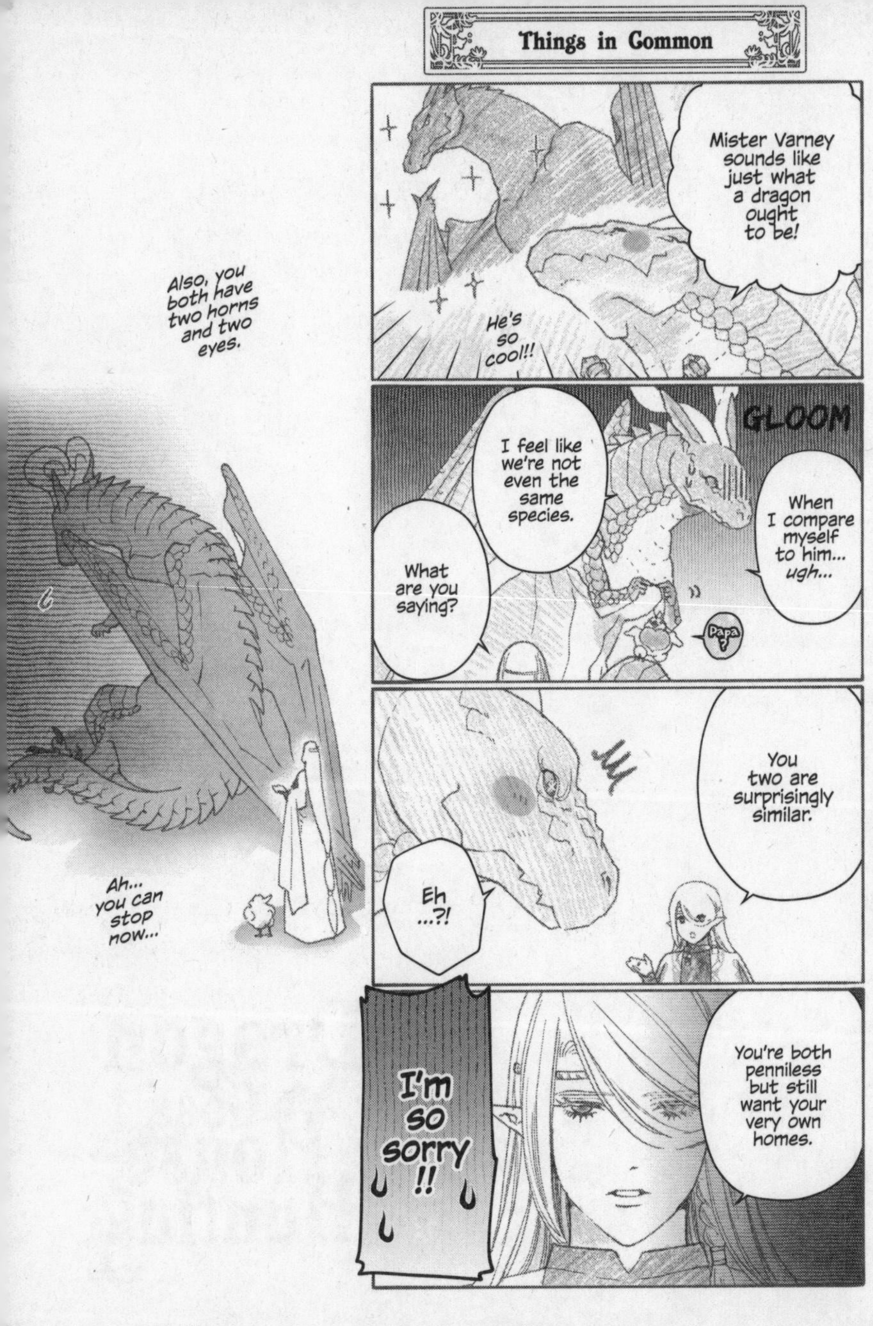
Things in Common
Mister Varney sounds like just what a dragon ought to be!
He's so cool!!
GLOOM
When I compare myself to him... ugh...
I feel like we're not even the same species.
What are you saying?
Papa?
You two are surprisingly similar.
Eh ...?!
You're both penniless but still want your very own homes.
I'm so sorry!!
Also, you both have two horns and two eyes.
Ah... you can stop now...

Dragon Goes House-Hunting

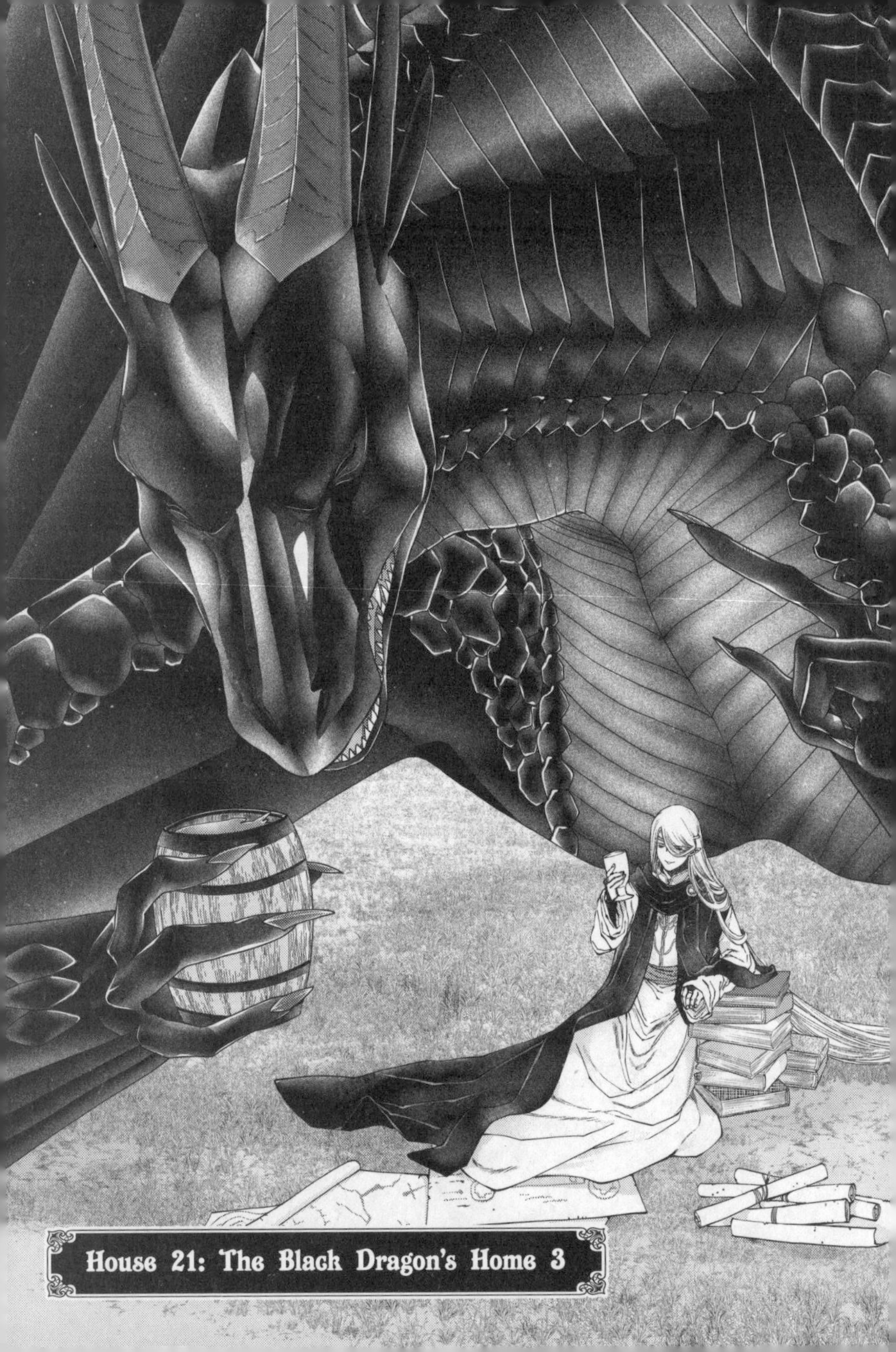

House 21: The Black Dragon's Home 3

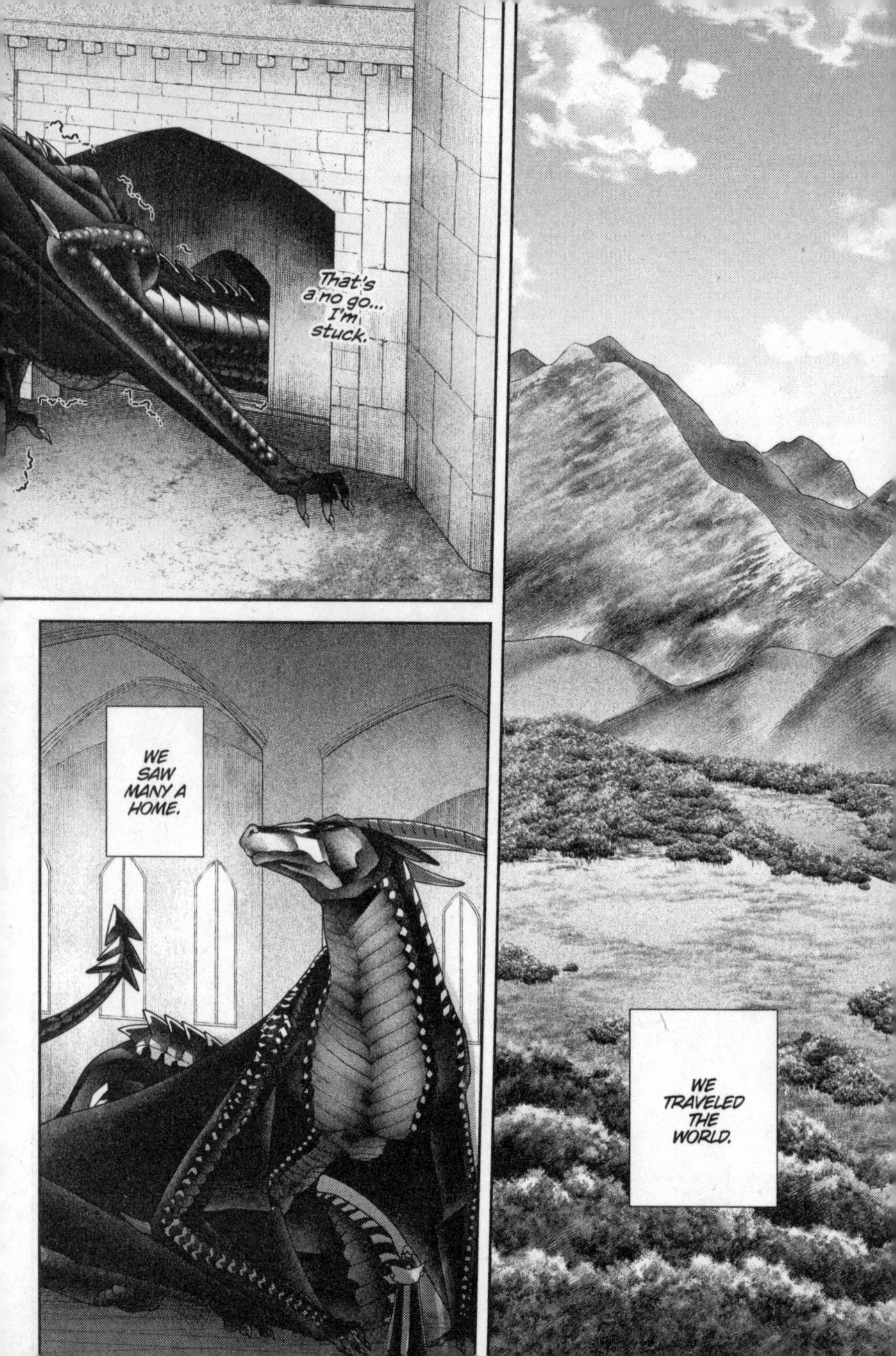
WE TRAVELED THE WORLD.
That's a no go... I'm stuck.
WE SAW MANY A HOME.

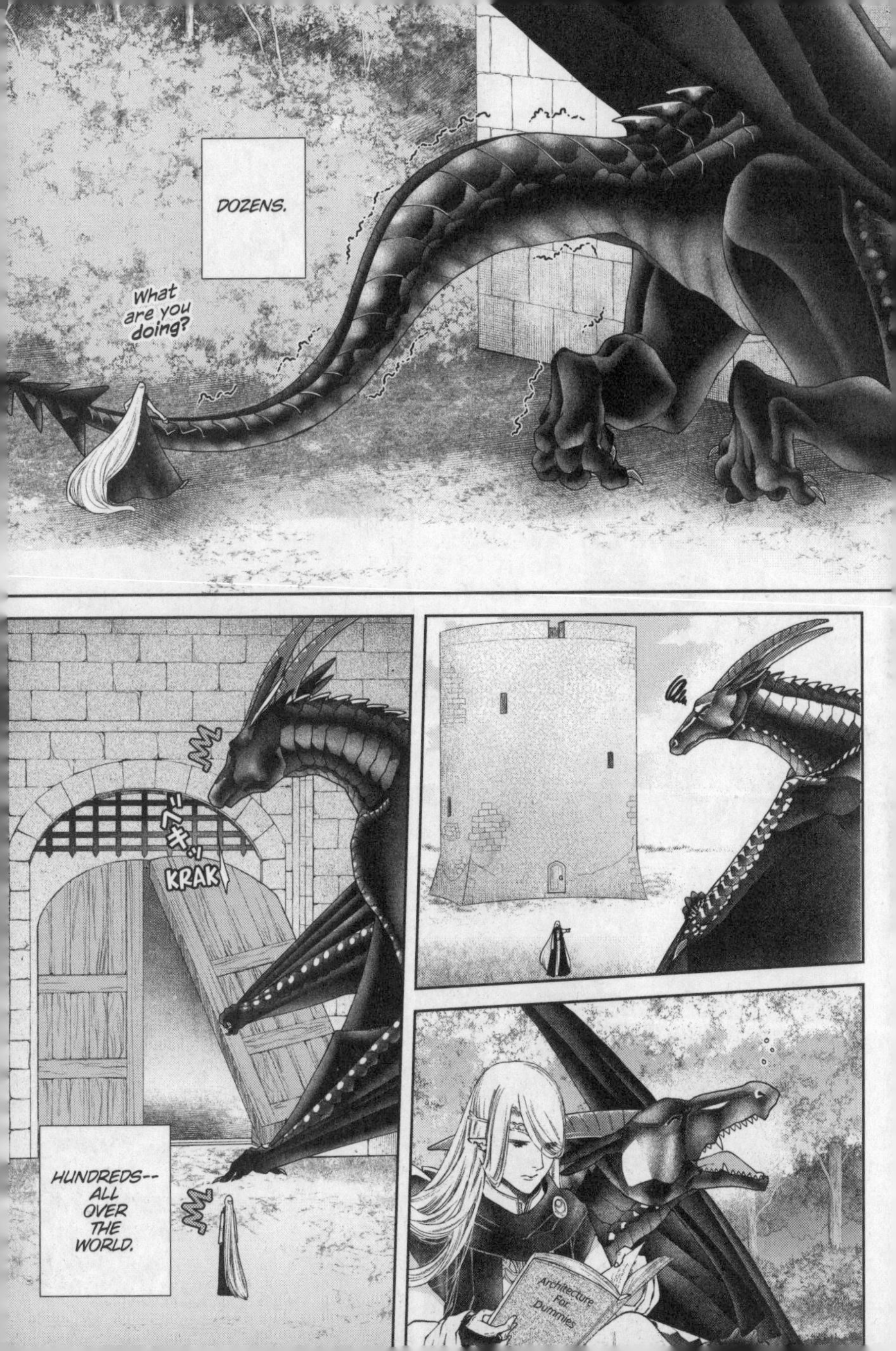
DOZENS.
What are you doing?
Architecture For Dummies
KRAK
HUNDREDS--ALL OVER THE WORLD.

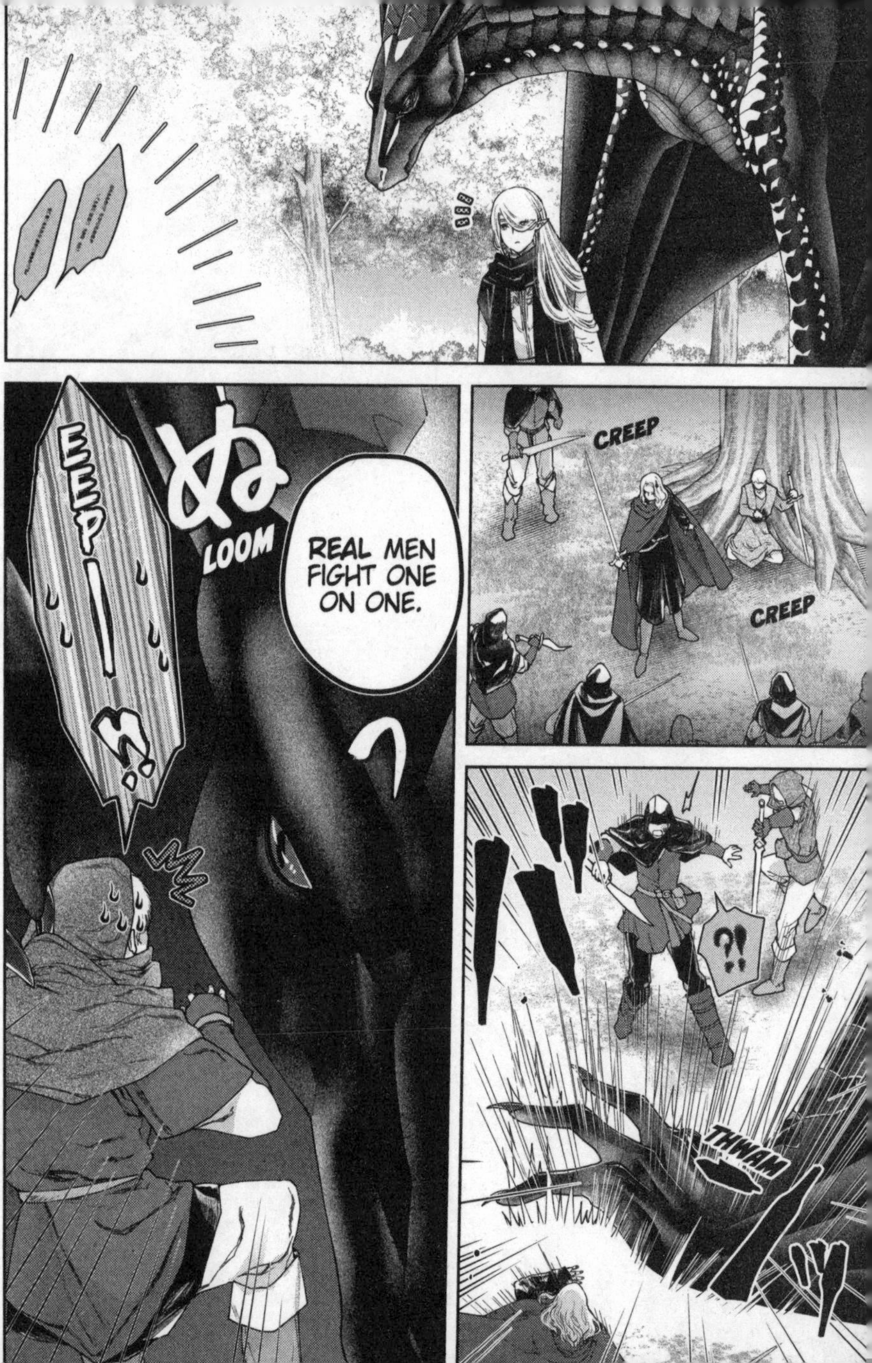
CREEP
CREEP
REAL MEN FIGHT ONE ON ONE.
ぬ
LOOM
EEP!!
THWAM
?!

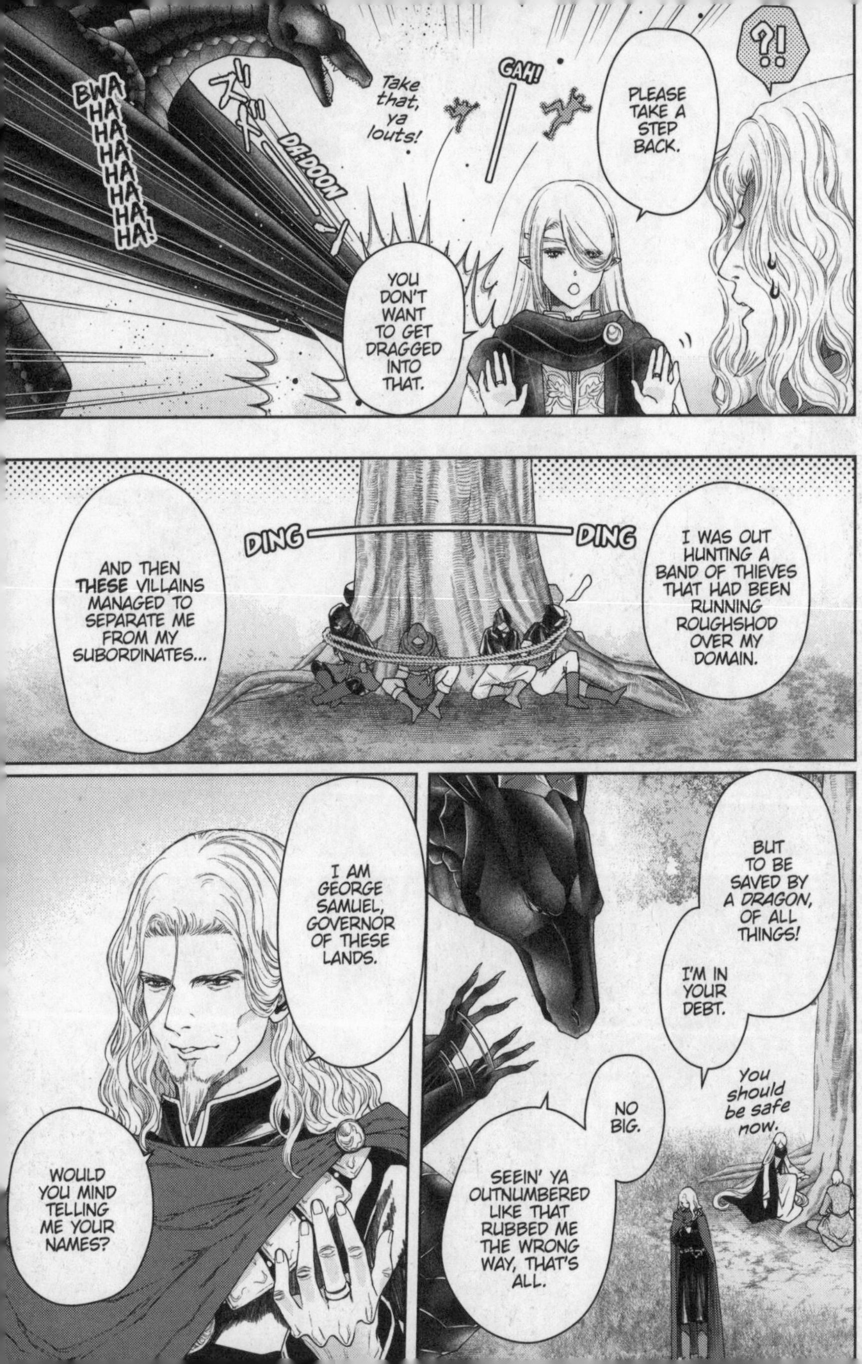
?!
PLEASE TAKE A STEP BACK.
YOU DON'T WANT TO GET DRAGGED INTO THAT.
GAH!
Take that, ya louts!
DA-DOON
BWA HA HA HA HA HA HA HA!
I WAS OUT HUNTING A BAND OF THIEVES THAT HAD BEEN RUNNING ROUGHSHOD OVER MY DOMAIN.
DING
DING
AND THEN THESE VILLAINS MANAGED TO SEPARATE ME FROM MY SUBORDINATES...
You should be safe now.
BUT TO BE SAVED BY A DRAGON, OF ALL THINGS!
I'M IN YOUR DEBT.
NO BIG.
SEEIN' YA OUTNUMBERED LIKE THAT RUBBED ME THE WRONG WAY, THAT'S ALL.
I AM GEORGE SAMUEL, GOVERNOR OF THESE LANDS.
WOULD YOU MIND TELLING ME YOUR NAMES?

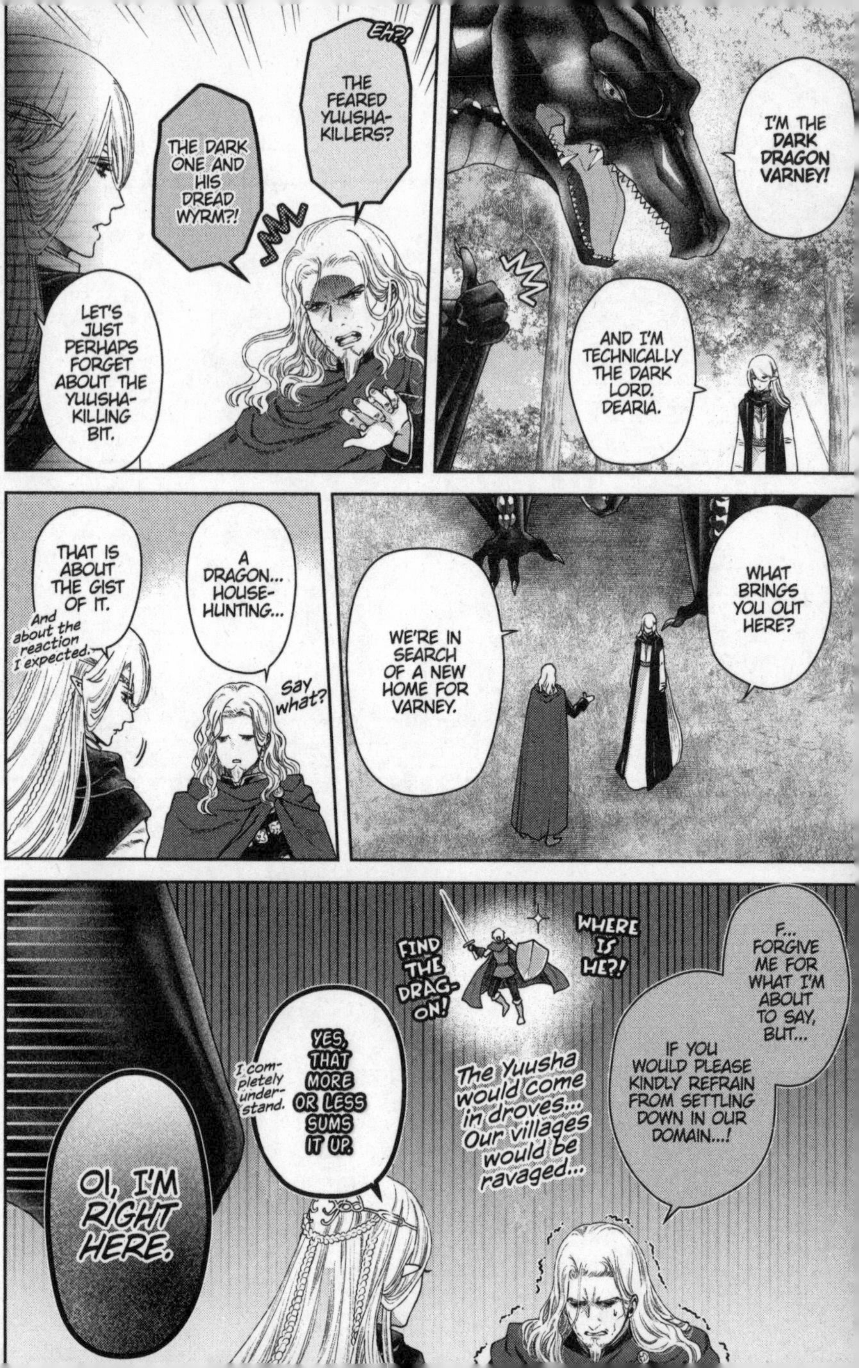
I'M THE DARK DRAGON VARNEY!
AND I'M TECHNICALLY THE DARK LORD. DEARIA.
EH?!
THE FEARED YUUSHA-KILLERS?
THE DARK ONE AND HIS DREAD WYRM?!
LET'S JUST PERHAPS FORGET ABOUT THE YUUSHA-KILLING BIT.
WHAT BRINGS YOU OUT HERE?
WE'RE IN SEARCH OF A NEW HOME FOR VARNEY.
A DRAGON... HOUSE-HUNTING...
Say what?
THAT IS ABOUT THE GIST OF IT.
And about the reaction I expected.
F... FORGIVE ME FOR WHAT I'M ABOUT TO SAY, BUT...
IF YOU WOULD PLEASE KINDLY REFRAIN FROM SETTLING DOWN IN OUR DOMAIN...!
WHERE IS HE?!
FIND THE DRAG-ON!
The Yuusha would come in droves... Our villages would be ravaged...
YES, THAT MORE OR LESS SUMS IT UP.
I completely understand.
OI, I'M RIGHT HERE.

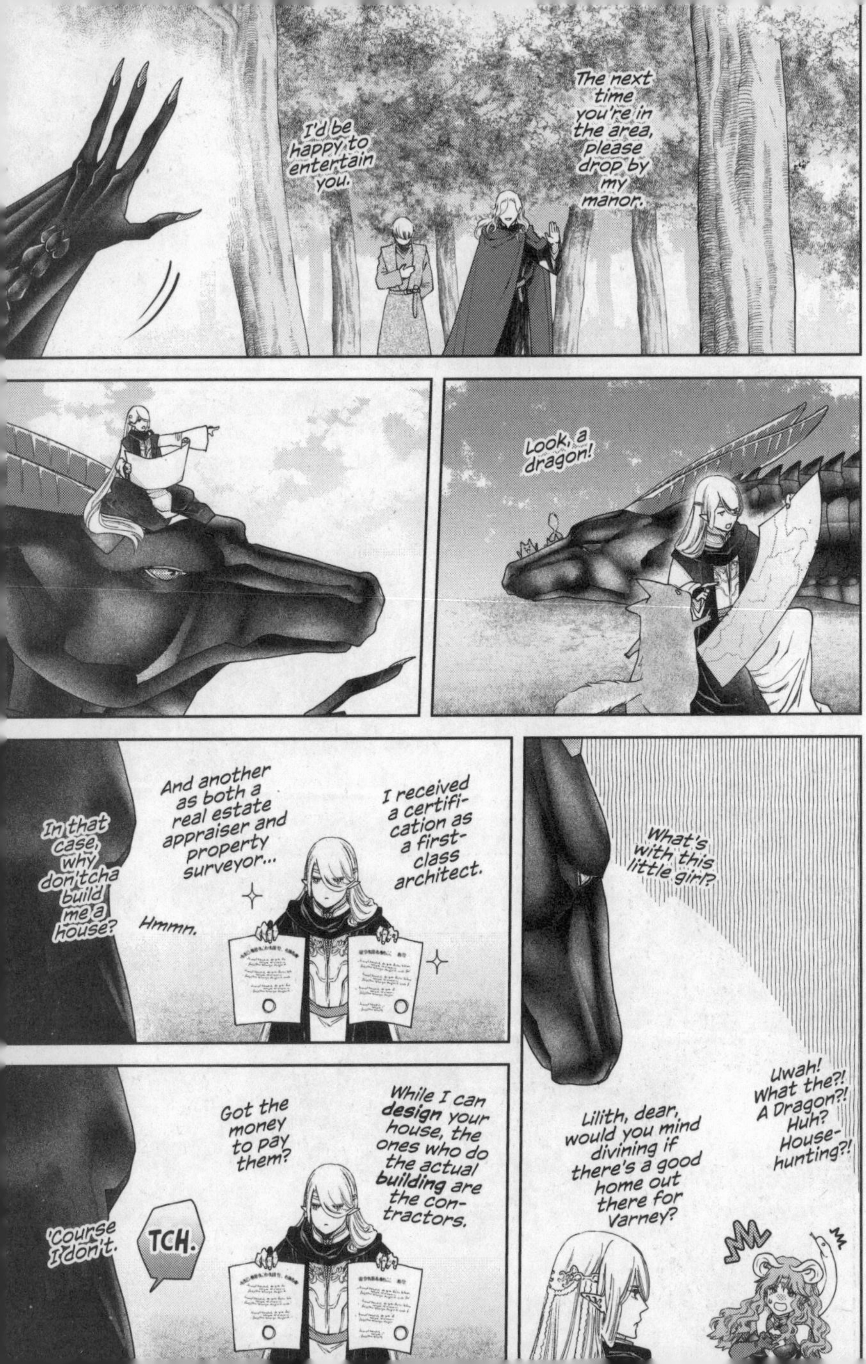

The next time you're in the area, please drop by my manor.
I'd be happy to entertain you.
Look, a dragon!
What's with this little girl!?
I received a certification as a first-class architect.
And another as both a real estate appraiser and property surveyor...
In that case, why don'tcha build me a house?
Hmmn.
While I can **design** your house, the ones who do the actual **building** are the contractors.
Got the money to pay them?
'Course I don't.
TCH.
Uwah! What the?! A Dragon?! Huh? House-hunting?!
Lilith, dear, would you mind divining if there's a good home out there for Varney?

THEY'RE PROBABLY JUST STARTING OUT.

LOOK OVER THERE.

IT'S A GROUP O' YUUSHA IN CHEAP GEAR.

!

OH? PICKING ON THE WEAK, ARE WE NOW?

HOW'S ABOUT WE GIVE 'EM A LITTLE SCARE, EH?

NO, NO, THIS IS JUST A SURPRISE.

SMIRK

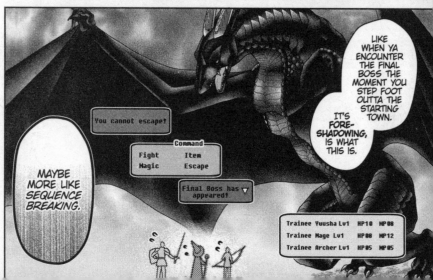

LIKE WHEN YA ENCOUNTER THE FINAL BOSS THE MOMENT YOU STEP FOOT OUTTA THE STARTING TOWN.

IT'S FORE-SHADOWING, IS WHAT THIS IS.

You cannot escape!

Command
Fight   Item
Magic   Escape

Final Boss has appeared!

MAYBE MORE LIKE SEQUENCE BREAKING.

Trainee Yuusha Lv1	HP 10	MP 08
Trainee Mage Lv1	HP 08	MP 12
Trainee Archer Lv1	HP 05	MP 05

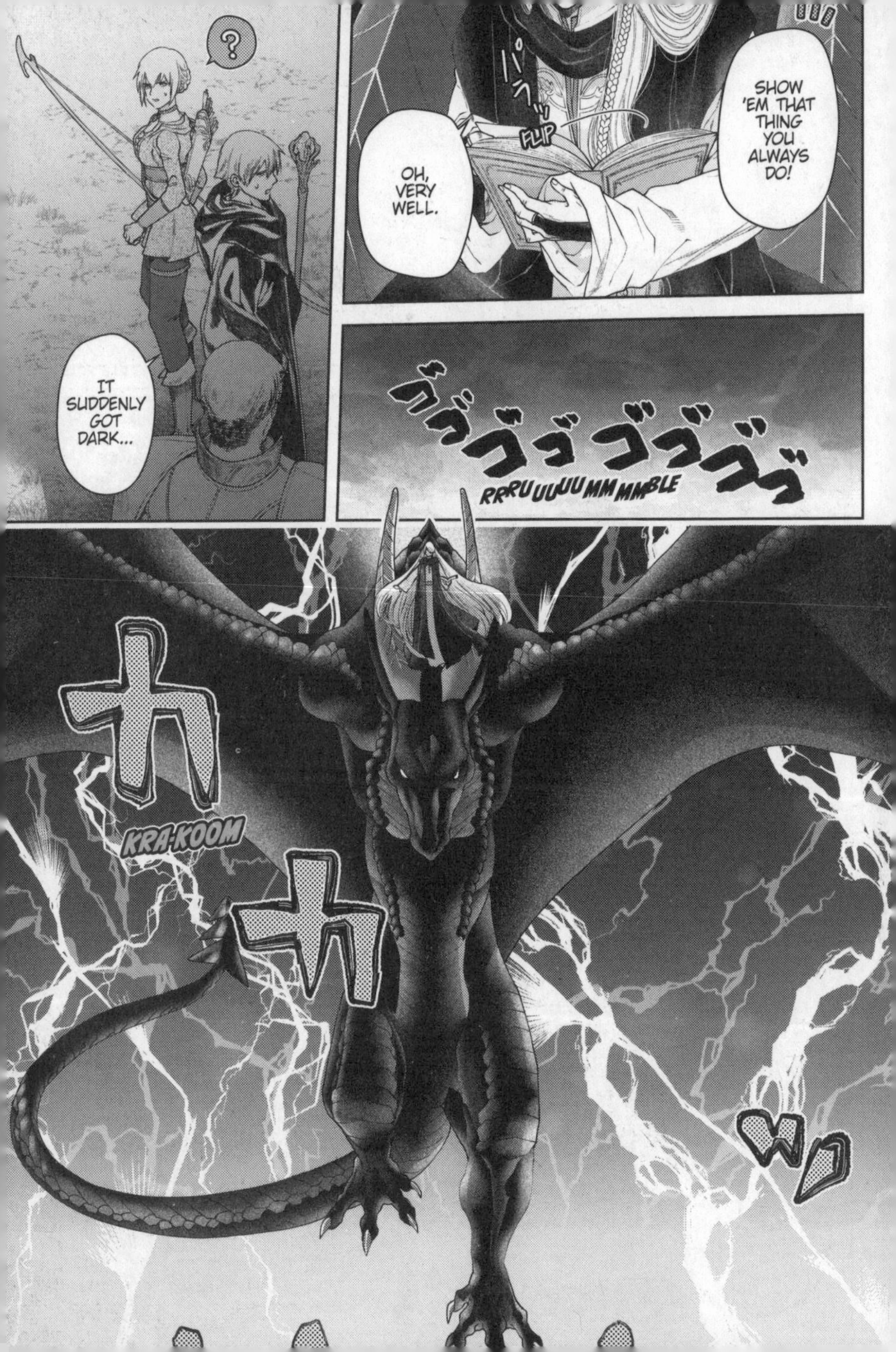
SHOW 'EM THAT THING YOU ALWAYS DO!
FLIP
OH, VERY WELL.
?
IT SUDDENLY GOT DARK...
RRRUUUUMMMMBLE
KRA-KOOM

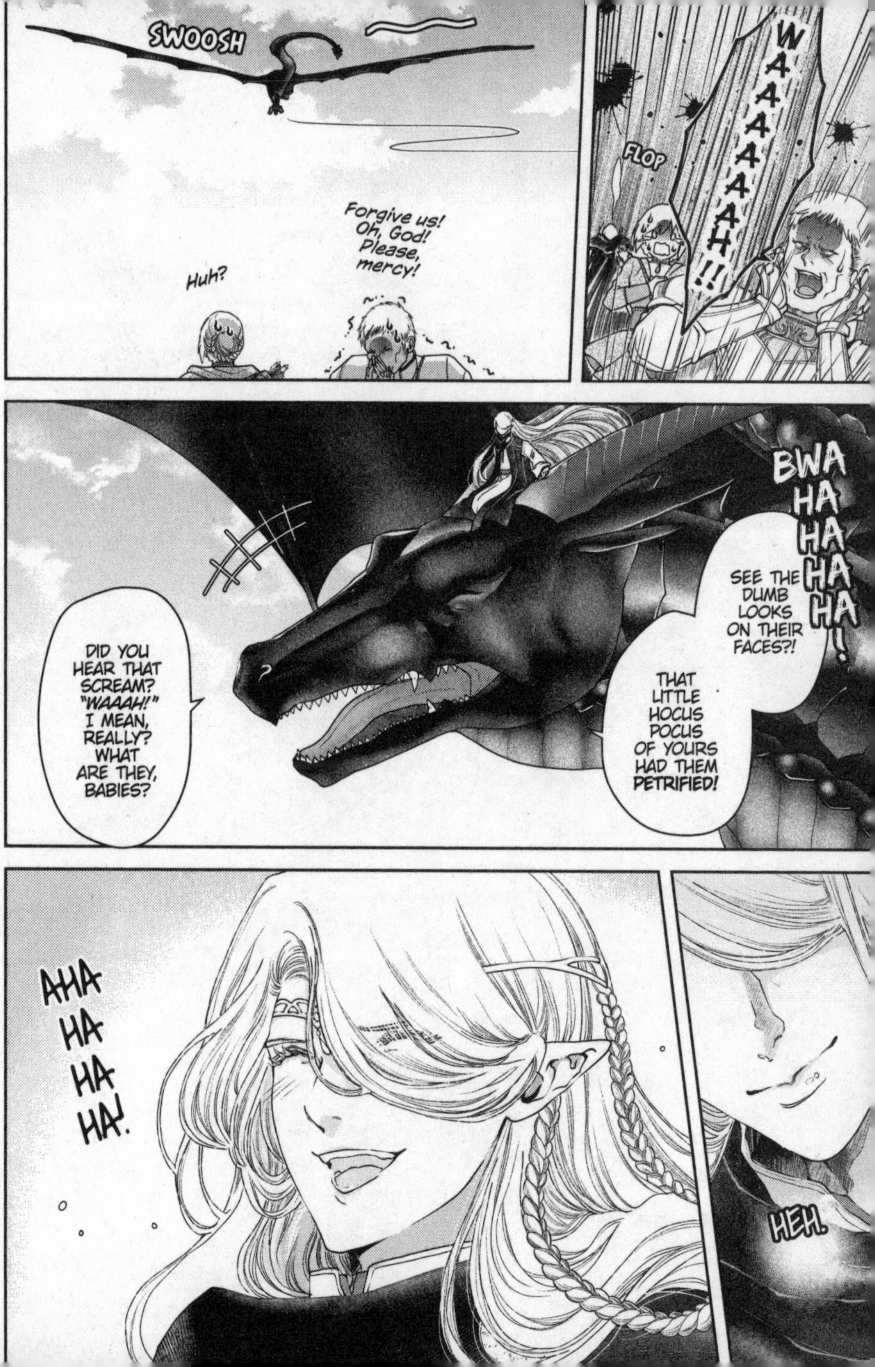
WAAAAAAAAH!!
FLOP
SWOOSH
Forgive us! Oh, God! Please, mercy!
Huh?
BWA HA HA HA HA!
SEE THE DUMB LOOKS ON THEIR FACES?!
THAT LITTLE HOCUS POCUS OF YOURS HAD THEM PETRIFIED!
DID YOU HEAR THAT SCREAM? "WAAAH!" I MEAN, REALLY? WHAT ARE THEY, BABIES?
HEH.
AHAHA HA HA HA.

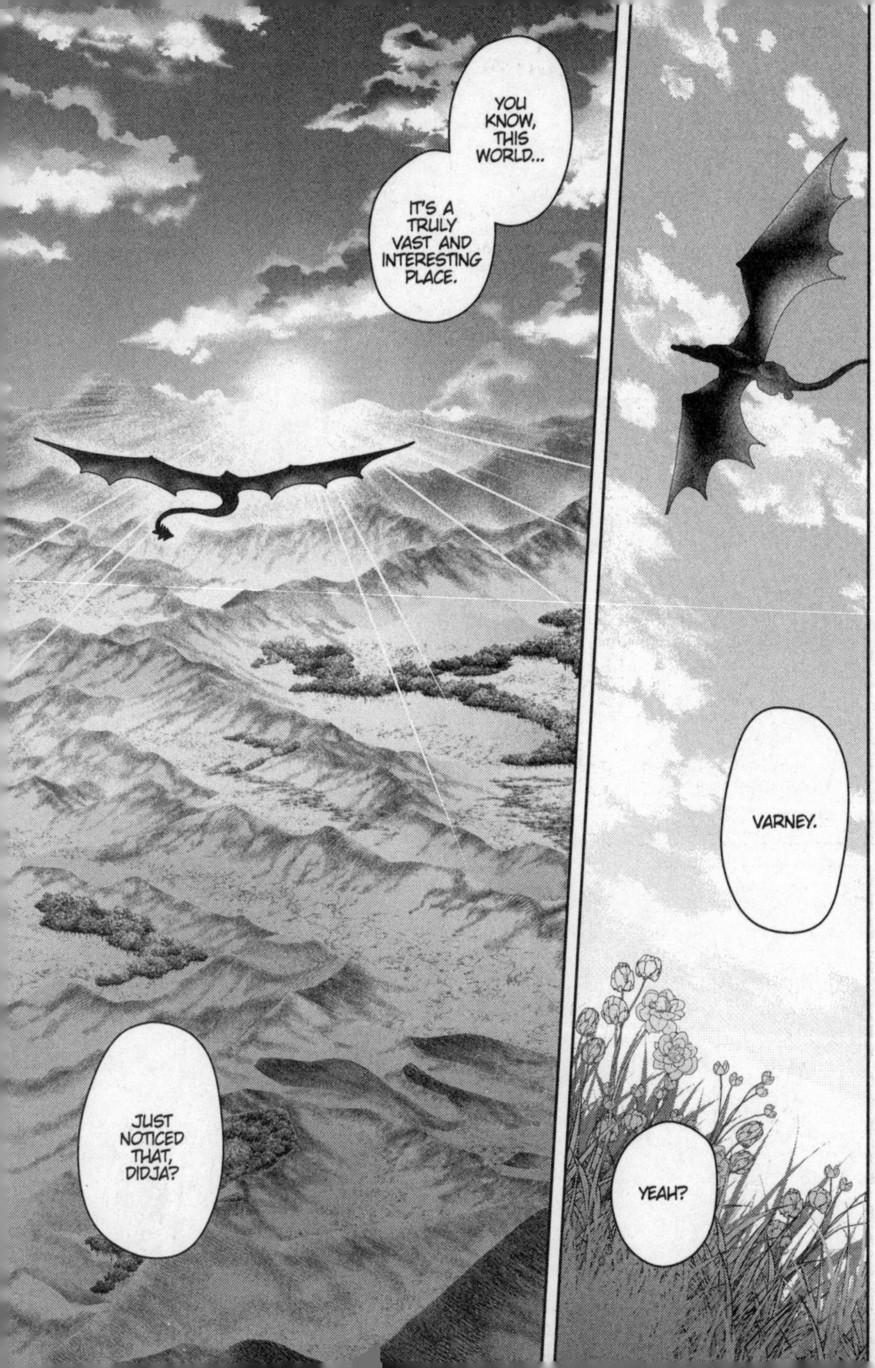
VARNEY.
YEAH?
YOU KNOW, THIS WORLD...
IT'S A TRULY VAST AND INTERESTING PLACE.
JUST NOTICED THAT, DIDJA?

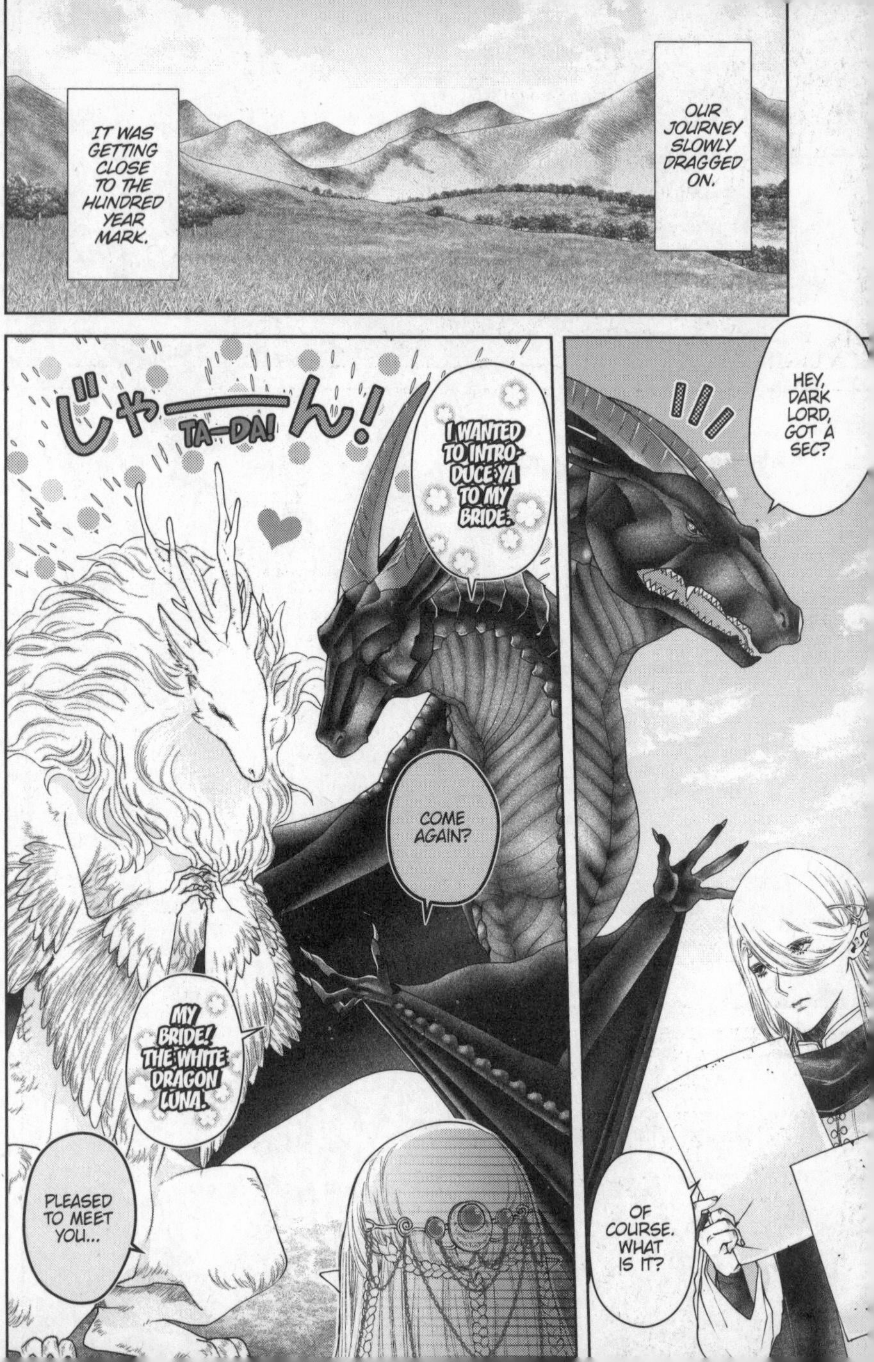
OUR JOURNEY SLOWLY DRAGGED ON.
IT WAS GETTING CLOSE TO THE HUNDRED YEAR MARK.
HEY, DARK LORD, GOT A SEC?
OF COURSE. WHAT IS IT?
じゃーーん!
TA-DA!
I WANTED TO INTRO-DUCE YA TO MY BRIDE.
COME AGAIN?
MY BRIDE! THE WHITE DRAGON LUNA.
PLEASED TO MEET YOU...

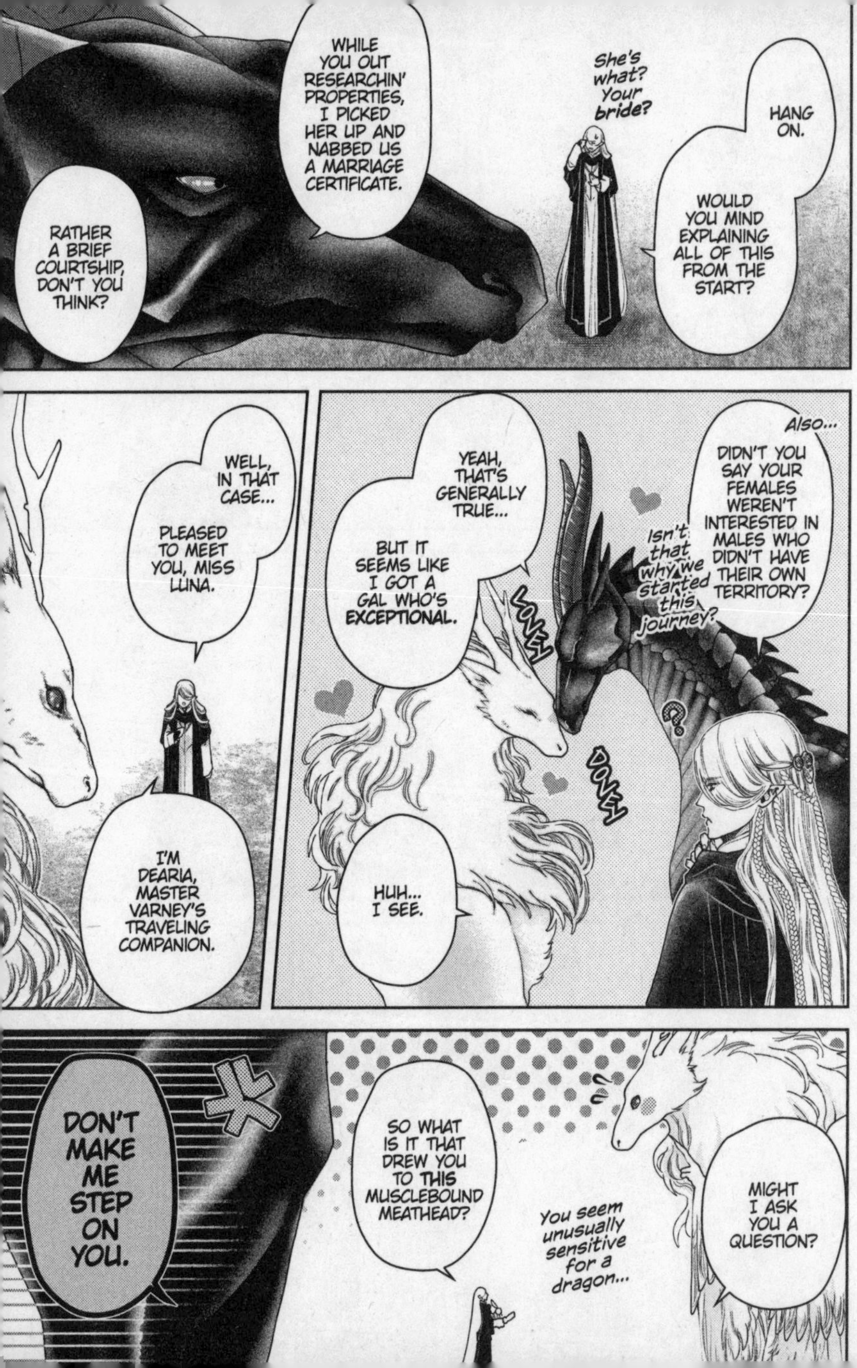

She's what? Your bride?
HANG ON.
WOULD YOU MIND EXPLAINING ALL OF THIS FROM THE START?
WHILE YOU OUT RESEARCHIN' PROPERTIES, I PICKED HER UP AND NABBED US A MARRIAGE CERTIFICATE.
RATHER A BRIEF COURTSHIP, DON'T YOU THINK?
Also...
DIDN'T YOU SAY YOUR FEMALES WEREN'T INTERESTED IN MALES WHO DIDN'T HAVE THEIR OWN TERRITORY?
Isn't that why we started this journey?
YEAH, THAT'S GENERALLY TRUE...
BUT IT SEEMS LIKE I GOT A GAL WHO'S EXCEPTIONAL.
LOVEY
DOVEY
HUH... I SEE.
WELL, IN THAT CASE...
PLEASED TO MEET YOU, MISS LUNA.
I'M DEARIA, MASTER VARNEY'S TRAVELING COMPANION.
MIGHT I ASK YOU A QUESTION?
You seem unusually sensitive for a dragon...
SO WHAT IS IT THAT DREW YOU TO THIS MUSCLEBOUND MEATHEAD?
DON'T MAKE ME STEP ON YOU.

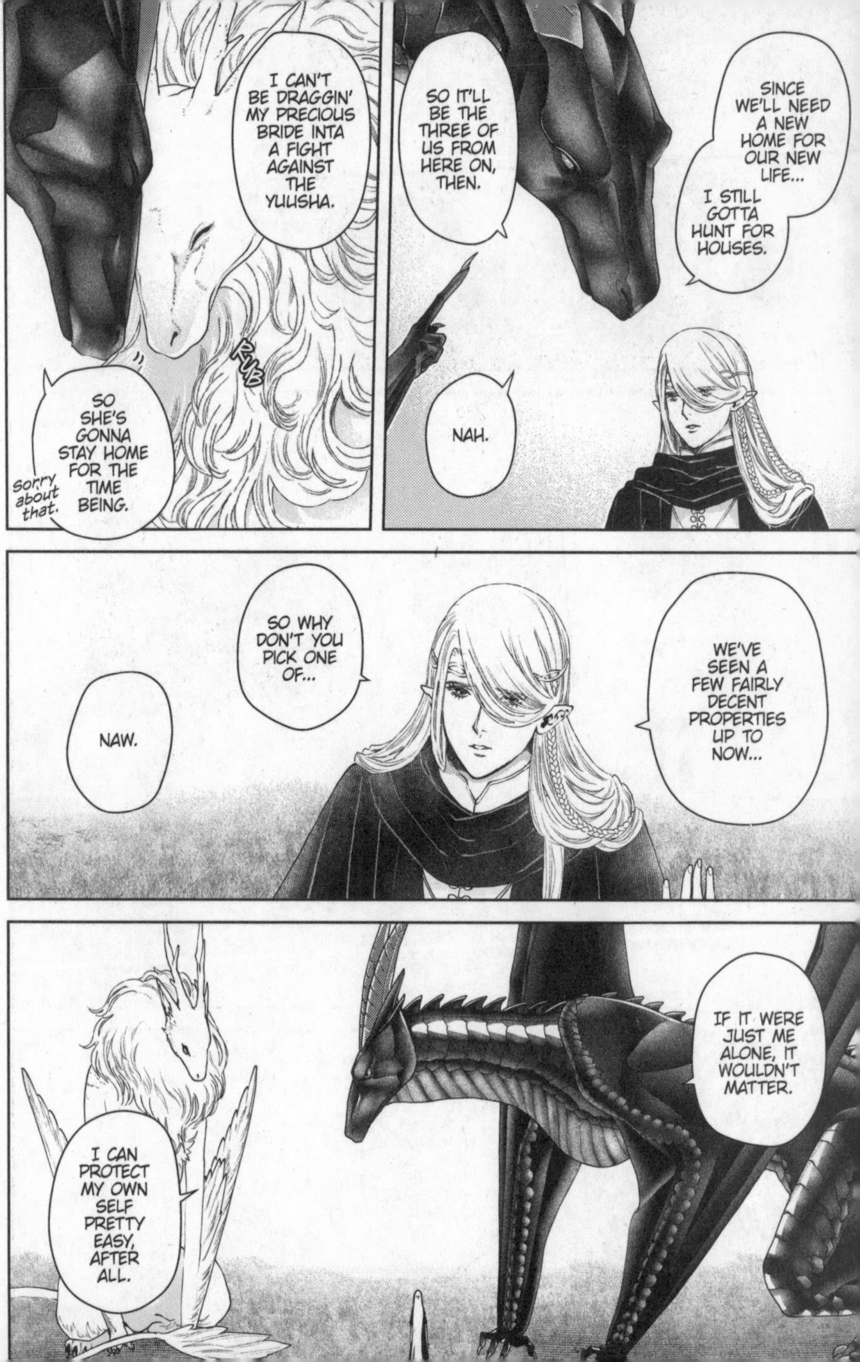
SINCE WE'LL NEED A NEW HOME FOR OUR NEW LIFE...
I STILL GOTTA HUNT FOR HOUSES.
SO IT'LL BE THE THREE OF US FROM HERE ON, THEN.
NAH.
I CAN'T BE DRAGGIN' MY PRECIOUS BRIDE INTA A FIGHT AGAINST THE YUUSHA.
RUB
SO SHE'S GONNA STAY HOME FOR THE TIME BEING.
Sorry about that.
WE'VE SEEN A FEW FAIRLY DECENT PROPERTIES UP TO NOW...
SO WHY DON'T YOU PICK ONE OF...
NAW.
IF IT WERE JUST ME ALONE, IT WOULDN'T MATTER.
I CAN PROTECT MY OWN SELF PRETTY EASY, AFTER ALL.

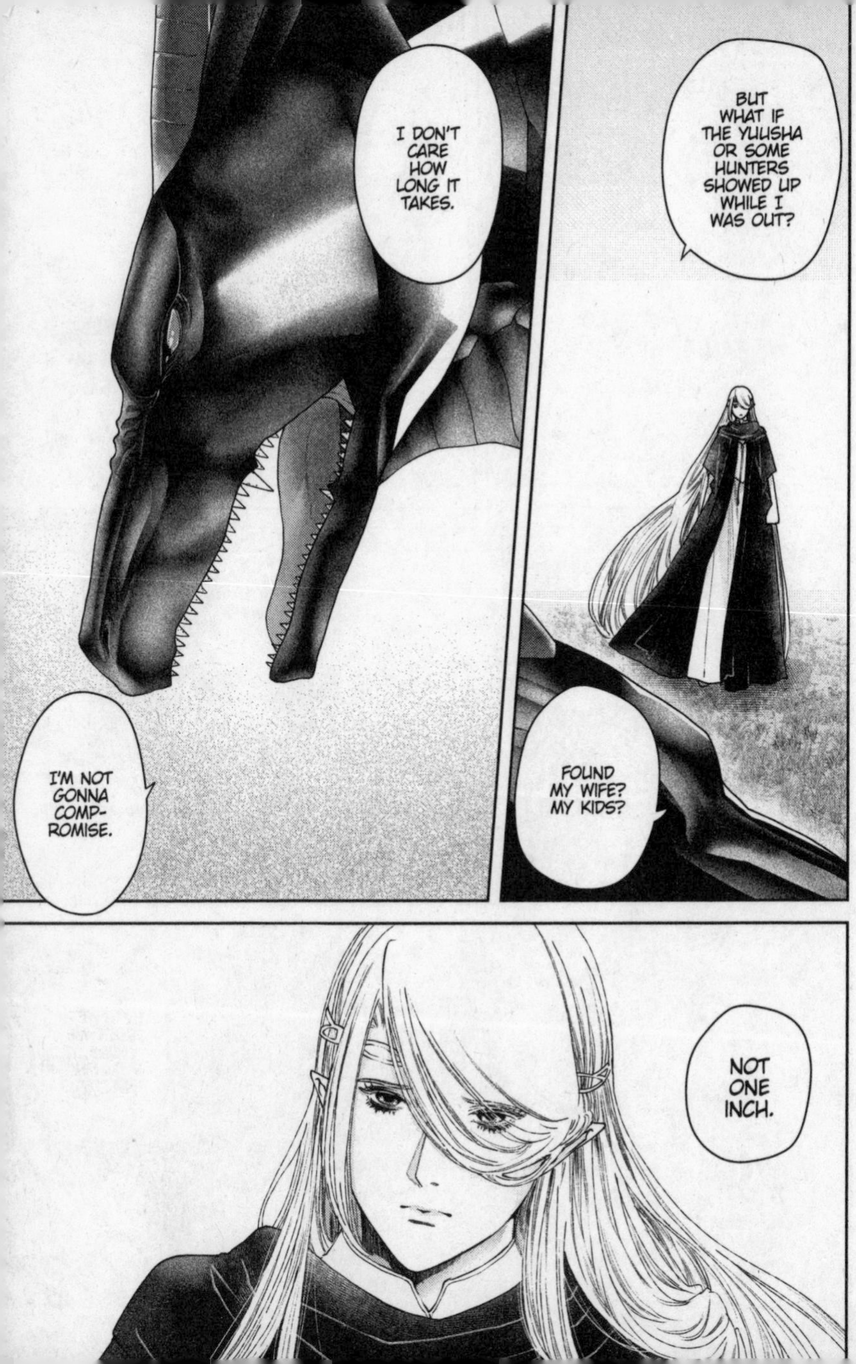
BUT WHAT IF THE YUUSHA OR SOME HUNTERS SHOWED UP WHILE I WAS OUT?
FOUND MY WIFE? MY KIDS?
I DON'T CARE HOW LONG IT TAKES.
I'M NOT GONNA COMP-ROMISE.
NOT ONE INCH.

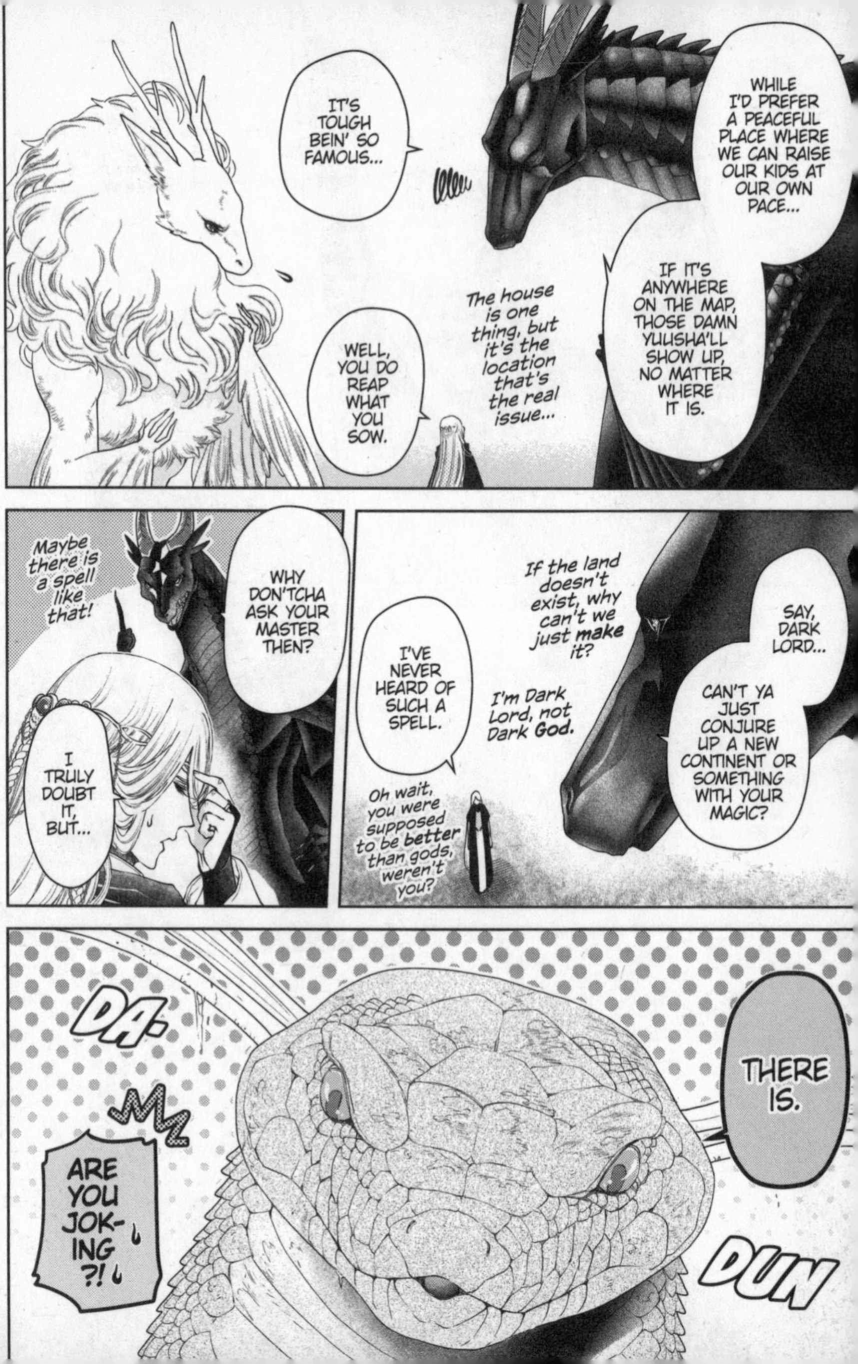
WHILE I'D PREFER A PEACEFUL PLACE WHERE WE CAN RAISE OUR KIDS AT OUR OWN PACE...
IF IT'S ANYWHERE ON THE MAP, THOSE DAMN YUUSHA'LL SHOW UP, NO MATTER WHERE IT IS.
The house is one thing, but it's the location that's the real issue...
IT'S TOUGH BEIN' SO FAMOUS...
WELL, YOU DO REAP WHAT YOU SOW.
SAY, DARK LORD...
CAN'T YA JUST CONJURE UP A NEW CONTINENT OR SOMETHING WITH YOUR MAGIC?
If the land doesn't exist, why can't we just make it?
I'm Dark Lord, not Dark God.
I'VE NEVER HEARD OF SUCH A SPELL.
Oh wait, you were supposed to be better than gods, weren't you?
WHY DON'TCHA ASK YOUR MASTER THEN?
Maybe there is a spell like that!
I TRULY DOUBT IT, BUT...
THERE IS.
DUN
DA-
ARE YOU JOK-ING?!

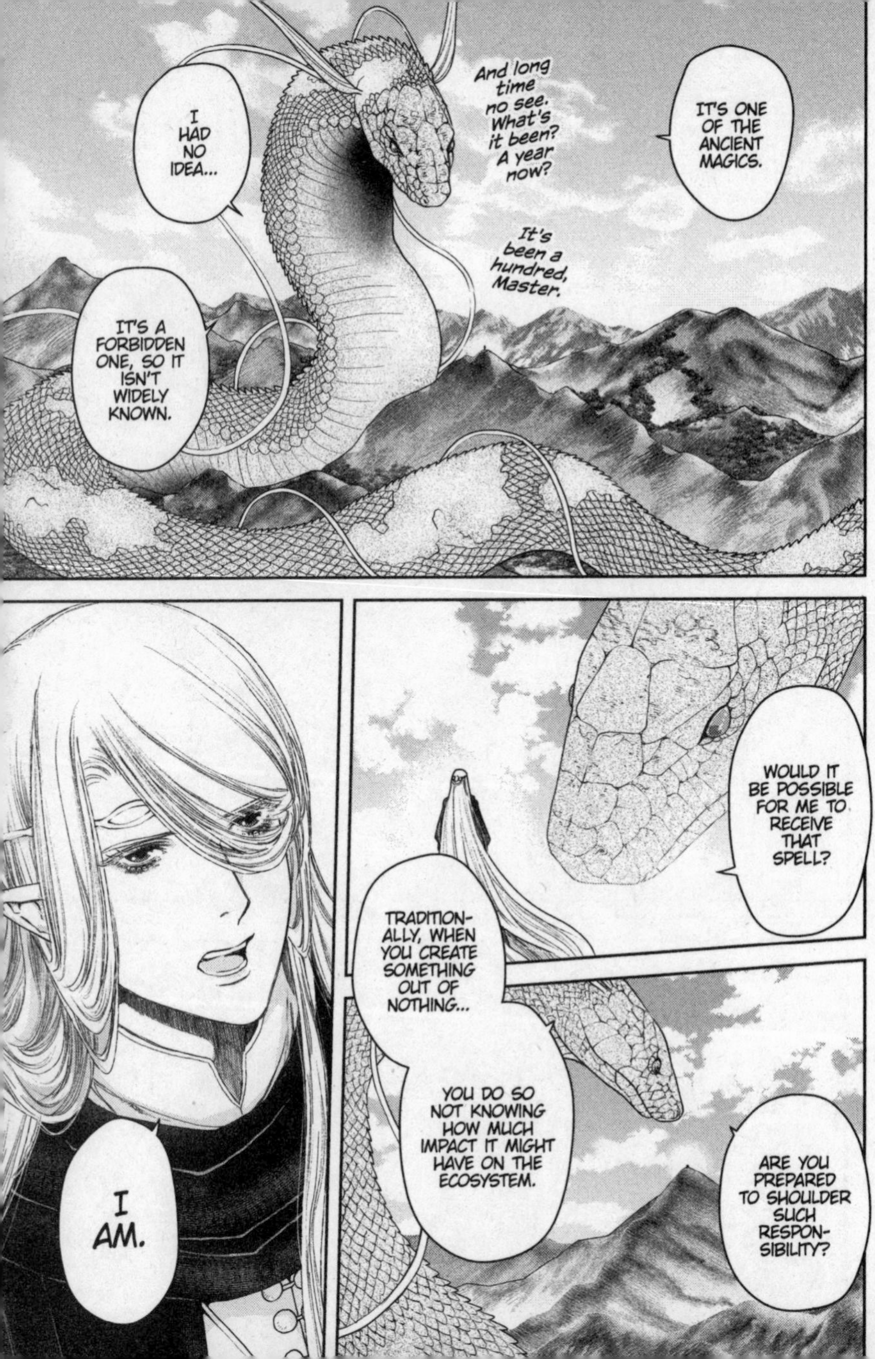
IT'S ONE OF THE ANCIENT MAGICS.
And long time no see. What's it been? A year now?
It's been a hundred, Master.
I HAD NO IDEA...
IT'S A FORBIDDEN ONE, SO IT ISN'T WIDELY KNOWN.
WOULD IT BE POSSIBLE FOR ME TO RECEIVE THAT SPELL?
TRADITION-ALLY, WHEN YOU CREATE SOMETHING OUT OF NOTHING...
YOU DO SO NOT KNOWING HOW MUCH IMPACT IT MIGHT HAVE ON THE ECOSYSTEM.
ARE YOU PREPARED TO SHOULDER SUCH RESPON-SIBILITY?
I AM.

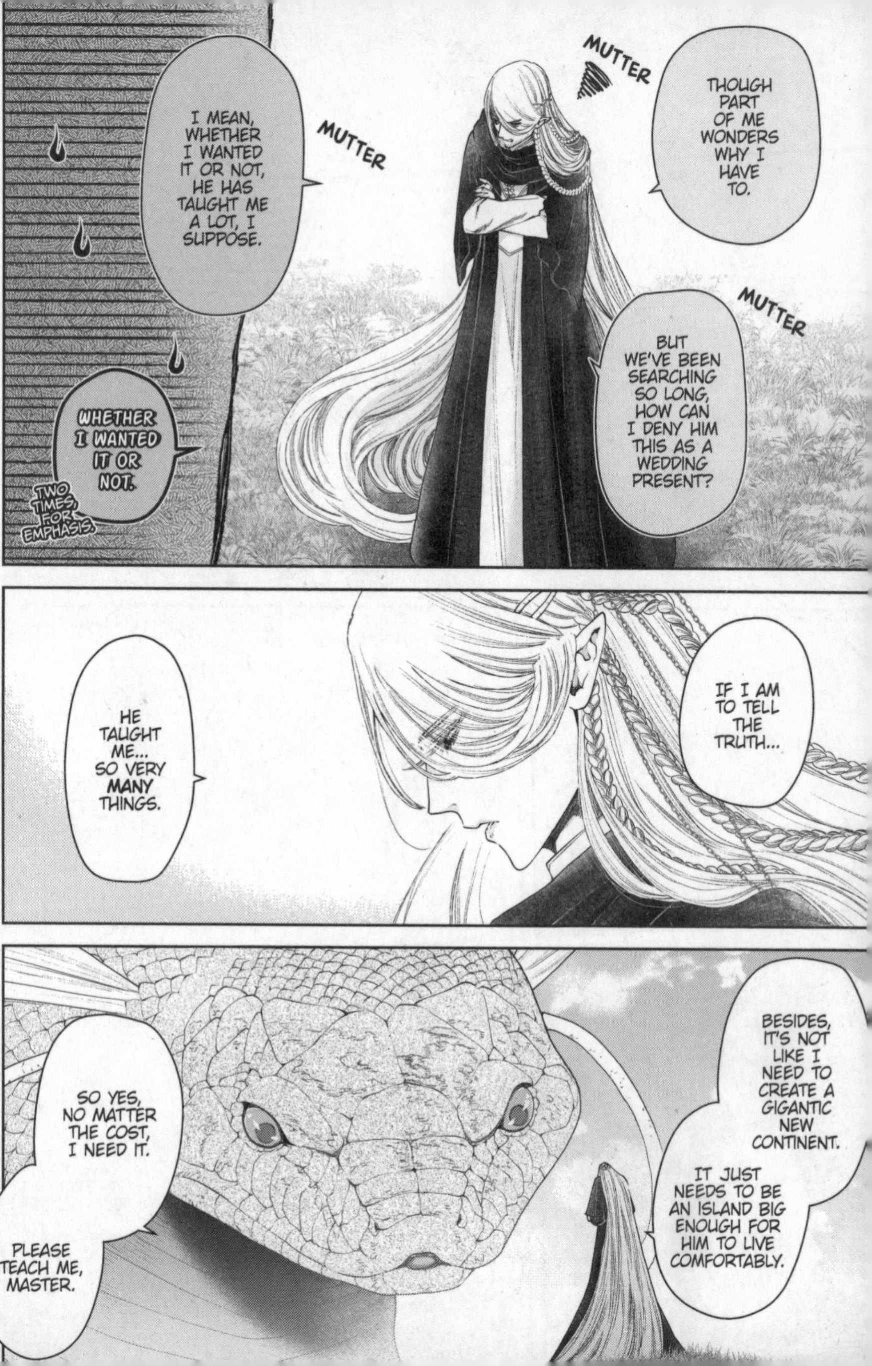
MUTTER
THOUGH PART OF ME WONDERS WHY I HAVE TO.
MUTTER
BUT WE'VE BEEN SEARCHING SO LONG, HOW CAN I DENY HIM THIS AS A WEDDING PRESENT?
MUTTER
I MEAN, WHETHER I WANTED IT OR NOT, HE HAS TAUGHT ME A LOT, I SUPPOSE.
WHETHER I WANTED IT OR NOT.
TWO TIMES, FOR EMPHASIS.
IF I AM TO TELL THE TRUTH...
HE TAUGHT ME... SO VERY MANY THINGS.
BESIDES, IT'S NOT LIKE I NEED TO CREATE A GIGANTIC NEW CONTINENT.
IT JUST NEEDS TO BE AN ISLAND BIG ENOUGH FOR HIM TO LIVE COMFORTABLY.
SO YES, NO MATTER THE COST, I NEED IT.
PLEASE TEACH ME, MASTER.

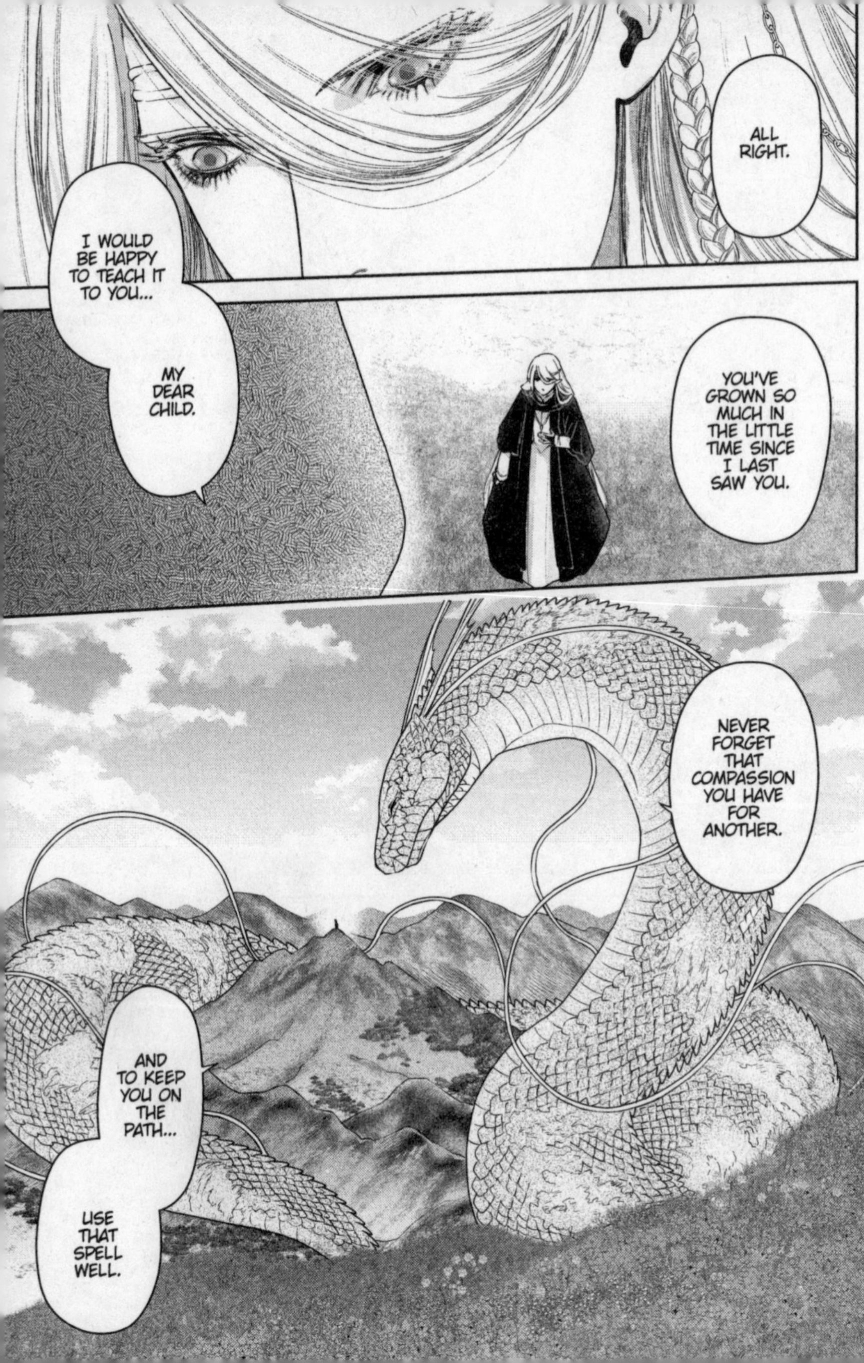

ALL RIGHT.
I WOULD BE HAPPY TO TEACH IT TO YOU...
MY DEAR CHILD.
YOU'VE GROWN SO MUCH IN THE LITTLE TIME SINCE I LAST SAW YOU.
NEVER FORGET THAT COMPASSION YOU HAVE FOR ANOTHER.
AND TO KEEP YOU ON THE PATH...
USE THAT SPELL WELL.

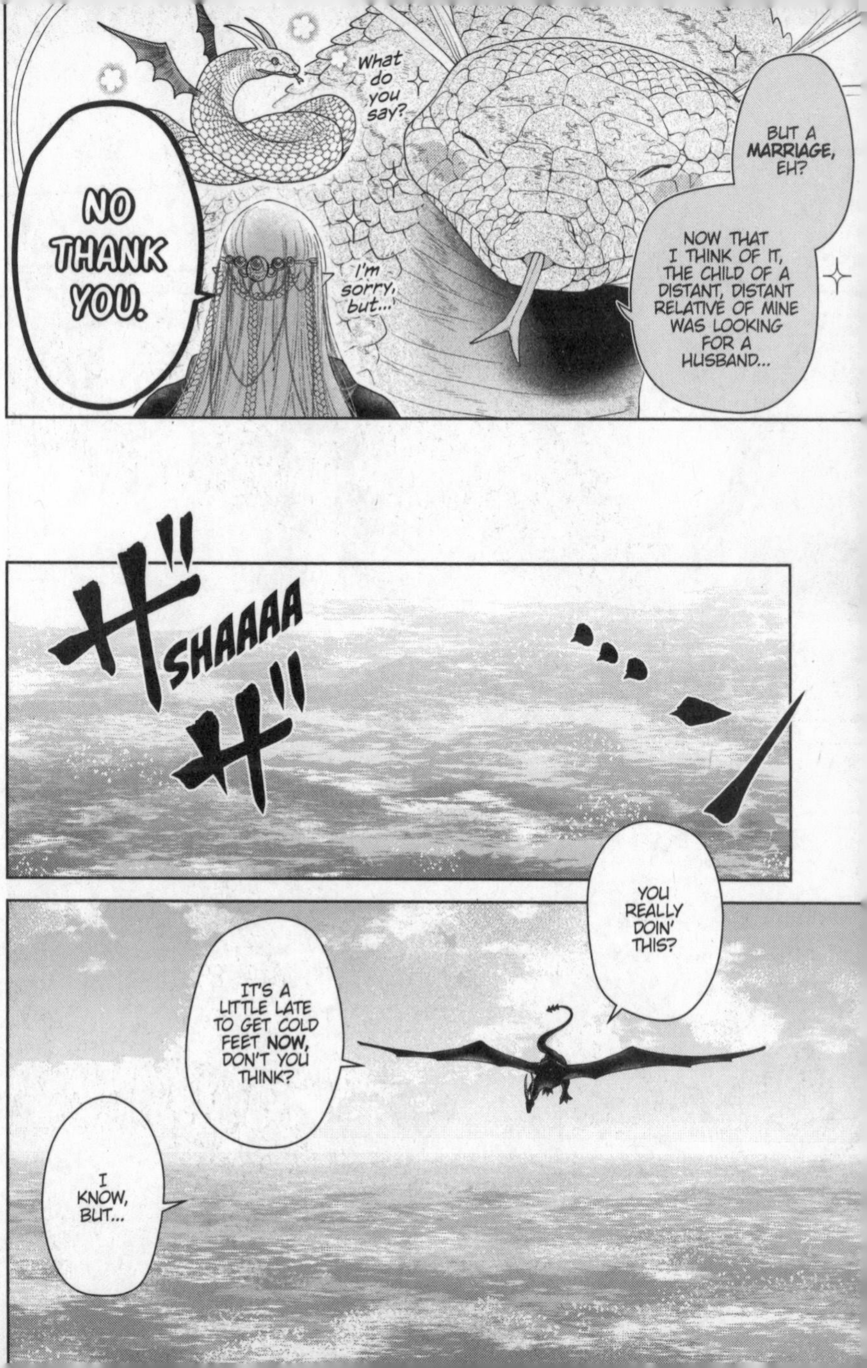
BUT A MARRIAGE, EH?
NOW THAT I THINK OF IT, THE CHILD OF A DISTANT, DISTANT RELATIVE OF MINE WAS LOOKING FOR A HUSBAND...
What do you say?
I'm sorry, but...
NO THANK YOU.
SHAAAA
YOU REALLY DOIN' THIS?
IT'S A LITTLE LATE TO GET COLD FEET NOW, DON'T YOU THINK?
I KNOW, BUT...

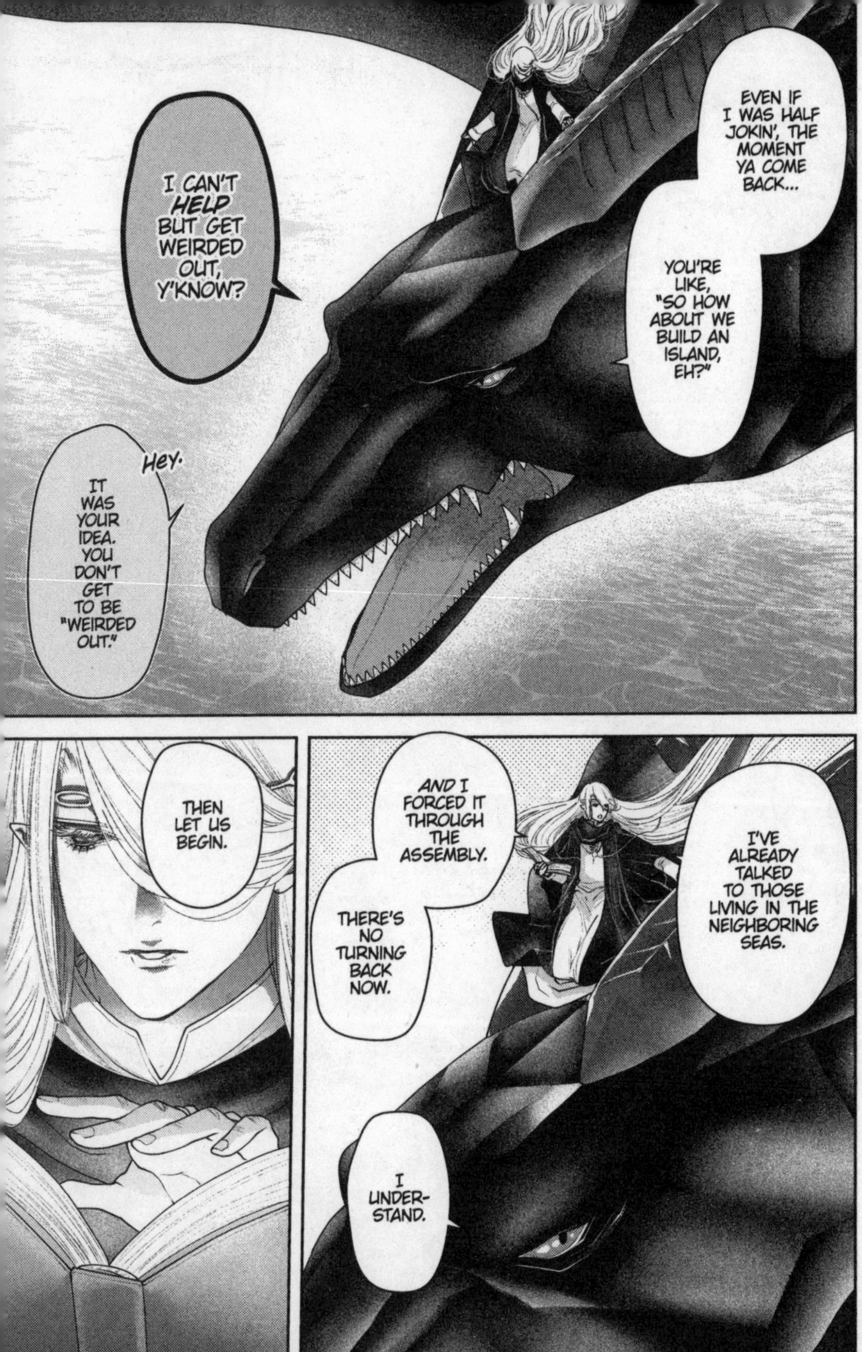
EVEN IF I WAS HALF JOKIN', THE MOMENT YA COME BACK...
YOU'RE LIKE, "SO HOW ABOUT WE BUILD AN ISLAND, EH?"
I CAN'T HELP BUT GET WEIRDED OUT, Y'KNOW?
Hey.
IT WAS YOUR IDEA. YOU DON'T GET TO BE "WEIRDED OUT."
I'VE ALREADY TALKED TO THOSE LIVING IN THE NEIGHBORING SEAS.
AND I FORCED IT THROUGH THE ASSEMBLY.
THERE'S NO TURNING BACK NOW.
I UNDER-STAND.
THEN LET US BEGIN.

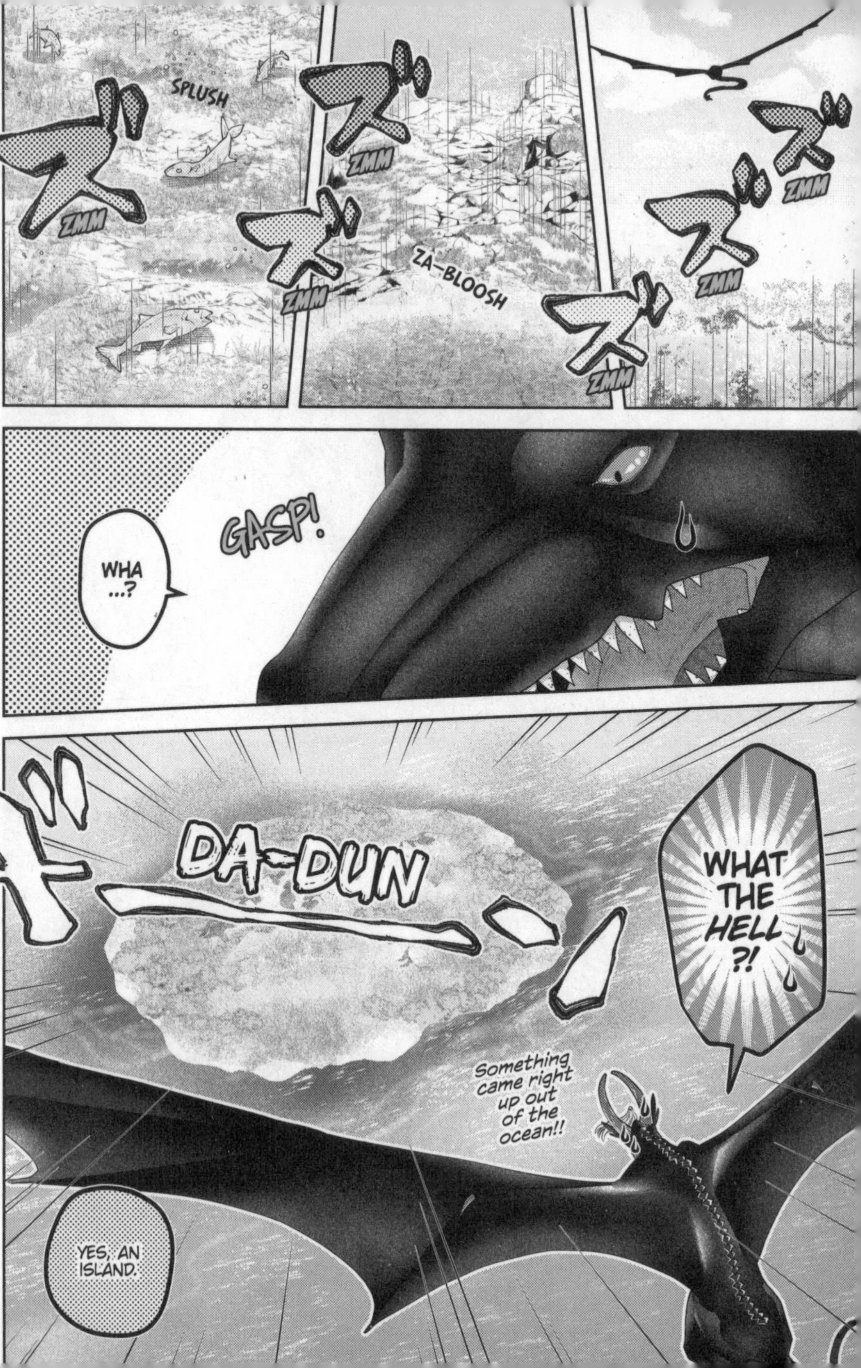
SPLUSH
ZMM
ZMM
ZMM
ZA-BLOOSH
ZMM
ZMM
ZMM
ZMM
GASP!
WHA ...?
DA-DUN
WHAT THE HELL ?!
Something came right up out of the ocean!!
YES, AN ISLAND.

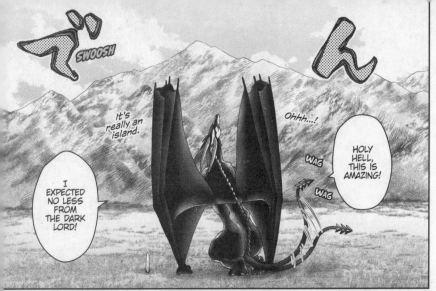

SWOOSH
HOLY HELL, THIS IS AMAZING!
Ohhh...!
WAG
WAG
It's really an island.
I EXPECTED NO LESS FROM THE DARK LORD!
BUT OF COURSE...
CRUMPLE
What happened?!
MP0
It does take quite a bit of magic to use...
So try your best, okay?
I STILL HAVE A WAY TO GO BEFORE I'VE GOT THE POWER OF A TRUE DARK LORD.
DRAINED...
DON'T DIE ON ME NOW. I STILL NEED YA AS BEST MAN, AFTER ALL.
AND I WAS PLANNIN' ON GETTIN' YA TO BE THE ENTERTAIN-MENT. DO US ALL A BELLY DANCE.
PLEASE ASK SOMEONE ELSE. FOR ALL OF IT.
No dancing. And definitely not that kind.

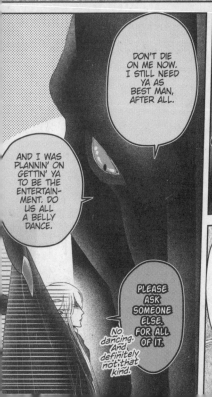

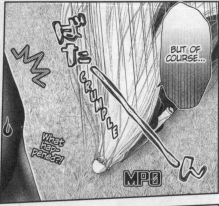

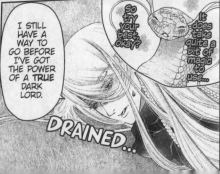

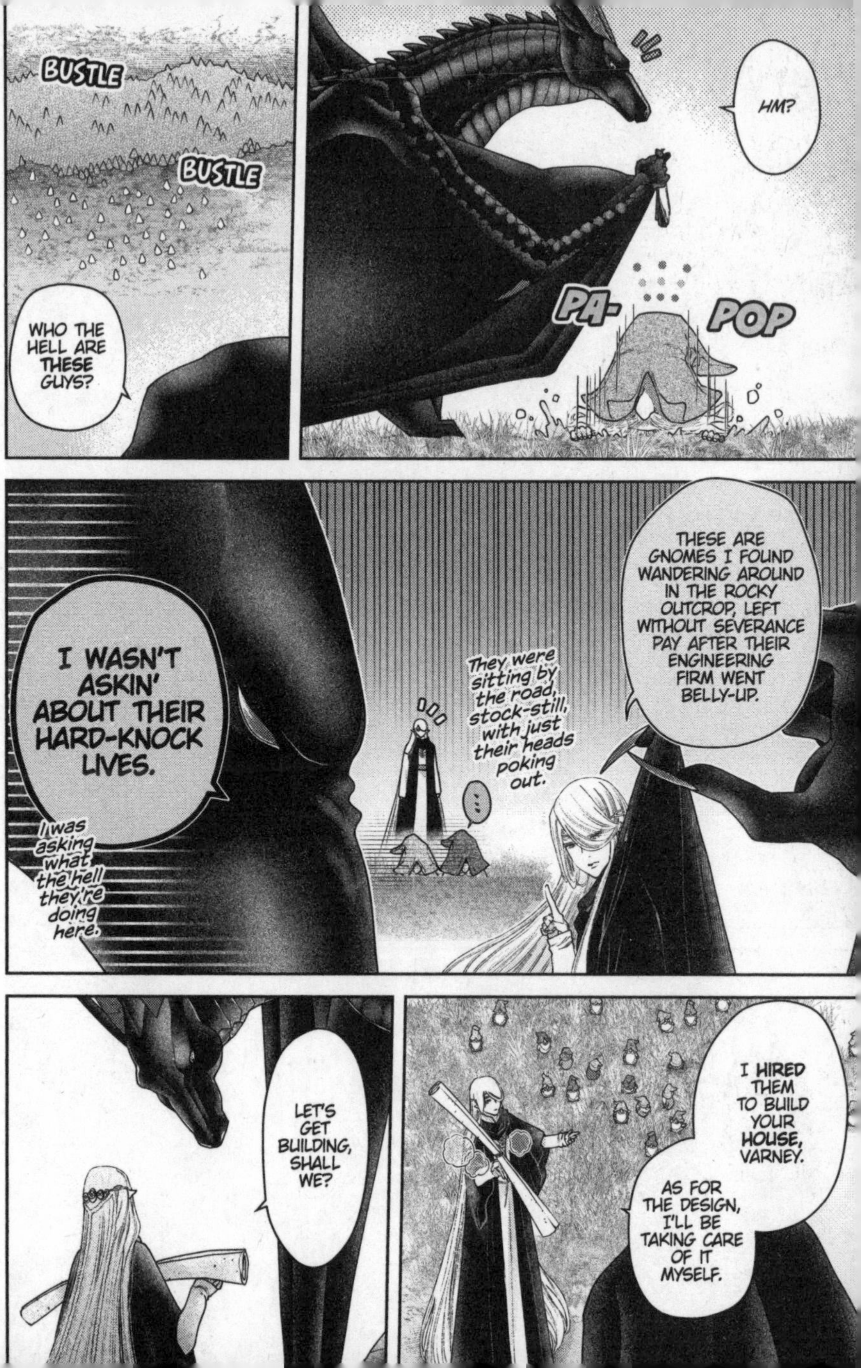
BUSTLE
BUSTLE
WHO THE HELL ARE THESE GUYS?
HM?
PA- POP
I WASN'T ASKIN' ABOUT THEIR HARD-KNOCK LIVES.
I was asking what the hell they're doing here.
They were sitting by the road, stock-still, with just their heads poking out.
THESE ARE GNOMES I FOUND WANDERING AROUND IN THE ROCKY OUTCROP, LEFT WITHOUT SEVERANCE PAY AFTER THEIR ENGINEERING FIRM WENT BELLY-UP.
LET'S GET BUILDING, SHALL WE?
I HIRED THEM TO BUILD YOUR HOUSE, VARNEY.
AS FOR THE DESIGN, I'LL BE TAKING CARE OF IT MYSELF.

A HOUSE BEFITTING THE DARK DRAGON.

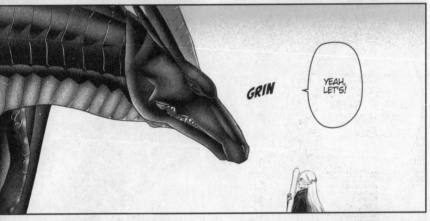

GRIN

YEAH, LET'S!

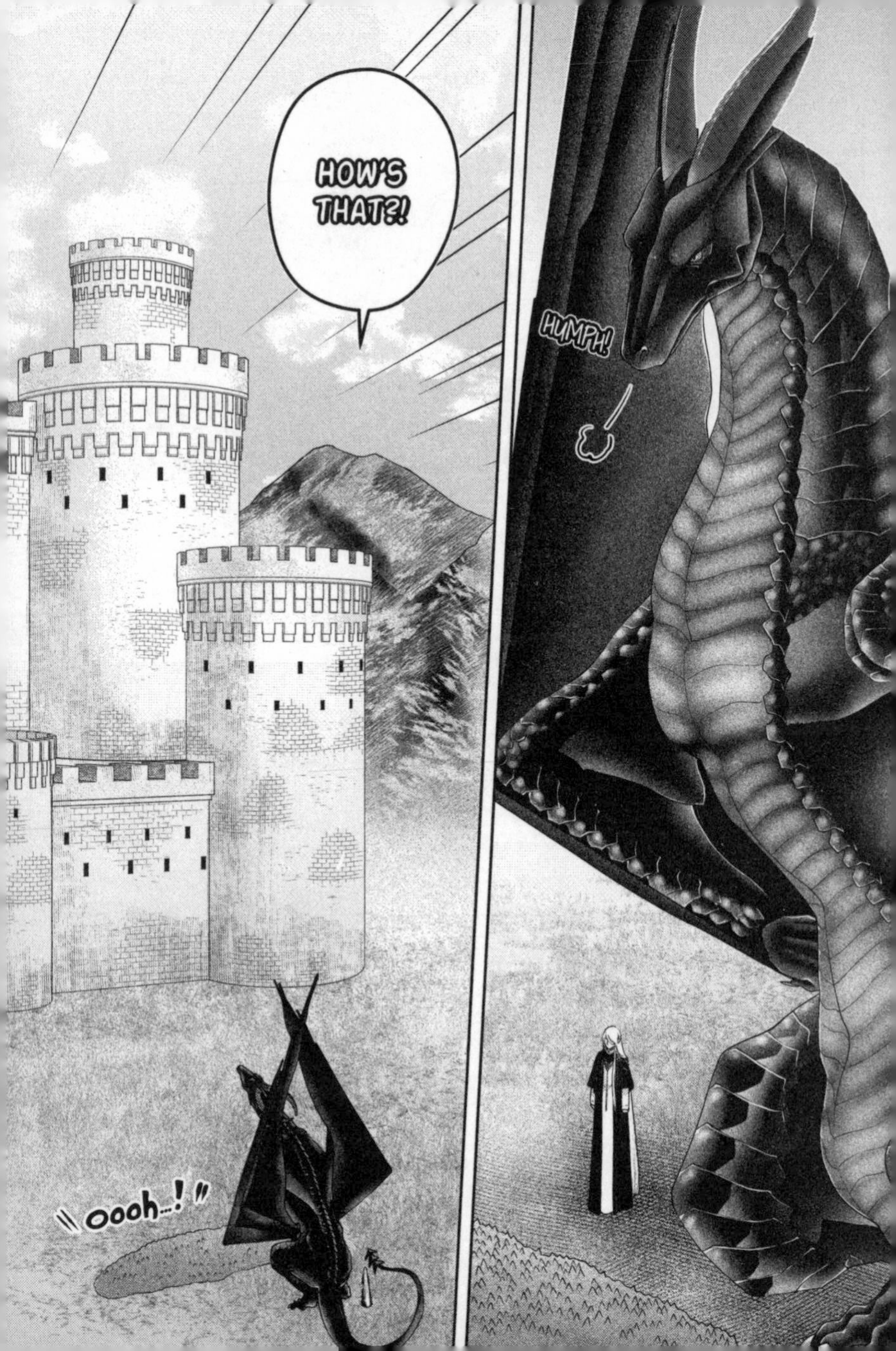
HUMPH!
HOW'S THAT?!
oooh...!

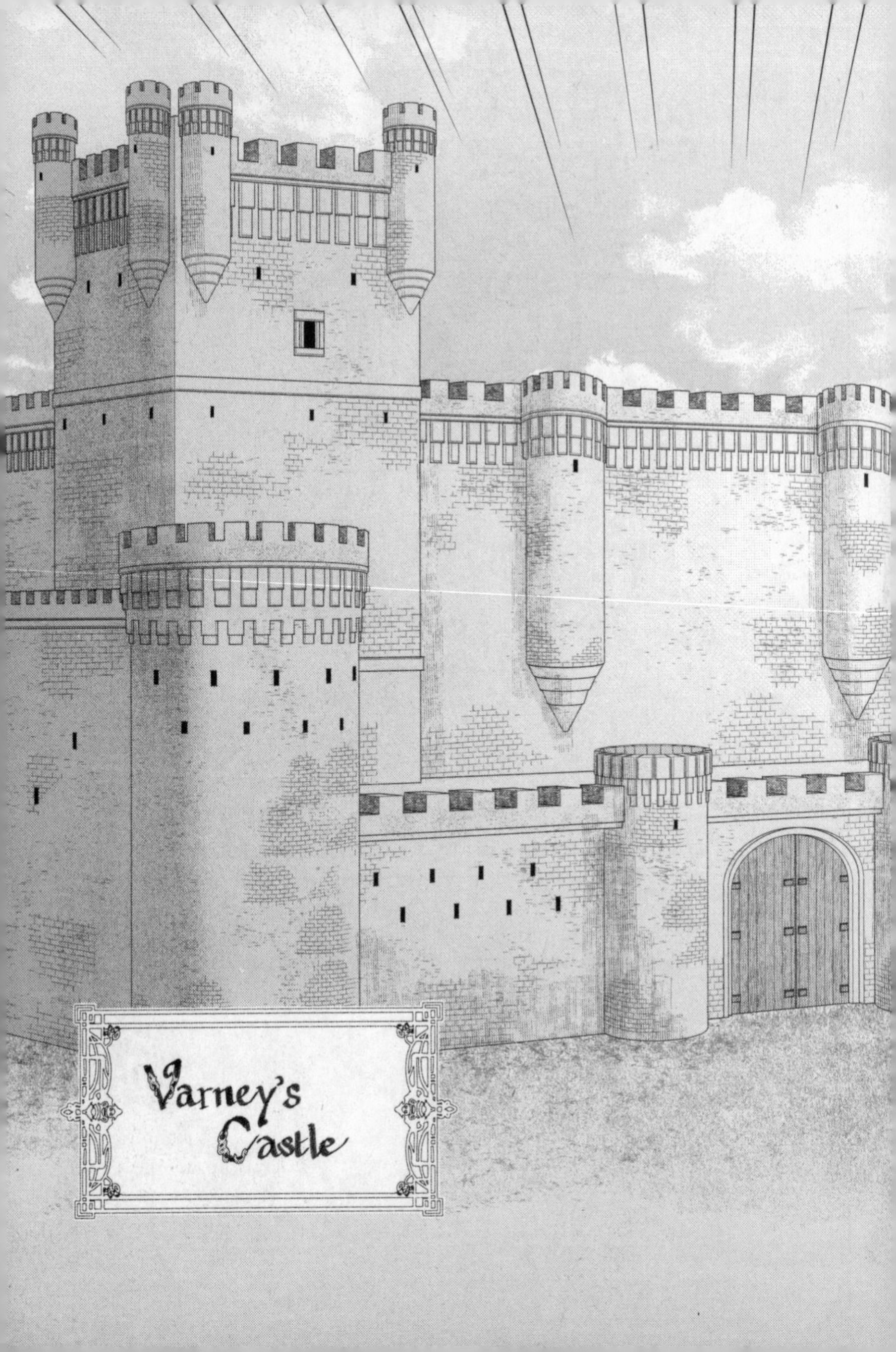
Varney's Castle

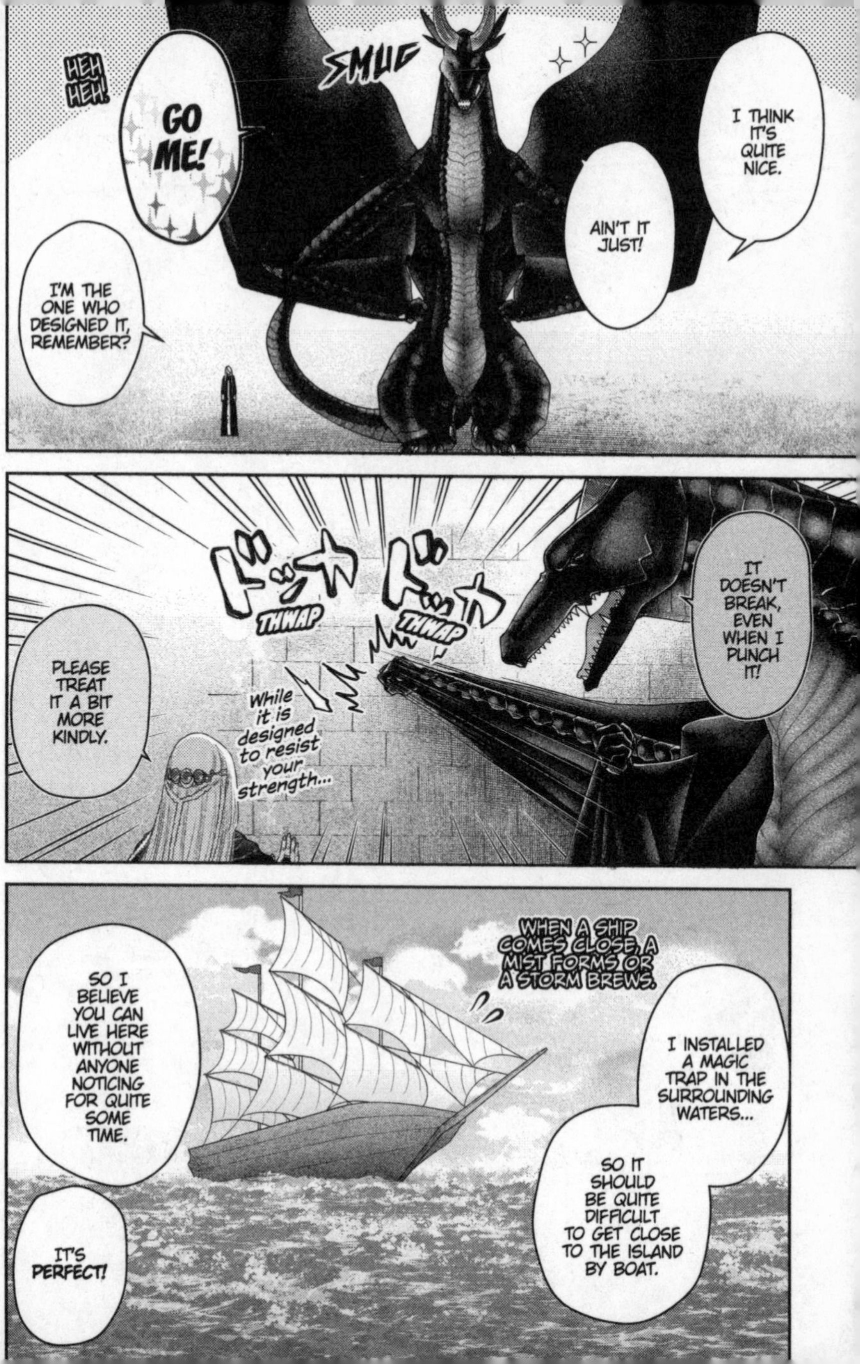
I THINK IT'S QUITE NICE.
AIN'T IT JUST!
SMUG
GO ME!
HEH HEH!
I'M THE ONE WHO DESIGNED IT, REMEMBER?
IT DOESN'T BREAK, EVEN WHEN I PUNCH IT!
ドッカ
THWAP
ドッカ
THWAP
While it is designed to resist your strength...
PLEASE TREAT IT A BIT MORE KINDLY.
WHEN A SHIP COMES CLOSE, A MIST FORMS OR A STORM BREWS.
I INSTALLED A MAGIC TRAP IN THE SURROUNDING WATERS...
SO IT SHOULD BE QUITE DIFFICULT TO GET CLOSE TO THE ISLAND BY BOAT.
SO I BELIEVE YOU CAN LIVE HERE WITHOUT ANYONE NOTICING FOR QUITE SOME TIME.
IT'S PERFECT!

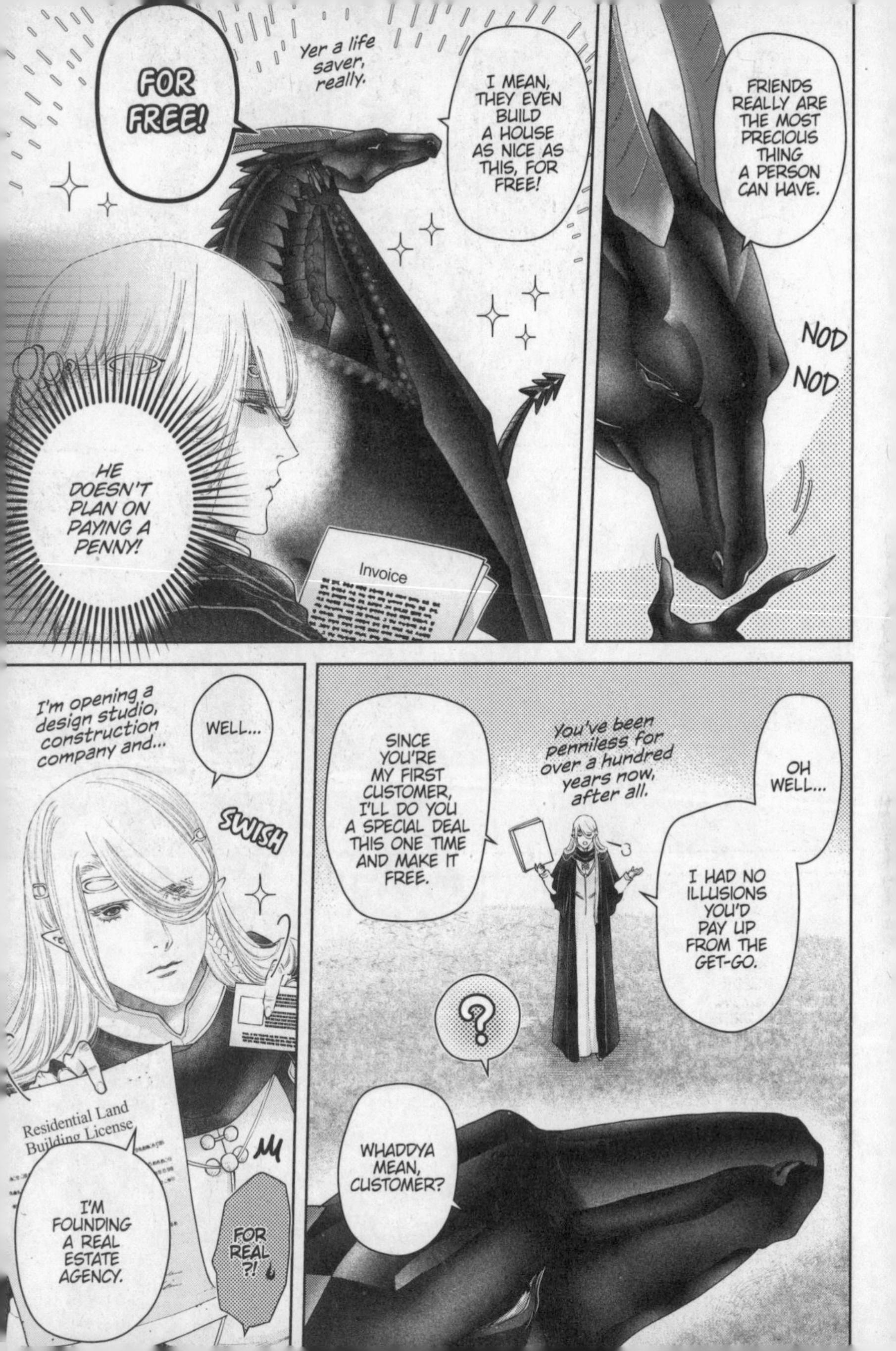
I MEAN, THEY EVEN BUILD A HOUSE AS NICE AS THIS, FOR FREE!
Yer a life saver, really.
FOR FREE!
HE DOESN'T PLAN ON PAYING A PENNY!
Invoice
FRIENDS REALLY ARE THE MOST PRECIOUS THING A PERSON CAN HAVE.
NOD
NOD
OH WELL...
I HAD NO ILLUSIONS YOU'D PAY UP FROM THE GET-GO.
You've been penniless for over a hundred years now, after all.
SINCE YOU'RE MY FIRST CUSTOMER, I'LL DO YOU A SPECIAL DEAL THIS ONE TIME AND MAKE IT FREE.
?
WHADDYA MEAN, CUSTOMER?
WELL...
I'm opening a design studio, construction company and...
SWISH
Residential Land Building License
I'M FOUNDING A REAL ESTATE AGENCY.
FOR REAL?!

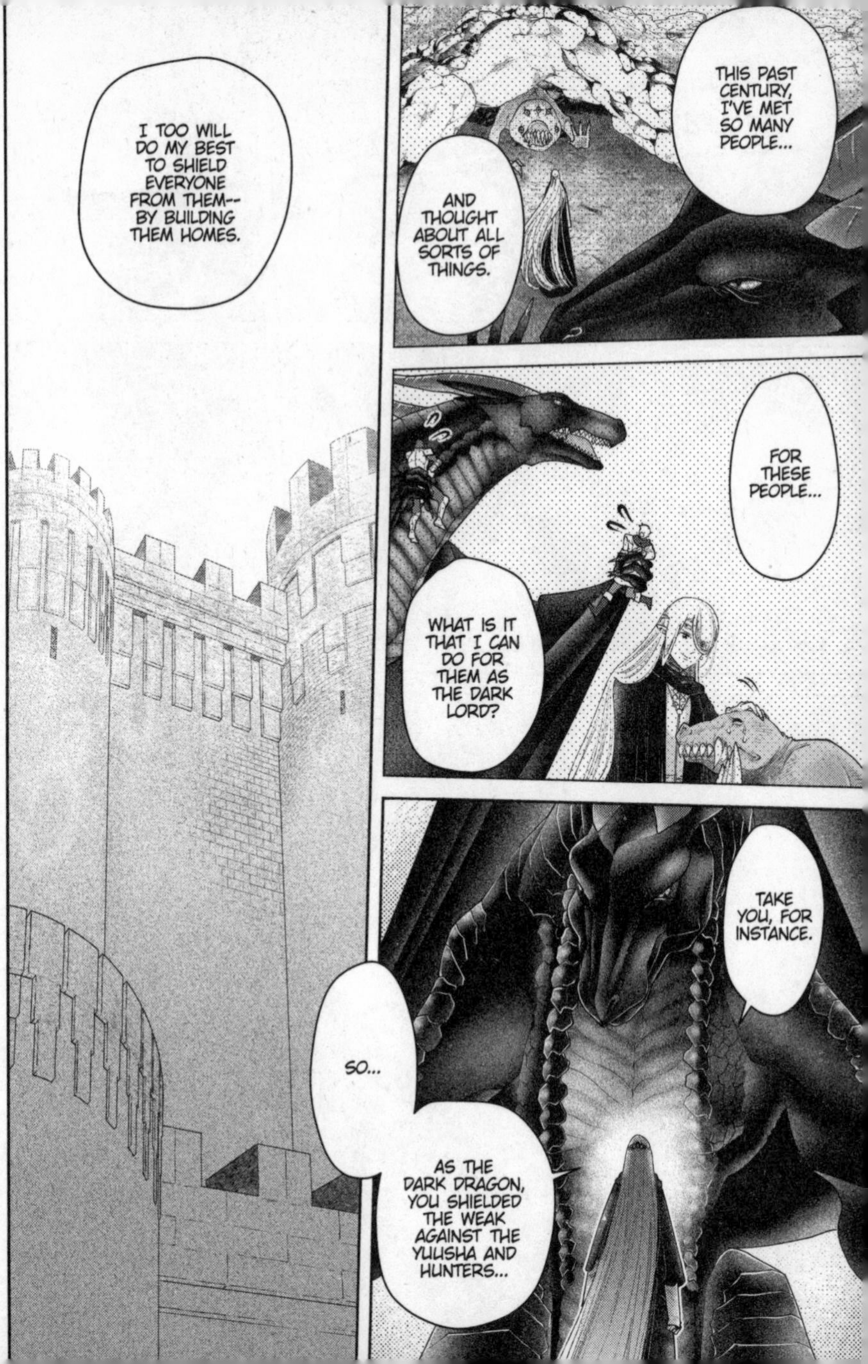
THIS PAST CENTURY, I'VE MET SO MANY PEOPLE...
AND THOUGHT ABOUT ALL SORTS OF THINGS.
FOR THESE PEOPLE...
WHAT IS IT THAT I CAN DO FOR THEM AS THE DARK LORD?
TAKE YOU, FOR INSTANCE.
SO...
AS THE DARK DRAGON, YOU SHIELDED THE WEAK AGAINST THE YUUSHA AND HUNTERS...
I TOO WILL DO MY BEST TO SHIELD EVERYONE FROM THEM-- BY BUILDING THEM HOMES.

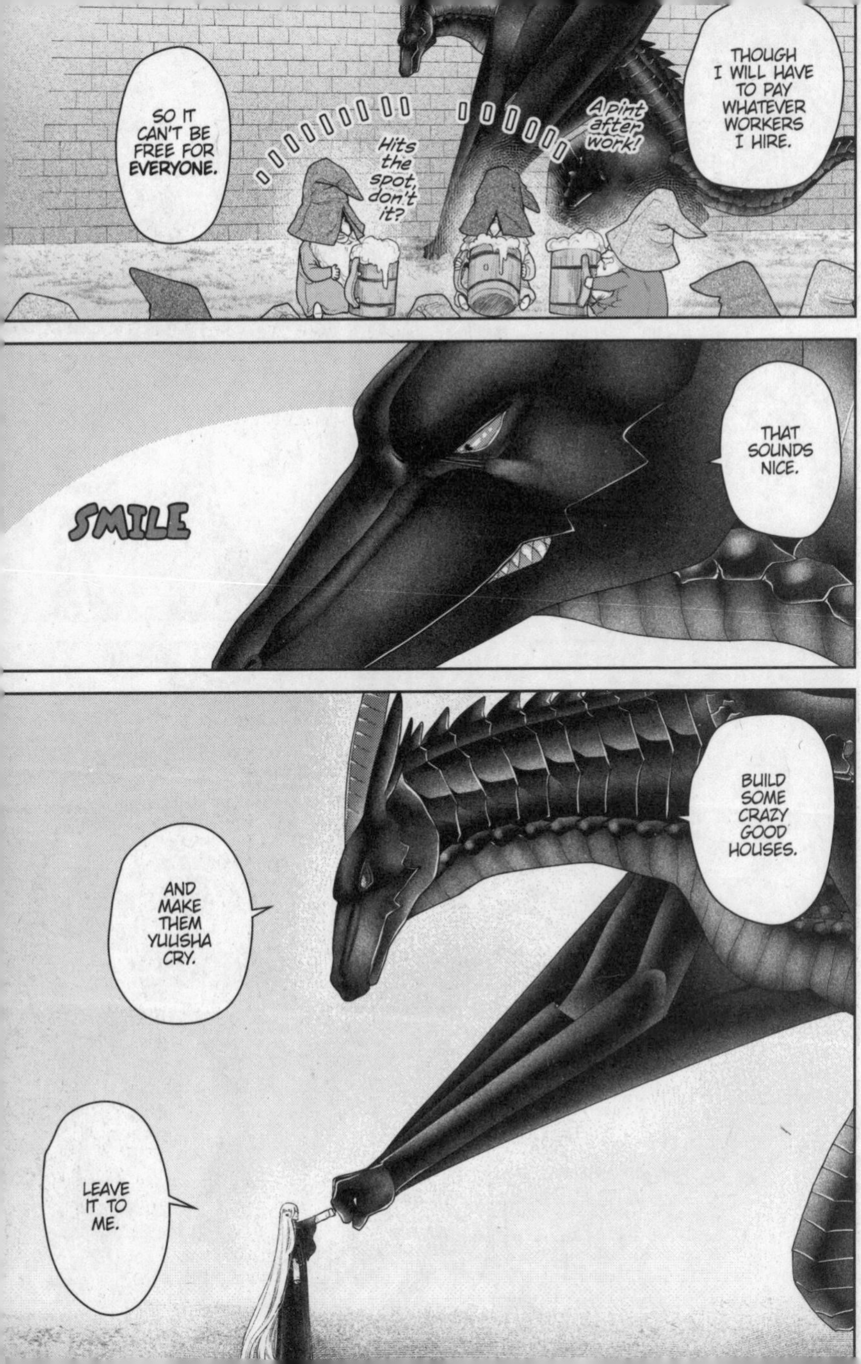
THOUGH I WILL HAVE TO PAY WHATEVER WORKERS I HIRE.
SO IT CAN'T BE FREE FOR EVERYONE.
A pint after work!
Hits the spot, don't it?
THAT SOUNDS NICE.
SMILE
BUILD SOME CRAZY GOOD HOUSES.
AND MAKE THEM YUUSHA CRY.
LEAVE IT TO ME.

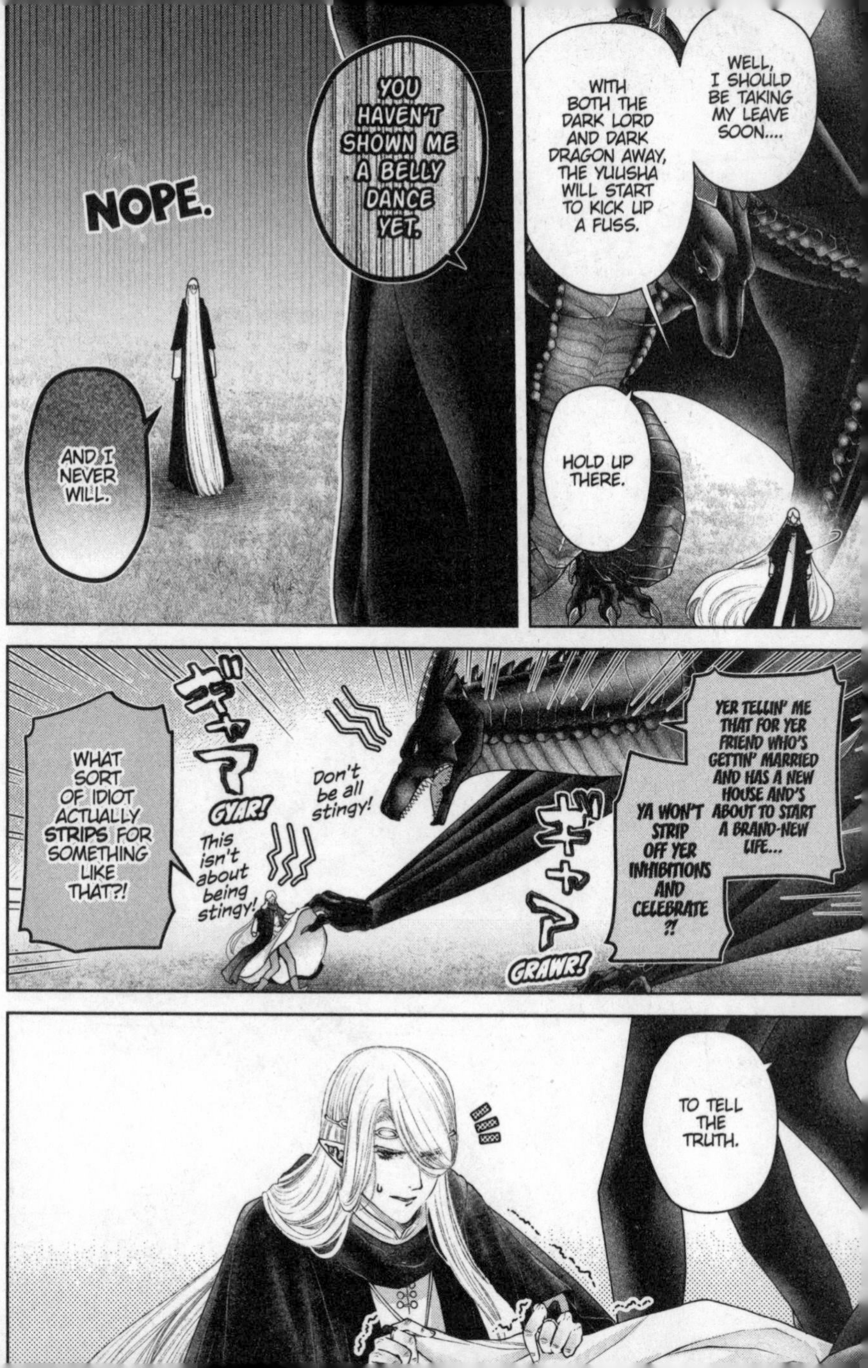
WELL, I SHOULD BE TAKING MY LEAVE SOON....
WITH BOTH THE DARK LORD AND DARK DRAGON AWAY, THE YUUSHA WILL START TO KICK UP A FUSS.
HOLD UP THERE.
YOU HAVEN'T SHOWN ME A BELLY DANCE YET.
NOPE.
AND I NEVER WILL.
YER TELLIN' ME THAT FOR YER FRIEND WHO'S GETTIN' MARRIED AND HAS A NEW HOUSE AND'S ABOUT TO START A BRAND-NEW LIFE...
YA WON'T STRIP OFF YER INHIBITIONS AND CELEBRATE?!
GRAWR!
Don't be all stingy!
GYAR!
This isn't about being stingy!
WHAT SORT OF IDIOT ACTUALLY STRIPS FOR SOMETHING LIKE THAT?!
TO TELL THE TRUTH.

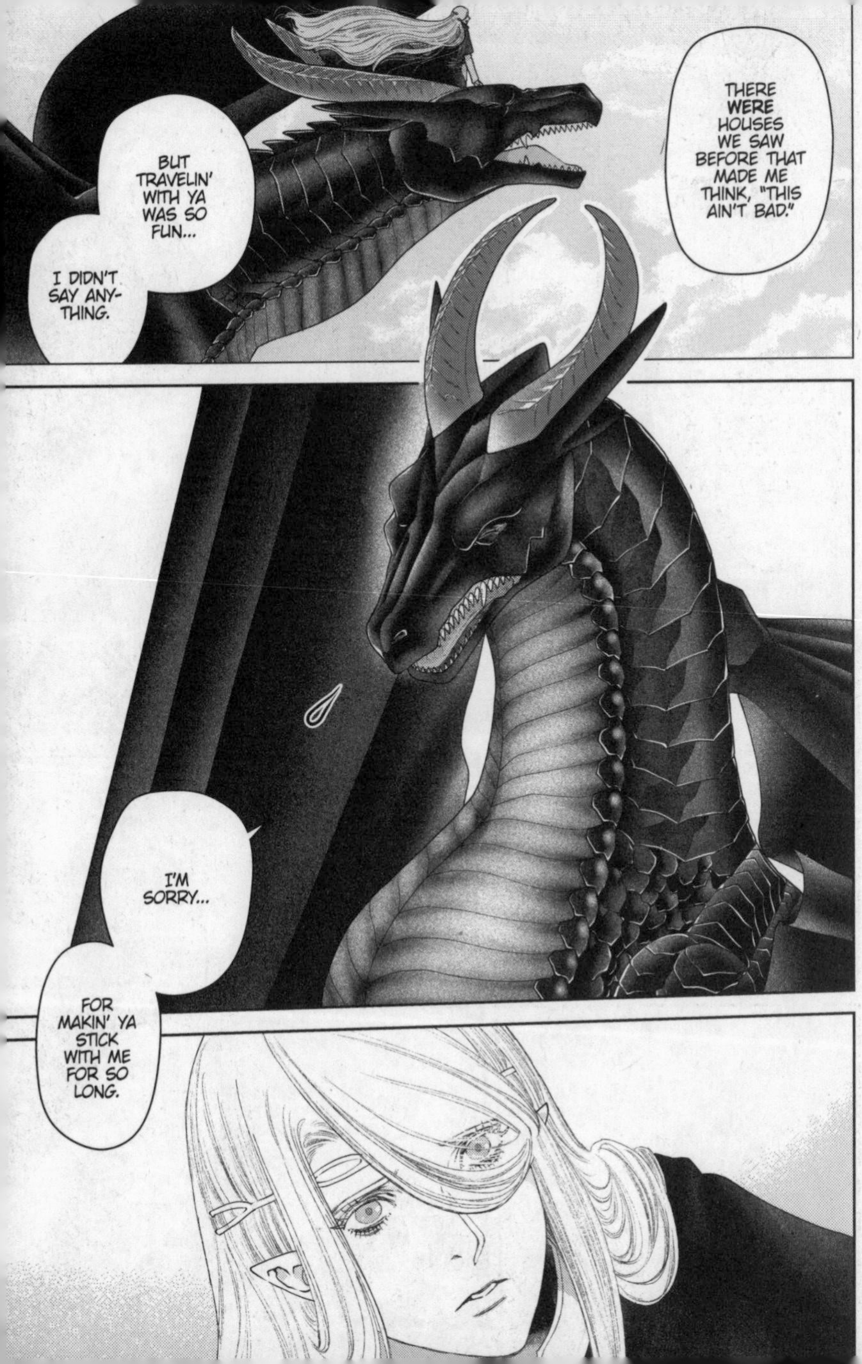
THERE WERE HOUSES WE SAW BEFORE THAT MADE ME THINK, "THIS AIN'T BAD."
BUT TRAVELIN' WITH YA WAS SO FUN...
I DIDN'T SAY ANY-THING.
I'M SORRY...
FOR MAKIN' YA STICK WITH ME FOR SO LONG.

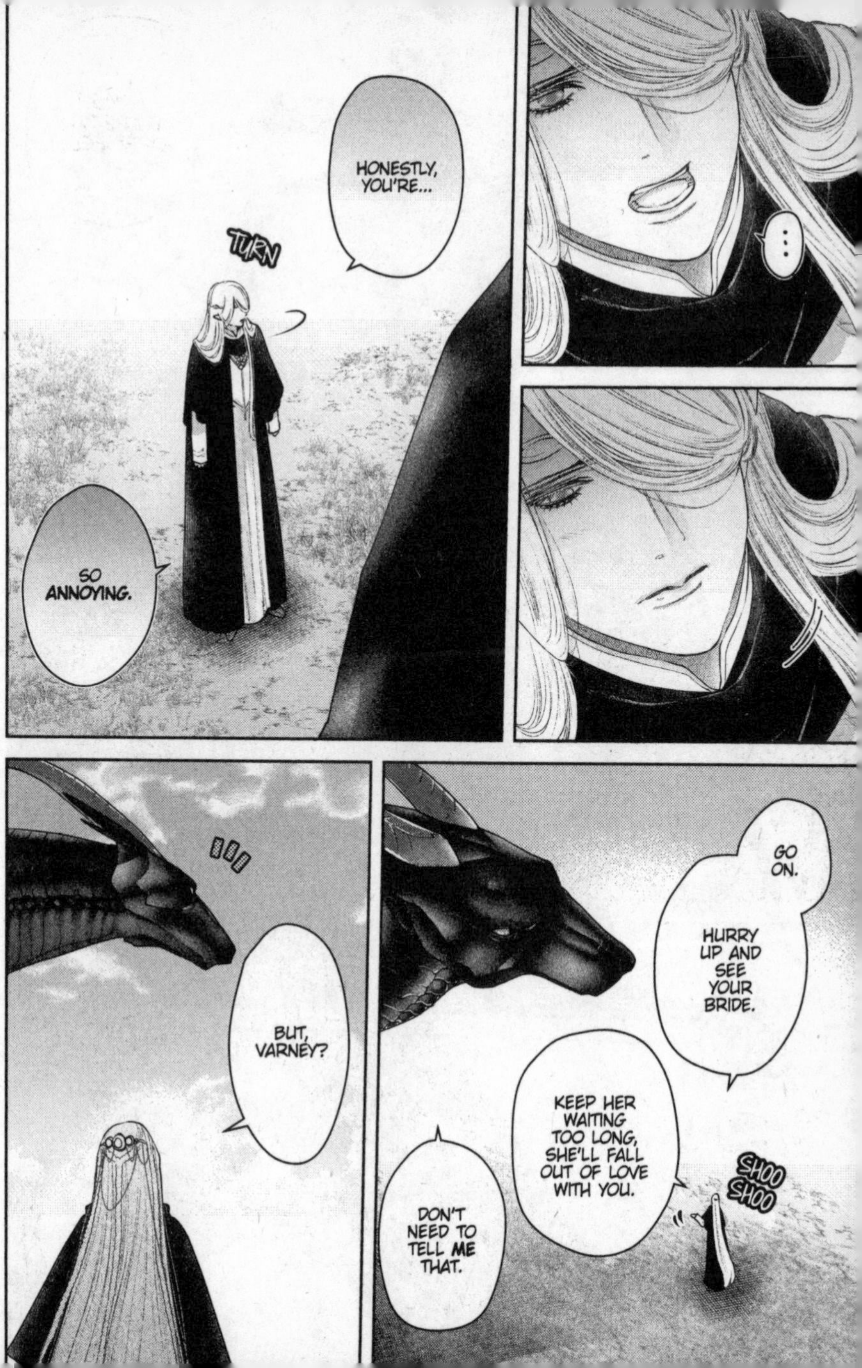
...
HONESTLY, YOU'RE...
TURN
SO ANNOYING.
GO ON.
HURRY UP AND SEE YOUR BRIDE.
KEEP HER WAITING TOO LONG, SHE'LL FALL OUT OF LOVE WITH YOU.
SHOO SHOO
DON'T NEED TO TELL ME THAT.
BUT, VARNEY?

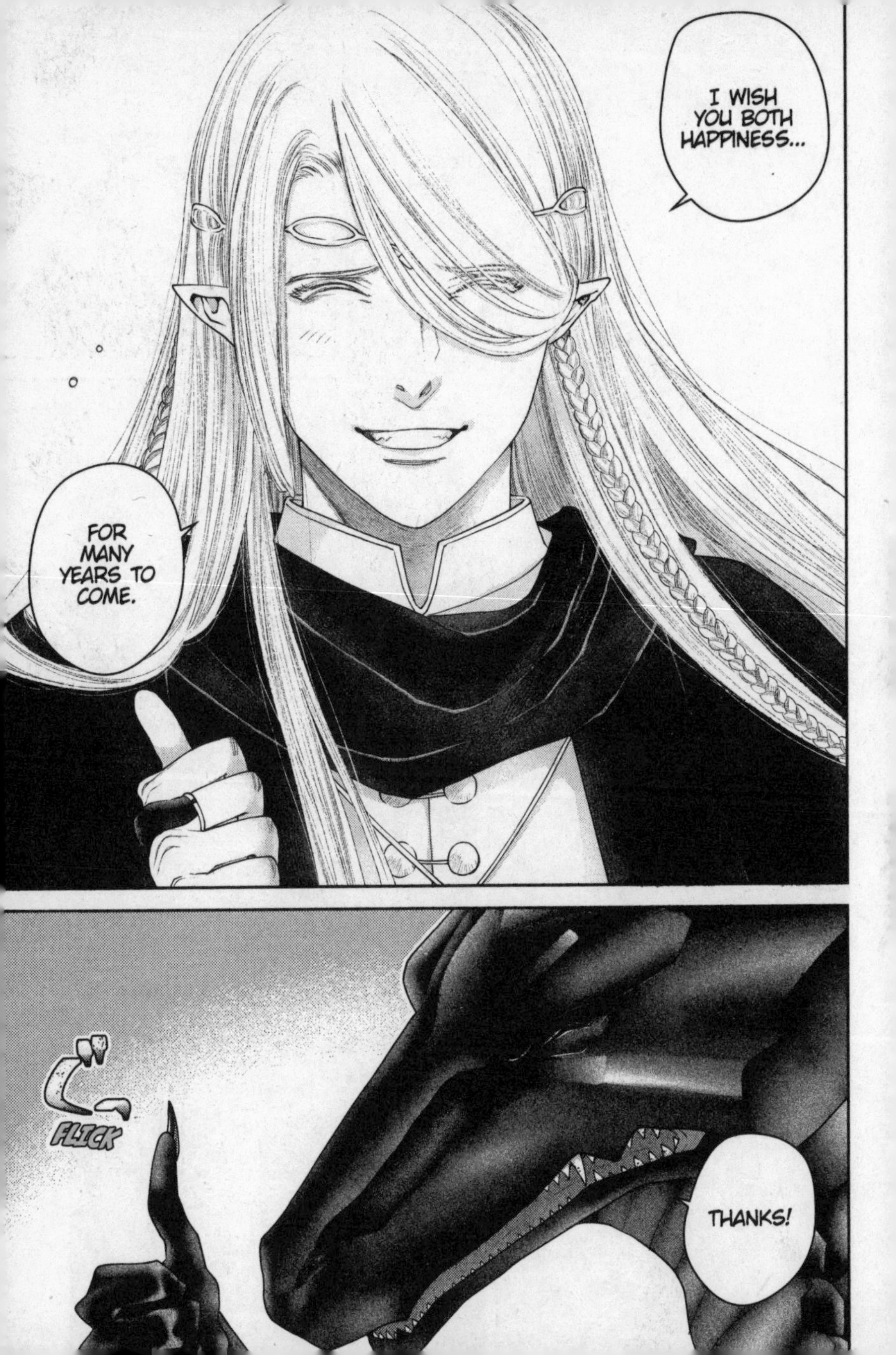
I WISH YOU BOTH HAPPINESS...
FOR MANY YEARS TO COME.
THANKS!
FLICK

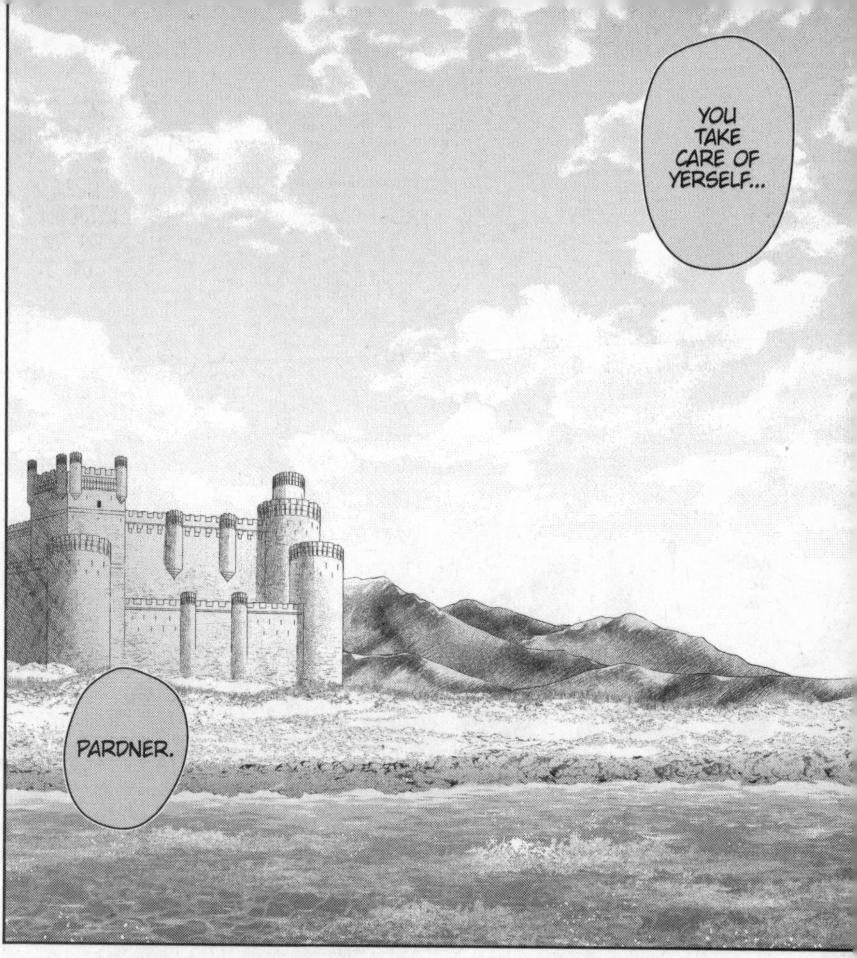
YOU TAKE CARE OF YERSELF...
PARDNER.
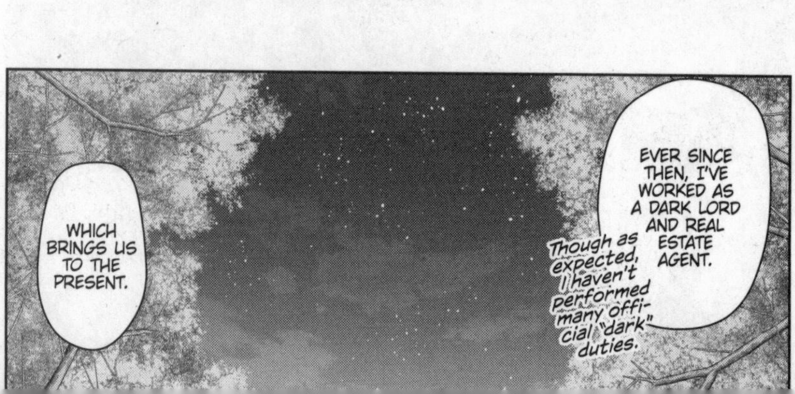
EVER SINCE THEN, I'VE WORKED AS A DARK LORD AND REAL ESTATE AGENT.
Though as expected, I haven't performed many offi-cial "dark" duties.
WHICH BRINGS US TO THE PRESENT.

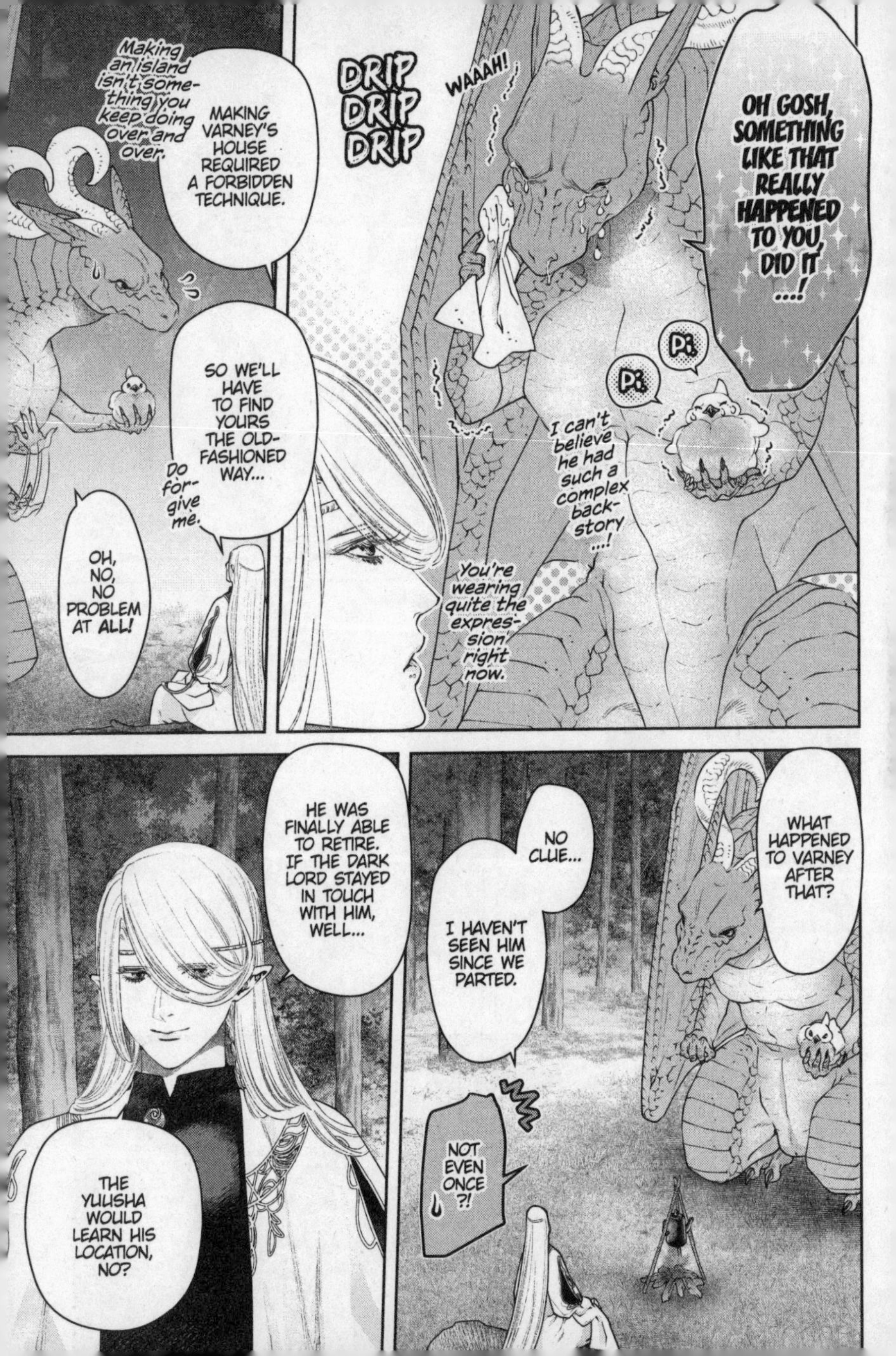
DRIP DRIP DRIP
WAAAH!
OH GOSH, SOMETHING LIKE THAT REALLY HAPPENED TO YOU, DID IT ...!
Pi
Pi
I can't believe he had such a complex back-story ...!
You're wearing quite the expres-sion right now.
Making an island isn't some-thing you keep doing over and over.
MAKING VARNEY'S HOUSE REQUIRED A FORBIDDEN TECHNIQUE.
SO WE'LL HAVE TO FIND YOURS THE OLD-FASHIONED WAY...
Do for-give me.
OH, NO, NO PROBLEM AT ALL!
WHAT HAPPENED TO VARNEY AFTER THAT?
NO CLUE...
I HAVEN'T SEEN HIM SINCE WE PARTED.
NOT EVEN ONCE ?!
HE WAS FINALLY ABLE TO RETIRE. IF THE DARK LORD STAYED IN TOUCH WITH HIM, WELL...
THE YUUSHA WOULD LEARN HIS LOCATION, NO?

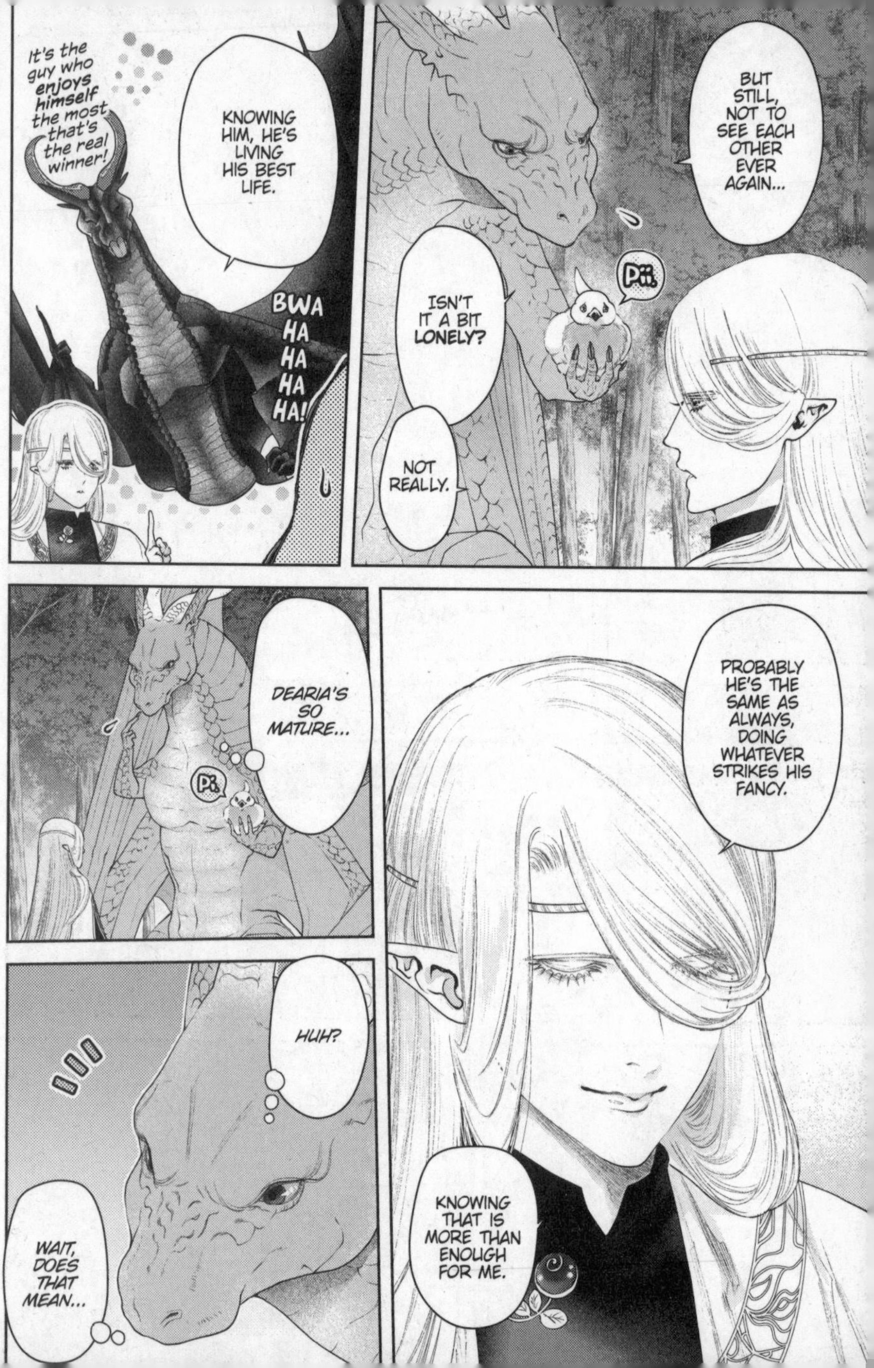
BUT STILL, NOT TO SEE EACH OTHER EVER AGAIN...
Pii
ISN'T IT A BIT LONELY?
NOT REALLY.
KNOWING HIM, HE'S LIVING HIS BEST LIFE.
BWA HA HA HA HA HA!
It's the guy who enjoys himself the most that's the real winner!
PROBABLY HE'S THE SAME AS ALWAYS, DOING WHATEVER STRIKES HIS FANCY.
KNOWING THAT IS MORE THAN ENOUGH FOR ME.
DEARIA'S SO MATURE...
Pi
HUH?
!!!
WAIT, DOES THAT MEAN...

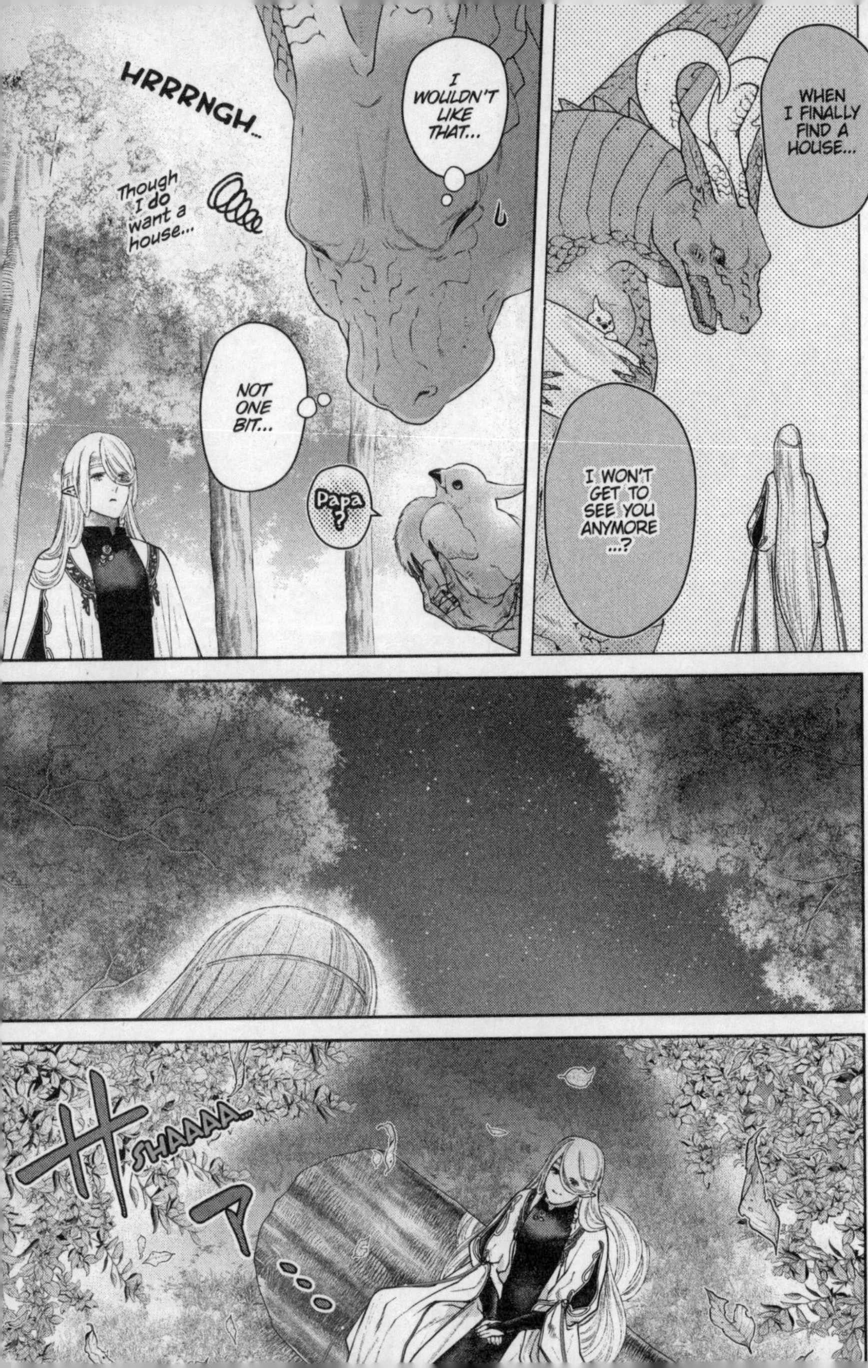
WHEN I FINALLY FIND A HOUSE...
I WON'T GET TO SEE YOU ANYMORE ...?
I WOULDN'T LIKE THAT...
NOT ONE BIT...
Papa?
HRRRNGH..
Though I do want a house...
HSHAAAA...
A
...

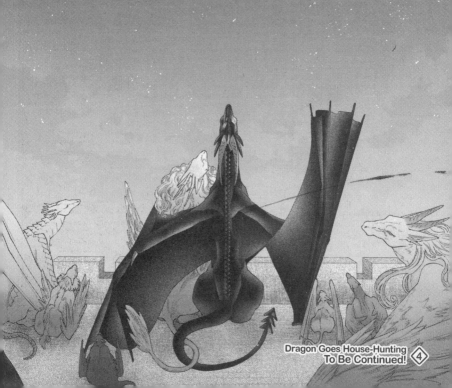

**Dragon Goes House-Hunting
To Be Continued!** ④

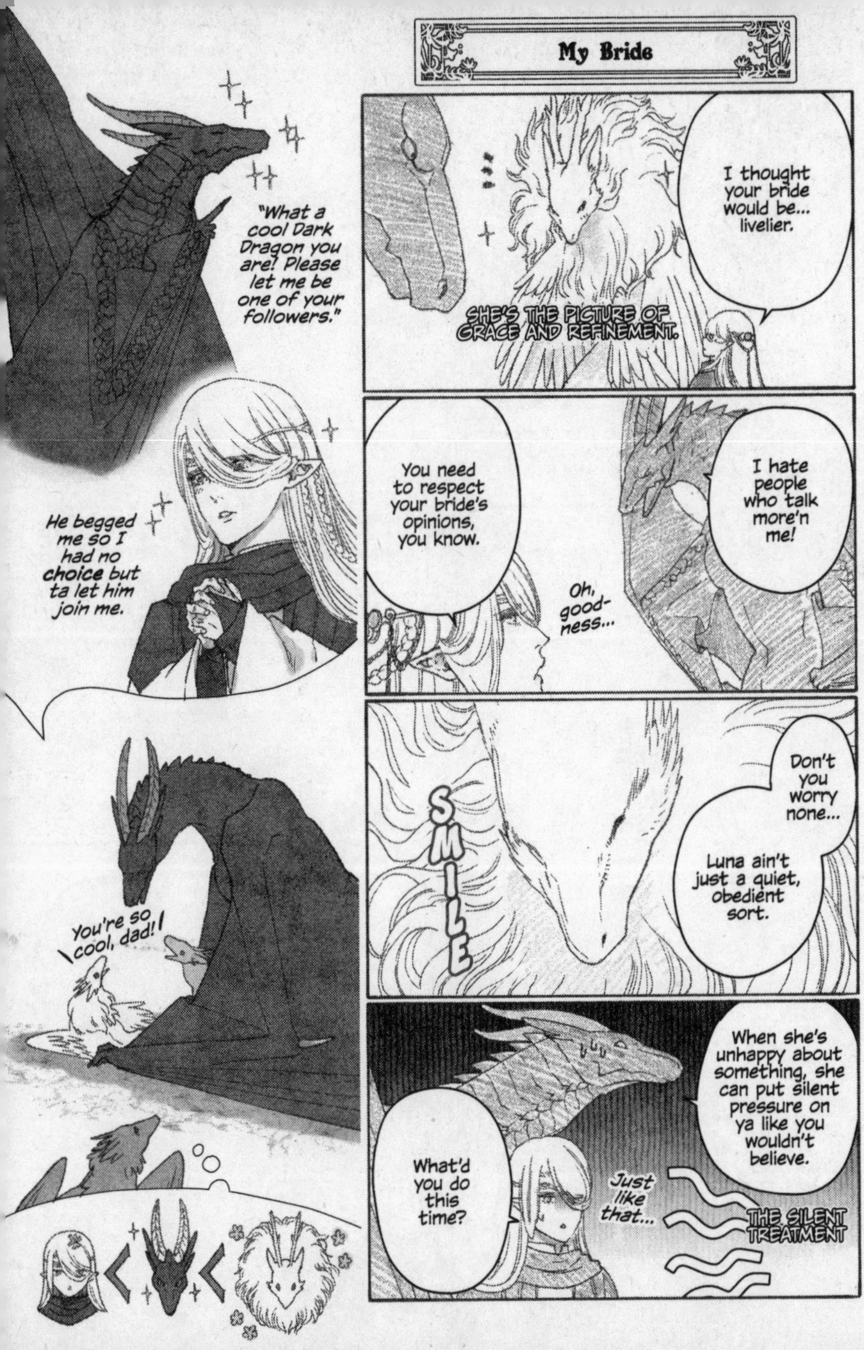
My Bride
...
I thought your bride would be... livelier.
SHE'S THE PICTURE OF GRACE AND REFINEMENT.
I hate people who talk more'n me!
You need to respect your bride's opinions, you know.
Oh, goodness...
Don't you worry none...
Luna ain't just a quiet, obedient sort.
SMILE
When she's unhappy about something, she can put silent pressure on ya like you wouldn't believe.
What'd you do this time?
Just like that...
THE SILENT TREATMENT
"What a cool Dark Dragon you are! Please let me be one of your followers."
He begged me so I had no choice but ta let him join me.
You're so cool, dad!!

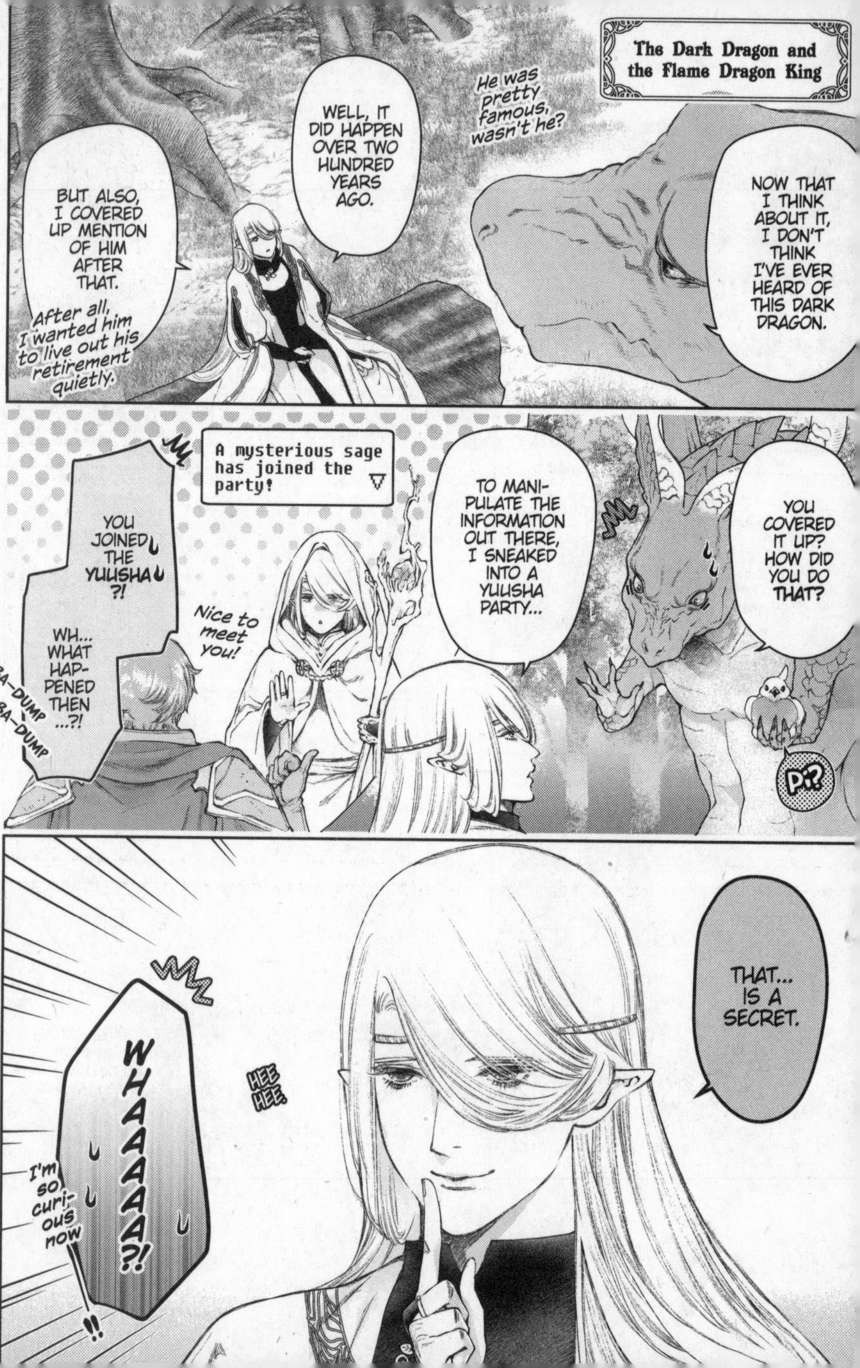
The Dark Dragon and the Flame Dragon King
NOW THAT I THINK ABOUT IT, I DON'T THINK I'VE EVER HEARD OF THIS DARK DRAGON.
He was pretty famous, wasn't he?
WELL, IT DID HAPPEN OVER TWO HUNDRED YEARS AGO.
BUT ALSO, I COVERED UP MENTION OF HIM AFTER THAT.
After all, I wanted him to live out his retirement quietly.
YOU COVERED IT UP? HOW DID YOU DO THAT?
Pi?
TO MANIPULATE THE INFORMATION OUT THERE, I SNEAKED INTO A YUUSHA PARTY...
A mysterious sage has joined the party!
Nice to meet you!
YOU JOINED THE YUUSHA?!
WH... WHAT HAPPENED THEN...?!
BA-DUMP BA-DUMP
THAT... IS A SECRET.
HEE HEE.
WHAAAAAAA?!
I'm so curious now!!